Master the™
Firefighter
Exam

18th Edition

PETERSON'S®

About Peterson's®

Peterson's has been your trusted educational publisher for over 50 years. It's a milestone we're quite proud of, as we continue to offer the most accurate, dependable, high-quality educational content in the field, providing you with everything you need to succeed. No matter where you are on your academic or professional path, you can rely on Peterson's for its books, online information, expert test-prep tools, the most up-to-date education exploration data, and the highest quality career success resources—everything you need to achieve your education goals. For our complete line of products, visit **www.petersons.com**.

For more information, contact Peterson's, 4380 S. Syracuse St., Suite 200, Denver, CO 80237; 800-338-3282 Ext. 54229; or visit us online at **www.petersons.com**.

ISBN-13: 978-0-7689-4374-0

Printed in the United States of America

10 9 8 7 6 5 4 3 2 1   22 21 20

Eighteenth Edition

Peterson's Updates and Corrections

Check out our website at **https://petersonsbooks.com/updates-and-corrections/** to see if there is any new information regarding the test and any revisions or corrections to the content of this book. We've made sure the information in this book is accurate and up to date; however, the test format or content may have changed since the time of publication.

Give Us Your Feedback. We welcome any comments or suggestions you may have about this publication. Contact us at **custsvc@petersons.com**. Your feedback will help us make education dreams possible for you—and others like you.

Contents

Contents

Before You Begin

OVERVIEW

- **How to Use This Book**
- **Preparing for the Firefighter Exam**
- **Six Test-Day Strategies**
- **Tips for Test Takers**
- **How This Book Is Organized**
- **Special Study Features**
- **More for You From Peterson's**
- **You're Well on Your Way to Success**

HOW TO USE THIS BOOK

You want to become a firefighter. That's great! Every city, town, and village needs qualified and enthusiastic new recruits to maintain a full firefighting staff. You've made a good start toward becoming a firefighter by buying this book.

Peterson's® *Master the™ Firefighter Exam* has been carefully researched and written to help you through the qualifying process. This book will show you what to expect on your written exam and will give you a speedy brush-up on the subjects covered. It will also provide valuable tips on how to prepare for the physical aptitude portion of the screening process.

Some subjects covered on the written exam are not taught in schools, so even if your study time is very limited, you should work toward the following goals:

- Improve your general test-taking skills.
- Improve your skills in analyzing and answering questions involving reasoning, judgment, comparison, and evaluation.
- Increase your speed and skills in reading and in understanding what you read (an important part of your ability to learn and a major part of most written tests).
- Pay close attention to exam eligibility criteria, requirements, and deadlines for the exam that you plan to take. Use the agencies' online resources for more detailed test information.

It is important that you become familiar with the type of examination you will take. Firefighter exams are administered either as pencil-and-paper-based tests using "bubble"-type answer sheets, or as computer-based tests (CBTs).

Paper-based tests may include auxiliary booklets that candidates will reference during the test. Computer-based exams may include multimedia presentations with audio or visual-themed questions.

This book presents different types of questions, many similar to those which have appeared on actual firefighter exams. Armed with this book, you will learn to do the following:

- **Find your weaknesses.** Once you know what subjects you need help with, you can concentrate on strengthening those areas. This kind of selective study yields the best test results.

- **Know what to expect on the exam.** All the questions in the practice tests—as well as the chapters that provide instruction in answering reading comprehension, reasoning and judgment, and spatial orientation questions—reflect the types of questions presented on firefighter exams and study handbooks from around the country. Working through this information will give you experience in answering actual test questions.

- **Build your confidence as you prepare for the test.** Whether the firefighter exam you're preparing for will be administered on paper or computer, practicing for the written exam with the questions in this book will build your self-confidence and will help prevent the test anxiety that sometimes contributes to low test scores.

NOTE
Fire departments in more than 31 states and Washington, D.C. administer their firefighter exam in designated testing centers throughout the United States.

Not all firefighter exams are alike; every city administers its own exam. The number of questions, the timing, and the actual content of each department's exam varies from one municipality to another. Nearly all firefighter exams, however, use the multiple-choice question format and cover the subject areas of reading comprehension, reasoning and judgment, use of maps and diagrams, basic mechanics, basic math concepts, and observation and memory. All these areas are covered in this book, so you can gain plenty of practice with each question type.

Every question in this book is followed by an answer key that provides the correct answer. Where applicable, detailed explanations are provided to aid in reasoning through a process, placing steps in a logical order, and solving math or mechanical problems. These explanations provide an excellent learning opportunity to understand why an answer is correct or incorrect.

PREPARING FOR THE FIREFIGHTER EXAM

Carefully read each chapter of Peterson's® *Master the™ Firefighter Exam* and do not skip over any information. You must know what to expect and then prepare yourself for it. The better prepared you are, the more confident you will feel about taking the exam. If you feel confident, you're more likely to answer questions quickly and decisively, complete the exam, and earn a high score. Greater confidence will also help you enter the physical performance test without hesitation, so you will be better able to prove that you are fit for the job. Here are seven tips to start you off:

1. **Set up a study schedule.** Assign yourself a period each day devoted to preparing for your firefighter exam. A regular schedule is best, but the important thing is to study daily, even if you can't do so at the same time every day.

2. **Study alone.** You will concentrate better if you work by yourself. Make a list of questions that you find puzzling and points of which you're unsure. Later, discuss

the items on the list with a friend who is preparing for the same exam. Exchange ideas and discuss more difficult questions at a joint review session shortly before the exam date.

3. **Eliminate distractions.** Choose a quiet, well-lit spot that is removed from distractions. Distance yourself from common areas where social activity or loud noises are common, and set aside your smartphone. Arrange as best you can to not be interrupted.

4. **Start at the beginning and read carefully.** Underline points that you consider significant. Make marginal notes. Flag the pages you think are especially important.

5. **Concentrate on the information and instruction chapters.** Learn the vocabulary of the job. Get yourself psyched to enter the world of firefighting. Learn how to handle reading-based questions. Focus on eliminating wrong answers; this is an important method for answering all multiple-choice questions, but it's especially vital for answering reasoning and judgement questions correctly.

6. **Answer the practice questions in each chapter.** Study the answer explanations. You can learn a great deal from them, even when you have answered correctly. The explanations might bring out points that had not occurred to you. This same suggestion applies throughout this book—not only to the practice tests, but to instructional chapters as well.

7. **Take the practice tests.** When you feel well prepared, move on to the practice exams. Take each exam in one sitting and time yourself to simulate your actual test day. If you're unable to do so, divide your time into no more than two sessions per practice test.

Consider each of the practice tests as a dress rehearsal for the real thing. Time yourself accurately and do not peek at the correct answers. Remember, you are taking these for practice. They will not be scored and do not count, so try to learn from them. Learn to think like a firefighter. Learn to reason like a firefighter. Learn to pace yourself so you can answer all the questions within the specified time limit. Then learn from the answer explanations and correct your mistakes.

SIX TEST-DAY STRATEGIES

Here are some quick tips to remember for test day:

1. **Focus only on the test.** Do not try to fit in taking the test between other activities.

2. **Arrive rested, relaxed, and on time.** In fact, plan to arrive a little bit early. Leave plenty of time for traffic tie-ups or other complications that might upset you and interfere with your test performance.

3. **Ask questions if there are any examiner's instructions you do not understand.** Make sure that you know exactly what to do. In the test room, the examiner will provide forms for you to fill out. The examiner will tell you how to fill in the grids on the forms. He or she will give you the instructions you must follow when taking the examination.

TIP

Do not memorize questions and answers. You might see questions on your exam that are very similar to the questions you encounter in this book but they won't be exactly the same.

4. **Follow instructions exactly during the examination**. If applicable, fill in the grids on the forms carefully and accurately. Filling in the grids inaccurately might lead to unfortunate consequences, such as a loss of veterans' credits to which you might be entitled, or your test results being sent to the wrong address. Do not begin until you are told to do so. Stop as soon as the examiner tells you to stop. Do not turn pages until you are told to do so or go back to parts you have already completed. Any infraction of the rules is considered cheating. If you cheat, your test paper will not be scored, and you will not be eligible for appointment. If you are taking a computer-based test, you will need to know how to use a mouse and keyboard to take each of the tests. You will need to enter your username and password to log in to your test and use the mouse to select the answers to each question. Administrators and technical assistance will be available to answer any questions you have.

5. **Read every word of every question.** Once the signal has been given and you begin the exam, be alert for exclusionary words that might affect your answer, such as *not, most, least, all, every*, and *except*.

6. **Read all the choices before you mark your answer.** It is statistically true that most errors are made when the last choice is the correct answer. Too many people mark the first answer that seems correct without reading all the choices to find out which answer is best.

TIPS FOR TEST TAKERS

Here's a list of general tips to help ensure that your score accurately reflects your understanding of content on the exam. Read these suggestions before you attempt the practice exams, and once again before you take the actual exam, to avoid any mishaps.

If you will be taking a paper-based test, keep these tips in mind:

- Mark your answers by completely blackening the answer space of your choice.

- Mark *only one* answer for each question, even if you think more than one answer is correct. If you mark more than one answer, the scoring machine will consider it a wrong answer, even if one of your answers is correct.

- If you change your mind, erase your first response completely. Leave no doubt as to which answer you've selected on the answer sheet.

- If you do any problem solving in the test booklet or on scratch paper, make sure to mark your answer on the answer sheet as well. Only the answer sheet is scored.

- Check often to make sure the question number matches the answer space number you're filling in. If you find that you have skipped a space earlier in the test, erase all the answers after the skip and fill in all the spaces again in the appropriate places.

- Answer every question in order, but don't spend too much time on any one question. If a question seems "impossible" to you, don't take it as a personal challenge. Make a guess and move on. Remember, your task is to answer correctly as many questions as possible. You must apportion your time wisely to give yourself a fair chance to read and answer all questions on the exam.

- Make an educated guess if possible. If you don't know the answer to a question, eliminate answers you know are wrong and guess from the remaining choices. If you have no idea at all what the correct answer is, guess anyway. Then make note of your guesses so you can give those questions a second look if time permits.

- If time is about to run out and you haven't answered all the questions, mark the remaining questions with the same answer choice. According to the law of averages, you should get 25 percent of them correct.

- If you finish before time is up, check to make sure that you filled in the answer sheet with each answer in the right space and that you have only one answer for each question. Then return to any difficult questions you marked in your booklet and try them again. There is no bonus for finishing early, so use all your time to perfect your exam.

The following is a list of suggestions for computer-based testing. Every CBT will be slightly different, so check for online tutorials to become familiar with the CBT controls.

- Follow all prompts on the computer screen. Fill in all required fields. Take notes, if allowed to do so, and read all questions carefully.

- Most questions will have only one correct answer. However, some CBTs present alternative item types that require a fill-in response or more than one correct response; in these cases, answer the item as directed.

- Determine ahead of time how the exam will be scored so you know whether to skip questions or guess.

- Find out if you can return to a question once you've moved to the next, or if the test allows only forward progress. Knowing that you can return to a difficult question can help you determine whether making a note and returning to it or making an educated guess is your best strategy.

- Pay attention to time constraints. The time remaining should be displayed on the computer screen. If time is about to run out and you haven't answered all the questions, mark the remaining questions with the same answer choice. According to the law of averages, you should get 25 percent of them correct.

- Confirm you've finished the exam and close out the test by going back to make sure you've followed all directions.

HOW THIS BOOK IS ORGANIZED

Taking the firefighter exam is a skill; it requires discipline and practice to succeed. These skills can be improved through coaching, but, ultimately, improvement requires practice. This book gives you both.

- **Part I** provides an in-depth look at the firefighting profession, including employment prospects, common job tasks, as well as information on training, advancement, and firefighter-related occupations. It also provides you with an extensive description of the screening process for becoming a firefighter, including information on applying for a position, medical and physical requirements, and job interviews.

- **Part II** is the diagnostic test, designed to help you identify your areas of strength and those areas where you need to spend more time in your review sessions.

- **Part III** is the coaching program. This part of the book analyzes each section of a typical firefighter exam—reading comprehension, reasoning and judgment, spatial orientation, observation and memory, mechanical reasoning, and math—and provides powerful strategies for attacking every question type headed your way.

- **Part IV** consists of three practice tests, each with the same average number and ratio of question types you'll encounter on a real firefighter exam. To accurately measure your performance, remember to adhere to the stated time limits for each test.
- **Part V** contains supplementary material. Appendix A lists common firefighting terms. Appendix B provides information related to the specialized field of wildland firefighting.

SPECIAL STUDY FEATURES

Peterson's® *Master the™ Firefighter Exam* is designed to be as user-friendly as it is complete. To this end, it includes several features to maximize the effectiveness of your preparation.

Summing It Up

Each chapter ends with a point-by-point summary that reviews the most important items in the chapter. The summaries offer a convenient way to review key points.

Bonus Information

As you work your way through the book, look to the margins for bonus information, including test-taking advice, strategies, important need-to-know information, and test pitfalls to avoid. This information will come in one of the following forms:

 Tips provide valuable strategies and hints to help answer the types of questions you will encounter.

 Alerts identify common pitfalls and misconceptions related to the exam.

 Notes highlight need-to-know information, whether it's details about the application process and scoring or the structure of certain test question types.

Looking for Additional Practice? Check out Peterson's Test Prep Subscriptions

Our subscription plans allow you to study as quickly as you can, or as slowly as you'd like. How does it work? Subscribers get unlimited usage of our entire test prep catalog for over 150 exams, including important exams for career-minded individuals like the Firefighter, EMT, Pharmacy Technician, and NCLEX-PN and NCLEX-RN exams. For more information, go to **www.petersons.com/testprep/**.

MORE FOR YOU FROM PETERSON'S

Peterson's publishes a full line of books—career preparation, education exploration, test prep, and financial aid. Peterson's publications can be found at local and college libraries and career centers and are available for purchase in stores and online at Amazon, Barnes & Noble, and other major retailers.

YOU'RE WELL ON YOUR WAY TO SUCCESS

Congratulations! You've made the decision to become a firefighter and have taken a significant step in that process. Peterson's® *Master the™ Firefighter Exam* will prepare you for everything you'll need to know come test day. Remember to study hard *and* smart; we wish you the best of luck.

PART I
FIREFIGHTING BASICS

What Firefighters Do

OVERVIEW

- The Nature of the Work
- Employment Outlook
- Places of Employment
- Essential Job Tasks of Firefighters
- Working Conditions
- First Responder and Emergency Medical Services
- Training and Advancement
- Firefighting in the Twenty-First Century
- Earnings
- Related Occupations
- Additional Information
- Summing It Up

THE NATURE OF THE WORK

Every year, fires destroy thousands of lives and damage property worth millions of dollars. Firefighters help protect the public against fire dangers through safety and fire prevention presentations and emergency response. This book describes the careers of paid firefighters; it does not cover the duties and responsibilities of the many thousands of volunteer firefighters in communities across the country.

When on duty, firefighters must be prepared to respond to fires and handle any emergency that arises. Firefighting is dangerous and complicated, so it requires organization and teamwork. At every fire, firefighters perform specific duties assigned by a company officer such as a lieutenant, captain, or other department officer. Firefighters connect hoselines to hydrants, operate pumps, and position ladders. Because duties can vary while the company is in action, all members must be skilled in many different firefighting activities, such as rescue, ventilation, and salvage. Some firefighters also operate emergency rescue vehicles, fireboats, and other heavy machinery. In addition, they take people out of harm's way and administer first aid.

Most fire departments are also responsible for fire-prevention activities in the community. The departments provide specially trained personnel to inspect public buildings for conditions that might lead to a fire. They may check building plans, the number and working condition of fire escapes and fire doors in buildings, the storage of flammable materials, and other issues related to potential fire hazards. Fire personnel may also inspect private homes for potential fire hazards. In addition, firefighters educate the public about fire prevention and safety measures by speaking at schools, coordinating with civic groups, holding car seat safety and installation clinics, and displaying equipment and trucks at public events.

Firefighters must hold regular practice drills and attend classroom training when not responding to emergencies. They're also responsible for cleaning and maintaining the equipment they use.

EMPLOYMENT OUTLOOK

The tragic events of September 11, 2001, highlighted both the dangers of being a firefighter and the courage of the men and women called to the profession. According to the US Fire Administration, 343 New York firefighters lost their lives that day. Because of their selfless actions, however, many more lives were saved. Since the 9/11 attacks, America has renewed her love for firefighters and first responders.

Even though the hazards of the profession have become all too clear, thousands of men and women strongly desire to join a fire service and serve their communities. It is an attractive career for many because the educational requirements are relatively low, salaries are relatively high, and a pension is guaranteed upon retirement. For these reasons, expect stiff competition for available job opportunities. The number of qualified applicants typically exceeds the number of available jobs, even though the written examination and physical requirements eliminate many candidates. Increasing competition for firefighter positions is expected to continue, especially as the demand for wildland firefighters increases.

According to the US Department of Labor's Bureau of Labor Statistics (BLS), firefighting jobs are expected to grow by 5 percent between 2018 and 2028. Most job growth will stem from volunteer positions being converted to paid positions. Additionally, a trend toward living in cities has increased the demand for firefighters.

Large, urban fire departments are expected to experience the slowest amount of growth. The turnover rate of firefighting jobs is particularly low at present. The low number is somewhat unusual when you consider that the role of a firefighter is hazardous and requires a relatively limited investment in formal education. Other job openings will arise, of course, as firefighters retire, leave the job for different reasons, or transfer to other occupations. Many city firefighter departments are looking for candidates with at least some college education in related fields, including emergency response. According to the BLS, physically fit applicants with high test scores, some post-secondary firefighter education, and paramedic training have the best prospects.

In recent years, firefighters have become involved in much more than preventing fires. In response to the expanding role of firefighters, some municipalities have combined fire prevention, public fire education, safety, and **emergency medical services** (EMS) into a single organization. Some local and regional fire departments have been consolidated into countywide public safety organizations. Consolidation has helped reduce overhead and administrative staff sizes and established more consistent training standards and work procedures.

PLACES OF EMPLOYMENT

According to the BLS, about 332,400 men and women worked as paid career firefighters in 2018. Nine out of ten firefighters worked in local fire departments. These fire departments vary widely in size; large cities can have several thousand workers on the payroll, whereas small towns can employ fewer than twenty-five. Most firefighters work in state and federal installations, including airports. Firefighting opportunities can also be found with private companies, such as manufacturing plants.

ESSENTIAL JOB TASKS OF FIREFIGHTERS

The following list of essential duties comes directly from a firefighter job posting:

Emergency Scene Response

Initial Response to Incidents

- Don protective turnout gear and equipment before and at emergency scenes.
- Proceed to assigned apparatus upon receiving a call for service.
- Make preliminary evaluations of incidents based on alarm information (e.g., alarm type, structure type, and so on).

Watch Duties

- Stand watch to receive incoming alarms and information, answer phones, and monitor access to the station house.
- Record administrative and general information messages from computer dispatch.
- Provide alarm communique to equipment operators/officers.
- Test alarms and dispatch equipment.
- Notify station personnel—over public address or through signals—of incoming alarms and required response.
- Field phone calls from outside and inside the department.

Driving

- Drive apparatus safely to and from emergency scene.
- Position apparatus upon arrival at emergency scene.
- Learn the most direct and expeditious routes by studying them before incident response; choose these routes when driving to an alarm site.
- Learn traffic laws and street conditions to allow safe and efficient apparatus operation.
- Plan route and position based on anticipated actions (e.g., arrival routes) of other companies when driving to multiple-alarm calls.

Pump Operations

- Connect apparatus to fire hydrant and operate pumps to supply water in appropriate pressure and volume using hydrant wrenches, couplings, hoses, spanner wrenches, and other tools.
- Connect and lay feeder line to supply water to fire; connect suction hose between hydrant and engine.
- Engage pumps and fill hose with water using hydrant pressure.
- Monitor control panel (e.g., water temperature, oil pressure gauge, fuel gauge, hydrant pressure).

ALERT

Remember, all traffic laws are applicable to emergency responders, including the fire department. An apparatus cannot be driven the wrong way down a one-way street, even if it is the closest route; nor can the vehicle drive through a red light. Optimally, citizens will move to the side of the road providing a safe space for an emergency vehicle. Still, the firefighter driving the apparatus is responsible for the safety of firefighters and the public no matter how dire the emergency.

1

- Pump pre-connected hoseline, master stream and sprinkler systems, wet or dry standpipe systems, specialty nozzles (e.g., drive-in, cellar distributor), aerial ladders, and booster lines.
- Connect ladder pipe to supply water during aerial ladder operations; adjust water pressure (by rule-of-thumb, according to pressure chart, or according to rules and regulations) in response to calls for increased or decreased pressure.
- Implement cold-weather procedures such as tank circulation when necessary.
- Maintain pressure by adjusting pressure relief valve or automatic pressure governor, then transfer from pressure stage to volume stage.
- Open and flush hydrants to ensure they're functional and drain properly.
- Shut down the pump when ordered by an officer.

Hose and Extinguisher Operations

- Stretch line or use extinguisher to deliver water, foam, and other extinguishing agents to the emergency scene.
- Operate nozzle at the front of the hoseline and spray water or other agent onto the fire or other hazards or into the involved structure to extinguish, contain, or control the fire-related incident.
- Locate the seat of the fire or alternate hazard (e.g., a gas leak) by observing, smelling, or listening for smoke, sound, flames, gas, vapors, and so on.
- Advance, or assist in advancing, the hose to the seat of fire or fire hazard.
- Disconnect hose from bed and attach to discharge gate.
- Determine type of hose and number of lengths needed for an operation.
- Connect hose to standpipe during high-rise incident command; connect hoselines to nozzles.
- Select type of extinguisher (e.g., foam, dry chemical, and so on) needed for an incident and use appropriate type to extinguish, contain, or control it.
- Feed hoseline to other fire personnel.
- Determine proper nozzle and nozzle setting.
- Operate stand on tower ladder to apply water to structures on fire.
- Pull hose off hose bed; flake out or unkink hoseline before charging or during extinguishment to ensure proper operations.

Mechanical Ladder Operations

- Stabilize ladder trucks; elevate and operate aerial ladders and platforms to rescue victims; provide access for ventilation; operate master stream devices.
- Climb mechanical ladders to perform search, rescue, and other operations.
- Operate ladder from ground or platform controls and elevate, rotate, and extend aerial or tower ladder for supported and unsupported operations while watching for power lines, trees, and other overhead obstructions.
- Stabilize elevating apparatus with wheel chocks; stabilize pads, jacks, and outriggers.
- Operate and direct ladder pipe to supply water during aerial ladder operations.

1

Manual Ladder Operations

- Determine manual ladder type and size needed at incident scene; carry manual ladder from apparatus to incident scene; anchor and secure manual ladders.
- Raise, extend, and climb manual ladders to perform search, rescue, and other operations.
- Return manual ladder to apparatus.

Forcible Entry

- Determine best location for forcible entry.
- Pry open, cut, or break down doors or otherwise enter structures, vehicles, aircraft, and other entrapments to search for and rescue victims and provide access to the emergency scene.
- Use pry bars, axes, sledgehammers, battering rams, Halligan tools, and other means to execute a forcible entry; cut through surfaces using power tools.
- Remove locks or hinges from doors and break holes in wooden, brick, and masonry walls using sledgehammers, battering rams, axes, and other forcible entry tools.

Ventilation

- Open or break windows; chop or cut holes in roofs; breach walls or doors; hang fans in windows or doors to remove heat, smoke, or gas from structures or entrapments.
- Determine best location for venting structure based on location of hazard and fire personnel, roof type, and building construction; hang fans from ladders and in doors, windows, and holes in roofs or walls.
- Use fans to create positive pressure.

Search

- Search assigned area for victims and to obtain further information about an incident; follow standard search procedures.
- Search area of fire-related hazard for conscious and unconscious victims; sweep assigned search area with arms, legs, or tools.
- Search floors above and below fire or other hazard, including stairwells and bulkheads, for victims who need to be moved or rescued.
- Examine perimeter of structure to determine whether any victims need assistance at windows, on ledges, or in the immediate vicinity of the structure.
- Identify hazardous conditions during a search and inform others of the problem(s).
- Determine search procedure or strategy required to accomplish objectives.
- Search main structures and extensions for the seat of a fire or other hazard.

Rescue

- Assist, hoist, carry, and drag victims away from emergency area using interior access (stairs, hallways, and so on), or, if necessary, by ladders, fire escapes, platforms, or other means of escape including rescue harnesses, ropes, and additional rescue equipment.
- Rescue drowning victims with lifesaving techniques.

1

- Conduct water rescues (e.g., a river rescue using boats) in accordance with established guidelines.
- Evacuate persons from incident scene to lessen risk of injury from fire, explosion, or chemical exposure.
- Move heavy objects and obstructions to access to trapped victims or bodies using air bags, chains and hoists, jacks, shoring materials, Hurst tools (also known as the "Jaws of Life"), and other hydraulic tools.
- Pry, break, or cut structures, vehicles, or aircraft to free victims involved in accidents, cave-ins, collapsed buildings, or other entrapments using door openers, jaws, axes, and other manual and mechanical equipment.
- Instruct persons on upper floors of an engaged structure about appropriate emergency actions, such as staying put, ascending to upper floors, and descending to lower floors via fire escapes.
- Dig to free victims trapped in tunnels, pipes, excavations, cave-ins, or other entrapments using shovels, picks, spades, and other equipment.
- Place victims on stretchers, backboards, Stokes baskets, or other rescue equipment.

Salvage

- Move and cover furniture, appliances, merchandise, and other property; cover holes in structures; stabilize damaged structural components; redirect or clean up water to minimize damage using plastic and canvas covers.
- Tear down/shore up weak and dangerous structural components; (e.g., floors, walls, roofs, over-hangs, and stairs) using hooks, axes, saws, and other tools.
- Spread salvage covers over property.
- Protect the integrity of the incident scene during salvage operations in case of suspected arson.
- Remove water from floors using brooms, squeegees, mops, water chutes, catchalls, and pumps.

Overhaul

- Open walls and ceilings, cut or pull up floors, move or turn over debris to check for hidden fires which could rekindle or spread using hooks, axes, saws, and pitchforks.
- Open ceilings and walls to expose hot spots and other hazardous conditions using axes, pike poles, and other fire rescue equipment.
- Search for and extinguish hidden fires by looking, feeling, or smelling for fire and smoke.
- Check open areas, walls, and other structures for fire extensions.
- Remove and neutralize or dispose of flammable or hazardous materials in buildings.
- Remove and extinguish burned or smoldering debris from buildings.
- Determine whether a smoke detector was present and functional before the fire.

Clean Up/Pick Up

- Pick up, clean, and return equipment to vehicle; roll or fold hose so the company can return to service.
- Control and clean up any medical waste products used by firefighters.
- Clean and return all tools, equipment, supplies, and property in usable condition to appropriate vehicles.

- Shut down and drain lines at pumps; see that all hoses used during response to incident are accounted for.
- Clean hoses using hose washers, brooms, and brushes.
- Back hoselines out of structures.

First Aid

- Provide direct medical assistance to persons requiring emergency attention or assist others in providing medical attention.
- Administer CPR if necessary; administer emergency medical treatment other than CPR as needed.
- Determine priority of emergency medical treatment for victims.
- Operate oxygen and other medical equipment; assist EMS personnel in administering medical treatment.

Station Duties and Maintenance

Equipment Maintenance

- Check, clean, and maintain personal gear and equipment to ensure proper and safe operation.
- Check self-contained breathing apparatus (SCBA) for proper operation and adequate air pressure.
- Check medical equipment.
- Check turnout gear for safety and structural integrity.
- Check the condition of generators, blowers, lights, cords, and fans.
- Check and maintain power equipment.
- Place turnout gear on or near apparatus.
- Check extension ladders.
- Check hose on apparatus (proper bedding and amount).
- Check and perform ordinary maintenance on other portable equipment (e.g., oil levels, greases, and so on).
- Clean, reload, and test hoses.
- Perform annual hose tests.
- Take inventory and perform regular maintenance on hand tools.
- Change over equipment and supplies from one apparatus to another.
- Paint and stencil equipment as needed.

Apparatus Maintenance

- Inspect, clean, and maintain apparatus to ensure proper and safe operation.
- Inspect engine to ensure the water pump works, then check engine pump pressure.
- Inspect aerial ladder sections and outriggers.
- Report mechanical or electrical problems to officer so apparatus can be taken out of service and repaired.
- Perform daily apparatus check (e.g., oil, fuel, and water levels; proper pressures and lubrications; inspection of batteries, lights, sirens, brakes, tires).

Chapter 1: What Firefighters Do

- Perform weekly apparatus check (e.g., hydraulic fuel levels); equip apparatus with traction devices (e.g., chains) as necessary.
- Check with equipment operator coming off duty regarding condition of apparatus.
- Perform annual pump test.

Facility Maintenance

- Check, clean, and maintain house facilities, including performing or assigning routine house-keeping chores.

Fire Prevention and Investigation

Inspection of Buildings and Fire Protection Devices

- Inspect buildings for fire prevention and hazardous materials code violations.
- Recognize and remedy code violations (e.g., blocked exits, improper storage of chemicals, and so on); inspect buildings (including schools) for code compliance.
- Inspect buildings upon request of occupants or owners.
- Conduct on-site inspections of fire protection devices (e.g., hydrants, alarms, sprinkler systems).

Pre-Fire Planning

- Review or prepare plans to provide information regarding hydrant locations, exposures, hazardous materials, and other areas or situations of high risk.
- Conduct site surveys in district.
- Tour buildings to identify or verify the presence of unusual fire hazards or situations.
- Recognize a target hazard (e.g., a new high-rise or a building with hazardous materials) that may warrant development of a pre-fire plan.
- Conduct familiarity inspections in district; become familiar with the layout of first- and second-alarm districts.

Investigations

- Examine incident scene, conduct interviews, collect and preserve evidence, and review forms and reports to help determine the cause of a fire or other emergency.
- Respond to incidents of suspicious or undetermined origin.
- Observe fireground conditions to detect possible arson.

Public and Community Relations

Public Relations

- Engage in activities that have an impact on the department's image in the community; provide information to the media and support for civilians.
- Deal with distressed individuals at emergency scenes.
- Meet civilians in the fire station, conduct tours, and provide information as requested.
- Make public presentations and conduct demonstrations of apparatus and equipment on behalf of the fire department.

Public Training and Education

- Oversee, develop, conduct, and evaluate fire prevention and other educational programs for the public.

Audiovisual Production

- Operate audiovisual equipment; develop and produce audiovisual materials for internal use or for public broadcasting.

Professional Development

- Participate in training drills and classes to enhance job-related skills and abilities; read internal memos and bulletins to stay current on new developments in departmental operations and procedures.
- Maintain knowledge of chemicals and other hazardous materials, building structures related to fire control, and latest firefighting equipment and techniques.
- Attend routine training drills and sessions; attend specialized training sessions on such topics as CPR certification, foam, ICS, and so on.
- Attend "live incident" training drills.
- Attend external seminars, workshops, and college courses to stay up to date on developments in fire service.
- Participate in external agencies and societies such as the National Fire Protection Association (NFPA).
- Keep abreast of developments in fire service by reading professional journals and publications such as *Fire Command*, *Wildfire*, and *Firehouse*.

Other Duties

- Operate generator to supply electricity to emergency scenes; set up electrical cords and lights as needed.
- Serve on special project committees as assigned.

WORKING CONDITIONS

Firefighters spend much of their time at fire stations, many of which have facilities for dining and sleeping. When an alarm sounds, firefighters must respond rapidly, regardless of the weather or hour. They may spend long periods outdoors fighting fires in adverse conditions.

Firefighting is among the most hazardous occupations. It involves risk of death or injury from cave-ins, toppling walls, and exposure to flames and smoke. Firefighters may also be exposed to poisonous, flammable, and explosive gases and chemicals.

In some cities, firefighters are on duty for 24 hours, then off for 48, receiving an extra day off at certain intervals. In other cities, they work a day shift of 10 hours for three or four days in a row, a night shift of 14 hours for three or four nights, have three or four days off, and then repeat the cycle. While in many large cities, particularly along the eastern United States, firefighters work a standard 40-hour week, others average as many as 56 hours per week. In addition to scheduled hours, firefighters often work the extra hours required to bring a fire under control. Fire lieutenants and captains work the same hours as the firefighters they supervise. Duty hours may include down time when firefighters are free to read, study, or pursue personal interests.

1

FIRST RESPONDER AND EMERGENCY MEDICAL SERVICES

New firefighters are typically eager to extinguish large blazes and perform daring feats of rescue in dangerous situations. While firefighters are certainly called upon to respond to all sorts of fires, they also assist with car accidents and the emergency treatment of serious injuries. Since the profession has accrued more and more duties over the years, fire departments now respond to more medical calls or cardiac emergencies than any other type of call, including fires.

Providing emergency medical care is often part of the firefighter's role. In fact, most firefighters are required to become certified as first responders, at a minimum. Firefighters deal with burns, broken bones, serious cuts and abrasions, and breathing stoppages—all of which may occur at the sites of major fires. Each recruit to a fire department receives training for these medical emergencies as part of his or her overall firefighter training. Since many municipalities merge firefighting sources with EMS, some firefighters are trained to be **emergency medical technicians (EMTs)**, and some EMTs and paramedics are trained as firefighters.

The initial open competitive exam—the one you're preparing for now in hopes of being accepted into the training program of your choice—will test your learning skills, common sense, judgment, and general awareness of safety measures and first aid. You will not be tested on advanced emergency techniques, as additional training for this area is included as part of the job.

Before providing anyone with emergency medical treatment, firefighters must ensure that the scene is safe and take proper **body substance isolation** (BSI) precautions to protect against infectious disease or other hazardous conditions. Firefighters put themselves at great risk when treating patients in pre-hospital settings. Because a patient's infection status is often unknown, firefighters may be exposed to infected blood or other body fluids.

An overzealous firefighter may not want to take the time for precautions such as wearing **personal protective equipment** (PPE) or cleaning surfaces stained with body fluids, especially when victims are in urgent need. However, firefighters who expose themselves unnecessarily to infectious diseases can pose a danger to those they intend to help.

Firefighters must be trained to assess patients rapidly at the scene of an emergency. This assessment involves quickly determining the following:

- The overall condition of the patient
- The extent of injury or illness
- The type of intervention and treatment required
- How to prioritize patients according to the seriousness of their injuries or illnesses
- The immediate transportation of seriously ill patients

The most important aspects of the initial assessment can be easily remembered with the acronym **ABCDE**, which stands for the following:

NOTE
Training doesn't stop once you've learned how to extinguish a fire. Firefighters often respond to medical emergency calls, such as cardiac events or car accidents.

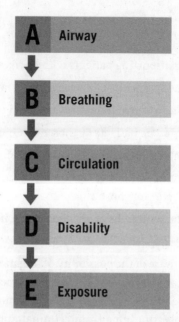

The elements of assessment involve the following steps:

Airway	Airway with cervical spine immobilization: <ul><li>Check for obstruction.</li><li>If trauma is present, immobilize cervical spine.</li></ul>
Breathing	Breathing (plus oxygen if needed) <ul><li>Ensure sufficient movement of air into the lungs.</li></ul>
Circulation	Circulation (with control of bleeding and IV fluids) <ul><li>Ensure oxygenated blood is being delivered to the tissues of the body (perfusion).</li><li>Check for life-threatening bleeding.</li></ul>
Disability	Disability (level of consciousness) <ul><li>Assess and protect brain and spinal functions.</li></ul>
Exposure	Exposure for examinations and protection from the environment <ul><li>Identify all injuries.</li><li>Avoid hypothermia.</li></ul>

Firefighters must be familiar with procedures to treat cardiac emergencies, as about 50 percent of deaths from cardiac disease occur outside of a hospital. The first responder plays a critical role in the treatment of these patients. The firefighter or EMT who encounters a cardiac patient in the field must perform lifesaving procedures. **Cardiopulmonary resuscitation (CPR)** skills are vital. However, studies have shown that CPR alone—although often a critical component of the lifesaving process—is not enough to resuscitate a patient. Defibrillation with an **automatic external defibrillator (AED)** is a relatively new, and, in some cases, legally mandated, responsibility of the first-aid provider. The computer systems of the AED help first responders diagnose and treat cardiac patients with electricity to help restore a regular heart rhythm. AEDs are simple to use and maintain, so more public safety professionals are now learning how to use this essential lifesaving device with only a few hours of training.

1

The following is a brief list of emergency medical procedures firefighters often use at emergency scenes:

- Treating and transporting patients with burns and smoke inhalation injuries
- Recognizing the symptoms of heat cramps, heat exhaustion, and heat stroke
- Treating patients with wounds, fractures, and other traumatic injuries
- Treating water rescue patients or those with hypothermia
- Treating patients suffering from respiratory ailments such as asthma
- Recognizing the symptoms of carbon monoxide poisoning and providing treatment and transport for those affected
- Recognizing the symptoms of an adverse reaction to hazardous materials and providing treatment for those affected

NOTE

Knowing what can and cannot be done during a medical emergency is a vital skill for firefighters.

Firefighters must be aware of the possibility of litigation as a result of providing emergency medical treatment. Lawsuits against people in the medical field—even those who provide first aid or pre-hospital care—have become more common in recent years, and public safety personnel are no longer immune from criminal and civil liability. All fire department personnel should be familiar with concepts of civil liability, tort liability, and negligence, as well as applicable laws and statutes regarding the provision of medical care. Firefighters can protect themselves from becoming the focus of a criminal or civil lawsuit by knowing their responsibilities at the scene of a medical emergency. They must follow all procedures carefully, document every action they take, and possess an understanding of patients' rights.

Common Sense

When you first think about fire-related injuries, you probably think of burns. A firefighter is much less likely to have to deal with burn injuries, however, than with respiratory arrest, cardiac arrest, or shock. If a fire victim's heart stops beating, he or she may survive only a few minutes without immediate medical attention. A victim in cardiac arrest will have no pulse. Your firefighter training will include CPR, and you must learn to initiate CPR immediately—with one exception: If the fire is gaining on you and a victim, you both must first escape immediately. Remaining in the path of a fire to apply CPR to a victim may create two victims instead of one. This is a matter of common sense. You might encounter a question about a scenario such as this on your exam. You might be asked which step of many you should take first in a given situation. The examiners are not really testing your knowledge of emergency medical practices and procedures here—they're looking for signs of logical reasoning and good judgment. Removing a victim from a fire is ALWAYS the first step.

Airway and Breathing

After a victim is removed from a fire, check his or her level of consciousness. If the victim is unconscious, open his or her airway. The next priority is the victim's breathing, regardless of any other injuries he or she might have sustained. Check for absence of breathing by observing the victim's chest or putting your ear to his or her nose to listen or feel for signs of breath. A person can live for only a short time without breathing, and a person who survives without breathing for an extended time may suffer severe brain damage.

Historically, the preferred method of attempting to restore breathing has been mouth-to-mouth resuscitation. The following table shows the steps for CPR with rescue breaths for all motionless victims with one rescuer present.

CPR with Rescue Breaths	Check
1. Check responsiveness. Tap and shout.	
2. Check for evidence of head or neck trauma. If none is evident, open the airway using the head tilt-chin lift or jaw thrust maneuver. Jaw Thrust Head Tilt-Chin Lift	
3. Check for breathing: Look, listen, and feel for normal breathing (not gasping) for 5 to 10 seconds.	
4. If the victim is breathing but unresponsive, place him or her in the recovery position.	
5. If the victim is not breathing, give two normal rescue breaths, each lasting one second*, with enough volume to produce visible chest rise.	
6. If rescue breaths go in, check the victim's pulse for up to 10 seconds.	
7. If the victim has no pulse, begin CPR: cycles of thirty chest compressions and two rescue breaths for 2 minutes (five cycles). Reassess after every five cycles.	
8. If a pulse is present but the victim is not breathing, provide rescue breathing only.	
9. If a rescue breath does not make the chest rise, re-tilt the head and try another rescue breath.	
10. If the rescue breath still does not make the chest rise, assume the airway is obstructed. Give cycles of thirty chest compressions, look for an object in the mouth, remove any visible object, and give two rescue breaths.	

*The one-second duration to make the chest rise applies to all forms of ventilation during CPR, including mouth-to-mouth, bag-mask ventilation, and ventilation through an advanced airway with or without supplemental oxygen.

In 2008, the American Heart Association (AHA) announced a major change in bystander CPR guidelines, declaring that untrained bystanders who perform chest compressions on cardiac arrest victims need not perform mouth-to-mouth resuscitation. The advisory changed 50-year-old guidelines that had combined chest compressions and "rescue breaths." Factors influencing the change included new studies showing that hard and fast chest pushes alone are as effective as—or even better than—traditional CPR in the moments after a collapse from cardiac arrest.

However, medical emergency personnel trained in CPR with mouth-to-mouth resuscitation should continue performing the procedure. Although there is now greater emphasis on the delivery of effective chest compressions, mouth-to-mouth resuscitation is still recommended for infants and children and for adult cardiac arrests caused by non-heart problems such as electrocution or near drowning.

1

You will not be asked how to perform mouth-to-mouth resuscitation on your exam, but you may encounter a question about when such a procedure is appropriate or for how long you should continue administering mouth-to-mouth resuscitation. These questions are intended to determine your level of awareness and the quality of your judgments.

Bleeding

Severe bleeding is not a direct result of exposure to fire, but among fire victims it is not uncommon. The bleeding is, of course, the result of an injury. People attempting to escape a fire might rush through a smoke-filled area with poor visibility and crash through jagged glass or impale themselves on fire-damaged wood or metal. The escape attempt might entail a fall or a jump that leads to injury. Bleeding often looks worse than it is, but spurting, bright-red blood from a severed artery (**arterial bleeding**) causes rapid, massive blood loss and is often fatal. Uncontrolled, long-term, heavy bleeding (**hemorrhaging**) from a large vein can also prove fatal.

NOTE

You will not be asked to name pressure points on the firefighter exam. Still, it's useful to know where they are. The exam might include a general question about control of bleeding to assess your priorities.

Treat a bleeding, injured person in a recline position if possible. If the bleeding is from a limb, elevate it to slow the blood flow. The firefighter, EMT, or other person offering aid should then cover the wound with the cleanest cloth readily available and press down hard. Pressure over the wound should slow the bleeding and limit the loss of blood so that a clot can form. You might need to maintain this pressure on the wound for a considerable time before a self-limiting clot can form. You will know that clotting is occurring when bleeding noticeably slows; the bloody area of the covering cloth will stop expanding, and the cloth may feel a bit drier. At this point you can secure the cloth over the wound by tying it snugly, but not tightly. If pressure over the wound stops the bleeding, this is the treatment of choice. Because maintaining pressure on a wound can take a considerable length of time, scan the area for an onlooker to assume the task so that you, the professional firefighter, can return to the fire scene to search for more victims or help fight the fire. Recognizing when and how to enlist nonprofessional help is another aspect of good judgment.

Arterial bleeding can sometimes be stopped, at least temporarily or in conjunction with direct pressure over the wound or **pressure points** (areas on the body where the artery lies close to bone). External pressure can narrow the artery against resistance from the bone. Pressure points are located at the temple (in front of the ear), below the jaw, behind the collarbone, in the upper and lower arms, at the wrist, in the groin, at the knee, and in the ankle. Apply pressure at the pressure point positioned between the wound and the heart and that's located closest to the wound. If you apply pressure at the appropriate pressure point and over the wound itself, you can slow the flow of blood and hasten clot formation. The diagram on the following page shows the locations of pressure points on the body.

A **tourniquet** is a tight, constricting band placed entirely around an extremity (arm or leg) to stop the flow of blood. A tourniquet is a method of last resort because it stops all blood flow to tissues beyond that point. Lack of blood eventually causes tissue death. After a tourniquet has been put in place and tightened, it should only be loosened or removed by a doctor. For these reasons, before placing a tourniquet, consider how soon the victim will receive qualified medical attention. If you find it impossible to stop arterial bleeding in any other way, it's better to lose the limb and save the life.

1

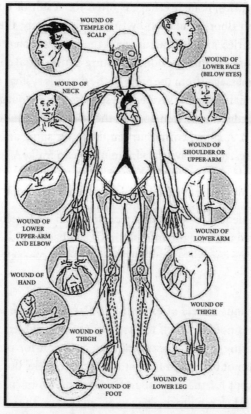

Pressure points for temporary control of aerterial bleeding.

Other Emergencies

Cardiac arrest, respiratory arrest, and hemorrhage represent three emergency situations in which firefighters must take immediate, decisive action. In these situations, time is of the essence. If you find yourself facing any one of these medical emergencies, you cannot wait for an EMT, paramedic, ambulance, or doctor. You must act. Be sure to remember this when answering questions on your exam.

Other emergency medical situations require immediate attention from firefighters and EMTs at the scene, but they don't require such instantaneous or proactive responses. These situations, while not immediately life threatening, can easily lead to shock and subsequent death. Two such examples are fractures and burns.

Fractures

A bone fracture can be in an extremity (arm, leg, hand, or foot), in the head, or in the torso (collarbone, rib, or pelvis). Fractures must be diagnosed and treated by a physician, and they can be extremely painful. A fracture victim in extreme pain may go into shock. The role of the firefighter at the scene is to lessen the chance or severity of shock by alleviating a victim's pain. The pain of a fracture is best alleviated by immobilizing the affected area. If it is safe to leave the victim wherever he or she is sitting or lying, instruct the person to stay put and move as little as possible. If the person must be moved, do so as gently as possible with minimal jarring to the affected area. When possible, fashion a makeshift splint extending beyond joints on either side of the break. Such a splint—made of a board or stick, padded with cloths or grass or moss, and secured with string or belts—should keep pieces of bone from moving about and spare the flesh from friction. The less motion, the less tissue damage that's likely to occur, in addition to bleeding, pain, and potential shock.

1

In fire emergencies, bone breakage is often the result of jumping from high windows or falling through floors weakened by fire. Unfortunately, these jumps and falls frequently cause back injuries, and the fracture with the greatest potential for grave damage is a spinal fracture. Enclosed within the bony structure of the spinal column is the spinal cord, which carries nerve messages from the brain to the nervous system and to the muscles of the entire body. If the spinal column is severed, these messages cannot get through. Broken bones have sharp, ragged edges. A broken bone in the spinal column, if a victim is moved, can injure the spinal cord. A spinal cord injury in the lower spine affects the lower extremities and, in extreme cases, it can leave the victim unable to walk. A spinal cord injury farther up on the spine can affect all parts of the body below the injury. A broken neck, for example, can leave the victim paralyzed from the neck down: a quadriplegic.

The general rule in first aid is that a person with a suspected back or neck injury should never be moved until totally immobilized on a backboard. In firefighting, however, there is always the one consideration that takes precedence—getting away from the fire.

Burns

The most obvious effects of exposure to fire are **smoke inhalation** and **burns**. Smoke inhalation does not lend itself to first aid. As a firefighter, you can administer oxygen as instructed during your academy training and wait for professional medical assistance. Burns also cannot be treated fully at the scene, but the burn victim can and must receive attention. Except for the most superficial burns, all burns should be considered serious. Body fluids are lost rapidly through exposed flesh in the wake of a burn, which can lead to dehydration, lowered blood pressure, and shock.

The intense pain of burns can also contribute to shock. After safely removing the burn victim from the fire area, make him or her lie down. Stop the burning process with cool water. Remove smoldering clothes and all jewelry. You should then loosely cover burned areas with a dry, sterile bandage or the cleanest cloth available. Do not break any blisters or use any ointments, lotions, or antiseptics on a burn victim. Do not give the patient anything by mouth. He or she may need advanced airway management or surgical procedures.

Shock

Shock is the body's involuntary response to major injury. It can occur immediately upon injury to the body or develop gradually. Shock is characterized by a swift and severe loss of blood pressure, rapid decrease in body temperature, bodily weakness, rapid heartbeat, and fainting. Lowered blood pressure is accompanied by decreased blood circulation and oxygen starvation of the cells, especially those of the vital organs. Therefore, the brain, liver, heart, and kidneys can quickly be damaged by shock. If shock deepens and continues, liver and kidney failure can result.

The injuries fire victims sustain (blood loss, burns, fractures, etc.) are often associated with a high risk of shock. For a fragile person, fear, fatigue, and pain are enough to initiate the onset of shock. In addition, fire victims often face legitimate apprehension about the fate of their loved ones, who might have been involved in the same fire, mixed with general anxiety about their future. The physical and mental pressures on fire victims are often overwhelming. One of the ways in which our bodies attempt to deal with the trauma is shock.

TIP

If you're given the option of possible paralysis for a victim or certain death, what choice do you have? Consider this as you prepare to take your exam.

1

Everyone who deals with fire victims must be aware of the symptoms of shock and the best ways to forestall, lessen, or reverse the symptoms. The medical treatment of choice is intravenous replacement of lost fluids—blood or plasma by transfusion and other fluids by infusion of saline, sucrose, or electrolyte solutions. Because this medical treatment follows the first-aid treatment by firefighters at the scene, the role of the firefighter is to accomplish these steps:

- **Relocate the victim.** Move the victim to a safe location and allay his or her fear of danger and additional pain.

- **Calm and convince the victim to lie down.** Unless the injuries themselves keep the victim off his or her feet, that person is likely to be highly agitated and prone to walk about frantically. This type of activity will only hasten the victim's shock.

- **Control bleeding.** This is often a lifesaving measure. Blood is necessary to sustain life, and a massive loss of blood is seriously life-threatening. Even moderate loss of blood contributes to shock. With loss of blood pressure and diminished circulation, lower blood volume can lead to a critical situation. As a firefighter, you can help prevent shock by stopping the bleeding.

- **Make the victim comfortable.** A common reaction to trauma is shivering. If the victim's clothing is wet, remove it. Loosen constricting clothing and cover the victim loosely. Keep him or her warm but avoid overheating, as extreme chilling or overheating adversely affect blood circulation. Watch for erratic changes in body temperature and adjust coverings accordingly.

- **Relieve pain.** The firefighter at the scene has limited resources for relieving pain. Immobilizing broken bones can help, as can covering open wounds to protect them from wind, water, or falling debris. Provide reassurance and moral support. Believe it or not, your calming words may help slow a victim's breathing and heart rate as much as anything. You may slow the onset of shock just by talking gently.

As a firefighter, you're the first at the scene of a fire. Thus, you face the primary mandate to save lives. You do so by removing people from danger caused by fire itself, but also by initiating first aid until other qualified personnel arrives to take over. Your task then turns back to extinguishing the fire.

First save lives, then save property. Help keep victims alive, then do what you can to alleviate injury, discomfort, and risk of additional harm. If you remember these simple rules, you should be able to easily answer most of the common sense and judgment questions on the exam.

Serving as an Emergency Medical Technician (EMT)

Fire departments typically have either dedicated EMTs or their firefighters respond to medical calls. Cost-cutting measures have forced more departments to certify firefighters as EMTs to handle large volumes of emergency calls. It's therefore a good idea to become familiar with the requirements for EMT certifications. When applying for firefighter positions, look carefully at all requirements and prerequisites for each department. The specific EMT certification requirements may vary from one department to another.

NOTE

Some fire departments require all applicants to have valid EMT certification; others award preference points to applicants who are already certified.

1

Levels of EMT Certification

There are three levels of EMT certification: **EMT-Basic**, **EMT-Intermediate**, and **EMT-Paramedic**. All three levels require you to complete an appropriate course based on the *National Standard Curriculum*. To become an EMT-Paramedic, you must have prior certification as an EMT-Basic or EMT-Intermediate. EMT certification varies by state.

EMT-Basic Certification involves training in BLS procedures and other tasks required to successfully fulfill the duties of the job. EMT-Basic responsibilities include the following:

- Operating vehicles
- Administering medical care to adult, pediatric, and trauma patients
- Administering CPR
- Using an automatic external defibrillator (AED)
- Treating wounds
- Assisting with childbirth
- Administering certain medications
- Responding to environmental emergencies

EMT-Intermediate Certification requires certification in EMT-Basic, additional training in advanced life support (ALS) procedures, and proficiency in the following skills:

- Giving intravenous therapy
- Treating respiratory emergencies
- Performing advanced airway procedures
- Interpreting cardiac rhythms
- Providing emergency pharmacology
- Managing obstetrical emergencies

EMT-Paramedic Certification requires the completion of all BLS and ALS skills that EMT-Basics and EMT-Intermediates have obtained. However, training in the following areas is also required:

- Patient assessment
- Drug therapy
- Airway management and ventilation
- Trauma and hemorrhage mitigation
- Advanced defibrillation techniques

EMT duties may vary by location and department.

Some applicants who lack the necessary EMT credentials required by a department believe that they can obtain these licensures in a short period. They soon discover, however, that these certifications require extensive training. The EMT-Basic and EMT-Intermediate levels generally require between 300 to 400 hours of instruction; the EMT-Paramedic level requires 1,000 to 1,200 hours of instruction. These certifications are usually valid for two

NOTE

All three levels of EMT certification require knowledge of the ethical and legal issues surrounding medical emergencies.

1

or three years, depending on your state. Most states, as well as most EMS positions, also require EMTs to participate in continuing education courses.

According to the US Department of Labor's online database Occupational Information Network, or O*NET, (**http://online.onetcenter.org**), some additional tasks performed by EMTs and paramedics are as follows:

- Administering emergency medical treatment and life support care to sick or injured persons in a pre-hospital setting as authorized by a physician
- Operating equipment such as electrocardiograms (EKGs), external defibrillators, and bag-valve mask resuscitators in advanced life-support environments
- Assessing the nature and extent of illness or injury to establish and prioritize medical procedures
- Maintaining vehicles and medical and communication equipment; replenishing emergency medical equipment and supplies
- Observing, recording, and reporting to the physician the patient's condition or injury, the treatment provided, and reactions to drugs and treatment
- Performing emergency diagnostic and treatment procedures such as stomach suction, airway management, or cardiac monitoring during the ambulance ride
- Administering drugs orally or by injection, and performing intravenous procedures under a physician's direction
- Comforting and reassuring patients
- Coordinating work with other emergency medical team members and police and fire department personnel
- Communicating with dispatchers and treatment center personnel to provide information about the emergency, to arrange reception of victims, and to receive instructions for further treatment
- Lifting and carrying patients

TRAINING AND ADVANCEMENT

Applicants for municipal firefighting jobs must pass a written test, a medical examination, and tests of strength, physical stamina, and agility, as specified by local regulations. These examinations are open to people who are at least 18 years old and have a high school education or the equivalent. Those who receive the highest scores on the examinations have the best chances for appointment. Extra credit usually is given for military service. Experience gained as a volunteer firefighter may also improve an applicant's chances for appointment.

As a rule, beginners in large fire departments are first trained for several weeks at the department's training center. Through classroom instruction and practical training, the recruits study firefighting techniques, fire prevention, hazardous materials, local building codes, and emergency medical procedures. They also learn how to use axes, saws, chemical extinguishers, ladders, and other rescue equipment. After completing this training, they are assigned to a fire company, where they are evaluated during a probationary period.

A small but growing number of fire departments have accredited apprenticeship programs that last for three to four years. These programs combine formal, technical instruction with on-the-job training under the supervision of experienced firefighters. Technical instruction covers subjects such as firefighting techniques and equipment, chemical hazards associated with various combustible building materials, emergency medical procedures, and fire prevention and safety.

1

Many fire departments offer continuing, in-service training to members of the regular force. This training may be offered during regular, on-duty hours at an easily accessible site connected to the station house alarm system. Such courses help firefighters maintain seldom-used skills and earn permits to operate new equipment the department acquires.

Most experienced firefighters continually study to improve their job performance and prepare for promotion examinations. To earn higher-level positions, firefighters must acquire expertise in the most advanced firefighting equipment and techniques, building construction, emergency medical procedures, writing, public speaking, management, budgeting procedures, and labor relations. Fire departments frequently conduct training programs, and some firefighters attend training sessions sponsored by the National Fire Academy on topics such as executive development, anti-arson techniques, and public fire safety. Most states also have extensive firefighter training programs.

Many colleges and universities offer courses in fire engineering and fire science, which can further a firefighter's education. Fire departments often offer members incentives such as tuition reimbursement or higher pay to pursue advanced training. Many fire captains and other supervisory personnel have college degrees.

Firefighters need to be mentally alert, courageous, and mechanically inclined. They must have endurance and a desire to serve the public. Initiative and sound judgment are crucial, as firefighters are often forced to make quick decisions in emergency situations. Because members of a crew eat, sleep, and work closely together under conditions of stress and danger, they should also be dependable and get along well with others. Leadership qualities are assets for officers, who must establish and maintain discipline and efficiency while directing the activities of firefighters in their companies.

Opportunities for promotion are good in most fire departments. Firefighters can advance to higher ranks as they gain experience. After three to five years of service, they might become eligible for promotion to lieutenant. The line of further promotion usually extends to captain, battalion chief, assistant chief, deputy chief, and chief. Advancement generally depends on a firefighter's scores from a written examination, on-the-job performance, and seniority. Increasingly, fire departments are using assessment centers—which simulate a variety of actual job performance tasks—to screen for the best candidates for promotion. However, many fire departments require that a candidate earn a master's degree, preferably in public administration or a related field, for promotion to positions higher than battalion chief.

FIREFIGHTING IN THE TWENTY-FIRST CENTURY

The terrorist attacks of 9/11 underscored the need for a strong incident command system and effective communications. As a result, nontraditional firefighter responsibilities are being emphasized, such as the investigation of potentially hazardous materials and suspicious activity. In many cases, fire departments must adapt to these new responsibilities without the benefit of additional human resources or funding. Consequently, fire department personnel must work even harder than before to learn new disaster-management techniques and streamline the department's emergency operations.

Before the events of 9/11, many fire departments—as well as the general public—were not prepared for the possibility of a large-scale disaster that could result in the deaths of hundreds of firefighters and thousands of civilians. Today, fire departments must develop plans to manage a variety of worst-case scenarios that include suicide bombings, airplane hijackings, and attacks with nuclear weapons.

To combat such plots and respond most effectively to catastrophes, fire departments have implemented extensive organizational changes with an emphasis on rescue and improved communications. Firefighting personnel must be able to take advantage of available state and federal resources and the assistance of neighboring departments. Each fire department must be willing to adopt and incorporate the policies and procedures of post-9/11 governmental agencies, such as the Department of Homeland Security. Other changes have included coordinating efforts with other departments and agencies, adopting common terminology for emergency situations, seeking additional funding when needed, and exploring new technology and procedures that make operations more efficient and help save lives.

Such changes cannot be implemented successfully without continuous, up-to-date training courses and materials. Cities large and small now devote time and energy to preparing for possible large-scale emergencies. This training is not limited to rookie firefighters. All personnel are required to refresh their knowledge on such topics and absorb new information throughout their careers.

We will never be able to eliminate the threat of terrorist attacks entirely, but the willingness of firefighting organizations to change their traditional operations and examine problems from new perspectives has led to the development of more effective disaster-response plans and increased large-scale disaster training for firefighters.

Note, however, that fire departments cannot neglect their responsibility to provide the community with basic fire safety education. Although it is necessary to plan for biological, chemical, or even nuclear attacks on our communities, it's just as important to make sure the public knows how to maintain smoke detectors, sprinklers, and other fire-prevention technology. All families should have a fire evacuation plan. Building owners and managers must be held accountable to local fire codes. As you might have gathered, new demands in the post-9/11 world must be balanced with a fire department's traditional responsibilities.

EARNINGS

According to the BLS, the median annual earnings of firefighters was $50,850 in 2019. Fire lieutenants, fire captains, and others may earn considerably more. The median annual earnings for fire inspectors in 2019, for example, was $60,230.

Firefighters who work more than a specified number of hours per week are required to be paid for overtime. Firefighters often earn overtime for working extra shifts to maintain minimum staffing levels or in the event of special emergencies.

Some of the benefits firefighters usually receive include the following:

- Medical insurance
- Liability insurance
- Sick leave
- Vacation
- Paid holidays

Almost all fire departments provide protective clothing, such as helmets, boots, and coats, as well as breathing apparatus. Many departments also provide dress uniforms. Firefighters are generally covered by pension plans that provide retirement at half pay after twenty-five years of service, or if disabled in the line of duty.

RELATED OCCUPATIONS

Related fire-protection occupations include wildland firefighters, who battle fires in forests, brush, vegetation, grasslands, and other uninhabited areas; fire-protection engineers, who identify fire hazards in homes; and fire inspectors. Fire-protection engineers also design automatic fire prevention, detection, and extinguishing systems. Fire inspectors examine buildings to detect fire hazards and ensure that federal, state, and local fire codes are met.

ADDITIONAL INFORMATION

Contact your local civil service office or local fire department for information about obtaining a job as a firefighter. Check job postings online or in your local newspaper for ads about available firefighting positions. You may also find listings for fire departments across the country by subscribing to the Industrial/Orgainzaitonal Solutions Fire Service Job Board. See **https://iosolutions.com/firefighter-jobs-fire-service-jobs** for more information.

Information about firefighter careers and qualifications can be obtained from the following resources and organizations:

International Association of Fire Fighters (IAFF)
1750 New York Avenue, NW Suite 300
Washington, DC 20006-5395
Phone: 202-737-8484
Fax: 202-737-8418
www.iaff.org

International Association of Fire Chiefs (IAFC)
4795 Meadow Wood Lane, Suite 100
Chantilly, VA 20151
Phone: 703-273-0911
Fax: 703-273-9363
www.iafc.org

National Registry of Emergency Medical Technicians
Rocco V. Morando Building
6610 Busch Boulevard
P.O. Box 29233
Columbus, OH 43229
Phone: 614-888-4484
Fax: 614-888-8920
www.nremt.org

US Fire Administration (USFA)
16825 S. Seton Avenue
Emmitsburg, MD 21727
Phone: 800-238-3358
Admissions Fax: 301-447-1441
www.usfa.fema.gov

International Association of Women in Fire and Emergency Service (Women in Fire)
1707 Ibis Dr.
Buffalo, MN 55313
Phone: 763-595-1207
Email: staff@womeninfire.org
www.womeninfire.org

National Fire Protection Association (NFPA)
1 Batterymarch Park
Quincy, MA 02169-7471
Phone: 800-344-3555
Fax: 800-593-6372
www.nfpa.org

Summing It Up

- Paid career firefighters must extinguish fires as well as maintain and repair equipment and facilities, conduct fire-prevention activities, and educate their communities about fire safety and prevention.

- About 90 percent of firefighters work in municipal fire departments. Some federal installations and private companies also have fire departments.

- When you apply for a position as a firefighter, you are not expected to know the specifics of driving a fire engine, using extension ladders, charging hoses, and so on. All recruits undergo rigorous training and must pass mastery exams before being appointed to a force. The initial exam tests your ability to learn, your common sense and judgment, and your awareness of general safety measures and emergency medical treatment.

- Providing **emergency medical care** is part of a firefighter's duty. Fire departments typically respond to more medical emergency calls than any other type of call, including fires. They assist with car accidents and give emergency medical treatment to the ill or injured.

- As **first responders**, firefighters are often required to perform vital life-saving procedures, such as treating patients in respiratory or cardiac arrest. You must know CPR and be able to operate automatic external defibrillator devices. You must also be able to recognize and treat burn and smoke inhalation injuries; heat cramps, heat exhaustion, and heat stroke; wounds, fractures, and other traumatic injuries; hypothermia and near-drowning; respiratory ailments; carbon monoxide poisoning; severe bleeding; shock; and adverse reactions to hazardous materials.

- Because cost-cutting measures have caused more fire departments to certify firefighters as **EMTs**, you should know the requirements for these certifications. There are three levels of EMT certification: **EMT-Basic**, **EMT-Intermediate**, and **EMT-Paramedic**. All require that you complete an appropriate course based on the *National Standard Curriculum*. All require extensive training and are valid for two to three years, depending on the state in which you work.

- To become a firefighter, you must pass a written test, a medical exam, and physical tests of strength, stamina, and agility, as specified by local regulations. As a recruit, you undergo several weeks of departmental training, including classroom instruction, practical training, and emergency medical procedures. Many departments also offer in-service training for experienced firefighters to maintain seldom-used skills and learn about new equipment and procedures.

- Opportunities for promotion are good in most fire departments. Since the 9/11 attacks, firefighters have undertaken new responsibilities such as investigating possible hazardous materials and suspicious activity; educating the public about what to do in the case of a large-scale disaster; and developing plans in the event of catastrophes such as suicide bombing attacks, multiple airplane hijackings, and/or attacks with weapons of mass destruction.

- Firefighter-related occupations include fire-protection engineers, who identify fire hazards in workplaces and homes and design fire prevention systems; fire inspectors, who examine buildings to detect fire hazards and ensure that federal, state, and local fire codes are met; and wildland firefighters, who focus on fires in uninhabited areas or large, open spaces.

Chapter 2

Firefighter Screening Process

OVERVIEW

- **Notice of Examination**
- **The Application**
- **Written Exam Contents**
- **Medical Standards**
- **Defining Fitness**
- **Tips for Staying Fit**
- **Physical Ability Tests**
- **The Candidate Physical Ability Test™**
- **Personality Tests and Psychological Evaluations**
- **The Interview**
- **Summing It Up**

NOTICE OF EXAMINATION

The first step on the path to becoming a firefighter is taking a written exam. You will need to know when and where the exam for the fire department in which you wish to serve will be administered. This information, as well as qualification requirements, test descriptions, and application instructions is provided in the **Notice of Examination** (NoE). It is important that you read the entire exam notice before beginning the application process. The following example is from San Marcos, Texas. It represents a typical notice of examination. Read it over and note everything a candidate will need prior to signing up for test day.

2

NOTICE OF CIVIL SERVICE EXAMINATIONS
FIREFIGHTER
San Marcos, Texas

The City of San Marcos will conduct a Civil Service Examination in order to establish an eligibility list for hiring Firefighters. This eligibility list will be in effect for a period of one year from the test date or until the list has been exhausted, whichever occurs first.

**See text box on page 2 for REQUIRED documents that must be submitted on-line by deadline: June 4th

Test Date: **June 10, 2019**
Time: NO ADMITTANCE TO THE TEST SITE AFTER 9:00 AM
Test site: San Marcos Activity Center, 501 E. Hopkins, San Marcos, Texas 78666
Starting Salary: $4,290 Monthly
Incentive Pay: Firefighters are eligible to receive incentive pay for Education, TCFP Certification, and/or Advanced EMS certifications (see below for more information)
Hiring Incentive: We are offering a hiring incentive to candidates holding a current Paramedic certification, and who are hired from this list, of $3,000 (half at hire and half at successful completion of the probationary period).
Lateral Entry: The Lateral Entry Program provides candidates with at least 2 years prior full-time work experience in a comparable fire/EMS agency, with no break in service of 180 days or more, with the ability to start above the first step of the pay scale. The Fire Chief makes the decision regarding eligibility for lateral entry. Placement may be up to step 19.3 of the pay scale based on years of experience in a comparable agency.

Physical Ability Exercise:
Candidates successfully completing the written exam should be prepared to complete the Physical Ability Exercise that same day. The swim exercise will occur immediately upon verification of a passing score on the written exam. Once the candidate has successfully completed the swim exercise, they will complete the Aerial Ladder exercise. The top scoring 30 candidates on the written exam, that have successfully completed both exercises, will be required to report to Station 5 for the Ability Course portion of the Exercise. Details are provided below:

Event: Ability Course Portion of the Physical Ability Exercise
Date: June 10, 2019
Time: Roll Call: TBD based on number of candidates
Place: San Marcos Fire Station #5, 100 Carlson Circle, San Marcos, Texas 78666

Candidates are encouraged to review the following: SMFD Physical Ability Exercise

MINIMUM QUALIFICATIONS INCLUDE:
- Must be at least eighteen (18) years of age and not over thirty-five (35) years of age on the date of the entrance examination.
- Must be a high school graduate or have an equivalency certificate certified by the issuing agency (i.e.: Texas Education Agency).
- Must possess a Basic (or above) Structure Fire Suppression Certification from the Texas Commission on Fire Protection or documentation from the Texas Commission on Fire Protection stating that the candidate is certified as a firefighter on the date of examination.
- Must hold a Texas Department of State Health Services "DSHS" Emergency Medical Services Certification EMT-Basic or higher (National Registry, Licensed, or Certification) on the date of examination.
- Must be able to obtain a Class B Texas Driver's License within one year of employment.
- Must comply with all applicable Civil Service Requirements and Regulations.

City of San Marcos Notice of Firefighter Entrance Examination   Page 1

OTHER REQUIREMENTS:
- Proof of valid driver's license with an acceptable driving record.

ADDITIONAL INFORMATION:

- Hire Preference: Preference in hiring shall be made based on DSHS Emergency Medical Services Certification (National Registry, Licensed, or Certification) level as follows:
  1. First preference – EMT-Paramedic
  2. Second preference –EMT- Advanced
  3. EMT-Basic (required)
- In order to properly train our personnel to provide Advanced Life Support (ALS) services, personnel who are hired that are not already Department of State Health Services (DSHS) and/or National Registry Paramedics **will be** detailed to attend Paramedic (EMT-P) level emergency medical training.
  - These individuals **will be** required to satisfactorily complete the Paramedic training and qualify for National Registry Certification.
  - Failure to satisfactorily complete and continuously maintain the Paramedic level certification and qualify for acceptance by the San Marcos Fire Department's Medical Director as such for the duration of employment constitutes good and sufficient cause for termination.
- The Fire Chief may consider the candidate's failure to remove his/her name from any and all other fire department's eligibility list(s), and provide verification as requested, as a good and sufficient reason to pass over that candidate for initial appointment to a beginning position.
- Employees receive up to $100/month for a College Degree or higher level TCFP Certification.
- EMT-Paramedics will receive an additional $150/month for maintaining their Paramedic Certification.

APPLICATION PROCESS

Candidates must have applied online by June 4, 2019 and present a valid picture identification (i.e. driver's license, ID card, etc.) to be admitted into the test site. Roll call will begin promptly at 9:00 AM. **Candidates not in attendance for roll call will not be permitted to take the test.**

Additional Points: Candidates who pass the examination with a score of 70% or more may be eligible to receive a maximum of five (5) additional points as outlined below. The required documents must be attached through the application process by June 4th to be eligible for the additional points:

- **Military Points (5 points):** Two (2) years prior honorable military experience (Honorable discharge from the United States Armed Forces). The DD-214 must reflect at least 2 years of active duty AND the word "Honorable" must be printed in the "Character of Service" section. The "Member-4" form includes the character of service.
- **Bachelor's Degree or greater (3 points):** A copy of the certified transcript must be provided.

> Required Certifications must be provided:
> The required certifications (highest level for each) must be attached through the application process by June 4th to be eligible to take the exam June 10th.
>   1. Texas Commission on Fire Protection Basic (or above) Structure Fire Suppression Certification.
>   2. DSHS Emergency Medical Services Certification EMT-Basic or higher (National Registry, Licensed, or Certification).

Candidates passing this written examination AND the physical ability exercise will be required to submit the Personal History Statement (PHS) to the San Marcos Fire Department. Candidates will have approximately three weeks to complete the PHS. The Personal History Statement, with additional instructions, will be emailed to you upon review of your application. Generally, candidates spend 12-15 hours to complete this thoroughly.

City of San Marcos Notice of Firefighter Entrance Examination   Page 2

2

TEST SITE INFORMATION

1. Absolutely no talking during the exam except directly to the proctor(s).
2. No reading the questions or answers out loud, for any reason.
3. Any person requiring reasonable accommodations to take the examination shall make such accommodations known to the Civil Service Director, in writing, no later than 10 business days prior to the examination.
4. **No electronic devices are permitted inside the room during the examination**.

TEST INFORMATION

The City of San Marcos' entry-level firefighter examination tests candidates' ability to learn, remember, and apply information, reading comprehension, interests, situational judgment, and logical and mathematical reasoning ability. The examination is a two-part process. The first part is reading and review of a study booklet containing firefighter-related information. You will be given exactly twenty (20) minutes to read the booklet. During this time you should read and learn as much of the information as you can. The second portion is a multiple choice written examination. You will be tested on how much of the information you can remember. You will not be able to take notes when reading the study materials or to refer to the study booklet during the test. A study guide is available for purchase from our test provider, IPMA-HR.

1. Personal items will not be allowed in the testing room (i.e. hats, purses, briefcases, cell phones, pagers, food, drinks, etc.). *No one* will be permitted to leave the building after the test has started until their test has been turned in.
2. Scoring:
   - A score of 70%, or more, is passing.
   - Candidates who pass and meet the criteria outlined above for additional points, receive a maximum of 5 additional points to increase their final score.
   - An eligibility list will be established by listing candidates in order by Texas Department of State Health Services "DSHS" Emergency Medical Services Certification and candidate's final score. In the event of a tie in final score, the order will be determined by the date of receipt of application with the earliest date and time taking priority.
3. The Eligibility List will be posted on the City's webpage by 5:00 p.m. Tuesday, June 11th.

WHO IS CERTIFIED AND WHAT DOES THIS MEAN?

A certified firefighter is a person who holds a Basic, Intermediate, Advanced, or Master Structure Fire Protection Personnel Certification from the *Texas Commission on Fire Protection*. To obtain a Structure Fire Protection Personnel Certification from the *Texas Commission on Fire Protection*, a person must comply with Section 423, Subchapter A of the *Texas Commission on Fire Protection's Standards Manual*.

Qualified candidates must hold a minimum certification of EMT-basic issued by the Department of State Health Services on the date of the examination. If you have any questions about your status with the Department of State Health Services, contact them through their website.

This does not include any volunteer certification, military training or certification, or a certification from another state. If you have any questions about your status with *the Texas Commission on Fire Protection*, contact the Commission through their website.

THE APPLICATION

While some departments still offer paper applications, it's easiest to locate the website for the fire department of your choice and apply online.

Regardless of whether you apply online or with a hand-written application, it's essential that you fill out your application completely and truthfully. It is also a good idea to keep the following points in mind as you complete your application.

- **Neatness counts.** If your application is misread, it is likely to be misfiled or misrepresented. If your application is sloppy, it brands you as careless. Sloppiness on an online application could include mistakes such as capitalizing all letters instead of just the first letter of proper nouns, or inappropriately using lowercase letters. An overly casual presentation could also count against you, so you should avoid chat acronyms, text message abbreviations, or slang on your application.

- **Accuracy is important.** One wrong digit in your Social Security number or exam number can misroute your application. And spelling matters, so proofread your application. Completeness is also a requirement; incomplete applications are often discarded before they're read, so fill in all required fields. Then review all information one last time before finalizing and submitting your application.

- **Telling the truth on your application is vital.** It's okay to describe past duties and responsibilities in the best possible light, but don't exaggerate. Don't list a degree you didn't receive or provide a graduation date if you haven't yet graduated. If your application form asks for reasons for leaving previous employment, give a brief but truthful explanation. Any statement you make on an application form is subject to verification. Staff members at civil service offices are trained to verify facts with schools and former employers. These investigators ask questions about your job performance, attendance record, duties, and responsibilities.

  Any misstatements that are not picked up by background investigators are likely to be unmasked during an interview. The last step of the screening process may be a personal interview with one person or a panel of interviewers. The interviewer(s) will have a copy of your application form and will ask questions based on your responses. The interview will be your opportunity to explain anything unfavorable in your employment history, such as dismissal from a job or frequent job changes. If you've made false claims or stretched the truth too far, the interview is likely to bring these inaccuracies to light.

Before you begin the application process, clean up your social media profiles, including Facebook, LinkedIn, Instagram, and Twitter. More and more employers have added social media investigation to their hiring process. If you wouldn't want someone you respect to see a post or a picture, then you probably wouldn't want your potential employer seeing it, either. Consider taking down posts that feature obscenities, racy photos, complaints about past employers or colleagues, intimate relationship details, and references to drug or alcohol use. Check your accounts not only for content that you have posted but also for links or connections to others for any content that could be considered unethical, immoral, illegal, vulgar, distasteful, or seem undesirable to a fire department. Don't go as far as locking

2

TIP

Be open and truthful on the application; promote your skills at the interview.

down or removing all your profiles, as employers may think that you're trying to hide something. You can use social media to boost your credibility and increase your appeal to an employer by being yourself and using discretion online.

WRITTEN EXAM CONTENTS

As mentioned previously, firefighter exams can vary by department, county, and municipality administering the exam. While the trend in larger departments is to use computer-based tests, many departments still administer paper-and-pencil tests with supplementary test booklets. Some computer-based tests integrate audio and video clips on which-certain question types are based. Regardless of the delivery method, the content on which candidates will be tested generally fall within the following categories:

Category	Skills Assessed
Reading Comprehension	• Understanding and drawing conclusions from written material
Reasoning and Judgment	• **Deductive Reasoning:** Applying general rules or regulations to specific cases or to proceed from stated principles to logical conclusions • **Inductive Reasoning:** Finding a rule or concept which fits a given situation; this would include coming up with a logical explanation for a series of events which seem to be unrelated • **Situational Judgment:** Determining the most suitable response to a given scenario • **Problem Sensitivity:** Recognizing or identifying the existence of problems (but not solving the problem) in a scenario; the problem could be procedural or involve witness/victim inconsistencies • **Information Ordering:** Applying rules to a situation for the purpose of putting the information in the best or most appropriate sequence; we seem to be lacking in the numerical ordering style question type
Spatial Orientation	• Using a map and answering questions that pertain to it
Observation and Memory	• Studying, memorizing, and answering questions about images (e.g., maps and diagrams)
Mechanical Reasoning	• Identifying tools and equipment and their functions
Mathematics	• Solving basic math problems, (primarily word problems) using addition, subtraction, multiplication, division, percentages, ratios, decimals, fractions, and averages • Using mathematical functions to answer question based on charts, graphs, diagrams and tables

Candidates may also be tested on their verbal expression, have their behavioral/interpersonal skills assessed, be given tests related to listening and personality, and be subjected to a psychological evaluation. You can find out more about the contents of the test you are interested in taking by contacting your local firefighter department.

Variations in Test Content and Structure

Many fire departments in recent years have outsourced their testing to third-party contractors. This means there's greater variation in the testing content and structure across states and municipalities than there used to be. This variation effects both physical and nonphysical portions of the test. The following is a selection of different requirements for firefighters arranged by state and county:

Florida

Miami

Miami requires prospects to take the Fire-Rescue Firefighter Exam, which consists of two parts: Lecture and Demonstration Test and Written Comprehension. This exam features three question types: multiple choice, agree-disagree, and lists.

Miami-Dade

Miami-Dade requires prospects to take the Audio-Written Screening Test (AWST), which has four sections: Math, Maps, Reading and Applying Technical Information, and Interpersonal Skills.

Orange County & Tampa

Prospects for the Orange County and Tampa fire departments must take the Ergometrics FireTEAM Exam, which is divided into four parts: Video-Based Human Relations, Mechanical Aptitude, Math, and Reading Ability.

Tallahassee

Tallahassee prospects are required to take the National Fire Select Test by FPSI. This entry-level written test features two main sections: General Aptitude and Personality Inventory.

Georgia

Atlanta

Prospects must take the ASSET Test, which features two components: Basic Skills and Advanced Mathematics.

Augusta

Prospects must take the CWH Firefighter Exam, which features three components: Cognitive Skills, Situational Questions, and a Personal Questionnaire.

New Jersey

In New Jersey, some counties require a firefighter training certificate prior to submitting a formal application.

Massachusetts

Prospects must complete the EB Jacobs Fire Service Assessment Battery (FSAB) as part of the Massachusetts Firefighter Exam. The FSAB is a standardized multiple-choice test designed to measure a candidate's ability and willingness to perform firefighter-related tasks.

The Written Ability portion features six sections: Written Comprehension, Written Expression, Information Ordering, Problem Sensitivity, Deductive Reasoning, and Inductive Reasoning.

2

Illinois

Each department in the state of Illinois has the freedom to administer the exam of its choice.

Chicago

Chicago requires prospects to pass a written test called the Chicago Firefighter test that features six sections: Math, Reading Comprehension, Mechanical Aptitude, Situational Judgment, Spatial Orientation, and General Knowledge.

MEDICAL STANDARDS

Firefighting is a physically demanding occupation. Firefighters may spend extended periods of time at the firehouse being sedentary, playing cards or watching television, or doing low-intensity tasks like cleaning equipment or cooking. Then, suddenly, the department will receive an emergency call that demands sustained and intense physical exertion. These rapid and extreme shifts in demands on a firefighter's body result in considerable physical stress, which is why the selection process places such a strong emphasis on medical conditioning and physical fitness.

FIREFIGHTING—PHYSIOLOGICAL DEMANDS

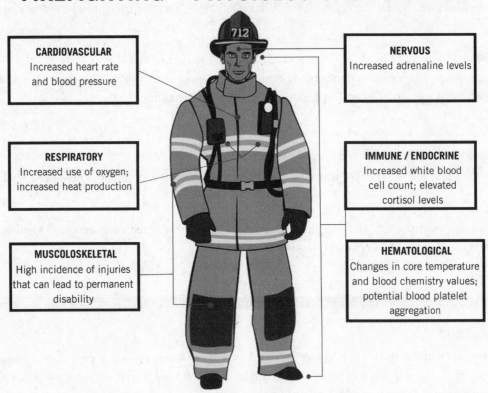

Firefighting requires lifting and carrying heavy objects while encumbered by heavy protective gear in the face of extreme temperatures, water exposure, and poor air quality. This work must be conducted speedily and with constant awareness of personal danger. Firefighters consistently face harsh, emotionally charged environments and physical demands that include the following:

- Excessive heat
- Extreme physical demands
- Wearing more than 70 pounds of equipment
- Toxic chemicals
- Dense smoke
- Breathing compressed air

Federal law prohibits discrimination against job applicants based on age. However, when youth is a bona fide prerequisite for the effective performance of job duties, employers are permitted to prescribe age limits. There is no question—the age limits for firefighter applicants is justified. Firefighter training requires a big investment of time, effort, and money. The goal is to hire and instruct healthy, capable young men and women who will serve many productive years as competent firefighters.

The following three medical standards are a matter of official policy for most fire departments:

1. A candidate must be fit to perform in a reasonable manner all the duties of the position. This position is physically demanding and affects public health and safety. Therefore, the department requires candidates to meet appropriately high standards of physical and mental fitness. The object of the pre-employment examination is to determine that a candidate meets the minimum medical standards. Appointees might be subject to re-examination at any time during their probationary periods.

2. A candidate will be medically disqualified upon a finding of physical or mental disability that renders the candidate unfit to perform in a reasonable manner the duties of this position or that might reasonably be expected to render the candidate unfit to continue to perform in a reasonable manner the duties of this position. (For example, a latent impairment or a progressively debilitating impairment may, in the judgment of the designated medical officer, reasonably be expected to render the candidate unfit to continue to perform the duties of the position.)

3. The fitness of each candidate is determined on an individual basis in relation to this position. The designated medical officer may employ diagnostic procedures, including the use of scientific instruments or other laboratory methods, that in his or her discretion would determine the true condition of the candidate before he or she is accepted. The judgment of the designated medical officer, based on his or her knowledge of the activities involved in the duties of this position and the candidate's condition, is determinative.

The following definitions apply:

- **Physical or Mental Disability:** A physical, mental, or medical impairment resulting from an anatomical, physiological, or neurological condition that prevents the exercise of a normal bodily function or that is demonstrable by medically accepted clinical or laboratory diagnostic techniques. Such impairment may be latent or manifest.

- **Accepted Medical Principles:** Fundamental deduction consistent with medical facts, based on the observation of many cases. To constitute an accepted medical principle, the deduction must be based on the observation of many cases over a significant time period and be so reasonable and logical as to create a certainty that can't be disproved.

- **Impairment of Function:** Any anatomic or functional loss, weakening of the capacity of the body, or any of its parts to perform that which is considered by accepted medical principles as normal.

- **Latent Impairment:** Impairment of function not accompanied by signs or symptoms, but of such a nature that there is a reasonable and moral certainty, according to accepted medical principles, that signs or symptoms will appear within a reasonable period or upon a change of environment.

- **Manifest Impairment:** Impairment of function accompanied by signs or symptoms.
- **Medical Capability:** Efficiency, fitness, or general ability to perform duty based on accepted medical principles.

As you can see, the medical standards for prospective firefighters are strict and rigorous. Conditions that would not deter a person's performance in a less strenuous occupation are disqualifying for firefighters. Some of these conditions are temporary, such as pregnancy; others, such as the use of drugs or being severely overweight, are correctable. Temporary or correctable conditions can cause the candidate to be barred from the physical performance test at any time and may effectively result in disqualification from competition or employment. Once the temporary or correctable conditions are overcome, however, any candidates still within the required age limit can compete the exam at a later date.

Several medical conditions can bar a candidate from employment as a firefighter, even if the candidate scored high on the physical performance test and is otherwise highly qualified. A person with any of these conditions might cause self-injury or suffer permanent complications as a result of undergoing strenuous physical exercise, participating in conditioning programs, or completing a physical performance test.

NOTE

Policies, regulations, and laws can change, as do medical advancements and treatments. The list of conditions shown here has been used by fire departments as grounds for disqualification in the past but may not be current or relevant to your circumstances; if in doubt, please check with the fire department of your choice to verify.

- Alcoholism
- Anemia
- Asthma
- Chronic gastrointestinal disorders
- Diabetes
- Drug dependence
- Heart disease
- High blood pressure
- Joint disease
- Kidney disease
- Liver disease
- Lung disease
- Muscular disorders
- Obesity (not simply being overweight)
- Epilepsy or other seizure disorder
- Sickle cell disease
- Ulcers
- Proneness to heat illness such as heat stroke or heat exhaustion

The preceding list represents conditions that are likely to be permanently disqualifying. Other conditions might not allow a potential candidate to take part in physical training or take the physical performance test until they are removed either by passage of time or through active, curative measures. Examples of such conditions include the following:

- Acute gastrointestinal disorder
- Dehydration
- Drug use
- Hernia
- Infections
- Being overweight
- Pregnancy
- Being severely underweight

Cooperation and assistance of a physician can help candidates attain the health and medical status required to participate in fitness programs and in the test itself. Individuals with any of these conditions should remain under the supervision of a doctor while undergoing vigorous physical training and should not attempt to participate in a physical performance test until given their doctor's approval.

Still other physical or medical conditions can disqualify a candidate by their presence and without regard to physical fitness:

- Severe hearing deficit
- Inability to perform job duties because of dependency on glasses, contact lenses, or hearing aids that can be lost, broken, or rendered dysfunctional under heat stress
- Severe allergies
- Cancer

People with the above conditions may be in excellent general health, but they could still be disqualified as firefighting candidates. Again, when in doubt, it's best to check directly with the fire department of your choice.

You're likely already aware of any disabilities or significant problems that would keep you from serving as a firefighter. If you're considering yourself as a firefighting candidate and think of yourself as a healthy, physically fit person, it's still wise to consult a doctor before investing time and money in the application process or in preparation for the written exam. Tell your doctor about the type of work you have in mind, describe the physical demands, and ask for an assessment of your potential to withstand these rigors. If your doctor foresees any potential problems, either in passing the exams or facing the physical demands, discuss corrective measures and remedial programs now. Follow the advice you receive. While speaking with your doctor, describe the firefighter physical performance test. You might be able to pick up special tips to prepare yourself to earn the top score on the test. Your doctor might even have a physical conditioning program to recommend.

The exam for which you are preparing yourself is the first step toward a career in firefighting. If all goes well, you can plan to spend the bulk of your working life in this rewarding career. But don't expect to prepare in a few weeks for a career that will last a lifetime. Start planning now!

Here's a three-step strategy to help start you on the right path:

Step One: Go to your doctor for a full medical exam. If you get the go-ahead from your doctor, you can begin an aggressive physical fitness training program. If your doctor has any reservations, take care of your health problems first. Follow your doctor's advice for improving your general health, addressing any specific issues, and building strength and stamina at a rate consistent with your overall condition.

Step Two: Take positive steps to be healthier. If you smoke, stop smoking now. Smoking has been linked to lung cancer, breathing disorders, heart disease, and circulatory diseases. Smoking begins to affect the body long before actual diseases develop. Smokers generally do not have the stamina of nonsmokers, because smoking reduces the power of the lungs to distribute oxygen. With less oxygen going to the muscles of the body, people who smoke generally cannot run or climb as long, cannot carry as much, and cannot sustain effort to the degree that nonsmokers can. For a top score on the physical performance test and a long career in firefighting, stop smoking now.

If you use drugs—inhaled, injected, ingested, or smoked—stop now. Different drugs affect the body in different ways, but all drugs alter your functioning. Regardless of

TIP

Because so much of the hiring decision is based on an applicant's physical status, we recommend working on your body *and* mind in preparation for the exams.

whether the drug you use affects your vision, hearing, emotions, or thinking, it creates an unnatural condition that decreases your chance of achieving a top score on the examination and thereby decreases your chances of being selected for a firefighter position. Drug testing, in fact, is part of the screening process for most firefighters, and candidates who test positive for drug use are typically disqualified from being hired.

Step Three: Control your weight. Excess weight requires your muscles, heart, and lungs to work harder. An overweight person tends to have less speed and stamina than a well-proportioned person and tends to be at greater risk of an early death. Rapid weight reduction, however, may shock your system. Weight must be lost gradually through a combination of calorie cutback and regular, sensible exercise.

Low body weight can also be a problem for prospective firefighters. Severely underweight candidates will unlikely be able to carry heavy loads for extended lengths of time and may tire easily. If being underweight does not stem from disease, an underweight person should be able to add weight slowly by consuming healthy foods and proteins that build muscle when combined with exercise and weightlifting.

Each fire department sets its own standards, but the following tables serve as a general guide to candidate weight requirements.

> **NOTE**
> In some states, smoking is grounds for disqualification as a firefighter.

> **NOTE**
> Although the tables begin at specified heights, no minimum height requirement has been prescribed for firefighters.

ACCEPTABLE WEIGHT IN POUNDS ACCORDING TO FRAME
MEN

Height		Small Frame	Medium Frame	Large Frame
Feet	Inches			
5	2	128–134	131–141	138–150
5	3	130–136	133–143	140–153
5	4	132–138	135–145	142–153
5	5	134–140	137–148	144–160
5	6	136–142	139–151	146–164
5	7	138–145	142–154	149–168
5	8	140–148	145–157	152–172
5	9	142–151	148–160	155–176
5	10	144–154	151–163	158–180
5	11	146–157	154–166	161–184
6	0	149–160	157–170	164–188
6	1	152–164	160–174	168–192
6	2	155–168	164–178	172–197
6	3	158–172	167–182	176–202
6	4	162–176	171–187	181–207

ACCEPTABLE WEIGHT IN POUNDS ACCORDING TO FRAME
WOMEN

Height		Small Frame	Medium Frame	Large Frame
Feet	Inches			
4	10	102–111	109–121	118–131
4	11	103–113	111–123	120–134
5	0	104–115	113–126	122–137
5	1	106–118	115–129	125–140
5	2	108–121	116–132	128–143
5	3	111–124	121–135	131–147
5	4	114–127	124–138	134–151
5	5	117–130	127–141	137–155
5	6	120–133	130–144	140–159
5	7	123–136	133–147	143–163
5	8	126–139	136–150	146–167
5	9	129–142	139–153	149–170
5	10	132–145	142–156	152–173
5	11	135–148	145–159	155–176
6	0	138–151	148–162	158–179

The civil service's examining physician may determine that weight exceeding that shown in the tables (up to a maximum of 20 pounds) is lean body mass and not fat. The examining physician will determine the frame size of the candidate.

Step Four: Embark on a positive program to build your strength, agility, speed, and stamina. The following section will give you some suggestions.

DEFINING FITNESS

Physical fitness is to the human body what fine-tuning is to an engine. It enables us to perform up to our potential. Fitness can be described as a condition that helps us look, feel, and do our best. More specifically, it is the ability to perform daily tasks vigorously and alertly, with energy left over for enjoying leisure-time activities and meeting emergency demands. It is the ability to endure, to bear up, to withstand stress, and to carry on in circumstances where an unfit person could not continue; and fitness is a significant basis for good health and well-being.

Physical fitness involves the performance of the heart and lungs and the muscles of the body. Because what we do with our bodies also affects what we can do with our minds, fitness influences, to some degree, qualities such as mental alertness and emotional stability.

As you undertake your fitness program, remember that fitness is an individual quality that varies from person to person. It is influenced by age, gender, heredity, personal habits, exercise, and eating practices. You can't do anything about the first three factors, but it is within your power to change and improve the others as necessary.

Knowing the Basics

Physical fitness is most easily understood by examining its components or parts. There is widespread agreement that the following five components are basic elements of being physically fit:

1. **Cardiorespiratory endurance:** The ability to deliver oxygen and nutrients to tissues and to remove wastes over sustained periods. Long runs and swims are among the methods employed in measuring this component.

2. **Muscular strength:** The ability of a muscle to exert force for a brief period. Upper-body strength, for example, can be measured by various weight-lifting exercises.

3. **Muscular endurance:** The ability of a muscle or a group of muscles to sustain repeated contractions or to continue applying force against a fixed object. Push-ups are often used to test the endurance of arm and shoulder muscles, for example.

4. **Flexibility:** The ability to move joints and use muscles through their full range of motion. The sit-and-reach test is a good measure of flexibility of the lower back and the backs of the upper legs.

5. **Body composition:** Refers to the makeup of the body in terms of lean mass (muscle, bone, vital tissue, and organs) and fat mass. An optimum ratio of fat to lean mass is an indication of fitness, and the right type of exercises can help decrease body fat and increase or maintain muscle mass.

Developing a Workout Schedule

Before starting a fitness program, it's wise to contact a certified fitness trainer, relay your goals, and secure a workout schedule. How often, how long, and how hard you exercise and what types of exercises you do should be determined by what you are trying to accomplish. Right now, your goal is to prepare your body to withstand the rigors of the physical performance test and make a top showing. Your goal also should be to be solidly prepared for the physical demands of firefighting.

Your exercise program should include something from each of the five basic fitness components just described. Each workout should begin with a warm-up period and end with a cool-down period. As a general rule, space your workouts throughout the week and avoid consecutive days of hard exercise.

The following is the amount of activity necessary for the average, healthy person to maintain a minimum level of overall fitness. Included are some of the popular exercises for each category.

- **Warm-up:** Five to ten minutes of exercises such as walking, slow jogging, knee lifts, arm circles, or trunk rotations. Low-intensity movements that simulate movements to be used in the activity can also be included in the warm-up.

- **Muscular strength:** A minimum of two 20-minute sessions per week that include exercises for all the major muscle groups. Lifting weights is the most effective way to increase strength.

NOTE

In 2003, the National Volunteer Firefighter Council (NVFC) launched the Heart-Healthy Firefighter Program (**https://healthy-firefighter.org/**). The website provides resources such as videos, tip sheets, exercises, and fitness information for firefighters and EMS personnel. The program's main goals are to battle heart disease and prevent heart attack, which is recognized as the leading cause of on-duty death for firefighters and EMS personnel.

2

- **Muscular endurance:** At least three 30-minute sessions each week that include exercises such as calisthenics (push-ups, sit-ups, pull-ups, etc.) and weight training for all the major muscle groups.
- **Cardiorespiratory endurance:** At least three 20-minute bouts of continuous aerobic (activity requiring oxygen), rhythmic exercise each week. Popular aerobic conditioning activities include brisk walking, jogging, swimming, cycling, rope-jumping, rowing, cross-country skiing, and some continuous-action games such as racquetball and handball.
- **Flexibility:** Ten to twelve minutes of daily stretching exercises performed slowly and without a bouncing motion. This exercise can be included after a warm-up or during a cool-down.
- **Cool-down:** A minimum of five to ten minutes of slow walking or low-level exercise combined with stretching.

Remembering Key Principles

The key to selecting the right types of exercises for developing and maintaining each of the basic components of fitness are found in these principles:

- **Specificity:** Pick the right type of activities to affect each component. Strength training results in changes to specific parts of the body. Train for the activity in which you're interested. For example, optimum swimming performance is best achieved when the muscles involved in swimming are trained for the movements required. It does not follow that a good runner is a good swimmer, because training for these activities builds different sets of muscles.
- **Overload:** To bring about improvement, work hard enough and at levels that are vigorous and long enough to overload your body above its resting level.
- **Regularity:** You can't "hoard" physical fitness or "cram" for a fitness test. At least three balanced workouts per week are necessary to maintain a desirable level of fitness.
- **Progression:** Increase the intensity, frequency, and/or duration of activity over time to see continued improvement.

Some activities can be used to fulfill more than one of your basic exercise requirements. In addition to increasing cardiorespiratory endurances, for example, running will build muscular endurance in the legs, and swimming will develop the arm, shoulder, and chest muscles. If you select the proper activities, it is possible to fit parts of your muscular endurance workout into your cardiorespiratory conditioning and save time.

Measuring Your Heart Rate

Heart rate is widely accepted as a good method for measuring intensity during running, swimming, cycling, and other aerobic activities. Exercise that doesn't raise your heart rate to a specific level and keep it there for a minimum of 20 minutes will not contribute significantly to reducing or preventing cardiovascular disease.

The **target heart rate** is the goal or the desired heart rate per minute. One of the simplest ways to arrive at the target figure is as follows:

maximum heart rate = (220 – age)

target heart rate = maximum heart rate × 70 percent

Thus, the target heart rate for a 40-year-old individual would be 126.

Measuring Your Progress

You will be able to observe the increase in your strength and stamina from week to week in many ways.

There is a two-minute step test you can use to measure and keep a running record of the improvement in your circulatory efficiency, one of the most important of all aspects of fitness.

The immediate response of the cardiovascular system to exercise differs markedly between well-conditioned individuals and others. The test measures the response in terms of pulse rate taken shortly after a series of steps up and down onto a bench or chair.

Although it does not take long, it is necessarily vigorous. Stop if you become overly fatigued while taking the step test. You should not try it until you have completed multiple weeks of conditioning. Please consult a physician before attempting any physical exercise.

The Step Test

Use any sturdy bench or chair 15–17 inches in height.

COUNT 1—Place right foot on bench.

COUNT 2—Bring left foot alongside right and stand erect.

COUNT 3—Lower right foot to floor.

COUNT 4—Lower left foot to floor.

REPEAT the four-count movement 30 times a minute for 2 minutes.

SIT DOWN on the bench or chair for 2 minutes.

AFTER RESTING for 2-minutes, TAKE YOUR PULSE for 30 seconds. (You can find your pulse by applying the middle and index fingers of one hand firmly to the inside of the wrist of the other hand, on the thumb or radial side.)

To find the per-minute rate, double the count.

Record your score for future comparisons. In succeeding tests—about once every two weeks—you probably will find your pulse rate becoming lower as your physical condition improves.

Remember three important points:

1. For best results, do not engage in physical activity for at least 10 minutes before taking the test. Take the test at about the same time of day and always use the same bench or chair.

2. Remember that pulse rates vary among individuals. What is important is not a comparison of your pulse rate with that of anybody else, but a record of how your rate is lowered as your fitness level increases.

3. As you progress, the rate at which your pulse is lowered should gradually level off. This leveling off is an indication that you are approaching peak fitness.

TIPS FOR STAYING FIT

When you have reached the level of conditioning you have chosen for yourself, you will want to maintain it. Although it has been found possible to maintain fitness with three workouts a week, exercise ideally should be a daily habit.

Broadening Your Program

You have a choice of many activities and forms of exercise to supplement a basic program. These include isometrics—sometimes called exercises without movement, water activities and swimming, weight training, and a variety of sports.

Isometrics

Isometric contraction exercises take very little time (6 to 8 seconds each) and require no special equipment. They're excellent muscle strengtheners and, as such, are valuable supplements to an exercise program. Isometric exercises work a muscle by pushing or pulling against an immovable object such as a wall, or by pitting it against the opposition of another muscle.

The basis for isometrics is the "overload" principle of exercise physiology, which holds that a muscle required to perform work beyond the usual intensity will grow in strength. Research has indicated that one hard, 6- to 8-second isometric contraction per workout can, over six months, produce a significant strength increase in a muscle.

The isometric exercises described here cover the major large muscle groups of the body. They can be performed almost anywhere and nearly any time. Note that there is no set order for doing them, nor must they all be completed at one time. You can, if you like, do one or two in the morning and others at various times during the day whenever you have half a minute or even less to spare.

For each contraction, maintain tension for no more than 8 seconds. Do little breathing during a contraction; breathe deeply between contractions. Start easily. Do not apply maximum effort in the beginning.

For the first three or four weeks, you should exert only about one-half of what you think is your maximum force. Use the first 3 or 4 seconds to build up to this degree of force and use the remaining 4 or 5 seconds to hold it.

For the next two weeks, gradually increase the force to more nearly approach maximum. After about six weeks, it will be safe to exert maximum effort.

Pain indicates that you're applying too much force; reduce the amount immediately. If pain continues, discontinue that exercise for a week or two. Then try it again with about 50 percent of maximum effort; if no pain occurs, you can gradually build up again toward the maximum.

TIP
If you can, continue your workouts on a five-days-a-week basis.

SOME COMMON ISOMETRIC EXERCISES

Target Area: Neck	Steps
Neck Flexing	1. Sit or stand with interlaced fingers of your hands on your forehead.
	2. Forcibly exert a forward push of your head while resisting equally hard with your hands.
Neck Extension	1. Sit or stand with interlaced fingers of your hands behind your head.
	2. Push your head backward while exerting a forward pull with your hands.
Side Bending	1. Sit or stand with the palm of your left hand on the left side of your head.
	2. Push with your left hand while resisting with your head and neck. Reverse using your right hand on the right side of your head.

Target Area: Upper Body	Steps
Wall Push-Off	1. Stand about three feet from a wall, and place your hands flat against it, about shoulder-width apart.
	2. Slowly lower your body toward the wall by flexing your elbows. When your elbows are aligned with your torso, push back up. Do 10 repetitions.
Shoulder Extension	1. Stand with your back to the wall, your hands at your sides, your palms toward the wall.
	2. Press your hands back against the wall, keeping your arms straight. Hold the pressure against the wall for 5 seconds, and then release slowly. Repeat the exercise 10 to 15 repetitions.
Shoulder Abduction	1. Stand in a doorway or with your side against a wall, with your arms at your sides, and your palms toward your legs.
	2. Press your hand(s) outward against the wall or door frame, keeping your arms straight. Repeat the exercise 10 to 15 repetitions.

Target Area: Arms and Chest	Steps
Hand Press	1. Stand with your feet slightly apart. Grasp your hands together in front of your chest.
	2. Firmly press your hands together. Hold for 10 seconds and then relax for 10 seconds. Repeat four more times.
Prayer Pose	1. Stand with your feet comfortably spaced and your knees slightly bent. Clasp your hands, palms together and close to your heart.
	2. Press your hands together and hold. Hold for 10 seconds and then relax for 10 seconds. Repeat four more times.
Arm Wrestle	1. Stand with your feet slightly apart and your knees slightly bent. Grip your fingers with your arms close to your chest.
	2. Pull hard and hold. Hold for 10 seconds and then relax for 10 seconds. Repeat four more times.

Target Area: Abdomen	Steps
Abdominal Squeeze	1. Stand with your knees slightly flexed and your hands resting on your knees.
	2. Contract your abdominal muscles.
Plank Hold	1. Start with your body in a horizontal position with your weight on your toes and forearms. Ensure your spine is straight. Tighten your abdominal muscles as hard as you can. Be mindful to flex your hips forward (buttocks clenched) and don't let your hips sink.
	2. Hold this position for 30 seconds. You should feel the most tension in your shoulders and core. Hold for 30-seconds. Repeat four times.
Target Area: Lower Back, Buttocks, and Back of Thighs	Steps
Wall Sit	1. Stand with your feet shoulder-width apart, hands clasped in front of your chest. Align your hips over your knees and your knees over your ankles. Put your arms out straight in front of you, palms down.
	2. Push your hips back and bend your knees until your thighs are nearly parallel to the ground. Hold for 30 to 60 seconds.
Glute Bridge	1. Lie on your back with your knees bent and your arms by your sides.
	2. Elevate your hips by pressing your weight down through your heels. Resist the urge to let your hips sink. Hold for 30-seconds. Repeat five times.

Water Activities

Water activities—from low-intensity walking, yoga, or tai chi to high-intensity aerobics or Zumba classes—are effective low-impact exercise options for many people with disabilities or physical limitations, such as arthritis, because the water's buoyancy reduces the pressure put on a person's joints. Swimming is one of the best physical activities for people of all ages, and as an exercise option for a firefighter candidate, it offers the benefits of providing a full-body workout by increasing the heart rate without stressing the body, toning muscles, and building endurance and strength. Swimming is also an efficient way to burn calories, as the water provides gentle muscle resistance during the workout.

With the body submerged in water, blood circulation automatically increases to some extent. The pressure of water on the body also helps promote deeper ventilation of the lungs. With well-planned activity, both circulation and ventilation increase still more.

Weight Training

Weight training is an excellent method of developing muscular strength and endurance. Barbells and weighted dumbbells—complete with instructions—are available at most sporting goods stores. A good rule to follow in deciding the maximum weight you should lift is to select a weight you can lift six times without strain. If you have access to a gym with sophisticated equipment, take advantage of the advice of professional trainers in establishing weight-training programs and goals.

2

Participatory Sports

Soccer, basketball, handball, squash, ice hockey, and other sports that require sustained effort can be valuable aids in building circulatory endurance. Games should be played with full speed and vigor only when your conditioning permits doing so with undue fatigue.

If you have been sedentary, however, it's important to pace yourself carefully in such sports. It might even be advisable to avoid them until you are well along in your physical conditioning program.

Past inactivity doesn't mean you should avoid all sports. There are many excellent conditioning and circulatory activities in which the amount of exertion can be easily controlled and in which you can progress at your own rate. Bicycling is one example. Others include hiking, skating, tennis, running, cross-country skiing, rowing, canoeing, water skiing, and scuba diving.

On days when you get a good workout in sports, you can skip part (or all) of your exercise program. Use your own judgment. For example, if you have engaged in a sport that exercises the legs and that stimulates the heart and lungs—such as skating—you can skip the circulatory activity for that day. However, you still should do some of the conditioning and stretching exercises for the upper body. On the other hand, weight-lifting is an excellent conditioning activity, but it should be supplemented with running or one of the other circulatory exercises.

Whatever your favorite sport, you will find your enjoyment enhanced by improved fitness. Every weekend athlete should invest in frequent workouts.

Establishing, implementing, and maintaining a fitness routine is vital to passing what's considered one of the most difficult aspects of the screening process: the physical ability test. In the next section, we will discuss what is involved in the test and some possible variations based on location.

PHYSICAL ABILITY TESTS

Almost all fire departments require successful candidates to pass some form of physical test. This physical test might be called a **physical ability test** (**PAT**) or it might be specifically the **Candidate Physical Ability Test** (**CPAT**). While these two tests feature considerable differences, they're both designed to ensure that candidates can perform the physically demanding tasks a firefighter faces in the regular line of duty.

Physical ability tests typically have a general fitness component and a "physical ability" component. It's not uncommon for the fitness portion to use different cutoff scores for men, women, and various age groups. These cutoff scores, however, are set at the same percentile for everyone. In other words, even if men and women aren't required to bench press the same amount of weight, the amount required of each can likely be pressed by about three-fourths (75 percent) of male *and* female applicants.

The "physical ability" portions usually require candidates to perform a series of linked exercises that simulate a firefighter's job, such as swinging an ax, climbing stairs with equipment, and dragging a human-form dummy. This type of physical test isn't intended to measure general fitness, but rather a candidate's ability to perform essential job tasks. Because the tasks are essential to the job, the same score (performance of these tasks within a reasonable timeframe) is required of all candidates to pass, regardless of age or gender.

Clothing and Equipment

The following is a list of clothing candidates must wear during a PAT and the equipment that is used. Note the weight of the various pieces of equipment.

Equipment	Weight (in pounds)
Turnout coat	5.5
Filled self-contained breathing apparatus (SCBA)	34
12-foot ladder	27
$1\frac{1}{2}$-inch standpipe rack	57
Ceiling pole simulator (up)	75
Ceiling pole simulator (down)	75
Human-form dummy	165

Common Tasks

The following nine tasks are commonly presented on physical ability tests across the country. Each task reflects a situation that an entry-level firefighter might encounter while on the job.

1. **Aerial Ladder Climb:** For this event, applicants must climb to the top of an aerial ladder set at 60 degrees to a height of 50 feet and then return to the bottom. Applicants will be attached to a safety line and will, upon instruction, ascend and descend the ladder without stopping. This activity is the first event of the PAT, and it is not timed. Applicants unable to successfully complete this event will not be allowed to continue the testing process. For this event only, applicants will not be required to wear the turnout coat or the SCBA; however, they will be required to wear the hard hat for safety.

2. **Hydrant Opening:** Applicants must use a hydrant wrench to open a functional hydrant completely (seventeen turns) and to close it completely (seventeen turns).

3. **Ladder Operations—Carry:** Applicants must remove a 12-foot plain ladder from a truck and carry it 50 feet, placing it against the drill tower. They must then pick up the ladder, carry it back, and replace it on the truck in its original position.

4. **Ladder Operations—Extension:** Applicants must extend a 30-foot ground ladder affixed to the side of the drill tower and bring it back down. You cannot drop the ladder without penalty.

5. **Charged Line Advance:** Applicants must pick up and advance a charged $1\frac{1}{2}$-inch hoseline with playpipe 100 feet. Pump pressure is set at 130 psi.

6. **Stair Climb with Equipment:** Applicants must pick up a $1\frac{1}{2}$-inch standpipe rack (a wrapped hose) and carry it up six flights of stairs. At the top of the stairs, applicants must place the standpipe rack on the floor. Applicants must then pick up the standpipe rack again and carry it back down to the bottom of the stairs. This aspect is an extremely challenging test component given the weight of the equipment applicants must wear and carry.

7. **Ceiling Pole:** Simulators have been constructed to replicate the action involved when using a ceiling pole to break apart ceilings in structures. Applicants must complete two sets of repetitions on both ceiling pole simulators (up and down), for four total sets of six repetitions each.

8. **Victim Rescue—Confined Space:** Applicants must wear a blackened facepiece to block their vision and are directed to enter a maze. Applicants must navigate the maze on their hands and knees and exit at the opposite end.

9. **Victim Rescue—Dummy Drag:** Applicants must drag a 165-pound human-form dummy 50 feet.

Whether you pass the test is primarily based upon the performance of current firefighters. Your time will be compared to that of incumbent firefighters who have done the exercise at the same pace they would have done during an actual fire or on the job.

Sample Test Site Layout

The following diagram illustrates the arrangement of a physical ability testing sequence. Each testing component is labeled with a number that corresponds to the components previously described in this section.

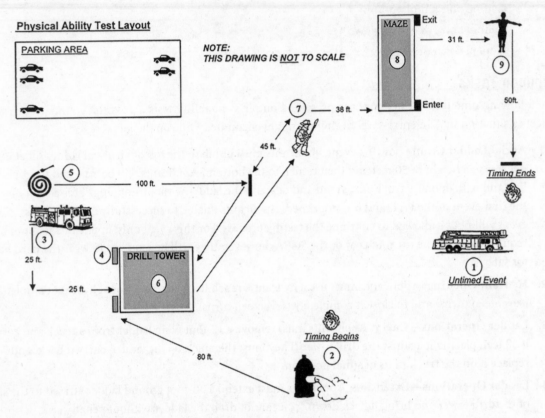

THE CANDIDATE PHYSICAL ABILITY TEST™

Many departments use the CPAT to measure candidate fitness, strength, and endurance. Developed by the International Association of Fire Fighters and the International Association of Fire Chiefs, the CPAT is a job-simulation, physical ability examination. In other words, candidates will complete tasks that mimic as closely as possible the everyday duties of real firefighters.

The CPAT consists of eight events: the stair climb, the hose drag, the equipment carry, the ladder raise and extension, the forcible entry exercise, the search event, the rescue exercise, and the ceiling breach and pull.

During the test, you will wear a 50-pound vest to simulate the weight of SCBA and protective garments. You must also wear long pants, a hard hat with a chinstrap, work gloves, and shoes with a closed heel or toe. You cannot wear a watch or jewelry that is restrictive or loose.

You will be required to walk—not run—from event to event along a marked path. Most departments require you to complete all eight events within **10 minutes and 20 seconds** (although you may find that some departments will use a slightly different cut-off time).

Following is a description of the eight CPAT events:

1. **Stair Climb:** This event is designed to replicate the task of climbing stairs while wearing protective gear and carrying firefighting equipment. During this event, you will be stepping on a StairMaster StepMill. Before the test begins, you're allowed to warm up for 20 seconds at a set stepping rate of 50 steps per minutes.

   During the warm-up, you're allowed to step off the StepMill, touch the wall, or hold onto the rail as you establish your walking rhythm. If you fall or step off the machine, you can restart your 20-second warm-up period up to two times. Fall off again and you've failed the test. You do not have a break between the warm-up period and the actual test.

   When the proctor says "Start," begin the timed test. Walk on the StepMill at a rate of 60 steps per minute for 3 minutes. If at any time during the timed test you fall, step off the StepMill, or grasp any testing equipment, you fail the test. You may momentarily touch the wall or handrail to keep your balance; however, you will be warned if you grasp the wall or rail for an extended period or use them to bear your weight. They will only warn you twice. You fail the test if you violate this rule a third time.

2. **Hose Drag:** During this event, you perform tasks that simulate dragging an uncharged hoseline from the fire apparatus to the site of the fire and pulling the hoseline around obstacles while remaining still and kneeling.

   You grasp an automatic nozzle attached to 200 feet of 1-inch hose. Place the uncharged hoseline over your shoulder or across your chest; you are not allowed to grab the hose past the 8-foot mark. You may run while dragging the hose 75 feet to a pre-positioned drum. Make a 90-degree turn around the drum and continue dragging the hose for an additional 25 feet. If you fail to go around the drum or stray outside of the marked path, you fail the test.

   Stop within a 5 × 7-foot box, drop to at least one knee, and pull the hoseline until the 50-foot mark is across the finish line. You must keep at least one knee on the ground during the hose pull, and you must stay within the marked boundary lines. You will receive one warning if your knees go outside of the marked boundary lines; a second violation constitutes a failure of the CPAT.

3. **Equipment Carry:** While on the job, firefighters frequently remove power tools from the fire apparatus, carry them to the fire site, and then later return them to the apparatus. This event simulates that task. You must remove two rescue circular saws (approximately 32 pounds each) from a cabinet one at a time and place them on the ground. You will then pick up both saws, one in each hand, and carry them 75 feet, walking around a prepositioned drum and then back to the starting point. At any point during the equipment carry, you may put the saws back on the ground to adjust your grip on them. However, if you drop either saw during the carry, you fail the test. You are not allowed to run during this event. You will receive one warning only; if you violate the rule a second time, you fail the test. When you return to the tool cabinet, you must place both saws on the ground, one at a time, and replace them in their proper places in the cabinet.

> **NOTE**
> In addition to the 50-pound vest, for the stair climb event you also will wear two 12.5-pound weights on your shoulders, which simulate the weight of a high-rise hose bundle.

4. **Ladder Raise and Extension:** During this event, you replicate the task of placing a ground ladder near a building and raising the ladder to the building's roof or window. Walk to the top rung of a 24-foot aluminum extension ladder, lift the unhinged end from the ground, and walk the ladder hand-over-hand until it is stationary against the wall. You may not use the ladder rails to raise the ladder. If you miss any rung during the raise, you are given a single warning. You fail if you violate this rule twice.

Next, place both feet inside a 36 × 36-inch box marked on the ground and extend the fly section of the prepositioned and secured 24-foot aluminum extension ladder hand-over-hand until the fly section hits the stop. Lower the fly section hand-over-hand to the starting position. If at any time your feet stray outside the marked boundary lines, you are given a warning. Straying outside the boundary lines twice constitutes a failure of the CPAT. Also, if you fail to raise or lower the ladder hand-over-hand or drop the ladder at any time during this event, you fail the test.

NOTE

A safety lanyard is attached to the 24-foot aluminum ladder to prevent injury. The lanyard will be activated should a candidate lose control of the ladder.

5. **Forcible Entry:** When entering a fire occupancy, firefighters are often required to open locked doors or breach walls with force. This exercise is designed to simulate that task.

You will use a 10-pound sledgehammer to strike a measuring device in the target area until the buzzer sounds. While striking the device, your feet must remain outside of the toe-box. After the buzzer is activated, place the sledgehammer on the ground. You fail the test if you lose control of the sledgehammer. You receive one warning if you step inside the toe-box; a repeat of this violation causes you to fail the test.

6. **Search:** This task simulates searching for a victim in an unfamiliar area with low visibility. During this exercise, you crawl on your hands and knees through a tunnel maze 3 feet high, 4 feet wide, and 64 feet long, with two 90-degree turns. You will face some obstacles at several points in the maze and must navigate your way over and under these obstacles. In two locations, the dimensions of the tunnel are reduced. Proctors observe your movements. If at any time you need to exit the tunnel before the event is completed, you call out or knock on the wall or ceiling of the maze, and the proctors will assist you. If you request such assistance, however, you fail the test.

7. **Rescue:** The purpose of this event is to replicate the experience of removing a victim or injured colleague from the scene of a fire. You grasp a 165-pound human-form dummy by the handle on the harness attached to a dummy's shoulders. You may grip either one or both handles. Drag the dummy 35 feet to a prepositioned drum, turn 180 degrees around the drum, and drag the dummy an additional 35 feet to the finish line. The dummy may touch the drum as you perform this task. However, you may not grasp or rest on the drum; a single warning is given if you violate this rule, and you fail the test if you do so twice. You're allowed to drop the dummy and adjust your grip. Keep in mind that the *entire* dummy must be dragged across the finish line for you to successfully complete this event.

8. **Ceiling Breach and Pull:** To see whether a fire has extended to other parts of a structure, firefighters often breach or tear down ceilings. This event is designed to measure your ability to perform this critical task.

Remove the pike pole from the bracket and, while standing within the boundary established by the frame of the equipment, you place the tip of the pole on the painted area of the hinged door in the ceiling. Completely push up the hinged door in the ceiling with the pike pole three times. Then hook the pike pole to the ceiling device and pull the pole down five times. Three pushes and five pulls constitute a "set." You must repeat this set four times. When you finish all your repetitions, the proctor calls out "Time!"

During this event, you're allowed to stop and adjust your grip on the pike pole, as needed. If you let your grip on the pike pole handle slip, you may readjust your grip without a warning or failure, *but only if the pike pole does not fall to the ground*. If you drop the pike pole, you receive only one warning. You must pick up the pike pole without help from the proctors and resume the event. If you violate this rule a second time, you fail the test. If you do not successfully complete a repetition, the proctor calls out "Miss!" and you must push or pull the apparatus to finish the repetition.

Preparing for the CPAT

Many candidates say, "I haven't run in a long time," or "I've never lifted this much weight before." Test administrators are not surprised when these candidates fail. Make sure you are physically fit and can meet all test requirements *before* the examination date. Spend the rest of the time before the test maintaining that level of fitness.

You can duplicate some of the CPAT events at home or in a gym. You can practice climbing on a step machine at a local health club, for example. But not all tests can be replicated. Some of the testing equipment, such as the 24-foor aluminum extension ladder, is outfitted with special safety gear in case a candidate drops or loses control of the device. If you are going to practice CPAT events at home, please be sure to *take all necessary safety precautions*. You will not be able to pass the real test if you injure yourself while practicing. The best way to replicate what you'll face on test day and maintain safety is to see if a fire department in your area offers practice CPAT course sessions and sign up for those. This way you can practice the exact maneuvers the test will cover while knowing your safety has been considered.

Also, be sure you know the specifics about the CPAT you will be taking. Make sure you know your department's cut-off time in case it differs from the 10 minutes and 20 seconds' passing time. Be sure to attend all orientation meetings and listen carefully to instructions that the department provides.

PERSONALITY TESTS AND PSYCHOLOGICAL EVALUATIONS

Many fire departments include personality or behavioral tests as part of their screening process. Personality tests help departments identify candidates who are motivated to be firefighters and who have good attitudes about their jobs. Psychological evaluations, on the other hand, are much more in-depth and often include both personality testing and an interview with a psychologist. These psychological evaluations are designed to determine a candidate's ability to deal with extreme stress and other emotionally challenging aspects of being a firefighter. The tests vary by fire department or national vendor, but most measure the following job-related behavioral predispositions:

TIP
The most important thing to do when preparing for any physical ability test is to begin practicing and training well in advance of exam day.

2

- **Stress Tolerance**—highlights the candidate's ability to deal with the on-the-job stressors of work as a firefighter
- **Team Orientation**—gauges the ability to function within the team dynamic of the firefighter position; the ability to work effectively with others
- **Motivation/Attitude**—measures the candidate's ability and desire to carry out the duties of a firefighter to the best of one's ability: to strive to maintain a positive attitude about the job.

The following graphic illustrates some of the personality characteristics and psychological traits required of a firefighter.

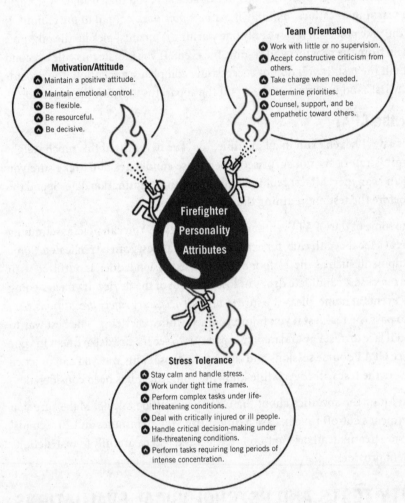

Motivation/Attitude
- Maintain a positive attitude.
- Maintain emotional control.
- Be flexible.
- Be resourceful.
- Be decisive.

Team Orientation
- Work with little or no supervision.
- Accept constructive criticism from others.
- Take charge when needed.
- Determine priorities.
- Counsel, support, and be empathetic toward others.

Firefighter Personality Attributes

Stress Tolerance
- Stay calm and handle stress.
- Work under tight time frames.
- Perform complex tasks under life-threatening conditions.
- Deal with critically injured or ill people.
- Handle critical decision-making under life-threatening conditions.
- Perform tasks requiring long periods of intense concentration.

Because there are no right or wrong answers to questions on personality tests, it is complicated to prepare for them. However, there are a few guidelines that can certainly improve your chances of doing well. Keep the following three tips in mind when answering questions on a personality test or when speaking with a psychologist:

1. **Always tell the truth.** Personality tests are designed in part to identify people who are not being candid. One of the main reasons some people do poorly on personality tests is that they answer questions in a way that they think makes them look perfect. No one is perfect. It is a mistake to act as if you know everything and have had experiences in every subject.

2. **Go with your first thought.** Because personality test questions have no right or wrong answers, it's easy to read too much into them. The questions are usually straightforward and should be answered as such. Don't try to second-guess the meanings of the questions or look for hidden meanings; doing so will certainly lower your performance.

3. **Do not be afraid to say how you feel.** Many questions on personality tests are answered in terms of the extent to which you agree or disagree with a given statement. Your choices to such questions might be something like: (1) Strongly Agree, (2) Agree, (3) Not Sure, (4) Disagree, (5) Strongly Disagree. If you feel strongly about a statement, don't be afraid to answer with a 1 or a 5. It is usually not wise to answer with too many 3s (Not Sure), unless you truly are not sure about how you feel.

THE INTERVIEW

An interview can take place at any time during the screening process, but when there are many applicants, the employment interview tends to be the last step. An interview takes a great deal of the interviewer's time, so it usually is extended only to candidates who appear fully qualified based on all other measures—written test, background investigation, medical examination, and physical fitness performance test.

If you have passed all the steps preceding the interview, you are very close—but you do not yet have a place on the fire force. The interview is a crucial step in the firefighter screening process.

The purpose of the interview is to gather information about you and add details that allow interviewers to gain a more complete picture of who you are. The following are some of the specific aims of the interview:

- **Supplement the application form.** The interviewer may ask about your childhood, education, and prior employment. This is your opportunity to explain employment gaps and abrupt terminations. If your record is anything less than perfect, this is your chance to indicate that you have learned from prior experience. Let the interviewer know that you have matured and explain how. Do not blame others for your mistakes. Take responsibility for impetuous behavior, personality clashes, and brushes with the law. Make clear that you have developed the self-control to abstain from such misbehaviors. You also might have an opportunity to expand on describing the kinds of work you did at previous jobs. If the application form gave you limited space in which to describe duties and responsibilities, you can now fill in details. You can convey enthusiasm for tasks you especially liked or at which you were notably skilled.

- **Learn more about your motivation level.** Firefighting is not easy work. The interviewer wants to know why you want to be a firefighter. Is your motivation strictly financial? Do you have an unhappy home life that you want to escape for long stretches? Do you care about people, or are you just seeking excitement? How do your interests coincide with those of current firefighters? Do your patterns of interest and motivation match those of successful, satisfied firefighters?

- **Assess your stability and personality.** This aspect of your ability to be a firefighter cannot be stressed enough. The interview may or may not provide a complete and accurate assessment. Firefighters live and work under stress. In the firehouse, firefighters live in close quarters with other men and women, sharing household and maintenance chores and sacrificing privacy. Firefighters must be able to cooperate with all members of their shift without showing undue conflict. Likewise, firefighters must not display habits or mannerisms that might create discord in the firehouse. In short, firefighters must get along and fit in. The stress that firefighters face is even greater when they are on the scene fighting fires. Interviewers will try to gauge how well you can follow orders

2

and how you will react under conditions of real physical pressure. The interviewer will look for signs telling how well you can juggle order-taking with initiative. Some of the questions might be hard to answer. The interview itself is a stressful situation. Consider all your alternatives and give a decisive answer. A firefighter must think before acting but must not spend too much time thinking about the next steps. Try to convey this same balance between deliberation and quick thinking as you answer tough questions. Try to give the impression that you can relay self-confidence and sustain strenuous activity under pressure as well as size up situations and deviate from prescribed routine when warranted by extreme emergency. Some fire departments supplement the interview with psychological tests to further screen out candidates who show a tendency to "crack" when in real danger or when faced with frustrating decisions.

Because this interview is usually the final step—the moment of decision as to whether you will be accepted on the force—you want to be at your very best. There are bound to be some surprises, but to a great extent, you can prepare yourself.

First, write down the date, time, and place of your interview on a wall calendar or in a hand-held planner. If you prefer an electronic calendar or use a smartphone app, record this information and set a reminder. Fold the interview notice and tuck it into your wallet or purse just in case you need to reference the original information later. If you are not sure how to get to the interview site, check out public transportation or automobile routes ahead of time. Do a dry run if necessary. On interview day, leave enough time for the unexpected. A 3-hour pile up on the way to the site will be reported in the newspaper and is an acceptable reason for missing an appointment, but a 20-minute bus breakdown is no excuse. If you arrive very early, go for a cup of coffee. Err on the side of caution. Go to the floor of your interview about 10 minutes ahead of time so you can use the restroom to refresh yourself.

Make sure you dress appropriately. You are not being interviewed for an executive position, so you need not wear a suit. However, your clothing should be businesslike, clean, and neat. Appropriate clothing and a well-groomed appearance will show the interviewer that you are taking the process seriously. You want to impress the interviewer as someone whom he or she would like as a person. Add to this favorable impression with a firm handshake, a natural smile, and frequent eye contact with the interviewer or interviewers.

Prepare yourself with answers to various questions. You might wonder how you can prepare the answers to questions you have not seen, but the questions are entirely predictable. Begin your preparation by looking over the application forms you filled out and any other papers you were required to file. You should be able to pick out points that an interviewer will want you to amplify or explain. Questions that might arise from the information you already have given include:

- Why did you choose your area of concentration in school?
- What particularly interests you about _____ (a specific subject)?
- Why did you transfer from X school to Y school?
- How did you get the job with _____?
- Which of the duties described in your second job did you like best? Which did you like least? Why?
- What did you do during the nine months between your second and third jobs?
- Please explain your attendance pattern at your first job.
- Explain the circumstances surrounding your departure from your second job.
- Please clarify your armed forces service/arrest record.

Other questions are routine and are included in almost all interviews. You can anticipate and prepare for them as well.

- Why do you want to leave the kind of work you are doing now?
- Why do you want to be a firefighter?
- How does your family feel about your becoming a firefighter?
- What do you do in your leisure time?
- Do you have hobbies? What are they? What do you particularly like about _____?
- What is your favorite sport? Would you rather play or watch?
- How do you react to criticism? What if you think the criticism is reasonable? What if you consider the criticism unwarranted?
- What is one of your pet peeves?
- Name your greatest strengths and weaknesses.
- What could make you lose your temper?
- Of what accomplishment in your life are you most proud?
- What act do you most regret?
- If you could start life over, what would you do differently?
- What traits do you value most in a coworker? Which do you value most in a friend?
- What makes you think you would be a good firefighter?

Still other questions might be more specific to a firefighter interview. Be sure to have prepared answers to the following questions:

- How much sleep do you need?
- Are you afraid of heights?
- How do you feel about irregular work hours?
- Do you prefer working alone or on a team?
- Are you afraid of dying?
- What would you do with the rest of your life if your legs were injured in an accident and you could no longer walk?
- How do you deal with panic? How do you handle your own? How do you deal with that of others?
- How do you feel about smoking, drinking, taking drugs, or gambling?
- What is your favorite TV program? How do you feel about watching the news, sports, or classical dramas? How do you feel about listening to rock music, country, or opera?

Now make a list of your own. The variety of interview questions is endless, but you can answer most with ease. Being well-prepared makes the whole process much more pleasant and less frightening.

There is one typical question that seems to make job candidates uncomfortable. The question is likely to be the first and, unless you are prepared, it might well throw you off guard: "Tell me about yourself." To answer this question, have a prepared script (in your head, not in your hand). Think well ahead of time about what you want to say. What might interest the interviewer? This question is not meant to gain information about your birth weight or your food preferences. The interviewer wants you to talk about yourself concerning your

2

interest in and qualifications for firefighting. Keep this in mind as you think about how to describe yourself. What information puts you in a good light related to the work for which you are applying? Organize your presentation and analyze what you plan to say. What is an interviewer likely to pick up on? To what other questions will your response lead? Be prepared to answer follow-up questions.

The temptation to talk too much is greatest with open-ended questions. Give complete answers but stop when you have fully answered the questions. Do not tell the interviewer more than he or she needs to know. Do not volunteer superfluous information. Do not get anecdotal, chatty, or familiar. Resist the urge to ramble on. Remember that the interview is a business situation, not a social one.

Toward the end of the meeting, the interviewer will most likely ask whether you have any questions. You undoubtedly will have had some before the interview began and should come prepared to ask others. If all your questions have been answered during the interview, tell the interviewer. If not, or if the conversation raises new questions, feel free to ask them. The interview is for your benefit, too, not just for the Personnel Division of the fire department.

Asking whether you have questions is usually a signal that the interview is nearly over. The interviewer is satisfied that he or she has gathered enough information about you. The time allotted to you is up. Be alert to the cues. Do not spoil the good impression you have made by prolonging the interview.

At the end of the interview, smile, thank him or her for the opportunity to have the meeting, and leave. Compose and send a brief thank you note to the interviewer or the chairperson of the interviewing panel. Such a note brands you as a courteous, thoughtful person, and indicates your continued interest in appointment.

Summing It Up

2

- Be sure to fill out your application form neatly, accurately, completely, and truthfully.

- Firefighting is a physically demanding occupation; therefore, candidates must meet high standards of physical and mental fitness. The pre-employment physical fitness exam is intended to determine whether you are fit to perform all the activities of the position. Review the general standards in this chapter and see your doctor for a full medical exam before you decide to apply for a firefighter position.

- To qualify as a firefighter, you must have five basic fitness components: cardiorespiratory endurance, muscular strength, muscular endurance, flexibility, and appropriate body composition.

- To prepare for the rigors of the physical performance test for firefighters, draw up an exercise program that includes elements for strengthening each of the five basic fitness components described above.

- Most fire department screening processes include a Physical Ability Test (PAT), but requirements vary from state to state. The Candidate Physical Ability Test™(CPAT), which consists of eight distinct parts, is used in many states and counties across the countries.

- Many fire departments employ personality and psychological tests to evaluate candidates. Personality tests help departments identify candidates who are genuinely motivated to be firefighters and who have a positive attitude about their work. Psychological evaluations assess a candidate's ability to handle extreme stress and other emotionally challenging aspects of being a firefighter.

- In addition to written, physical, and psychological exams and a background check during the firefighter screening process, you may also be called for an interview. Interviews are usually offered only to candidates who appear fully qualified. The interview helps the department supplement the information on your application form, learn more about your motivation, and assess your stability and personality. Because it is usually the final step in being accepted on the force, be sure you carefully prepare for the interview. Arrive on time (or early); dress appropriately; prepare yourself to answer various questions about yourself, your work history, your experience, and your application; and make a list of questions you may have for the interviewer(s). Be polite, personable, and tell the truth. After the interview, be sure to thank the interviewer or chairperson of the interviewing panel in a brief note.

PART II
DIAGNOSING YOUR STRENGTHS AND WEAKNESSES

Chapter 3   Diagnostic Test

Chapter 3

The Diagnostic Test

OVERVIEW

- **Introduction to the Diagnostic Test**
- **Diagnostic Test Answer Sheet**
- **Diagnostic Test**
- **Answer Key and Explanations**
- **Diagnostic Test Assessment Grid**

INTRODUCTION TO THE DIAGNOSTIC TEST

Before you begin preparing for your firefighter exam, it's important to know your areas of knowledge strengths and areas in which you need improvement. If you find the reading comprehension questions easy, for example, it would be a mistake to spend hours practicing them. Taking the Diagnostic Test in this chapter and then working out your scores will help you determine how you should apportion your study time.

Preparing to Take the Diagnostic Test

If possible, take the Diagnostic Test in one sitting. At 60 questions, this test is shorter than the average exam, but you should give yourself at least 2 hours to complete it. The actual tests usually contain between 110 to 120 questions, and last for 3 to 4 hours. The purpose of this test is to give you an idea of what areas of study you need to focus on. The full-length practice tests that come later will give you the real-time pacing experience once you've strengthened your skills in the needed areas.

First, assemble all the things you will need to take the test, including the following items:

- No. 2 pencils, at least three
- A timer
- The answer sheet—provided on the following page

Set a timer for the time specified at the top of the first page of the test. Stick to that time so that you are simulating the average per-question time allotted on an actual exam. At this point, it's as important to know how many questions you can answer in the time allotted as it is to answer questions correctly. Good luck!

DIAGNOSTIC TEST ANSWER SHEET

1. Ⓐ Ⓑ Ⓒ Ⓓ   13. Ⓐ Ⓑ Ⓒ Ⓓ   25. Ⓐ Ⓑ Ⓒ Ⓓ   37. Ⓐ Ⓑ Ⓒ Ⓓ   49. Ⓐ Ⓑ Ⓒ Ⓓ

2. Ⓐ Ⓑ Ⓒ Ⓓ   14. Ⓐ Ⓑ Ⓒ Ⓓ   26. Ⓐ Ⓑ Ⓒ Ⓓ   38. Ⓐ Ⓑ Ⓒ Ⓓ   50. Ⓐ Ⓑ Ⓒ Ⓓ

3. Ⓐ Ⓑ Ⓒ Ⓓ   15. Ⓐ Ⓑ Ⓒ Ⓓ   27. Ⓐ Ⓑ Ⓒ Ⓓ   39. Ⓐ Ⓑ Ⓒ Ⓓ   51. Ⓐ Ⓑ Ⓒ Ⓓ

4. Ⓐ Ⓑ Ⓒ Ⓓ   16. Ⓐ Ⓑ Ⓒ Ⓓ   28. Ⓐ Ⓑ Ⓒ Ⓓ   40. Ⓐ Ⓑ Ⓒ Ⓓ   52. Ⓐ Ⓑ Ⓒ Ⓓ

5. Ⓐ Ⓑ Ⓒ Ⓓ   17. Ⓐ Ⓑ Ⓒ Ⓓ   29. Ⓐ Ⓑ Ⓒ Ⓓ   41. Ⓐ Ⓑ Ⓒ Ⓓ   53. Ⓐ Ⓑ Ⓒ Ⓓ

6. Ⓐ Ⓑ Ⓒ Ⓓ   18. Ⓐ Ⓑ Ⓒ Ⓓ   30. Ⓐ Ⓑ Ⓒ Ⓓ   42. Ⓐ Ⓑ Ⓒ Ⓓ   54. Ⓐ Ⓑ Ⓒ Ⓓ

7. Ⓐ Ⓑ Ⓒ Ⓓ   19. Ⓐ Ⓑ Ⓒ Ⓓ   31. Ⓐ Ⓑ Ⓒ Ⓓ   43. Ⓐ Ⓑ Ⓒ Ⓓ   55. Ⓐ Ⓑ Ⓒ Ⓓ

8. Ⓐ Ⓑ Ⓒ Ⓓ   20. Ⓐ Ⓑ Ⓒ Ⓓ   32. Ⓐ Ⓑ Ⓒ Ⓓ   44. Ⓐ Ⓑ Ⓒ Ⓓ   56. Ⓐ Ⓑ Ⓒ Ⓓ

9. Ⓐ Ⓑ Ⓒ Ⓓ   21. Ⓐ Ⓑ Ⓒ Ⓓ   33. Ⓐ Ⓑ Ⓒ Ⓓ   45. Ⓐ Ⓑ Ⓒ Ⓓ   57. Ⓐ Ⓑ Ⓒ Ⓓ

10. Ⓐ Ⓑ Ⓒ Ⓓ   22. Ⓐ Ⓑ Ⓒ Ⓓ   34. Ⓐ Ⓑ Ⓒ Ⓓ   46. Ⓐ Ⓑ Ⓒ Ⓓ   58. Ⓐ Ⓑ Ⓒ Ⓓ

11. Ⓐ Ⓑ Ⓒ Ⓓ   23. Ⓐ Ⓑ Ⓒ Ⓓ   35. Ⓐ Ⓑ Ⓒ Ⓓ   47. Ⓐ Ⓑ Ⓒ Ⓓ   59. Ⓐ Ⓑ Ⓒ Ⓓ

12. Ⓐ Ⓑ Ⓒ Ⓓ   24. Ⓐ Ⓑ Ⓒ Ⓓ   36. Ⓐ Ⓑ Ⓒ Ⓓ   48. Ⓐ Ⓑ Ⓒ Ⓓ   60. Ⓐ Ⓑ Ⓒ Ⓓ

DIAGNOSTIC TEST

60 questions—136 minutes

Directions: The following 60 questions are similar to those you will find on an actual firefighter exam. Be sure to read the questions carefully and follow any specific instructions that precede them. Choose the best answer to each question and fill in the corresponding circle on the answer sheet. The Answer Key and Explanations follow this diagnostic test.

Questions 1–5 are based on the following passage. Choose the best answer to each question.

When a disaster happens, leadership for emergency management of the situation is typically assumed by local government officials. However, because disasters are unpredictable and vary wildly in scope, the assistance of state and federal agencies is often necessary; that's where the
Line Incident Command System (ICS) comes in.
5   The ICS is a standardized, coordinated management structure that commands and controls emergency responses. While emergency response can look slightly different for agencies across local, state, and federal lines, the ICS maintains and executes a response hierarchy designed to get everyone involved in agreement and coordinated in the most efficient manner possible.
        The ICS enables diverse organizations to integrate capabilities and achieve shared goals us-
10   ing three main framework components: Resource Management, Command and Coordination, and Communications and Information Management.
        Because the ICS affects the job of all emergency responders, every firefighter must be trained—not just captains and lieutenants. Still, due to the chaotic nature of emergency events, it's important to appoint a single leader who can sign off on all decisions and direct all respond-
15   ers. In cases involving the ICS, the leader will be a designated Incident Commander. The Incident Commander is given complete control of the scene and has the authority to remove anyone from the site, including fellow officers.

1. What is the Incident Command System?

    A. A standardized approach to firefighter collaboration.

    B. A standardized, coordinated management system that commands and controls emergency responses.

    C. An approach to coordinated breaks among fire stations that increases efficiency.

    D. A system for the implementation of martial law.

2. Why is the ICS important?

    A. It controls how firefighters get paid.

    B. It's a means for advancement within the department.

    C. It increases the efficiency of emergency response by ensuring everyone is coordinated and in agreement.

    D. It replaced the Unified Command.

3. For whom is ICS training mandatory?

   A. The captain and lieutenant assigned to Incident Command Watch.

   B. Each member of the fire department.

   C. The captains and lieutenants from each fire station.

   D. The captains from each fire station.

4. During a large-scale event requiring the ICS, who has authority to remove anyone—even other officers—from the scene?

   A. The Duty Officer

   B. The Duty and Resource Officers

   C. The Resource Officer

   D. The Incident Commander

5. Which of the following is among the three main framework components of ICS?

   A. Insurance Claims

   B. Preparedness

   C. Finance and Administration

   D. Resource Management

Questions 6–10 are based on the following diagram. Study and memorize the details of the buildings on Water Street for five minutes, cover the diagram, and answer the questions. Do not refer to the diagram while answering the questions.

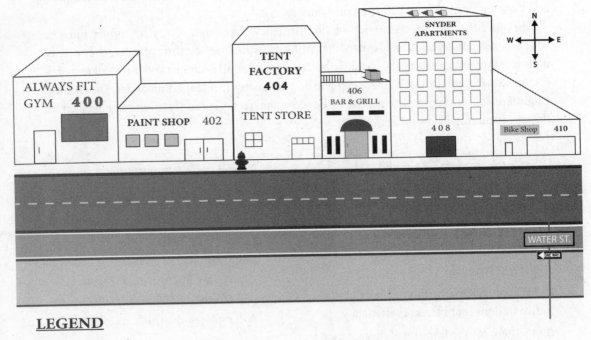

LEGEND

▥ – Balcony

◳ – Chimney

◀ – Skylight

⛽ – Hydrant

6. Which building has the most people in residence?

   A. 402 Water Street

   B. 406 Water Street

   C. 408 Water Street

   D. 410 Water Street

7. Which business most likely keeps volatile chemicals in its inventory?

   A. 400 Water Street

   B. 402 Water Street

   C. 406 Water Street

   D. 410 Water Street

8. The fire hydrant is located in front of the

   A. Paint Shop.

   B. Bike Shop.

   C. Tent Factory.

   D. Always Fit Gym.

9. Which building has a chimney?

   A. Snyder Apartments

   B. Paint Shop

   C. Bike Shop

   D. Bar & Grill

10. Traffic flows in what direction on Water Street?

    A. Two lanes going west

    B. One lane going east, one lane going west

    C. Two lanes going east

    D. One lane going east

11. One gallon of water weighs 8.34 pounds. How many pounds would 4,800 gallons of water weigh?

    A. 38,040 lb.

    B. 40,032 lb.

    C. 42,075 lb.

    D. 48,032 lb.

12. Solve: $\frac{1}{3} + \frac{1}{3} + (8 - 5)$

    A. $2\frac{2}{3}$

    B. $3\frac{1}{3}$

    C. $3\frac{1}{9}$

    D. $3\frac{2}{3}$

13. The fire department is called to a rural residential fire. When they arrive, a six-story building is actively burning on all sides. When more water is ordered, a firefighter is directed to count the number of gallons of water as the trucks arrive. A water tender arrives with 1,200 gallons, which are transferred to a drop tank that can hold 2,000 gallons. A second water tender arrives with 1,000 gallons of water, followed by another, carrying 750 gallons. The firefighter will report the number of gallons on the scene is

    A. 2,950.

    B. 3,050.

    C. 3,950.

    D. 4,950.

14. Five firefighter hopefuls weigh in before training. Alvarez weighs 180 lb.; Funt, 155 lb.; Johnston, 170 lb.; Hindle, 165 lb.; and Milburn, 190 lb. What is the mean weight of the potential firefighters?

    A. 168 lb.

    B. 172 lb.

    C. 175 lb.

    D. 178 lb.

Diagnostic Test

Chapter 3: Diagnostic Test

15. $8^2 =$

A. 16

B. 49

C. 64

D. 80

16. In 2017, the number of fire deaths per 100 fires was 0.1 in France, 0.2 in Spain, 0.5 in Denmark, 0.3 in the United States, 0.2 in Great Britain, and 0.4 in Sweden. From the highest number of deaths per 100 fires to the lowest, what is the correct order?

A. France, Great Britain/Spain, United States, Sweden, Denmark

B. Denmark, Sweden, United States, Great Britain/Spain, France

C. Great Britain, Spain, France, Denmark, United States, Sweden

D. Sweden/Great Britain, United States, Spain, Denmark, France

17. Fire Station #5 is analyzing data for all the response calls for one year. Of a total of 1,600 responses, 289 were for motor vehicle accidents (MVAs), 89 for pedestrians injured by motor vehicles, 612 residential fires, 254 bicycle accidents, 334 delivery/newborns, and 22 boating accidents. What percentage of the total calls were motor vehicle, pedestrian-motor vehicle, and boating accidents combined?

A. 18%

B. 21%

C. 22%

D. 25%

18. There are six firefighters in one crew, and their ages are 24, 29, 33, 36, 41, and 47. What is the mean age of the crew?

A. 33 years

B. 35 years

C. 37 years

D. 39 years

19. If a crate has the dimensions of 15 ft. × 15 ft. × 12 ft., what is the volume of the crate in cubic yards?

A. 100 cubic yards

B. 145 cubic yards

C. 245 cubic yards

D. 370 cubic yards

20. Which of the following fractions is equal to .40?

A. $\dfrac{2}{5}$

B. $\dfrac{4}{40}$

C. $\dfrac{2}{10}$

D. $\dfrac{4}{100}$

21. The town of Azureville uses a color-coding system for its fire hydrants, as seen in the table below.

Fire Hydrant Color	Hoseline Diameter	Hydrant Flow Capacity
Light Blue	2.5 inches	Less than 500 gallons
Medium Blue	3 inches	Between 500 and 1,000 gallons
Dark Blue	5 inches	Greater than 1,000 gallons

According to the information presented, which of the following statements most accurately describes the relationship between the colors of the hydrants, their hoseline diameters, and their water-flowing capacity?

A. As the color of the hydrants gets lighter, the hoseline diameter increases, and the flowing capacity doubles.

B. As the color of the hydrants gets lighter, the hoseline diameter decreases, and the flowing capacity increases.

C. As the color of the hydrants gets darker, the hoseline diameter decreases, and the flowing capacity decreases.

D. As the color of the hydrants gets darker, the hoseline diameter increases, and the flowing capacity increases.

22. Life-threatening packages bear certain characteristics, such as restricted endorsements such as "Personal" or "Private"; misspelled names; soft spots, bulges, or irregularities in shape; excessive postage; and poorly done wrapping, protruding wires, and buzzing or ticking noises. If you ever encounter a suspicious package or item, take the following steps:

1. Do not touch, move, or alter the object.

2. Once you have left the immediate area, call 911. Provide your name, location, object location, and a physical description of the package.

3. Inform others and keep people away from the area.

4. Write down any information you have about the object and provide this to Emergency Personnel when they arrive.

An office worker at Whilshire & Marz found an oddly shaped package in the building's front lobby addressed to "The Personal Office at Whilshure & Mars." It had no return address and was heavily wrapped in duct tape. The office worker considered the package suspicious; he left the immediate area and called 911.

Of the following options, which step would be best for the office worker to take next?

A. Take a picture of the package and record any details he can think of about the object for the Emergency Personnel.

B. Tell his manager about the situation so that knowledge of the package can be spread widely while also actively directing people away from the lobby.

C. Move the package to an empty office where it can be isolated.

D. Announce that a bomb has been found and pull the fire alarm to start a building-wide evacuation.

Chapter 3: Diagnostic Test

23. Put the following instructions for using a fire extinguisher in the proper order:

    1. Squeeze the extinguisher trigger.

    2. Slowly back away from the fire.

    3. Sweep the fire extinguisher from side to side; keep doing so until the fire is completely out.

    4. Aim the nozzle low at the base of the fire while keeping the extinguisher in an upright position.

    5. Remove the pin from the handle.

    A. 5–3–4–2–1

    B. 4–3–1–5–2

    C. 5–4–1–3–2

    D. 4–3–2–1–5

24. Smoke detectors should be on every level of a house. Detectors need to be located both inside bedrooms and outside the sleeping areas. To prevent false alarms, do not position smoke alarms within 10 feet (3 meters) of a cooking appliance or where drafts might interfere with their operation.

    Based on the information given, where in the home would you want to avoid having a smoke detector?

    A. Inside living rooms and near basement closets

    B. Inside the kitchen and next to air conditioning/heating ducts

    C. Inside bedrooms and near hallways

    D. Inside basement rooms and near a home office

25. The procedure for removing and preparing a firefighter's personal protection equipment (PPE) for next use can be broken down into four basic steps. Put these steps in the correct order.

    Step 1: Place clothing in a ready state.

    Step 2: Inspect PPE for damage and need for cleaning.

    Step 3: Remove protective clothing.

    Step 4: Clean equipment as needed, remove damaged equipment from service, and report to company officer, if applicable.

    A. 1–2–3–4

    B. 2–4–1–3

    C. 3–2–4–1

    D. 4–3–2–1

26. Last June, 25 percent of all fires in a city were in buildings of Type A, 40 percent were in buildings of Type B, and 15 percent were in buildings of Type C.

    Of the following, the most accurate statement for the number of fires in June is that

    A. the total number of fires was equal to the number of fires in the three types of buildings.

    B. a fourth building type accounted for 20 percent of fires in the city.

    C. fires in buildings of Type B were responsible for more fires than other building types combined.

    D. the total number of fires was four times the number of fires in Type A buildings.

27. The act of arson is purposely setting fire to property, either personal or belonging to someone else. A fire is considered arson only after all accidental causes have been ruled out, which means investigators must prove an individual caused a fire deliberately and with harmful intent. Some common indicators of arson that investigators look for are as follows:

1. A large amount of damage.

2. No "V" burn pattern present, or unusual burn patterns and high heat stress.

3. Lack of accidental causes.

4. Evidence of forced entry.

5. The same person showing up at unconnected fires.

6. Low burning point with unidentifiable point of origin.

7. Multiple points of origin.

In the aftermath of a large fire at an abandoned warehouse, an investigator observes significant damage to the structures and cannot determine any accidental causes for the fires. To label this case as potential arson, which additional discovery would be most helpful?

A. Identification of multiple places of frayed electrical wiring in the structure

B. Video recordings from nearby security cameras of multiple people loitering near the warehouse around the estimated time of ignition

C. Findings of fire code violations, such as unsafe building materials and flammable substances on site

D. Detection of multiple locations in the warehouse from which the fire spread

28. Station 12 responds to a fire at a four-story commercial building. Witnesses reported an explosion, but it's unclear with the state of the fire where the blast originated. Firefighter Maloney begins taking eyewitness accounts to better assess the situation. Each witness describes the event as follows:

Witness 1: "I was walking by and heard a huge blast. I turned and saw flames shooting from the fifth floor on the northeast side."

Witness 2: "I looked out my window and saw glass shatter and a fireball on the northwest side of the top floor."

Witness 3: "The fourth floor lit up on the northeast side. All the glass crashing to the street sounded like small bells."

Witness 4: "There was this big flash of light on the first floor. Just look at the glass all over the sidewalk on the northeast side."

Considering the eyewitness accounts, Firefighter Maloney recognizes that she should relay information to other responders based on the descriptions of witnesses

A. 1, 2, 3

B. 1, 2, 4

C. 1, 3, 4

D. 2, 3, 4

29. An emergency situation earlier in the day disrupted standard daily activities at the fire house. Your supervisor has provided a set of instructions for multiple tasks to complete. Your shift ends soon, and you're not sure you'll have time to complete everything before needing to depart. You've communicated this, and your supervisor would like you to prioritize certain tasks before departing. In order to make the best use of your time and attend to mission critical duties, you

    A. complete one hour of physical fitness.

    B. clean the living facilities.

    C. inspect personal protective equipment for damage.

    D. wash the fire engine and clean equipment.

30. On the first day you report for work as a firefighter, you're assigned to routine duties that seem mundane and boring. You should

    A. consider these duties an opportunity to become thoroughly familiar with the firehouse.

    B. explain to your superior that you are capable of greater responsibility.

    C. perform your assignment perfunctorily while conserving energy for more important work in the future.

    D. try to get someone to take care of your assignment until you have become thoroughly acquainted with your new associates.

31. A firefighter's foremost duty is to protect life and property.

    An off-duty firefighter walks down the street about six blocks from a firehouse. Suddenly, a woman runs out of an apartment saying there was a fire in the building. He immediately follows the woman into the burning building and tries to put the fire out. The firefighter's action were:

    A. proper, because even though he was off duty, he was willing to help.

    B. improper, because by going into a fire without any backup, he endangered both his life and that of the woman.

    C. proper, because the other apartment residents needed to be alerted and evacuated.

    D. improper, because he was off duty and needed to rest after his shift.

32. According to the Bloomberg City Hall policy, confidentiality is of the utmost importance and should not be compromised under any circumstances.

    Consider the following situation: A visitor to the Bloomberg City Hall tells one of the aides that he has an appointment with the office supervisor, who is expected shortly. The visitor asks permission to wait in the supervisor's private office, which is currently unoccupied. For the office aide to allow the visitor to do so would be

    A. proper; the visitor would be less likely to disturb the other employees or to be disturbed by them.

    B. improper; it is not courteous to permit a visitor to be left alone in an office.

    C. proper; the supervisor might want to speak to the visitor in private.

    D. improper; the supervisor might have left confidential papers on the desk.

33. The fire department is called to the scene of a fire in a new apartment complex. While the firefighters are setting up hoses and moving aerial ladders into place, the owner of the building arrives, and he is nearly hysterical. As the firefighters move in, the owner is hindering them as he tries to enter the building. Another firefighter escorts the owner to a safe area and tells him he must stay out of harm's way. The owner is upset because he states he doesn't have insurance for the building, and he doesn't want any damage done to the doors or walls from "ax happy firemen." Meanwhile, law enforcement has been requested to assist with the owner. What is the most appropriate response to the owner in this moment?

A. "Sir, please leave or we'll have you arrested!"

B. "Not everyone is as lucky as you are to have such talented firefighters respond to their call. The faster we work the better we can protect your property."

C. "Firefighters have to take measures to extinguish the fire. All efforts are required. Please speak with the captain after we extinguish the fire."

D. "The fire department does not care that you do not have insurance. We'll do anything necessary to contain the situation."

34. Answering a call to a duplex fire, firefighters find flames coming from the windows of both residences. A woman is attempting to run into one of the doors. Firefighters yell warnings and then physically remove the woman from harm. She is crying, frantic, and keeps saying her cat is in the house. What would be the best action for the firefighters who are with the woman to take?

A. Ignore the woman, as the animal is already likely dead.

B. Pass the information along to the firefighters working on the woman's house.

C. Offer the woman their condolences about her cat.

D. Advise the woman to get a "pet in the house" window sticker next time.

Diagnostic Test

35. Firefighters use specialized tools for forcible entry when they need emergency access into a building. They select which tool to use based on a given situation. They want to select the tool that is most appropriate for their task and environment, creating as little risk as possible.

A firefighter has gained access to a three-story house and needs to confirm if the fire has reached the third story before proceeding any further down the second-floor hallway. Which of the following tools would be most appropriate to use in such a situation?

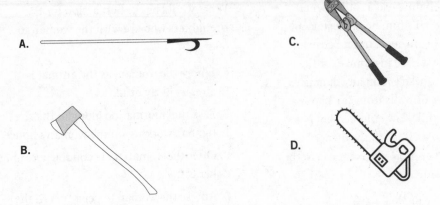

A.

B.

C.

D.

36. A firefighter's tools have specific uses. The following table lists some of these tools and their functions.

Type	Tools	Uses
Cutting	Pickhead axe	Cuts through doors, breaks windows; pointed end can be used to pierce materials
	Rotary saw, chain saw, reciprocating saw, power saw	Cuts through doors, walls fences, gates, security bars, and other barriers
	Bolt cutter	Cuts off padlocks or cuts through obstacles such as fences
Prying	Halligan tool, Flat bar, Crowbar	Breaks windows, forces doors open
Pushing/ Pulling	Pike pole	Punches holes to search for fires behind walls and ceilings; pulls items from intense heat and flames; breaks windows for ventilation
Striking	Flathead axe	Breaks open doors, windows; used with Halligan tool to force doors open
	Sledgehammer	Breaches walls and windows; used with other tools to force doors open or break padlocks

Which of the following would be used as a striking tool for forcible entry?

A. Bolt cutter

B. Flathead axe

C. Reciprocating saw

D. Halligan tool

37. The drawing shown represents a building as viewed from the front.

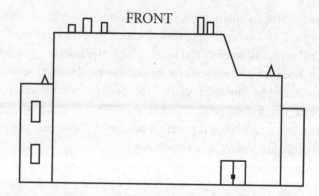

FRONT

Which drawing represents the same image from behind?

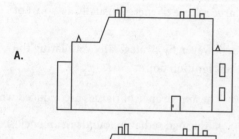

A.

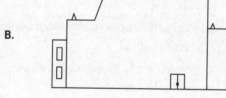

B.

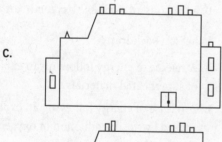

C.

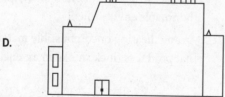

D.

Questions 38–41 are based on the following passage.

Flashovers and backdrafts are distinct yet often confused fire-related events that pose a fatal risk to firefighters on duty. Part of the confusion stems from the fact that flashovers and backdrafts produce similar results: in both instances, a large fire instantly envelops an entire room or area. Flashovers, however, are temperature-driven events, whereas backdrafts are air-driven.

Line
5   Flashovers are caused by thermal radiation feedback in an enclosed area. When fire heats a given area, all objects in that area will absorb heat until they reach their ignition temperature threshold. Once the heat pushes objects past that threshold, they ignite and the area is suddenly engulfed floor-to-ceiling in flames, i.e., a flashover.

    A backdraft occurs when a fire uses all the available oxygen in a given area—reducing the
10 appearance of flames while pushing all objects in the vicinity to their ignition point—and an additional source of oxygen is then introduced. The introduction of additional oxygen, such as opening a window to the area on fire, allows the fire to "breathe" again and all superheated gases in the area instantly explode. This results in a large release of energy, usually as a gust of smoke and debris, known as a backdraft.

15   Both flashovers and backdrafts can be prevented, however, by strategically ventilating the area in question before combustible contents reach their ignition point.

38. Which of the following could cause a backdraft?

  A. Training a hoseline on the center of a fire

  B. Using the wrong hose size when fighting a fire

  C. Opening a window to an area that's on fire

  D. A brush fire that's spreading rapidly

39. A flashover occurs when

  A. a door or window is opened, introducing new oxygen to an oxygen-deficient area.

  B. combustible material in an enclosed area is heated beyond its ignition point.

  C. the volume of smoke surpasses the volume of an enclosed area that's on fire.

  D. flames shoot toward firefighters through gaps in a building.

40. The appearance of flames are reduced when

  A. thermal radiation builds in an enclosed area.

  B. combustible objects are heated beyond their threshold.

  C. new oxygen is introduced to an environment that's on fire.

  D. a fire uses all available oxygen in an area.

41. What is a backdraft?

  A. A release of energy following an explosion of superheated materials

  B. A release of energy following an explosion caused by the introduction of oxygen to a flammable environment

  C. A rapid heating of combustible material that produces thick smoke in an enclosed area

  D. An introduction of cool air to a warm environment

Questions 42–44 are based on the following map.

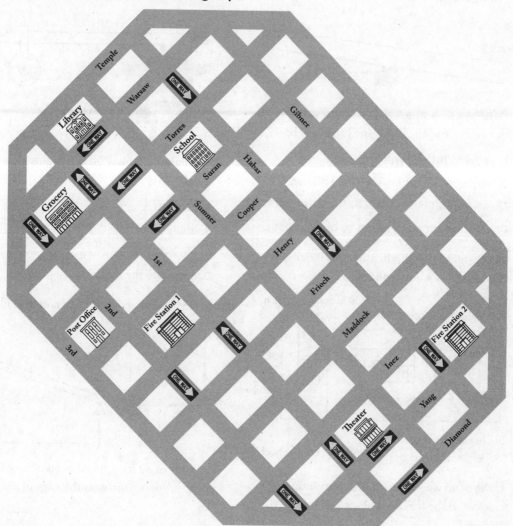

42. If there is a fire at the library, what is the quickest way to respond from Fire Station 1?

    A. Henry to 1st to Warsaw

    B. 1st to Torres to Sumner to Warsaw

    C. Henry to 1st to Cooper to Sumner to Warsaw

    D. Henry to 1st to Temple to Sumner to Warsaw

43. If there is a fire at the theater, what is the quickest way to respond from Fire Station 2?

    A. Yang to Gibner to Habar to Yang

    B. Yang to Habar to Inez to 1st

    C. Yang to Gibner to Sumner to Maddock

    D. Yang to Gibner to Inez to 2nd to Yang

44. How many blocks from Fire Station 1 to Fire Station 2?

    A. 4

    B. 5

    C. 6

    D. 8

45. The figure below shows a first-class lever.

If the block on which the lever is resting is moved close to the brick, the brick will be

A. easier to lift and will be lifted higher.

B. harder to lift and will be lifted higher.

C. easier to lift but will not be lifted as high.

D. harder to lift and will not be lifted as high.

46. In the figure shown, the threaded block can slide in the slot but cannot revolve.

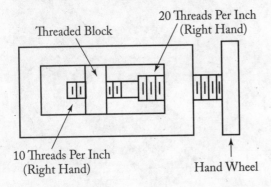

If the hand wheel is turned 20 revolutions clockwise, the threaded block will move

A. 1 inch to the left.

B. $\frac{1}{2}$ inch to the left.

C. $\frac{1}{2}$ inch to the right.

D. 1 inch to the right.

47. The figure below shows a lever-type safety valve.

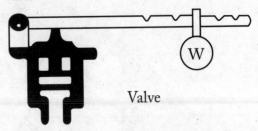

The valve will blow off at a higher pressure if weight W is

A. decreased.

B. doubled.

C. moved to the left.

D. moved to the right.

48. A pry bar is used to move a concrete block.

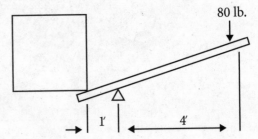

A force of 80 lb., applied as shown, will produce a tipping force on the edge of the block of

A. 80 lb.

B. 160 lb.

C. 240 lb.

D. 320 lb.

Questions 49–50 refer to the drawing shown.

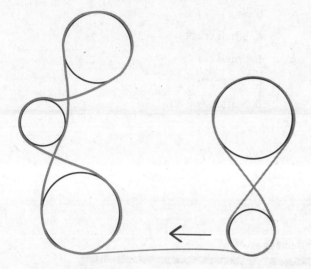

49. How many pulleys are moving in the clockwise direction?

   A. 2

   B. 3

   C. 4

   D. 5

50. How many pulleys are moving in the counterclockwise direction?

   A. 5

   B. 4

   C. 3

   D. 2

Questions 51–55 are based on the following passage. Study and memorize the details of the information presented in the passage for five minutes and then answer the questions. Do not refer to the passage while answering the questions.

Mr. Smith is having coffee in his home when he is rocked by a loud explosion. His dog, Pumpkin, is excitedly barking and running in circles. He moves to the large window facing the street and sees multiple vehicles involved in an accident. There are flames coming from the front end of a station wagon. Another vehicle involved is a large truck, which is leaking a greenish-blue liquid.

Line 5 Before calling 911, Mr. Smith counts the vehicles—and sees five. Mr. Smith makes the call, giving dispatch his full name and address and describes everything he can see from his window.

Mr. Smith tells his dog to stay in the house as he goes outside to see if he can help. He grabs a blanket off of the sofa and steps outside. There is a crowd gathering around, and children are close to the leaking liquid. Someone has a fire extinguisher and is working to put out the vehicle

10 fire. Mr. Smith told dispatch there were five vehicles involved, but now he can see there is a sixth vehicle as well. He moves to assist a woman from the burning vehicle who has slumped to the ground. Just as he is wrapping the blanket around her, Engine Company 477 arrives to take care of the victims. Mr. Smith returns to his house and pets his dog.

51. What kind of vehicle is on fire?

   A. A large truck

   B. A sedan

   C. A station wagon

   D. A small truck

52. What is Mr. Smith's dog's name?

   A. Plump

   B. Poppy

   C. Puppy

   D. Pumpkin

53. What is the Engine Company number?

A. 455

B. 477

C. 407

D. 404

54. How many cars are involved in the collision?

A. Three

B. Four

C. Five

D. Six

55. Which vehicle is leaking a greenish-blue liquid?

A. Small truck

B. Small car

C. Large truck

D. Station wagon

Questions 56–58 are based on the following chart and passage.

Flammable Liquids: Hazard Classifications

CLASS	FLASH POINT	BOILING POINT	EXAMPLES
I-A	Below 73°F / 23°C	Below 100°F / 38°C	Diethyl Ether, Pentane, Ligroin, Petroleum Ether
I-B	Below 73°F / 23°C	At or Above 100°F / 38°C	Acetone, Benzene, Cyclohexane, Ethanol
I-C	73—100°F / 23—38°C	— — —	P-Xylene

Combustible Liquids: Hazard Classifications

II	101—140°F / 39—60°C	— — —	Diesel Fuel, Motor Oil, Kerosene, Cleaning Solvents
II-A	141—199°F / 61—93°C	— — —	Paints (oil-based), Linseed Oil, Mineral Oil
II-B	200°F / 93°C and Above	— — —	Paints (oil-based), Neatsfoot Oil

Flammable and combustible liquids are categorized as hazardous materials according to their flashpoints. A flashpoint is the minimum temperature required for a liquid to produce vapor dense enough to ignite. The lower a liquid's flashpoint, the more dangerous, and the higher its hazard classification; this is because liquids with lower flashpoints require less heat and energy to catch fire. Classifications range from II-B for combustible liquids—like certain oil-based paints and neatsfoot oil—to I-A for the most hazardous flammable liquids, like pentane and petroleum ether. Such hazardous liquids are to be stored in containers according to their classifications. While outside factors like temperature impact various conditions of hazardous material fires, the actual flashpoint of a given liquid always stays the same.

Part II: Diagnosing Your Strengths and Weaknesses

56. Which statement about flammable and combustible liquids is true?

   A. The flashpoint is the maximum temperature at which a liquid emits vapor that's dense enough to be ignitable.

   B. The rate at which a liquid produces flammable vapor depends entirely on external factors.

   C. The type of container used to store a flammable or combustible liquid is irrelevant.

   D. The vaporization rate for flammable and combustible liquids increases as temperatures rise.

57. A liquid is a Class II combustible liquid if its flashpoint is greater than

   A. 39°C.

   B. 60°C.

   C. 141°F.

   D. 199°F.

58. Ethanol boils at

   A. 23°C.

   B. 35°C.

   C. 73°F.

   D. 101°F.

Questions 59 and 60 are based on the following floor plan.

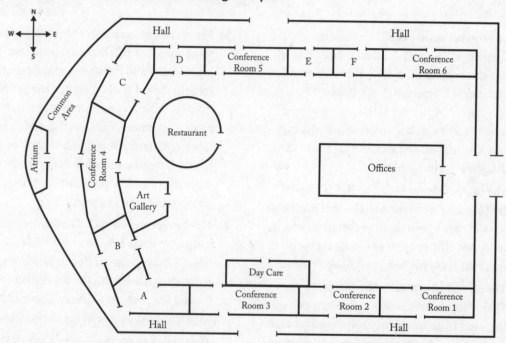

59. The entrance on the south side is

   A. closer to Room A than it is to Conference Room 6.

   B. closer to Room D than it is to Conference Room 1.

   C. farther from Conference Room 2 than it is from Room C.

   D. farther from Conference Room 3 than it is from Room B.

60. Firefighters responding to a fire in Conference Room 4 find the entrance on the north side blocked. The next closest entrance is on the

   A. east side of the building.

   B. north side of the building.

   C. west side of the building.

   D. south side of the building.

ANSWER KEY AND EXPLANATIONS

1. B	13. A	25. C	37. A	49. B
2. C	14. B	26. D	38. C	50. D
3. B	15. C	27. D	39. B	51. C
4. D	16. B	28. A	40. D	52. D
5. D	17. D	29. C	41. B	53. B
6. C	18. B	30. A	42. C	54. D
7. B	19. A	31. B	43. D	55. C
8. C	20. A	32. D	44. C	56. D
9. D	21. D	33. C	45. C	57. A
10. A	22. B	34. B	46. D	58. D
11. B	23. C	35. A	47. D	59. A
12. D	24. B	36. B	48. D	60. D

1. **The correct answer is B.** The Incident Command System is a standardized, coordinated management system that commands and controls emergency responses. The ICS is used by fire departments, emergency medical services, law enforcement, disaster services, and other agencies that respond to disasters or emergencies.

2. **The correct answer is C.** The ICS is important because it provides a standard protocol for all types of emergency responses, which increases efficiency by ensuring everyone involved is coordinated and in agreement.

3. **The correct answer is B.** The Incident Command System works only when everyone involved in an emergency response knows the protocol. ICS is a highly organized and structured approach to incident management that requires all involved to know their job and understand who's in control of various issues and resources across all departments.

4. **The correct answer is D.** The Incident Commander has complete control of the scene, including who's present. In an emergency, it's critical to have one leader who can sign off on all decisions and confidently direct all responders.

5. **The correct answer is D.** Three framework components of ICS that enable diverse organizations to integrate capabilities and achieve shared goals, as stated in the text, are Communication and Information Management, Command and Coordination, and Resource Management. While choices A, B, and C may be included under the large umbrella of ICS responsibilities, none are a main framework component.

6. **The correct answer is C.** The Snyder Apartments, which is located at 408 Water St., has the most people living in residence. The paint shop (choice A), the bar & grill (choice B), and the bike shop (choice D), would not have the most people living in residence.

7. **The correct answer is B.** While any of the buildings could potentially contain volatile materials, a paint shop would contain large amounts of paint, a known volatile material, and could contain other volatile liquids such as paint thinners, paint removers, solvents, and oils as well. The gym (choice A), the bar & grill (choice C), and the bike shop (choice D) are not the most likely places to keep larger amounts of volatile chemicals as a regular part of their inventory.

8. **The correct answer is C.** The fire hydrant is located on the sidewalk in front of the Paint Shop, an essential detail that firefighters should identify when arriving on scene.

9. **The correct answer is D.** The Bar & Grill has a chimney. The apartments, paint shop, and the bike shop do not have a chimney.

10. **The correct answer is A.** Water St. has two lanes, both going west. One-way streets may present additional difficulties in reaching and staging for a fire or other emergency. Emergency vehicles, including the fire department must observe traffic laws.

11. **The correct answer is B.** A gallon of water weighs 8.34 lb. Multiply:

    8.34 lb. × 4,800 gallons = 40,032 lb.

12. **The correct answer is D.** Remember the order of operations (PEMDAS).

    Solve the equation in the parentheses first:

    $$(8 - 5) = 3$$

    Then add the fractions together: $\dfrac{1}{3} + \dfrac{1}{3} = \dfrac{2}{3}$

    Finally, add the whole number and the fraction: $3 + \dfrac{2}{3} = 3\dfrac{2}{3}$

13. **The correct answer is A.** Add the gallons of water that are brought to the scene: 1,200 + 1,000 + 750 = 2,950 gallons. Be careful to avoid arithmetic errors and don't be misled by extra information in the question. The drop tank can hold 2,000 gallons, but its capacity does not figure into the total amount of water on the scene.

14. **The correct answer is B.** To determine the mean (or average), add the weight of the firefighters:

    180 + 155 + 170 + 165 + 190 = 860 lb.

    Then divide the total weight (860) by 5, the number of firefighters:

    860 ÷ 5 = 172 lb.

15. **The correct answer is C.** $8^2 = 8 \times 8 = 64$. Basic math skills are required in firefighting every day. Familiarity with addition, subtraction, multiplication, division, and skills with fractions, exponents, percentages, area, volume, and more are mandatory.

16. **The correct answer is B.** Based on the statistics listed, the correct order from highest to lowest is Denmark, Sweden, United States, Great Britain/Spain (tied with 0.2 each), and France.

17. **The correct answer is D.** Of the 1,600 response calls for the year, 289 were for MVAs, 89 for pedestrian-MVAs, and 22 for boating accidents. Add these three numbers to get the combined total:

    $$289 + 89 + 22 = 400$$

    You might have recognized right away that 400 divides into 1,660 equally 4 times, and as such would mean that the total of the three quantities would make up $\dfrac{1}{4}$ or 25% of the total calls. But to solve a problem in which you need to find what percentage one number is of another, follow these steps:

    Let m = unknown percentage.

    $\dfrac{m}{100} = \dfrac{400}{1,600}$ Set up the proportion and cross mulitply.

    $1,600m = 40,000$ Divide by m.

    $m = 25\%$

18. **The correct answer is B.** To find the mean or average age, begin by adding the ages of the crew members:

    $$24 + 29 + 33 + 36 + 41 + 47 = 210$$

    Then, divide the total of the ages by 6 (the number of firefighters):

    $$210 \div 6 = 35$$

19. **The correct answer is A.** Begin by finding the volume of the crate in cubic feet. Multiply:

    $$15 \times 15 \times 12 = 2,700 \text{ cubic feet}$$

    To find the cubic yards, divide the volume by 27:

    $$2,700 \div 27 = 100 \text{ cubic yards}$$

20. **The correct answer is A.**

$.40 = \dfrac{4}{10}$, which can be reduced to $\dfrac{2}{5}$.
Remember, to convert a decimal into a fraction, set up the decimal as a fraction with a denominator of 1 and multiply both the numerator and denominator by 100. Then simplify.

$$.40 = \dfrac{0.40}{1} \times \dfrac{100}{100} = \dfrac{40}{100} = \dfrac{4}{10} = \dfrac{2}{5}$$

21. **The correct answer is D.** The pattern established by the colors is as the hydrants get darker, both the hoseline diameter and the water-flowing capacity increase.

22. **The correct answer is B.** Once Emergency Personnel has been contacted through 911, the office worker should calmly inform those around him to stay away from the area where the package is located. He can record information about the package (choice A) in a variety of ways after informing the other workers, thus assuring protection of others first. Under no circumstances should he move the package (choice C); doing so could potentially activate a detonating mechanism. Pulling the fire alarm (choice D) is not necessary, as 911 has already been called and doing so may create unnecessary panic.

23. **The correct answer is C.** The acronym PASS (pull, aim, squeeze, and sweep) will help you remember the correct sequence. The instructions should be placed in the following order: 5–4–1–3–2. Remove the pin from the handle. Aim the nozzle low at the base of the fire while keeping the extinguisher in an upright position. Squeeze the extinguisher trigger. Sweep the fire extinguisher from side to side; keep doing so until the fire is completely out. Slowly back away from the fire.

24. **The correct answer is B.** Smoke detectors should not be placed in the kitchen where cooking could trigger a false alarm or near windows, doors, or ducts where drafts might interfere with their operation.

25. **The correct answer is C.** The steps for removing and preparing PPE for next use should be placed in the following order: 3–2–4–1. Written out, those steps are as follows: Remove protective clothing; inspect PPE for damage and need for cleaning; clean equipment as needed, remove damaged equipment from service, and report to company officer, if applicable; and place clothing in a ready state.

26. **The correct answer is D.** Remember that the total number of all fires in June (including those that did *not* occur in building types A, B, or C) must equal 100 percent. If 25 percent of all fires were in buildings of Type A, then the total number of fires in June was four times the number of fires in Type A buildings.

27. **The correct answer is D.** Fire behavior is well documented regarding point of origin. As mentioned in the information, an established point of proof that arson has occurred is multiple points of origin, such as three separate and spontaneous sources of ignition. No other answer choices provide substantial evidence of arson.

28. **The correct answer is A.** Witnesses 1, 2, and 3 all report that the explosion occurred at the top of the building somewhere on the north side. Even as Witness 1 improperly says the explosion took place on the fifth floor (the building has only four), the account aligns with the information from Witness 2 and 3, that the explosion occurred on the top floor. Witness 4's description should be excluded, as even though it identified broken glass as properly occurring on the north side of the building, the account of the blast on the first floor is challenged by three other accounts.

29. **The correct answer is C.** Certain activities are performed at the beginning of new shifts, like inspection of personal protective

equipment and maintenance of the fire engine. In the event of an emergency, such routines will be altered. When considering which of the duties ordered by your supervisor take priority, it is important to consider which tasks would have an immediate impact during your shift or, if another emergency were to occur, for those taking your place. All tasks listed in the answer choices represent important duties for safety and team preparedness; however, in this case, the priorities of a firefighter demand that personal protective equipment be maintained to ensure the safety of firefighters on duty.

30. **The correct answer is A.** The question clearly states that you are new to the job. Therefore, it would be wise to use this opportunity to become acquainted with firehouse procedures and demonstrate your abilities. This choice outlines a course of action that will benefit you and the firehouse in which you are working because it gets needed work done. Considering that it is your first day on the job, telling your supervisor of your capacity for greater things (choice B) while showing an unwillingness to handle your first assignment would not be the best way to make a favorable impression. Performing in a perfunctory manner (choice C) would show a lack of enthusiasm and will not help you complete your assigned work in the best possible manner or in the shortest possible time. This would be your responsibility as a newly appointed firefighter. The course of action in choice D isn't likely to lead to the completion of the assignment or to enhance your image among fellow firefighters.

31. **The correct answer is B.** While the firefighter's actions might sound heroic, choices A and C support a quick yet rash decision. Since he's alone, it's unwise for the firefighter to rush into the building without knowing that backup is on the way; he might not

be able to alert all the tenants before the fire gets out of control. Also, by asking the woman to go back into the burning building, he unnecessarily risks her life. Choice D offers no sound reason for not helping the woman. The proper course of action would be for the firefighter to direct the woman to call 911 and stay put while he goes into the building to begin evacuating immediately.

32. **The correct answer is D.** First evaluate the course of action on part of the office aide. Permitting the visitor to wait in the supervisor's office is highly improper. You know nothing about the nature of the visit; it might not be for a friendly or congenial purpose. Moreover, there might be confidential papers on the supervisor's desk that should not be seen. Therefore, you must pick between choices B and D. This is not a question of courtesy. Although all visitors should be treated with courtesy, permitting the visitor to wait in the supervisor's office is a question of privacy and security.

33. **The correct answer is C.** All firefighters should show respect for citizens. However, civilians cannot be allowed to interfere with ongoing fire work. A firefighter's response should diffuse the situation and direct the citizen to a mutually beneficial resolution, in this case: containing the fire and addressing the citizen's concerns. In many situations, not only could the owner be injured, he could also cause a firefighter to be injured or interfere with firefighting efforts. Even though the owner makes disparaging remarks about firefighters in general, the firefighter who speaks with him must show restraint and direct the individual to address concerns with a superior so that the firefighter's priorities, preservation of life and property, can be met.

34. **The correct answer is B.** Firefighters may empathize with people at an emergency, but they must maintain a professional distance

for the safety of all concerned. The woman cannot be allowed into the burning house, no matter how tragic it will be to lose her cat. However, it is appropriate to pass along the information to the firefighters working directly on the residence. In some cases, pets have been resuscitated after suffering smoke inhalation. Educating the woman about potential ways to protect any future pets she may have would be helpful, but compassion for her emotional state would dictate holding off until a later time.

35. **The correct answer is A.** A pike pole is used to punch holes to search for fires behind walls and ceilings. Given the situation, that a firefighter on the second floor of the building wishes to gather information about the floor above, a pike pole would allow the firefighter to safely puncture a hole in the ceiling above without risking directly whatever conditions exist on the third floor. A flathead axe (choice B) is used for breaking down doors and windows; bolt cutters (choice C) are used for cutting through padlocks and other obstacles; a chain saw (choice D) is used for cutting through doors, walls, and other barriers.

36. **The correct answer is B.** A flathead axe is a striking tool used to forcibly open doors and windows. With the information provided by the table, it is the only "striking" tool available among the listed answer options and thus would be the best tool for the situation.

37. **The correct answer is A.** While all the buildings are similar, the ability to visualize a situation from all angles is critical. Hazards can be anywhere on the scene, no matter the size or location. Knowing the location of the doors, windows, and other features is mandatory (often, even buildings with double doors in front have only a single door in back).

38. **The correct answer is C.** Opening a window to an area that's on fire would introduce new oxygen to that environment and could result

in a backdraft. Hose size (choice B) and hose position (choice A) are irrelevant regarding backdraft, and as backdrafts occur only in closed areas, a brush fire (choice D) would not be a cause.

39. **The correct answer is B.** A flashover is the result of thermal radiation in an enclosed area eclipsing the ignition point of combustible objects in that area. Introducing oxygen (choice A) could create a backdraft, not a flashover. Flashovers aren't dependent on volume or density of smoke (choice C), and while flames shooting from a building (choice D) could result from a flashover, they aren't likely to cause one.

40. **The correct answer is D.** The passage states, "when a fire uses all available oxygen in a given area—reducing the appearance of flames"; this implies that flames are reduced once a fire uses the available oxygen in an enclosed space. Lack of oxygen has this effect, not its introduction (choice C) or thermal radiation (choice A), and heating combustible objects beyond their threshold (choice B) will create flames, not quell them.

41. **The correct answer is B.** When oxygen enters an oxygen-starved and highly flammable environment, the contents of the environment burst into flames and release a wave of energy known as a backdraft. Choice A is plausible but doesn't provide enough detail; backdrafts only result from explosions caused by the introduction of new oxygen. Choice C is a tell-tale sign that a backdraft could occur, but fails to define the phenomena itself. Choice D is irrelevant.

42. **The correct answer is C.** The quickest way to respond to a fire at the library is Henry to 1st to Cooper to Sumner to Warsaw. The fire department cannot break laws just because they respond to emergencies. All traffic laws still apply, including one-way streets.

43. **The correct answer is D.** The quickest way to the theater is Yang to Gibner to Inez to 2nd

to Yang. Even fire departments must obey traffic laws. A fire truck cannot drive the wrong way down a one-way street simply because it is a closer route to the emergency.

44. **The correct answer is C.** The closest route is six blocks. The route to Fire Station 2 on Yang Street via Henry (two blocks) and Habar (four blocks) is the closet route that obeys all traffic signs.

45. **The correct answer is C.** If the block is moved toward the brick, the moment for a given force exerted will increase (being farther from the force) making it easier to lift; the height will be made smaller, hardly raising the brick when moved to the limit (directly underneath it).

46. **The correct answer is D.** The hand wheel tightens to the left when rotated clockwise since it has a right-handed thread. If the hand wheel is turned 20 revolutions, it moves one inch to the left, pulling the threaded-block one inch in the opposite direction (to the right).

47. **The correct answer is D.** By moving the weight to the right and thus increasing the length of the level arm, the effort is increased, enabling the valve to blow off at a higher pressure.

48. **The correct answer is D.** Let x = tipping force produced on the edge of the block.

$$80 \times 4 = 1 \times x; x = 320 \text{ lb.}$$

49. **The correct answer is B.** There are three pulleys moving clockwise. Study the drawing to determine the correct answer.

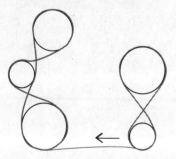

The arrow indicates direction for one pulley. Based on this information, follow the belt around the pulleys and count how many pulleys are moving clockwise.

50. **The correct answer is D.** There are two pulleys moving counterclockwise. Study the drawing for the answer.

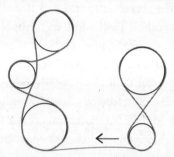

Follow the belt around the pulleys to determine how many are moving counterclockwise.

51. **The correct answer is C.** The station wagon is on fire. Read the narrative carefully and memorize the material. It is important to answer the questions without referring to the paragraphs. Assessing the situation is a must before you enter the scene.

52. **The correct answer is D.** Mr. Smith's dog's name is Pumpkin.

53. **The correct answer is B.** The responding engine company is number 477.

54. **The correct answer is D.** There are six vehicles involved in the accident. Although Mr. Smith initially tells dispatch there are five vehicles, he sees the sixth once he is on the scene.

55. **The correct answer is C.** The large truck is leaking greenish-blue liquid. Mr. Smith sees the truck leaking the fluid and reports that information to dispatch.

56. **The correct answer is D.** Flammable and combustible liquids stored above room temperature are considered more hazardous because they reach their flashpoints more quickly. The size and type of storage container is determined by the hazard

classification of the material (choice C); the flashpoint of a given material is the minimum temperature (choice A) at which it emits a vapor dense enough to ignite; and the rate at which a liquid produces flammable vapor depends on the liquid itself (choice B), not just external factors.

57. **The correct answer is A.** A liquid is a Class II combustible liquid if its flashpoint is equal to or greater than 101°F/39°C and below 140°F/60°C. A liquid with a flashpoint greater than 141°F or 60°C (choices B and C) would labeled Class II-A or higher, and a liquid with a flashpoint greater than 199°F (choice D) would be labeled Class II-B.

58. **The correct answer is D.** Ethanol is a Class I-B flammable liquid, which means it has a boiling point of 100°F; 23°C (choice A), 35°C (choice B), and 73°F (choice C) temperatures aren't hot enough to boil this hazardous material.

59. **The correct answer is A.** Study the drawing carefully. There are three entrances to the building. There are conference rooms and smaller rooms intermingled in a horseshoe shape. The south entrance is positioned at the bottom of the drawing. The only true statement of the choices given is that the south exit is closer to Room A than it is to Conference Room 6.

60. **The correct answer is D.** If the north entrance to the building is blocked, then the next closest outside door is on the south side of the building. Firefighters should always be prepared for the possibility that the first choice may not be available and have a backup plan, in advance. The east side entrance (choice A) would take the firefighters to the opposite side of the building. The north side entrance (choice B) is blocked. There is no west side entrance (choice C).

DIAGNOSTIC TEST ASSESSMENT GRID

Now that you've completed the diagnostic test and read through the answer explanations, you can use your results to target your studying. Find the question numbers from the diagnostic test that you answered incorrectly and highlight or circle them below. Then focus extra attention on the chapters dealing with those topics.

Category	Questions	Chapter
Reading Comprehension	1–5, 38–41, 56–58	4
Reasoning and Judgment: Deductive Reasoning	22, 24, 27, 36	5
Reasoning and Judgment: Inductive Reasoning	21, 26, 35	5
Reasoning and Judgment: Information Ordering	23, 25	5
Reasoning and Judgment: Problem Sensitivity	28, 29, 31, 32	5
Reasoning and Judgment: Situational Judgment	30, 33, 34	5
Spatial Orientation	37, 42–44, 59, 60	6
Observation and Memory	6–10, 51–55	7
Mechanical Reasoning	45–50	8
Math	11–20	9

PART III
TEST PREPARATION

Chapter 4

Reading Comprehension

OVERVIEW

- **About Reading Comprehension Questions**
- **Sample Reading Program**
- **Five Common Types of Reading Comprehension Questions**
- **Tackling Reading Comprehension Questions**
- **Summing It Up**
- **Exercise 1: Reading Comprehension**
- **Exercise 2: Reading Comprehension**
- **Answer Keys and Explanations**

ABOUT READING COMPREHENSION QUESTIONS

A recent nationwide survey of firefighter examinations indicates wide variations in the subject matter of these exams. One topic common to all exams, however, is reading comprehension. Some exams include classic reading comprehension questions that present a passage and then ask questions about the details of the text and, perhaps, its meaning. Other exams require candidates to indicate proper behavior based on their reading of printed procedures and regulations. A third type of reading-based question requires candidates to reason and predict the logical next steps in a scenario based on information presented in a reading passage. Of course, questions of judgment in emergency and nonemergency situations rely heavily on reading as well. There are nearly as many variations of the reading-based question as there are test makers.

Before you devote attention to strategies for dealing with reading-based questions, give some thought to your reading habits and skill-level. How do you read best? Do you have to read something multiple times to understand it, or do you get the point of the passage on your first pass? Do you notice details, or do you concentrate on the overall meaning of the passage?

Between now and test day, work to improve deficits in your reading concentration and comprehension. A daily newspaper provides excellent material to improve your reading. Make a point of reading all the way through any article you begin; don't be satisfied with the first paragraph or two, and read with a pencil in hand so you can underline details and ideas that seem crucial to the its meaning. Notice points of view, arguments, and supporting

> **NOTE**
>
> As mandated by federal law, fire service agencies cannot require candidates to know firefighting procedures when taking their entrance exams; however, some firefighter departments consider questions of firefighter procedure as nothing more than common sense questions and include them in the test. If you encounter questions of this type, keep in mind that what most people consider to be common sense may not always be the best answer in firefighting situations.

information. When you've finished the article, summarize it for yourself. Can you identify its purpose? What main idea is presented? What is the writer's attitude? Did you find certain information lacking?

As you answer these questions, review what you underlined. Did you focus on important words and ideas? Did you read with comprehension? As you repeat this process you'll find that your reading becomes more efficient. You'll read with greater understanding and get more out of your newspaper.

You can't sit down the night before a test that involves reading comprehension and cram for it. The only way to build your reading skill is to practice systematically. The gains you make will show in an increased score on the test, as well as in your reading for study and pleasure.

Trying to change reading habits you've had for a long time can be difficult and discouraging. Try applying these suggestions one at a time rather than overwhelm yourself by attempting to implement them all at once. Change can be challenging. Remember, though, that changes you make for the better will stay with you for a lifetime.

SAMPLE READING PROGRAM

- Set aside 15 minutes each day to practice new reading techniques.

- Start with a short, easy-to-read article from a newspaper or magazine. Time yourself. At the end of your practice session, time yourself on another short article and keep a record of both times.

- Select a news story. Read it first, then practice an eye-scan exercise. Work on reducing the number of times your eye stops on each line (try limiting this number to two).

- Read an editorial, a book review, or a movie or drama review in a newspaper or literary magazine. This type of article typically expresses the author's point of view and is therefore good practice for searching out main ideas. After you read, see whether you can write a good title for the article and jot down a one-sentence summary of the author's main idea. You can also try to make up a test question based on the article, with four answer choices. This is excellent practice for determining main ideas (and you can use your own questions to test your friends).

- Find a new word and write the sentence in which it appears. Guess its meaning from the context, then look up its definition in a dictionary. Try to write a sentence of your own using the word. Then try to use the word in conversation at least twice the following day.

A major aspect of your daily reading that deserves special attention is vocabulary building. The most effective readers have rich, extensive vocabularies. As you read, make a list of unfamiliar words. Include words that you understand within the context of the article but that you can't define. In addition, mark words you don't understand. When you put aside your newspaper, find a dictionary and look up every new word. Write the word and its definition in a special notebook (writing down words and their definitions helps seal them in your memory far better than reading alone—the notebook can serve as a handy reference for your own use). A sensitivity to the meaning of a greater number of words will

NOTE
If you follow this sample program daily, your test score will serve as proof of the gains you've made in reading comprehension.

make reading easier and more enjoyable, even if these specific words don't crop up on your exam. Mastering reading-based questions depends on more than just reading comprehension. You must also know how to parse out answers from the text and be able to choose the best answer from a list of possibilities, all of which may be good ones.

FIVE COMMON TYPES OF READING COMPREHENSION QUESTIONS

1. **Best title or main idea.** The answer might be obvious, but incorrect choices to the "main idea" question are often half-truths that get easily confused with the main idea. They might misstate the idea, omit part of the idea, or even offer a supporting idea quoted directly from the text. The correct answer is the one that addresses the largest part of the passage, or, ideally, the whole thing.

2. **Question of fact or detail.** You might have to mentally rephrase or rearrange, but you should find the answer stated in the body of the passage.

3. **Interpretation.** This question type asks you what a passage means, not just what it says. On firefighter exams, for example, questions based on categories of building styles might fall into the realm of interpretation.

4. **Inference.** This is the most difficult type of reading-based question, as it asks you to go beyond what the passage says and to predict what might happen next. Your answer must be based on a combination of the information in the passage and your own common sense, but not on outside information you might have about the subject. A variation of the inference question might be presented as follows: "The author would expect that. . ." To answer this question, you must understand the author's point of view and make an inference from that viewpoint based on the information presented.

5. **Vocabulary.** A passage may directly or indirectly ask about the meaning of certain words used in the passage.

TIP

Vocabulary building is an excellent habit to develop and practice throughout your lifetime.

TACKLING READING COMPREHENSION QUESTIONS

It's a good idea to approach reading comprehension questions by reading the questions, rather than the answer choices, before the passage. The questions will alert you to look for certain details, ideas, and points of view. Use your pencil and underline key words in the questions. These will help direct your attention as you read.

Next, skim the passage rapidly to get an idea of subject matter and organization. If key words or ideas pop out at you, underline them, but don't consciously search out details in the preliminary skimming.

Then, read the passage carefully with thorough comprehension as your main goal and underline the important words as you have been doing in your newspaper reading.

Finally, return to the questions. Read each question carefully. Be sure you know what it asks. Misreading questions is a major cause of error on reading comprehension tests. Then read all the answer choices. Eliminate the obviously incorrect answers first. You might be left with only one possible answer. If you find yourself with more than one possible answer, reread the question. Focus on catch-phrases or words that might destroy the validity of a seemingly acceptable answer, like *under all circumstances, at all times, never, always, under no condition, absolutely, entirely,* or *except when.* Finally, skim the passage once more, focusing on the underlined segments. By now, you should be able to conclude which answer is best.

Using a Four-Step Approach

It's time to work through some typical reading comprehension question sets together. We'll follow the four steps we've just discussed to locate the answers within the passages:

STEP 1: Skim the questions and underline key words.

STEP 2: Skim the passage.

STEP 3: Read the passage carefully and underline words that seem important or that you think hold clues to the question's answers.

STEP 4: Reread the question carefully, then choose the best answer choices based on your underlined passage.

Let's begin.

Questions 1–4 are based on the following passage.

The best kind of limestone for printing is Bavarian. Light-colored and perfectly smooth, it is porous and absorbs both water and greasy substances equally. The stone used is about 6 inches thick, up to 90 × 65 cm (35 × 25 inches), and it can weigh up to 175 pounds. Grinding the stone smooth creates a clean printing surface. This allows a drawing to be made on the surface with a greasy lithographic pencil or crayon. The drawing is then fixed by rinsing the stone with a weak solution of nitric acid and gum arabic. The stone is wiped with water before each impression is taken and, for each print, it is inked with a leather-covered roller. During this process, the porous limestone retains the grease of the crayon where the drawing has been made, and the parts that are not drawn upon become impregnated with water. The ink, which is greasy, is repelled by the water-wet areas and adheres only to the areas marked by the crayon.

1. What is the best title for this paragraph?

   A. "Where Good Limestone Is Found"

   B. "The Process of Lithographic Printing"

   C. "Watercolor Drawings on Limestone"

   D. "How to Make a Printing Stone"

2. According to the paragraph, Bavarian limestone is used because it

   A. can be cut into very large blocks.

   B. has a spongelike surface.

   C. contains nitric acid and gum arabic.

   D. will repel grease.

3. The aspect of this process NOT described by the paragraph is

   A. the finished product.

   B. how to ink the stone.

   C. creating a printing surface.

   D. what kind of limestone to use.

4. According to the paragraph, the purpose of the nitric acid and gum arabic is to

   A. make the limestone light-colored.

   B. erase previous drawings.

   C. make the drawing permanent.

   D. repel the printing ink.

STEP 1: Skim the questions and underline key words.

Your underlined questions should look something like the following four items:

1 The <u>best title</u> for this paragraph is

2 According to the paragraph, <u>Bavarian limestone</u> is used because it

3 The aspect of this process <u>NOT described</u> by the paragraph is

4 According to the paragraph, the purpose of the <u>nitric acid</u> and <u>gum arabic</u> is to

STEP 2: Skim the passage.

This quick reading should give you an idea of the structure of the passage and its overall meaning.

STEP 3: Read the passage carefully and underline words you find important or that you think hold clues to the question's answers.

You could also underline words and phrases that are found in the questions you've read already. Your underlined passage should look something like this:

The best kind of <u>limestone for printing is Bavarian</u>. Light-colored and perfectly smooth, it is <u>porous and absorbs both water and greasy substances</u> equally well. The stone used is about 6 inches thick, up to 90 × 65 cm (35 × 25 inches), and it can weigh up to 175 pounds. Grinding the stone smooth <u>creates a clean printing surface</u>. This allows a drawing to be made on the surface with a <u>greasy lithographic pencil or crayon</u>. The <u>drawing is then fixed</u> by rinsing the stone with a very weak solution of <u>nitric acid and gum arabic</u>. The stone is wiped with water before each impression is taken and, <u>for each print</u>, <u>it is inked</u> with a leather-covered roller. During this process, the <u>porous limestone</u> retains the grease of the crayon where the drawing has been made, and the parts that are not drawn upon become impregnated with water. The ink, which is greasy, is repelled by the water-wet areas and adheres only to the areas marked by the crayon.

STEP 4: Reread each question carefully and select the best answer choice based on your underlined passage.

Once you've selected your answer choices, compare your answers with those provided.

Answers and Explanations

1. **The correct answer is B.** The best title for any passage is the one that encompasses all ideas presented without being too broad or too narrow. Choice B provides the most inclusive title for this passage. A look at the other choices shows you why. The first sentence mentions where to find good limestone, but the rest of the paragraph clearly indicates that this isn't the main idea. Therefore, choice A can be eliminated. Watercolor drawing isn't mentioned, so choice C can be eliminated. Although the paragraph emphasizes the importance of the stone, it doesn't specifically discuss how to create a printing stone. The passage is clearly devoted to the process of creating a print, not to the creation of a printing stone. Therefore, choice D also can be eliminated.

2. **The correct answer is B.** The capability of Bavarian limestone to absorb water and greasy substances indicates that its spongelike surface is important for the printing process. Therefore, choice B is the best answer. Although the paragraph indicates that the limestone is often cut into very large blocks, nothing in the passage suggests that this is important to the printing process. Therefore, choice A can be eliminated. The passage states that the stone is rinsed with a solution of nitric acid and gum arabic. Nothing indicates that the nitric acid and gum arabic come from the stone itself, so choice C can be eliminated. The beginning of the passage clearly states that Bavarian limestone absorbs greasy substances. Because the meaning of *repel* is most nearly the opposite of *absorb*, choice D can be eliminated.

3. **The correct answer is A.** The ideas you underlined should help you with this question of fact. The finished product is never mentioned in the passage. Inking the stone (choice B), creating a printing surface (choice C), and choosing a type of limestone (choice D) are all mentioned and can be eliminated.

4. **The correct answer is C.** The answer to this question is in the following sentence: "The drawing is then fixed by rinsing the stone with a very weak solution of nitric acid and gum arabic." Here, the word *fixed* means "to make permanent." The best way to figure out the meaning of a word used in an unfamiliar way is to decide what meaning would make the most sense based on the rest of the passage. This sentence makes the most sense when we replace the word *fixed* with choice C, "made permanent."

You can see how using this method can help you to navigate through the different types of reading comprehension questions. The previous question set presented the three more straightforward question types: title/main idea, facts and details, and vocabulary. In the next set, we'll tackle some interpretation and inference questions as well.

Questions 5–9 are based on the following passage.

Weatherproofing wooden deck surfaces with the XYZ Process results in a surface that's far superior to those treated with other, less effective methods. XYZ Process-treated surfaces are durable to heavy walking traffic, resistant to wear from heavy rains and runoff from overhanging roofs, resistant to bleaching from excessive exposure to the sun, and maintain a "fresh wood" look for several years. In addition to producing a wooden surface that's attractive and durable, the XYZ Process also has several safety and environmental benefits. Surfaces treated with the XYZ Process are noncombustible, odorless, safe for children and pets, and free from splinters. Any wooden surface can be treated with the XYZ Process and done by anyone with access to a garden hose, a scrub brush, and a paintbrush. The application process is safe for surrounding vegetation, animal life, and anyone without major respiratory problems.

5. It's most accurate to state that the author of this passage presents

   A. facts, but reaches no conclusion concerning the value of the process.

   B. a conclusion concerning the value of the process unsupported by facts.

   C. neither facts nor conclusions, but merely describes the process.

   D. a conclusion concerning the value of the process and facts to support that conclusion.

6. If the XYZ Process were used for a surface other than a deck, it would be most useful for a

   A. cement sidewalk.

   B. plastic mailbox.

   C. wooden door.

   D. metal handrail.

7. The aspect of the XYZ Process NOT discussed in the paragraph is

   A. resistance to wear from snow and ice.

   B. safety concerns for animals.

   C. effects on surrounding plants.

   D. how it compares to other methods.

8. The main reason for treating wooden surfaces with the XYZ Process is to protect

   A. children from harmful odors.

   B. surrounding vegetation.

   C. wooden surfaces from weathering.

   D. animals from splinters.

9. Which of the following might be negatively affected by the XYZ Process?

   A. Plants surrounding the treated area

   B. Someone with respiratory problems

   C. Children walking on a treated surface

   D. Animals walking on a treated surface

STEP 1: Skim the questions and underscore key words.

Your underscored questions should look something like the following five items:

1. It is most accurate to state that the author of the passage <u>presents</u>

2. If the <u>XYZ Process</u> were used for a <u>surface other than a deck</u>, it would be most useful for a

3. The <u>aspect</u> of the XYZ Process <u>NOT discussed</u> in the paragraph is

4. The <u>main reason for treating</u> wooden surfaces with the XYZ Process is to protect

5. Of the following, one that might be <u>negatively affected</u> by the XYZ Process is

STEP 2: Skim the passage.

This quick reading should help you to get an idea of the subject matter of the passage and how it is organized.

STEP 3: Read the passage carefully and underline the words you find important or that you think hold clues to the question's answers.

You could also underline words and phrases that are found in the questions you've read already. This fact-filled passage might be underlined like this:

<u>Weatherproofing</u> wooden deck surfaces <u>with the XYZ</u> Process results in a surface that's <u>far superior</u> to those treated with other, <u>less effective methods</u>. XYZ Process-treated surfaces are <u>durable to heavy walking traffic, resistant to wear</u> from heavy rains and runoff from overhanging roofs, <u>resistant to bleaching</u> from excessive exposure to the sun, and <u>maintain a "fresh wood" look</u> for several years. In addition to producing a wooden surface that's <u>attractive and durable</u>, the XYZ Process also has several <u>safety and environmental benefits</u>. Surfaces treated with the XYZ Process are <u>noncombustible</u>, <u>odorless</u>, <u>safe for children and pets</u>, and free from <u>splinters</u>. <u>Any wooden surface</u> can be treated with the XYZ Process and done by anyone with access to a garden hose, a scrub brush, and a paintbrush. The application process is <u>safe</u> for <u>surrounding vegetation</u>, <u>animal life</u>, and anyone <u>without major respiratory problems</u>.

STEP 4: Reread each question carefully and select the best answer choice based on your underlined passage.

Once you've selected your answer choices, compare your answers with those provided.

Answers and Explanations

5. **The correct answer is D.** This is a combination of a main idea and interpretation question. If you cannot easily answer this question, reread the passage. The author clearly states his or her opinion about the XYZ Process in the first sentence. The rest of the passage provides an abundance of facts to support the conclusion.

6. **The correct answer is C.** This item is an example of an inference question. Toward the end of the passage, the author claims, "Any wooden surface can be treated with the XYZ Process." Because a wooden door is the only wooden surface mentioned, you can infer that the XYZ Process would be most useful in treating it.

7. **The correct answer is A.** The ideas you underlined should help you with this factual statement. Resistance to wear from snow and ice is the only aspect not mentioned. Safety concerns for animals

(choice B), effects on surrounding plants (choice C), and how it compares to other methods (choice D) are all explicitly noted in the text.

8. **The correct answer is C.** Protecting wooden surfaces from weathering is the main reason for treating wooden surfaces with the XYZ Process. The fact that the XYZ Process protects children (choice A), plants (choice B), and animals (choice D) is just an added benefit.

9. **The correct answer is B.** Underlining under what circumstances the process is safe to use should help you to determine this detail and interpretation question. By stating that the process is safe for any-one *without* major respiratory problems, the passage, in effect, is saying that the XYZ Process might not be safe for people *with* major respiratory problems.

4

Now that you've had some guided practice, branch out and test yourself with the reading comprehension practice exercises located after the Summing It Up section. Use the four-step process to work your way through the passage sets and try to answer each question before you read the answer explanation.

Summing It Up

4

- Reading comprehension questions appear on all firefighter exams in various forms, so be prepared to encounter them when you take your written exam.

- Before you develop strategies for answering reading-based questions, be sure to ask yourself how well you read, whether you concentrate fully, and whether you completely understand what you're reading.

- Work to improve your concentration and comprehension skills by following a program that will sharpen your focus and help you develop new reading techniques.

- Vocabulary building is one of the most important aspects of improving your reading comprehension. Knowing what words mean is a big step toward better understanding what you read.

- Five of the most common types of reading comprehension questions that appear on firefighter exams are those that ask about fact or detail, those requiring you to choose an appropriate title or find the main idea in a passage, those requiring you to interpret what a passage means, those that ask you to make inferences based on the information presented, and those that require you to choose the correct definitions of specific words.

- Use the following four-step method to work through the reading comprehension questions:

  STEP 1: Skim the questions and underscore key words.

  STEP 2: Skim the passage.

  STEP 3: Read the passage carefully and underscore words that seem important or that you think hold clues to the question's answers.

  STEP 4: Reread the question carefully, then choose the best answer choices based on your underscored passage.

EXERCISE 1: READING COMPREHENSION

20 Questions—37 Minutes

> **Directions:** Each of the passages in this practice exercise are followed by questions about the passage's content. After reading the passage, choose the best answer to each question. Base all answers on what's *stated* or *implied* in the passage.

4

Questions 1–3 are based on the following passage.

Shafts extending into the top story, except those stair shafts in which the stairs do not continue to the roof, shall be carried through and at least 2 feet above the roof. Every shaft extending above the roof, except open shafts and elevator shafts, shall be enclosed at the top with a roof of materials having a fire-resistance rating of one hour and a metal skylight covering at least three quarters of the area of the shaft in the top story. Skylights over stair shafts shall have an area not less than one tenth the area of the shaft in the top story but shall have an area not less than 15 square feet. Any shaft terminating below the top story of a structure and those stair shafts not required to extend through the roof shall have the top enclosed with materials having the same fire-resistance rating as required for the shaft enclosure.

1. Based on the paragraph, elevator shafts that extend into the top story are

   A. not required to have a skylight but are required to extend at least 2 feet above the roof.

   B. neither required to have a skylight nor to extend above the roof.

   C. required to have a skylight covering at least three quarters of the area of the shaft in the top story and to extend at least 2 feet above the roof.

   D. required to have a skylight covering at least three quarters of the area of the shaft in the top story but are not required to extend above the roof.

2. Of the following skylights, the one that meets the requirements of the paragraph measures

   A. 4 feet by 4 feet over a stair shaft that, on the top story, measures 20 feet by 9 feet.

   B. $4\frac{1}{2}$ feet by $3\frac{1}{2}$ feet over a pipe shaft that, on the top story, measures 5 feet by 4 feet.

   C. $2\frac{1}{2}$ feet by $1\frac{1}{2}$ feet over a dumbwaiter shaft that, on the top story, measures $2\frac{1}{2}$ feet by $2\frac{1}{2}$ feet.

   D. 4 feet by 3 feet over a stair shaft that, on the top story, measures 15 feet by 6 feet.

3. Suppose a shaft that does not go to the roof is required to have a three-hour fire-resistance rating. Based on the paragraph, it could be inferred that, for the material enclosing the top of the shaft,

   A. a one-hour fire-resistance rating is required.

   B. a three-hour fire-resistance rating is required.

   C. no fire-resistance rating is required.

   D. the fire-resistance rating cannot be determined.

Questions 4–10 are based on the following passage.

Fire regulations require that every liquefied petroleum gas installation be provided with the means for shutting off the supply to a building in case of an emergency. The installation of a shut-off valve immediately inside a building, which sometimes is done for the convenience of the user, does not comply with this regulation. An outside shut-off valve just outside the building seems to be the logical solution. However, the possibility of tampering illustrates the danger of such an arrangement. A shut-off valve so located might be placed in a locked box. There is no advantage over a valve provided within the locked cabinet containing the cylinder or an enclosure provided over the top of the cylinder. Keys can be carried by firefighters or, in an emergency, the lock can be broken. When no valve is visible, the firefighters should not hesitate to break the lock to the cylinder enclosure. The means for shutting off the gas varies considerably among the numerous types of equipment used. When the cover to the enclosure has been opened, the gas can be shut off as follows:

Close the tank or cylinder valves to which the supply line is connected. Such valves always turn to the right. If the valve is not provided with a handwheel, an adjustable wrench can be used. If conditions are such that shutting off the supply at once is imperative and this can't be accomplished as previously mentioned, the tubing commonly employed as the supply line can be flattened to the extent of closure by a hammer. If the emergency requires the removal of the cylinder, the supply line should be disconnected, and the cylinder moved to a safe location. A tank buried in the ground is safe against fire. When conditions indicate the need to remove a cylinder or tank and this cannot be done due to the severity of exposure, pressures within the container can be kept within control of the safety valve by means of a hose stream sprayed on the surface of the container. The melting of the fuse plug also can be prevented in this way.

4. According to the passage, in an emergency, a firefighter should break the lock of a cylinder enclosure whenever the shut-off valve

   A. fails to operate.

   B. has no handwheel.

   C. has been damaged.

   D. can't be seen.

5. According to the passage, shut-off valves for liquefied petroleum gas installations

   A. always turn to the right.

   B. always turn to the left.

   C. sometimes turn to the right and sometimes to the left.

   D. generally are pulled up.

6. According to the passage, if a cylinder needs to be moved but can't be due to severity of exposure, the pressure can be kept under control by

   A. opening the shut-off valve.

   B. spraying a hose stream on the cylinder.

   C. disconnecting the supply line to the cylinder.

   D. removing the fuse plug.

7. The passage states that the supply line should be disconnected when the

   A. fuse plug melts.

   B. cylinder is moved to another location.

   C. supply line becomes defective.

   D. cylinder is damaged.

8. The passage states that the shut-off valves for liquefied petroleum gas installations are sometimes placed inside buildings

   A. so that firefighters will be able to find the valves more easily.

   B. because it is more convenient for the occupants.

   C. to hide the valves from public view.

   D. because this makes it easier to keep the valves in good working condition.

9. It is suggested in the passage that, during an emergency, the supply line tubing should be flattened to the extent of closure when the

   A. supply line becomes defective.

   B. shut-off valve cannot be opened.

   C. shut-off valve cannot be closed.

   D. supply line is near a fire.

10. According to the passage, fire regulations require that liquefied petroleum gas installations should

   A. be made in safe places.

   B. be tamperproof.

   C. have shut-off valves.

   D. not exceed a certain size.

Questions 11–20 are based on the following passage.

Air-conditioning systems are complex and are made up of several processes. The circulation of air is produced by fans and ducts. The heat is produced by steam, hot water coils, coal, gas, or oil fire furnaces. The cooling is done by ice or mechanical refrigeration. And the cleaning is done by air washers or filters.

Line

5   Air-conditioning systems in large buildings generally should be divided into several parts with wholly separate ducts for each part or floor. The ducts are then extended through fire partitions. As a safeguard, whenever ducts pass through fire partitions, automatic fire dampers should be installed in the ducts. Furthermore, the ducts should be lined on the inside with fire-resistant materials. In addition, a manually operated fan shut-off should be installed at a

10 location that is readily accessible under fire conditions.

    Most air-conditioning systems recirculate a considerable portion of the air. When this is done, an additional safeguard must be taken to have the fan arrange to shut down automatically in case of fire. A thermostatic device in the return air duct will operate the shut-off device whenever the temperature of the air coming to the fan becomes excessive. The air filters frequently

15 are coated with oil to help catch dust. Such oil should be of a type that does not ignite readily. Whenever a flammable or toxic refrigerant is employed for air cooling, coils containing such a refrigerant should not be inserted in any air passage.

11. According to the passage, fan shutoffs in the air-conditioning system should be installed

    A. near the air ducts.

    B. next to fire partitions.

    C. near the fire dampers.

    D. where they can be reached quickly.

12. Based on the passage, whenever a fire breaks out in a building containing an air-conditioning system that recirculates a portion of the air, the

    A. fan will shut down automatically.

    B. air ducts will be opened.

    C. thermostat will cease to operate.

    D. fire partitions will open.

13. The passage states that, on every floor of a large building in which air-conditioning systems are used, there should be a(n)

    A. automatic damper.

    B. thermostatic device.

    C. air filter.

    D. separate duct.

14. The conclusion can be drawn that, in an air-conditioning system, flammable refrigerants

    A. can be used if certain precautions are observed.

    B. should be used sparingly and only in air passages.

    C. should not be used under any circumstances.

    D. might be more effective than other refrigerants.

15. The spreading of dust by means of fans in the air-conditioning system is reduced by

    A. shutting down the fan automatically.

    B. lining the inside of the air duct.

    C. cleaning the circulated air with filters.

    D. coating the air filters with oil.

16. According to the passage, the purpose of a thermostatic device is to

    A. regulate the temperature of the air-conditioning system.

    B. shut off the fan when the temperature of the air rises.

    C. operate the fan when the temperature of the air falls.

    D. assist in the recirculation of the air.

17. Which part of the air-conditioning system passes through a fire partition?

    A. Ducts

    B. Air filters

    C. A thermostatic device

    D. The cooling fan

18. The parts of an air-conditioning system that should be made of fire-resistant materials are the

    A. hot water coils.

    B. automatic fire dampers.

    C. air duct linings.

    D. thermostatic devices.

19. According to the passage, automatic fire dampers should be installed

    A. on oil-fired furnaces.

    B. on every floor of a large building.

    C. in ducts passing through fire partitions.

    D. next to the hot water coils.

20. Based on the passage, the coils containing toxic refrigerants should be

    A. used only when necessary.

    B. lined with fire-resistant materials.

    C. coated with nonflammable oil.

    D. kept out of any air passage.

EXERCISE 2: READING COMPREHENSION

20 Questions—37 Minutes

Directions: Each of the passages in this practice exercise are followed by questions about the passage's content. After reading the passage, choose the best answer to each question. Base all answers on what's *stated* or *implied* in the passage.

4

Questions 1–3 are based on the following passage.

It shall be unlawful to place, use, or maintain in a condition intended, arranged, or designed for use any gas-fired cooking appliance, laundry stove, heating stove, range, water heater, or combination of such appliances in any room or space used for living or sleeping in any new or existing multiple dwelling unless such room or space has a window opening to the outer air or such gas appliance is vented to the outer air. All automatically operated gas appliances shall be equipped with a device that shuts off automatically the gas supply to the main burners when the pilot light in such appliances is extinguished. A gas range or the cooking portion of a gas appliance incorporating a room heater shall not be deemed an automatically operated gas appliance. However, burners in gas ovens and broilers that can be turned on and off or ignited by nonmanual means shall be equipped with a device that shall shut off automatically the gas supply to those burners when the operation of such nonmanual means fails.

1. According to this paragraph, an automatic shut-off device is NOT required on a gas

   A. hot water heater.
   B. laundry dryer.
   C. space heater.
   D. range.

2. According to this paragraph, a gas-fired water heater is permitted

   A. only in kitchens.
   B. only in bathrooms.
   C. only in living rooms.
   D. in any type of room.

3. An automatic shut-off device shuts off

   A. the gas range.
   B. the pilot light.
   C. the gas supply.
   D. all of the above.

Questions 4–6 are based on the following passage.

A utility plan is a floor plan that shows the layout of a heating, electrical, plumbing, or other utility system. Utility plans are used primarily by the persons responsible for the utilities, but they are important to the craftsman as well. Most utility installations require the leaving of openings in walls, floors, and roofs for the admission or installation of utility features. The craftsman pouring a concrete foundation wall, for example, must study the utility plans to determine the number, sizes, and locations of the openings he must leave for piping, electrical lines, and the like.

4. Of the following items of information, the one that is least likely to be provided by a utility plan is the

   A. location of the joists and frame members around stairwells.

   B. location of the hot water supply and return piping.

   C. location of light fixtures.

   D. number of openings in the floor for radiators.

5. According to the paragraph, of the following, the persons who most likely will have the greatest need for the information included in a utility plan of a building are those who

   A. maintain and repair the heating system.

   B. clean the premises.

   C. put out the fires.

   D. advertise the property for sale.

6. According to the paragraph, a repair crew member should find it most helpful to consult a utility plan when information is needed about the

   A. thickness of all doors in the structure.

   B. number of electrical outlets located throughout the structure.

   C. dimensions of each window in the structure.

   D. length of a roof rafter.

Questions 7–9 are based on the following passage.

Most people first encounter grammar in connection with the study of their own language in school. This kind of grammar is called prescriptive grammar because it defines the role of the various parts of speech (such as nouns, verbs, adjectives, and so on). The purpose of prescriptive grammar is to define the norms, or rules, of correct usage. This kind of grammar states how words and sentences are to be put together in a language so the speaker will be perceived as having good grammar skills. When people are said to have good grammar skills, the inference is that they obey the rules of accepted usage associated with the language they speak.

4

7. According to the paragraph, what is the purpose of grammar?

   A. It's not actually that important in our language.

   B. It's the "glue" that holds sentences together.

   C. It indicates how to use language properly.

   D. It obeys the rules of proper language.

8. The author of this paragraph is primarily concerned with

   A. the different parts of speech.

   B. the purpose of prescriptive grammar.

   C. who has good grammar.

   D. the study of grammar in school.

9. According to the paragraph, someone who is considered to use the rules of prescriptive grammar properly

   A. has studied his or her own language in school.

   B. defines the various parts of speech.

   C. did well in language class.

   D. obeys the rules of accepted usage.

Questions 10–13 are based on the following passage.

Information theory deals with the numerical measurement of information, the representation of information (such as data encoding), and the capacity of communication systems to transmit, receive, and process information. We use—and may even be part of—many communication systems in our daily lives. A typical communication system has of several components. First, there must be a source that produces the information or message to be transmitted. One source with which we're all familiar is human speech. Second, a transmitter, such as a telephone and an amplifier or television camera, converts the message into electronic or electromagnetic signals. Third, these signals are transmitted through a channel, or medium, such as a wire or the atmosphere. The channel is the component of the system most susceptible to interference. Distortion and degradation of the signal can originate from many sources. (Some examples of interference, known as "noise," include the static in radio and telephone reception, the fading of a cellular phone signal, and the "snow" experienced in poor TV reception.) The fourth component of a communication system is the receiver, such as a television or radio. A TV or radio can act as a receiver by reconstructing the signal into the original message. The final component is the destination, such as a person watching or listening to the message that the television or radio receives.

10. Which of the following is the best title for this passage?
    A. "The Basics of Information Theory"
    B. "Humans and Data Transmission"
    C. "Communication System Components"
    D. "Transmission and Signal Interference"

11. According to the passage, the signal is converted by the
    A. source.
    B. transmitter.
    C. receiver.
    D. channel.

12. According to the passage, a human being can act as a
    A. source only.
    B. transmitter and a receiver.
    C. source and a destination.
    D. destination only.

13. According to the passage, what is likely to happen to a telephone signal transmitted through a faulty wire?
    A. It will result in static.
    B. It will sound the same.
    C. It will be amplified.
    D. It will result in "snow."

4

Questions 14–17 are based on the following passage.

PREPARING FOODS FOR STORAGE: MEAT, POULTRY, AND FISH

Always keep your refrigerator at about 40°F and your freezer at 0°F or colder. You should check the temperature periodically with an appliance thermometer. Temperature is very important because if you don't store these items properly, your customers could become ill from contaminated food. Refrigerate meat and poultry in the original packaging. For long-term freezer storage, it's best to remove the original packaging and wrap these items tightly in moisture- and vapor-proof material. You can use heavy foil, freezer bags, freezer plastic wrap, or freezer containers. Tightly wrap fresh fish in moisture- and vapor-proof material before refrigerating or freezing.

14. Assume that you, as the head chef of a major restaurant chain, are responsible for the proper storage of large amounts of meat, poultry, and fish. One of your duties as head chef is to teach your cooks how to store these items. Today, one of your cooks asks you what she should do with a new shipment of fresh fish. You should tell her to

    A. refrigerate the fish in its original packaging.

    B. store it in the freezer at about 40°F.

    C. freeze the fish in its original packaging.

    D. wrap it in heavy foil and put it in the freezer.

15. When the storage instructions refer to using vapor-proof and moisture-proof materials, they mean using materials that

    A. do NOT allow liquids or odors to leak out.

    B. allow liquids but NOT odors to leak out.

    C. allow odors but NOT liquids to leak out.

    D. allow odors and liquids to leak out.

16. According to the instructions for long-term storage, removing meat or poultry from the original package and wrapping it tightly in freezer plastic wrap is

    A. inadvisable because you should freeze meat or poultry in the original packaging.

    B. advisable because freezer plastic wrap is moisture- and vapor-proof.

    C. inadvisable because you should not store meat or poultry in the freezer.

    D. advisable because you should not refrigerate meat or poultry in the original packaging.

17. According to the storage instructions, the action that would NOT be practicing proper food storage is

    A. storing food in a freezer with a temperature below 0°F.

    B. wrapping meat or poultry in heavy foil before freezing.

    C. removing fish from its packaging and storing it in a freezer container.

    D. freezing meat or poultry in the original packaging.

Questions 18–20 are based on the following passage.

Citizens interested in filing a property damage claim totaling less than $5,000 are required to fill out Minor Claim Form LG-203 in duplicate and return it to the Secretary of Minor Claims in the District Court Building. If the citizen seeks compensation for emotional damage in ad-
Line
5   dition to the property damage, he or she also is required to fill out Intermediate Claim Form K-46. This form is to be filled out in duplicate and sent to the Secretary of Minor Claims. Minor Claim Form LG-203 will then be compared to Intermediate Claim Form K-46. The Secretary of Minor Claims will then forward both copies of Form K-46 to the Division Office, which will send one copy to the State Office of Minor Claims. When the information on Form LG-203 indicates that the claim is of a minor nature, the case is thoroughly reviewed by the Secretary of Minor
10 Claims. If this review indicates that the complaining party is entitled to an emotional-damage hearing, Witness Form R-11 must be completed by a witness to the incident. Once this form is returned to the Secretary of Minor Claims, the defending party is sent a copy of the Summons Form S-4 and asked to return it to the State Office of Minor Claims. When the State Office of Minor Claims receives the Summons Form, an office representative will compare it to Form
15 K-46 and decide whether the case may be heard in District Court.

18. According to the paragraph, for the State Office of Minor Claims to decide whether a case may be heard in the District Court, it must have received which documents?

   A. Form K-46

   B. Forms K-46 and LG-203

   C. Forms K-46 and S-4

   D. Forms K-46, LG-203, R-11, and S-4

19. Of the forms mentioned in the paragraph, the defending party is responsible for preparing the

   A. Intermediate Claim Form.

   B. Summons Form.

   C. Witness Form.

   D. Minor Claim Form.

20. According to the paragraph, the Division Office

   A. keeps one copy of Form LG-203.

   B. sends out both copies of Form K-46.

   C. keeps one copy of Form K-46.

   D. sends out both copies of Form LG-203.

ANSWER KEYS AND EXPLANATIONS

Exercise 1

1. A	**5.** A	**9.** C	**13.** D	**17.** A
2. B	**6.** B	**10.** C	**14.** A	**18.** C
3. B	**7.** B	**11.** D	**15.** D	**19.** C
4. D	**8.** B	**12.** A	**16.** B	**20.** D

4

1. **The correct answer is A.** The answer to part of the question lies in information that is not explicitly stated. The first sentence states that *all shafts except stair shafts* in which the stairs do not continue to the roof must be carried at least 2 feet above the roof. Thus, elevator shafts must extend those 2 feet, which eliminates choices B and D. The second sentence makes the exception that elevator shafts need not have a skylight, which eliminates choice C.

2. **The correct answer is B.** First, calculate the area of the skylights given in the answer choices. (Remember that area is the length multiplied by the width.) Since the passage says that a skylight must be at least 15 square feet, choices A and B meet this requirement at 16 sq. ft. and 15.75 sq. ft., respectively.

   The next step is to see if the skylight has an area not less than one tenth the area of the shaft in the top story. This is calculated by finding the area of the shaft and dividing this number by the area of the skylight. The skylight in choice A measures 16 sq. ft. and the shaft measures 180 sq. ft. , or $\frac{16}{180} = 0.088$, which is less than the one-tenth requirement. This means that only the skylight in choice B meets the requirements listed in the passage: the 15.75 sq. ft. skylight over the 20 sq. ft. pipe shaft covers more than three quarters of the area (0.7875) of the shaft.

3. **The correct answer is B.** According to the last sentence in the paragraph, a shaft terminating below the top story of a structure must have a top with the same fire-resistance

   rating as that required for the shaft enclosure (in this case, three hours).

4. **The correct answer is D.** Sentence 8 of paragraph 1 (lines 9–10) states that, where no valve is visible, the firefighters should break the lock to the cylinder enclosure.

5. **The correct answer is A.** Sentence 2 (lines 13–14) of paragraph 2 states that these tank valves always turn to the right.

6. **The correct answer is B.** Sentence 7 of paragraph 2 (lines 20–22) states that "pressures within the container can be kept within control of the safety valve by means of a hose stream sprayed on the surface of the container."

7. **The correct answer is B.** Sentence 5 of paragraph 2 (lines 17–18) says: "*If the emergency requires the removal of the cylinder*, the supply line should be disconnected, and the cylinder moved to a safe location."

8. **The correct answer is B.** Sentence 2 of paragraph 1 (lines 2–4) states that the shut-off valve placed inside a building for the convenience of the user does not satisfy the emergency shut-off requirements.

9. **The correct answer is C.** If the shut-off valve cannot be closed, the supply of gas can be shut off by flattening the supply line tubing.

10. **The correct answer is C.** The answer is given in the passage's opening sentence: "Fire regulations require that every liquefied petroleum gas installation be provided *with the means for shutting off the supply to a building in case of an emergency.*"

11. **The correct answer is D.** The last sentence of paragraph 2 (lines 9–10) states that manual

fan shut-offs should be installed where they are readily accessible.

12. **The correct answer is A.** Sentence 3 of paragraph 3 (lines 13–14) describes a thermostatic device that automatically shuts off recirculation of air in case of fire.

13. **The correct answer is D.** Sentence 1 of paragraph 2 (lines 5–6) provides the answer: "Air-conditioning systems in large buildings generally *should be divided into several parts with wholly separate ducts for each part or floor.*"

14. **The correct answer is A.** The last sentence of the passage (lines 16–17) states that, when flammable refrigerants are used, the coils containing the refrigerant should not be inserted in the air passages. This practice constitutes a precaution that makes the use of flammable refrigerants acceptable.

15. **The correct answer is D.** Sentence 4 of paragraph 3 (lines 14–15) tells us that "air filters frequently are coated with oil to help catch dust."

16. **The correct answer is B.** The answer is in sentence 3 of paragraph 3 (lines 13–14): "A

thermostatic device in the return air duct *will operate the shut-off device whenever the temperature of the air coming to the fan becomes excessive.*"

17. **The correct answer is A.** The passage clearly states that the "ducts are … extended through fire partitions" (lines 6–7).

18. **The correct answer is C.** The passage clearly states that "the ducts should be lined on the inside with fire-resistant materials" (lines 8–9). There may be other fire-resistant materials involved, but the passage mentions only one fire-resistant *lining.*

19. **The correct answer is C.** Sentence 3 in paragraph 2 (lines 7–8) tells us that "automatic fire dampers should be installed in the ducts."

20. **The correct answer is D.** While other options seem plausible, the last sentence of the passage (lines 16–17) tells us that when "a flammable or toxic refrigerant is employed for air cooling, coils containing *such a refrigerant should not be inserted in any air passage.*"

Exercise 2

1. D	5. A	9. D	13. A	17. D
2. D	6. B	10. C	14. D	18. C
3. C	7. C	11. B	15. A	19. B
4. A	8. B	12. C	16. B	20. C

1. **The correct answer is D.** An automatic shut-off device is required on all automatically operated gas appliances; however, a gas range is not considered to be an automatically operated gas appliance.

2. **The correct answer is D.** A gas-fired water heater is permitted anywhere, provided that the space has a window opening to the outer air or the appliance is vented to the outer air.

3. **The correct answer is C.** The automatic shut-off device shuts off the gas supply to the burners when the pilot light goes out. This prevents the room from filling with gas.

4. **The correct answer is A.** The utility plan shows the layout of a utility system, not the structure of the building itself.

5. **The correct answer is A.** The heating system is one of the utility systems, so the people concerned with its maintenance and repair would find it most useful.

6. **The correct answer is B.** Again, consider the definition of a utility. The electrical system is a utility system. Structural information appears on a utility plan only where it is incidental to the layout of utilities.

7. **The correct answer is C.** The paragraph states that the purpose of prescriptive grammar is to define the rules of correct usage, which is another way of saying that grammar indicates how to use language correctly.

8. **The correct answer is B.** The purpose of this passage should be clear as you read the paragraph. If you were unsure, try working backward by eliminating the wrong answers first. (Hint: "The purpose of prescriptive grammar …" begins one of the sentences in the text.)

9. **The correct answer is D.** The answer to this question is in the last sentence. While the wording differs slightly, the meaning is the same.

10. **The correct answer is C.** Although this passage starts with a comment about information theory (choice A), that's not the primary focus here. The relationship between humans and information technology (choice B) is not the focus either. While topics of transmission and interference (choice D) are discussed, they too are not the focus of the passage. This leaves "Communication System Components" as the best title for this passage.

11. **The correct answer is B.** Sentence 5 (lines 6–8) clearly states that the second component of a communication system, the transmitter, converts the message into a signal.

12. **The correct answer is C.** Human beings are mentioned in the last sentence of the passage as possible sources and destinations in communication systems.

13. **The correct answer is A.** This question requires you to go beyond the available information and guess which answer is most likely to be true given the information provided. A damaged wire is likely to have some negative effects, so choices B and C can be eliminated. The experience of "snow" is specifically described interfering with TV reception, so choice D can be eliminated as

well. It is reasonable to infer then, that a telephone signal transmitted through a faulty wire will result in static.

14. **The correct answer is D.** The last sentence of the passage says to wrap fresh fish in moisture- and vapor-proof material. The previous sentence mentions that heavy foil is a vapor-proof material.

15. **The correct answer is A.** This question is about vocabulary. Storage materials that do NOT allow odors to leak out are called vapor-proof. Storage materials that do NOT allow liquids to leak out are called moisture-proof.

16. **The correct answer is B.** The instructions clearly state that meat and poultry should be removed from their original packaging and wrapped in moisture- and vapor-proof material before *long-term* storage. Freezer plastic wrap is moisture-and vapor-proof and therefore suitable for long-term storage.

17. **The correct answer is D.** The instructions clearly state that meat and poultry should be removed from their original packaging and wrapped in moisture- and vapor-proof material before freezing. Freezing meat or poultry in the original packaging—as opposed to refrigeration—is not proper food storage.

18. **The correct answer is C.** The last sentence of the paragraph confirms that the State Office of Minor Claims must receive Form K-46 from the Division Office and Form S-4 from the defending party before deciding if the case can be heard in court.

19. **The correct answer is B.** Lines 11–13 indicate that the defending party is responsible only for the Summons Form.

20. **The correct answer is C.** According to sentence 5 (lines 6–8), the Division Office receives both copies of Form K-46 and sends one to the State Office of Minor Claims. This procedure implies that the Division Office keeps a copy of Form K-46.

Chapter 5

Reasoning and Judgment

OVERVIEW

- What Are Reasoning and Judgment Questions?
- Reasoning and Judgment Strategies
- Guided Practice: Reasoning and Judgment
- Summing It Up
- Exercise: Reasoning and Judgment
- Answer Key and Explanations

WHAT ARE REASONING AND JUDGMENT QUESTIONS?

While a firefighter's life is filled with routine and repetition, the nature of firefighting means that any call can turn to chaos. And firefighters need to be flexible to be able to transform disarray into order. That often means processing large amounts of information to arrive at strong conclusions. On the firefighter's test, Reasoning and Judgment questions assess your ability to come to reasonable conclusions using available data, given rules, firefighting situations, procedures, and the priorities of every fire department: preserve life and property, and do so efficiently.

There are five types of questions that fall under the category of Reasoning and Judgment: information ordering, deductive reasoning, inductive reasoning, problem sensitivity, and situational judgement. Each of those question types has specific qualities and objectives that you'll explore in the guided practice that follows.

Fire Department Priorities: The Foundation for Reasoning and Judgment Questions

Perhaps the most important foundation for answering reasoning and judgment questions successfully is to know fire department priorities. These priorities are straightforward—a fire department is expected to protect life and property and to run efficiently. Being efficient is important in any work, but it is less important than protecting life and property. Hence, the goals of a fire department in order of importance are as follows:

1. **Protecting life.** If a life is at risk in the question scenario, then protecting that life is the best reason to justify any practice.

2. **Protecting property.** If the protection of life is not an issue, the second-best reason for any practice is to protect property, including fire department property. Property can be sacrificed when someone's life is at stake, but if there is no real threat to anyone's life, property should be protected.

3. **Being as efficient as possible.** If there is no real question of life or death and no real threat to property, then the best reason for taking an action is that it is efficient. If you encounter several answer choices based on efficiency, you must judge which answer choice is most suitable.

Remember that reasons must be realistic. To justify a practice for protecting life, there must be something in the question scenario to support the idea that someone's life is at stake. Similarly, a proposed answer based on efficiency must have the appearance of being possible and efficient.

REASONING AND JUDGMENT STRATEGIES

Before seeing the reasoning and judgment questions, let's look at some key strategies for ensuring that you work through these questions in a step-by-step, well-reasoned manner. Almost everything you need to answer a reasoning and judgment question is present in the question itself, so you're responsible for gathering that information and then processing it in order to adequately address the goal of the question. Along the way, you can take several actions that will allow you to eliminate answer choices to efficiently answer the question.

1. **Pinpoint Your Goal.** While this is generally true for any question, a reasoning and judgment question's goal will directly determine which information you decide to use and what you ignore. When you see that your goal is to come to a logical conclusion independent of mathematic computation or verbal and written expression, it's likely that you're in the realm of reasoning and judgment and you can employ the other strategies that follow. Consider underlining the goal of the question for easy reference.

2. **Gather What You Know.** Regardless of the kind of reasoning and judgment question you're answering, the question or an associated passage will provide you with the details you need to answer correctly. Whether those details are instructions for a procedure, common firefighting practice, a data set, witness accounts, or a common firefighting situation, you need to identify them so that you have all the information you need to answer accurately. The stated goal of the question will direct you to what details are pertinent. At the same time, you can make use of previous knowledge to make simple inferences based on what you know of basic firefighting technology and a firefighter's priorities.

3. **Look for Relationships.** The most challenging step in answering reasoning and judgment questions is processing all the details that have been provided in order to arrive at a conclusion. Often, this process focuses on comparing different pieces of information to determine what's missing, what should come next, or what describes what you're seeing in the situation. In addition, you may need to combine different details, which will then need to be compared to available answer options.

4. **Track Information.** You're going to be juggling a lot of details while working through reasoning and judgment questions, so by taking any opportunity you have to summarize a witness' testimony or mark what steps have already been completed in a procedure, you're saving your working memory a lot of trouble and limiting the number of times you need to look back and reread any passages.

5. **Predict the Answer.** Before you look at answer choices, take the time to gather and process details from the question. Given the exam's time limit, you won't have a lot of time to do this, but enough for you to pause before looking and make a prediction based on what you've already seen. That small step can help you avoid distractions in the answers.

6 **Eliminate Answers.** As is the case for most question types, you'll have a great reason to eliminate each wrong answer. You can eliminate any answer choice that contradicts information presented by the passage and the goal of the question. If possible, physically cross off weak answer choices.

You'll see all these strategies put into practice in the guided practice that follows. You'll also get to practice them yourself in the practice questions later in this chapter.

GUIDED PRACTICE: REASONING AND JUDGMENT

The following guided practice uses the reasoning and judgment questions seen in Chapter 3: Diagnostic Test. Regardless of whether you answered them correctly, work through the questions using the previously introduced strategies and read the answer guides to see exactly how an expert completes the questions efficiently and effectively.

Example 1: Information Ordering (Question 23, Diagnostic Test)

Put the following instructions for using a fire extinguisher in the proper order:

1. Squeeze the extinguisher trigger.

2. Slowly back away from the fire.

3. Sweep the fire extinguisher from side to side; keep doing so until the fire is completely out.

4. Aim the nozzle low at the base of the fire while keeping the extinguisher in an upright position.

5. Remove the pin from the handle.

A. 5–3–4–2–1

B. 4–3–1–5–2

C. 5–4–1–3–2

D. 4–3–2–1–5

> **TIP**
> **Information Ordering** questions ask you to put information in the best or most appropriate sequence.

With this information ordering question, you must select the logical sequence of steps for a series of actions. To begin, identify the goal of the situation from the question, here: the operation of a fire extinguisher. Thereafter, consider the purpose of such an action. In this case, you would use a fire extinguisher to put out a fire. With that knowledge in mind, read through and process the steps, and you may be able to quickly identify the logical first and/or last step in the sequence.

For this situation, it's likely that one of the last steps of using a fire extinguisher would be to extinguish the fire. With that prediction, that means that Step 3 should come toward the end of the sequence. When you evaluate the answer options, no choice places Step 3 last; however, three of the four choices (A, B, and D) place extinguishing the fire as the second step, which would precede enabling use of the fire extinguisher or aiming at the fire. When you read through the steps in the order suggested by choice C, you see a clear path from enabling the extinguisher to function and operating the extinguisher efficiently to practicing good fire safety. **The correct answer is C.**

Example 2: Deductive Reasoning (Question 24, Diagnostic Test)

Smoke detectors should be on every level of a house. Detectors need to be located both inside bedrooms and outside the sleeping areas. To prevent false alarms, do not position smoke alarms within 10 feet (3 meters) of a cooking appliance or where drafts might interfere with their operation.

Based on the information given, where in the home would you want to avoid having a smoke detector?

A. Inside living rooms and near basement closets

B. Inside the kitchen and next to air conditioning/heating ducts

C. Inside bedrooms and near hallways

D. Inside basement rooms and near a home office

> **TIP**
>
> **Deductive Reasoning** questions ask you to apply general rules to specific situations or to draw logical conclusions from stated principles or regulations.

With deductive reasoning questions, you will be provided common premises or rules for handling certain tasks, procedures, tools, and other firefighting related topics. Using those established rules, you must come to a specific conclusion for a given situation. Just like with other reasoning and judgment questions, you must understand the goal of the question, gather information from the question or accompanying passage, and make a reasonable judgment. For this question, you are asked to determine where smoke detectors should *not* be placed within a home. The question has provided multiple pieces of information related to where smoke detectors should and should not be placed. The question itself has provided everything you need in order to answer accurately. For your goal, which piece of information bears the strongest relationship? You're told to "not position smoke alarms within 10 feet (3 meters) of a cooking appliance or where drafts might interfere with their operation." You can predict that the correct answer is related to kitchens or even windows and ducts.

Upon examining the answers, you see that choice B aligns with your prediction. However, you still need to evaluate all answer choices. In doing so, you know that you can eliminate choice C, as "detectors need to be located" inside bedrooms. And while the question provided little information related to basement rooms, such locations are not part of a kitchen nor necessarily affected by drafts. Eliminating such answers requires some inference on your part, but notice that our predicted choice is still valid. **The correct answer is B.**

Example 3: Inductive Reasoning (Question 21, Diagnostic Test)

The town of Azureville uses a color-coding system for its fire hydrants, as seen in the table below.

Fire Hydrant Color	Hoseline Diameter	Hydrant Flow Capacity
Light Blue	2.5 inches	Less than 500 gallons
Medium Blue	3 inches	Between 500 and 1,000 gallons
Dark Blue	5 inches	Greater than 1,000 gallons

According to the information presented, which of the following statements most accurately describes the relationship between the colors of the hydrants, their hoseline diameters, and their water-flowing capacity?

A. As the color of the hydrants gets lighter, the hoseline diameter increases, and the flowing capacity doubles.

B. As the color of the hydrants gets lighter, the hoseline diameter decreases, and the flowing capacity increases.

C. As the color of the hydrants gets darker, the hoseline diameter decreases, and the flowing capacity decreases.

D. As the color of the hydrants gets darker, the hoseline diameter increases, and the flowing capacity increases.

TIP
Inductive Reasoning questions ask you to use the specific details of a given situation to arrive at a general conclusion.

5

Inductive reasoning questions provide details about a specific situation and ask you to come to a general conclusion based on the given data. Inductive reasoning is nearly the opposite of deductive reasoning (general to specific), but your approach to the questions will be similar. As always, identify the goal of the question: finding the relationship between the color of hydrants, hoseline diameters, and water-flowing capacity. The table provides specific information for each component of the question. It's important to examine each piece of information in the table and then consider the relationships present. You can ask, "What happens as the color changes?" To answer that, compare the data for each color. As the color shifts from light blue to medium blue, the hoseline increases, as does the hydrant flow capacity. When comparing medium blue to dark blue, the same relationship is clear. There appears to be a direct relationship between how dark the hydrant is and how big a hoseline diameter it supports, as well as the hydrant flow capacity. You should expect to see those relationships reflected in the correct answer.

As always, you can eliminate answers that contradict the information in the table. Choice A reverses the relationship between color and hoseline diameter while also mischaracterizing the relationship with flowing capacity. Choice B properly indicates the relationship between color and hoseline diameter (if darker equals an increase, then lighter equals a decrease) but inverts the rule for flowing capacity. Choice C reverses the relationship between hydrant color and both hoseline diameter and flowing capacity. That leaves only one possible answer. **The correct answer is D.**

Example 4: Problem Sensitivity (Question 28, Diagnostic Test)

Station 12 responds to a fire at a four-story commercial building. Witnesses reported an explosion, but it's unclear with the state of the fire where the blast originated. Firefighter Maloney begins taking eyewitness accounts to better assess the situation. Each witness describes the event as follows:

Witness 1: "I was walking by and heard a huge blast. I turned and saw flames shooting from the fifth floor on the northeast side."

Witness 2: "I looked out my window and saw glass shatter and a fireball on the northwest side of the top floor."

Witness 3: "The fourth floor lit up on the northeast side. All the glass crashing to the street sounded like small bells."

Witness 4: "There was this big flash of light on the first floor. Just look at the glass all over the sidewalk on the northeast side."

Considering the eyewitness accounts, Firefighter Maloney recognizes that she should relay information to other responders based on the descriptions of which witnesses?

A. 1, 2, 3

B. 1, 2, 4

C. 1, 3, 4

D. 2, 3, 4

With problem sensitivity questions, your goal is to determine the nature of the problem as presented by the situation, often resulting from mismatched or inconsistent information when comparing multiple accounts. Of course, your method of processing the information will be largely consistent with other reasoning and judgment questions. Read through the question and any additional information, establish your goal—determine which witnesses are reliable—and start to gather information. From the question, you know there was an explosion at a four-story building. You have four eyewitness accounts. You'll want to summarize each story. Witness 1 says there was a blast on the fifth floor on the northeast side. Witness 2 says a fireball could be seen on the top floor on the northwest side. Witness 3 says there was a flash of light on the fourth floor on the northeast side. And witness 4 says there was a flash of light on the first floor on the northeast side. After you've adequately gathered information, you have to build some relationships or process what's been given.

In this situation, that means comparing each account. Through comparison, you see the accounts differ as to on what floor and on which side of the building the explosion occurred. Then consider which similarities and differences are most significant. While witnesses 2 and 3 disagree on what side of the building the explosion was on, they agree that it was on the top or fourth floor, as you learned from the question that the building has four floors. Witness 1 states the explosion was on the northeast side, agreeing with witnesses 3 and 4, but says that the explosion was on the fifth floor. You know that cannot be the case, as the building has only four floors, but it's entirely possible he or she was mistaken. You can hold on to witness 1 until you examine the account of witness 4. Witness 4 aligns with 1 and 3 for the side of the building but provides the greatest contradiction to the other three witnesses: that the explosion was on the first floor. All other witnesses agree that the explosion was toward the top of the building. As such, any answer that includes witness 4 is likely incorrect. **The correct answer is A.**

Example 5: Situational Judgment (Question 29, Diagnostic Test)

An emergency situation earlier in the day disrupted standard daily activities at the firehouse. Your supervisor has provided a set of instructions for multiple tasks to complete. Your shift ends soon, and you're not sure you'll have time to complete everything before needing to depart. You've communicated this, and your supervisor would like you to prioritize certain tasks before departing. In order to make the best use of your time and attend to mission critical duties, you

A. complete one hour of physical fitness.

B. clean the living facilities.

C. inspect personal protective equipment for damage.

D. wash the fire engine and clean equipment.

TIP

Problem Sensitivity questions ask you to recognize or identify a problem (e.g., procedural, witness/victim inconsistencies) in a given scenario.

A situational judgment question asks you to apply what you know of a firefighter's priorities and come to a reasonable decision about what action is important to take in a given situation. The question itself will provide enough detail to describe the situation, but you need to recall that a firefighter prioritizes life above property, then efficiency. In this situation, you know that you have time to complete only a few tasks. Your job is to select the task that will provide the greatest benefit to a firefighter's mission and as such, the firefighter's team members or those impacted by an emergency. Since the situation referenced relates basic firehouse duties, choices made here will have a direct impact on a fire department's ability to render services to a community, fight fires, and guarantee the upkeep of equipment that protects firefighters in the line of duty. Because no options are provided by the question itself, you'll be unable to directly predict the correct answer for the situation, but you will be able to establish that any action that relates to the ability to save lives in the community or protect your fellow firefighters will take precedence. Then, you can evaluate the answers in relation to other firefighting priorities.

Physical fitness (choice A) is important for firefighters and the physical nature of their jobs; your physical fitness can have a direct impact on your ability to save lives and prevent dangerous situations for your team members. The cleanliness of living facilities (choice B) directly impacts your team and proper functioning of the firehouse, impacting efficiency and team morale. Personal protective equipment (choice C) can be the difference between life and death in emergency situations and must be checked for damage daily. The fire engine is a critical tool for transporting and supporting firefighters on calls, and over time, inattentiveness and lack of care can lead to damage and malfunction; as such, it is cleaned daily (choice D).

Of those options, which choice provides the greatest impact on the safety of firefighters and those they serve? As PPE directly impacts the safety of your team members and their ability to serve life and property when responding to calls, it takes precedence over other duties. Should a call come in before another team member is able to check PPE, firefighters would be at risk of injury or death should damage be present. Neglecting an hour of physical fitness is unlikely to impact you in a way that would run counter to a firefighter's mission, unless it is a regular occurrence. However, it is also a task that can be accomplished while off-duty. Regular maintenance and cleaning of fire department facilities is standard daily practice. But in the event of an emergency, it is unlikely to impact the ability of firefighters to serve their community. Daily maintenance of the fire engine is a mission critical task for firefighters, and firefighters should always present themselves and their equipment in the best condition possible. However, in relation to the inspection of PPE, this task would be secondary. **The correct answer is C.**

Reasoning and judgement questions can be one of the most challenging aspects of the firefighter exam, but if you remember to systematically apply the strategies presented in this chapter, you can successfully work your way through them. For more practice with these question types, work through the practice exercise following the chapter summary.

5

TIP
Situational Judgment questions ask you to determine the most suitable response to a given scenario.

Summing It Up

- Reasoning and judgment questions include information ordering, deductive reasoning, inductive reasoning, problem sensitivity, and situational judgment situations. The questions will provide steps, rules, details describing a specific situation, and other information to assess your ability to come to reasonable conclusions and express understanding of firefighting priorities.

- As a foundation to answering reasoning and judgment questions, remember the three priorities of every fire department:

    1. Protect life.

    2. Protect property.

    3. Be as efficient as possible.

- Reasoning and Judgment questions can be answered accurately using variations on the following steps:

    - **Pinpoint your goal** so that you know what information can be ignored and prioritized.

    - **Gather what you know** as stated by the questions or passages.

    - **Look for relationships** by comparing information in the question or passage.

    - **Track information**, marking important details or writing down your thinking.

    - **Predict the answer** based on what you have gathered and processed.

    - **Eliminate answers** that contradict information from the passage and/or firefighting priorities.

EXERCISE: REASONING AND JUDGMENT

20 Questions—30 minutes

Directions: The following questions are based on scenarios designed to test your reasoning and judgment skills. Read each scenario and choose the best answer to the question or questions that refer to it.

1. High rise fires create complex situations for firefighters, often involving multiple companies, and thus interconnected stages of operation. The first company on scene often begins the fire attack. Place the following steps in the most logical order:

   Step 1. Travel to the floor in question.

   Step 2. Transport equipment such as hose packs, adaptors, and SCBA to the building.

   Step 3. Investigate the alarm panel and confer with building personnel.

   Step 4. Enter the building.

   Step 5. Communicate conditions to command.

   Step 6. Commence fire attack.

   A. 2–3–5–1–4–6

   B. 2–4–3–5–1–6

   C. 4–3–2–1–6–5

   D. 5–3–4–1–6–2

Questions 2–4 are based on the following information.

Fires can be classified into different types, based on the kind of material that has combusted. Different materials require different types of extinguishers to safely combat the fire without creating greater risk for responders. The following table outlines different classes of fires, their materials, and appropriate extinguisher types.

Fire Type	Materials	Suggested Types of Extinguisher
Class A	Solid combustible materials (wood, paper, cloth, plastic, etc.)	Water, foam
Class B	Ignitable liquids and gases (gasoline, petroleum, alcohol, paint, etc.)	Foam, powder, carbon dioxide
Class C	Energized electrical equipment (wiring, electronics, appliances, etc.)	Carbon dioxide, dry powder
Class D	Alkali metals (potassium, magnesium, aluminum, sodium, etc.)	Dry powder
Class K	Cooking oils and animal fats	Wet chemical

2. You find a fire extinguisher labeled with an A. Which of the following materials would the extinguisher be suitable to be used on should the material combust?

   A. An active fuse box at an apartment building

   B. A grease fire in a restaurant kitchen

   C. A barrel of powdered aluminum at an industrial site

   D. A small fire in the storage area of a clothing store

3. You've arrived at the scene of a fire at a fuel depot at which fires have occurred in the past due to faulty wiring and fuel spills. The immediate cause is unclear. To prepare for the likely causes of the fire, which type of extinguisher would be most appropriate?

   A. Carbon dioxide

   B. Water

   C. Foam

   D. Wet chemical

4. Firefighter Hernandez and his company have responded to a fire alarm in the server room of a telecommunications company. Before firefighters arrived on site and turned off the power, an employee attempted to use an on-site wet chemical extinguisher to put out the fire. Following its use, the flames spread, destroying many of the servers. After the situation was brought under control, Hernandez explained that

   A. wet chemical extinguishers are appropriate for all kinds of fires.

   B. liquid extinguishers conduct electricity and risk greater harm when used on energized electronics.

   C. there are multiple kinds of dry powder extinguishers that are applicable for most classes of fires.

   D. fire blankets and appropriate extinguishers should be present to combat Class K fires.

5. A ladder company arrives on scene at a fire in a residential dwelling. With no hoselines available and a victim trapped inside, the company is going to use a tactic for extracting victims in just such a scenario. Place the following steps in the most logical order:

   Step 1. Enter the structure.

   Step 2. Create a vent at a predetermined point of entry.

   Step 3. Evaluate the structure from the exterior.

   Step 4. Search the room and extract the victim.

   Step 5. Identify and control the interior door.

   A. 2–3–1–5–4

   B. 3–1–4–2–5

   C. 3–2–1–5–4

   D. 1–3–2–4–5

6. As a bystander at a fire at a multi-story apartment building, you see several firefighters enter the building. Another company on the fireground begins placing ladders at various windows on different floors, including a ladder to the roof with several rungs visible above the lip of the building. No firefighters travel up these ladders. The most likely reason for placing such ladders in situations like this is to

   A. prepare for firefighters to use hoselines on the ground should the fire spread.

   B. create new potential exits for firefighters should the original point of entry become impassable.

   C. give victims of the fire an opportunity to quickly reenter the building once the fire is extinguished.

   D. prepare for the inevitable extinguishing of the fire and the inspection of the structure for stability and initial cause.

7. Firefighters Stanley and Takata arrive on scene at a small fire on the lot of a residential structure. The fire has set alight a gazebo, a shed, and fence line during a backyard barbecue but seems unlikely to spread to nearby houses because of the distance between homes. Guests take video of the firefighters as Stanley and Takata move their gear through the crowd, evaluate the safety of individuals and structures, determine the sources of fuel, and begin to extinguish the fire. During their actions, the firefighters should have but neglected to

   A. alert residents of the neighborhood to evacuate their homes.

   B. call for additional support when they saw the scale of the fire.

   C. ask not to be filmed while completing their work.

   D. clear bystanders from the fireground.

8. A firefighter is on his way home from duty late on a Sunday night. As he rounds a bend in the road, he sees a man on the sidewalk frantically waving his arms, shouting, and pointing toward the ground floor of a nearby apartment complex. There appears to be smoke billowing from multiple windows. The firefighter stops his vehicle and exits. In this situation, the firefighter should

   A. run to the apartment complex, pull a fire alarm, and direct tenants to safety away from the structures.

   B. call the fire department directly and run to the apartment complex to arouse tenants and start an evacuation.

   C. call 911 and wait for the fire department to arrive before contributing to the fire attack and evacuation.

   D. direct the pedestrian to call 911 and await arrival of the fire crews while the firefighter alerts residents.

9. The first firefighting unit to arrive at the scene of an incident assumes command until it requires transfer or termination. The first unit will take the following steps (steps are not presented in order):

Step 1. Create a plan and assign units.

Step 2. Provide continuing command.

Step 3. Assume command.

Step 4. Evaluate the incident and conditions.

Step 5. Return units to service and terminate command.

Step 6. Request additional units as needed.

What is the most logical sequence of steps for commanding?

A. 3–4–1–2–6–5

B. 4–6–3–1–2–5

C. 3–1–6–2–5–4

D. 1–3–4–6–2–5

10. The table below indicates the amount of water, measured in gallons per minute, produced by hoses of different diameters and tip sizes.

Hose Number	Hose Diameter	Nozzle Pressure	Nozzle Size	Gallons Per Minute (GPM)
1	1.75 in.	50	0.875 in.	161
2	1.75 in.	50	0.9375 in.	185
3	2.5 in.	50	1 in.	210
4	2.5 in.	50	1.125 in.	266
5	2.5 in.	50	1.25 in.	328

Which factor can be said to have the most significant impact on the amount of water produced per minute, based on the data available?

A. Hose diameter, which dramatically increases the GPM as the diameter increases

B. Nozzle size, which dramatically decreases the GPM as the size increases

C. Hose diameter, which decreases the GPM as the diameter decreases

D. Nozzle size, which increases the GPM as the size increases

11. The combination of a fuel source, oxygen, and heat is known as the fire triangle. All three elements are necessary for standard ignition and combustion to occur.

While attacking a wildfire in a state park, firefighters decided to dig a long trench between the fire and a large meadow of long grasses untouched by the flames. The most logical reason for doing so in the given situation is

A. firefighters want to separate the fire from further sources of fuel and begin containment.

B. the trench will redirect the flow of oxygen toward the fire to strengthen it.

C. cool air will be drawn into the trench, thus lowering the temperature of the fire.

D. firefighters can take cover within the trench should the blaze become uncontrollable.

12. A multi-car traffic incident has occurred on a local freeway. Multiple companies are on scene to extinguish reported vehicle fires as well as to remove motorists who may be trapped inside their vehicles. The fires are quickly extinguished and Firefighter Fratelli has been tasked with prioritizing extraction and transport of victims to nearby medical facilities. In his assessment of the situation, Fratelli discovers four victims in need of removal from their vehicles and medical care. Victim 1 is an elderly male with lacerations on both arms and potential fractures in his hands. Victim 2 is a middle-aged female with a head injury from her airbag and visible and cognitive symptoms of a mild concussion. Victim 3 is an unconscious female in her early twenties who, firefighters are told by another passenger, is eight months pregnant. Victim 4 is a male child with bruising on his neck and abdomen beneath his seat belt. Firefighter Fratelli should prioritize extraction and transportation of which victim?

   A. 1
   B. 2
   C. 3
   D. 4

13. Your fire company arrives at a fire involving drum containers of hazardous substances. The fire is behaving strangely, and no one on site has information related to the nature of the materials. You remember that not all fires can be treated in the same way. The most reasonable course of action is to

   A. begin active firefighting to extinguish the flames.

   B. move the fuel sources away from the fires.

   C. avoid using water on substances until the material has been identified.

   D. establish a containment process to avoid having water runoff spread hazardous materials.

14. A backdraft is a sudden and rapid expansion of superheated gases within a structure, often resulting in an explosion. Backdrafts result from a sudden influx of oxygen into an oxygen-depleted environment that then accelerates the combustion of heated gasses and unburned particulate matter in the space. The low-oxygen environment inside a space results in the incomplete combustion of material, creating yellow and brown smoke, among other features. Additionally, because of the pressure inside, smoke tends to escape through the cracks around doors and windows in puffs. To prevent backdrafts, firefighters will often try to remove further sources of fuel and limit access to new oxygen sources.

   Firefighters have responded to a fire at an unoccupied mobile home. In assessing the situation, firefighters can see yellowish smoke escaping the structure through cracks around the windows and the front door, but the flames appear to be at a low level inside. The best course of action for firefighters to take in this situation would be to

   A. break windows on the structure to allow firefighters to access the interior.

   B. create holes in the ceiling of the structure for unburned particulate matter in the smoke to escape.

   C. open the front door of the building to create a point of entry for fire attack.

   D. douse the exterior of the space with water to slow the spread of the fire and let the internal blaze continue until the temperature has fallen.

Chapter 5: Reasoning and Judgment

15. As a bystander at a fire, you stand at a safe distance and watch first responders as they establish the scene and extract victims from the structure. As firefighters begin to withdraw from the structure after their primary search, you think you see a silhouette in a window close to the source of the flames. The best course of action to take in this situation is to

    A. rush into the structure and seek out the victim for extrication.

    B. get the attention of a responder on scene and describe what you saw.

    C. ask other bystanders if they saw what you saw.

    D. call 911 to report to an operator directly so that they can pass along the information.

16. An illegal campfire ignited a forest fire in some nearby public lands. The fire spread from the camp-fire in a v-shape, extending to a dry, grassy ravine and wooded inclines in the immediate area. But within a few acres of the point of origin, the fire swerved and began traveling up a nearby mountain at a rapid speed, outpacing firefighters in the area who had started creating fire breaks. The fire-fighters were unable to hike the mountain quickly enough to get ahead of the blaze because of the extreme heat, and the fire grew uncontrollably. Firefighters descended and began preparing their defense at base of the slope. Based on this information, what conclusion can be drawn about the behavior of fires?

    A. Fires travel faster downhill as burning materials roll ahead of the flames to ignite other sources of fuel.

    B. Fires travel faster uphill as the heat they generate rises to pre-heat fuel and increase the speed of combustion.

    C. Fires travel faster uphill as fuel sources were present at a higher density on the mountain.

    D. Fires move indifferent to elevation and incline and continue spreading from the point of origin uniformly.

17. Witnesses of an early morning fire at a small electronics store reported seeing a person fleeing the scene just before the fire crews arrived. The nature of the fire has elevated the case to a suspected arson. Upon interviewing the witnesses, the following information is recorded:

    Witness 1: "He came running out from behind the store, tall guy, at least 6' 2". He had cool sunglasses and was wearing a green jacket."

    Witness 2: "He ran right towards me from behind the store and down the alley. I'm pretty sure he was wearing a green shirt and had light hair. His eyes, I remember, were bright blue."

    Witness 3: "I saw him run out the side door. He looked like he was going to hit his head, he was so tall. He had a jacket on, light blue, I think."

    Witness 4: "I saw a man in a green jacket with light hair, probably a bit older, but it was hard to tell because of his sunglasses. It looked like he escaped from the back of the store."

    Which witness testimonies will the fire investigator record in the report?

    A. 1, 2, 3

    B. 1, 2, 4

    C. 1, 3, 4

    D. 2, 3, 4

18. Advancing hoselines to the point of fire attack can be achieved through a variety of methods, some of which will change as based on hose storage and form. The following steps (not in order) describe the process for advancing a flat hose with loops:

Step 1. Flake out the hose in line with the entry point and commence fire attack.

Step 2. Walk away from the storage, pulling the hose from the bed.

Step 3. Grasp the nozzle and pull the hose partially out of the hose bed.

Step 4. Advance to desired location until loops pull taut and drop the hose.

Step 5. Pull the loops of the hose down and place one arm through each loop.

Which option lists the most logical sequence of steps?

A. 3–4–5–2–1

B. 2–3–4–5–1

C. 3–2–1–5–4

D. 3–5–2–4–1

19. While returning to the firehouse from a late-night call, the fire engine passes a dirt field that sometimes serves as an extended parking lot for a nearby western events center. There are several vehicles scattered around the lot. You notice that one vehicle has its lights on and is coasting toward a concrete barrier that divides parking lanes. The vehicle does not brake and crashes into the barrier. For a moment, you think you see a small burst of flames beneath the car. No one else in the engine cab saw the event, but you convince the driver to divert into the dirt lot and stop. You run to the stopped vehicle. You see smoke building in the cabin and a woman with her head resting on the steering wheel. The best next step to take in the situation is to

A. break the driver's side window to the car.

B. signal your crew and attempt to open the door to the vehicle.

C. run back to the fire engine to retrieve an extinguisher for the fire and Halligan tool to access the car interior.

D. open the hood of the car to search for the source of the smoke.

20. At noon on a Friday, four calls are received simultaneously by 911 operators within the response area of a fire house. Which of the following events requires the most urgent attention from fire and rescue?

A. The head-on collision of two school buses in a school parking lot

B. A fire inspection for the renovations of a 150-year-old church prior to reopening

C. A report of a fuel spill and multi-car pileup on the freeway

D. A bike crash and possible unconscious cyclist in a local park

ANSWER KEY AND EXPLANATIONS

1. B	5. C	9. A	13. C	17. C
2. D	6. B	10. D	14. B	18. D
3. A	7. D	11. A	15. B	19. B
4. B	8. D	12. C	16. B	20. C

1. **The correct answer is B.** In order to properly extinguish the fire in a high rise and address the priorities of any fire department, firefighters must work efficiently. In the most logical order, firefighters must transport all essential gear to the building (2), enter the building (4), check building alarms (3), communicate known conditions to command so that further assistance may be rendered (5), travel to the floor indicated by alarms (1), and then begin extinguishing the fire (6). Other options incorrectly place entering the building in a not so logical order.

2. **The correct answer is D.** You can infer that a fire extinguisher labeled with an A would address the same class of fires, using either water or foam. The table shows that a Class A fire consists of materials such as wood, paper, cloth, plastic, and more. Of the available choices, only choice D depicts a setting in which you would likely find solid combustible material, probably cloth or paper. Choice A is a Class C fire, choice B is a Class K fire, and choice C is a Class D fire, which would require a fire extinguisher labeled with a C, K, or D, respectively.

3. **The correct answer is A.** Details from the question make it clear that the fire likely resulted from either energized electrical devices or ignitable liquids. When comparing the suggested types of extinguishers, the only overlapping extinguisher type is carbon dioxide. Water (choice B) runs the risk of conducting electricity from the energized devices. Foam (choice C) is applicable to Class B fires, but not Class C. Wet chemical extinguishers (choice D) apply only to Class K fires.

4. **The correct answer is B.** According to the table, energized electrical equipment requires a carbon dioxide or dry powder extinguisher. A wet chemical extinguisher would conduct the electricity and potentially spread the fire. The table makes it clear that wet chemical extinguishers are not appropriate for every situation (choice A). While it is true that dry powder extinguishers are useful for a variety of fire classes (choice C), that information does not apply in this situation. Similar logic applies to choice D: the information is valid but not applicable to the situation.

5. **The correct answer is C.** It's clear that certain steps must occur earlier than others and some later. Firefighters must evaluate the structure before entering, which eliminates choices A and D. Between choices B and C, choice B has the firefighter create a vent after securing and extracting the victim, at which point the firefighter has already left the structure.

6. **The correct answer is B.** Firefighters prioritize the safety of bystanders, victims, and fellow firefighters. The positioning of ladders at windows and rooftops is a common precaution in situations where initial points of entry may turn unstable. When evaluating the answer options, several may be eliminated as they do not represent alignment with firefighting priorities. Choice A is illogical, as ground floor access is possible without the use of ladders. Choice C creates an unnecessary safety hazard for victims, asking that they use ladders rather than stairs or servicing elevators to return to their homes. Choice D speaks to efficiency but redirects resources away from combatting an active fire (a top priority) to a post-fire task.

7. **The correct answer is D.** Firefighters Stanley and Takata take an efficient approach to determining the nature of the fire and working to combat it. However, the firefighters neglected to ensure the safety of those in proximity to the fire (choices A and D). Since the passage states that there was sufficient distance between homes in the neighborhood, alerting residents would take time away from active firefighting, which means that choice A is not the best answer. The passage describes how bystanders were able to take video of the firefighters, implying that they were still present in the backyard during the fire, and thus near firefighting operations. Having bystanders on the fire-ground increases the chance of injury or interference with firefighting. As such, bystanders should be cleared in the initial stages of firefighting.

8. **The correct answer is D.** Even off duty, the firefighter's concern is for the well-being of others. A firefighter knows that efficient work can save lives, so the firefighter will look to work as efficiently as possible, which means delegating tasks to others while seeking to take action that suits his or her specific skill set. Choice A would allow the firefighter to immediately begin alerting residents, but the decision would skip the notification of fire and rescue workers. Choice B is effective but could sacrifice time to communicating with emergency operators and leave firefighters to waste time searching for the proper location. Choice C would be an important choice for a bystander to take to prevent needless risk; however, because the firefighter is trained and capable, he or she could begin assisting residents while minimizing risk to others.

9. **The correct answer is A.** Assuming command at the location of an incident follows a logical series of steps: assume command, evaluate the incident and conditions, create a plan and assign units, provide continuing command, request additional units as needed, and return units to service and terminate command. Step 5, returning units to service and terminating command, must be the last step in the process, thus eliminating choice C. Similarly, assuming command (step 3) must occur as soon as possible. Choices A, B, and D all place it early on, but choice D has the command unit creating a plan prior to assuming command, which could create operational disarray, as it would be unclear whose plan to follow. The sequences in choices A and B appear logical, but choice B has command requesting additional units before it is clear what the plan for operations is, thus resulting in decreased efficiency as units may be requested that are unnecessary.

10. **The correct answer is D.** There are only two different hose diameters listed in the table, 1.75 and 2.5 inches. Nozzle pressures are consistent, but nozzle size and gallons per minutes gradually increase. The objective of the question is to infer which factor, hose diameter or nozzle size, has the greatest impact on water produced in gallons per minute (GPM). GPM increases as both hose diameter and nozzle size increase, but one factor has a greater impact than the other. When examining hose diameter, a .75-inch increase in hose diameter from hose 2 to hose 3 correlates with an increase of 25 GPM. A similar increase in GPM is apparent from hose 1 to hose 2 (24 GPM). When looking closely at the numbers of hose 3 and 4, the nozzle size change of 1 inch to 1.125 inches results in a change of 56 GPM, more than from hose 1 to 2 or 2 to 3. But the nozzle size change is twice the change from hose 2 to hose 3. With that in mind, it appears that double the nozzle size change only doubles GPM. That is a constant rate of growth, meaning that it is nozzle size and not hose diameter that has a greater effect on GPM.

11. **The correct answer is A.** The question provides you with information related to the fire triangle. The course of fire attack is an attempt to deprive a fire of its contributing elements: oxygen, fuel, and/ or heat. The question establishes that the trench separates the fires from a large meadow. The most logical reason for doing so is to prevent the fire from accessing a large new source of fuel. Choice B

is contradictory to the purpose of most firefighting activities. Choice C is possible but defies basic reasoning for the situation; if cool air were to be drawn into the trench, there is not guaranteed interaction with the fire, at least nothing that is indicated by information presented by the passage. Choice D is reasonable but also disconnected from the information in the passage; in addition, firefighters would be better off fleeing the fire on foot than taking the time to construct a trench if their primary purpose was self-protection.

12. **The correct answer is C.** In evaluating the situation, there are four victims with varying levels of trauma and responsiveness. A responder must select the victim who requires the greatest level of care in specifics of the situation and aligns with departmental priorities. A nonresponsive victim will largely be prioritized over other victims, especially those who can move and respond on their own accord. Victim 3 presents the greatest cause for concern, at least as related to the other victims. Victim 3 is unconscious which likely indicates a head injury, and she is also pregnant, thus increasing both the risk of her condition and raising to a higher priority for responders.

13. **The correct answer is C.** To prioritize safety and efficiency, a firefighter is best served by taking only necessary actions to guarantee to the best of his or her ability the safety of civilians on site and the fire crew. Lacking information that may affect the ability of the fire crew to safely combat the fire, choice A assumes that the fire will respond to standard firefighting practices despite the unknown composition of the fuel source. The passage reminds readers that not all fires can or should be treated equally. As such, following a normal course of action could prove dangerous. Moving the fuel sources away from the fire (choice B) risks both approaching the fire, uncertain of its nature, and moving hazardous materials whose nature is also unknown, also putting responders at risk. Choice D presupposes that water will be used for containment as opposed to other methods and thus may waste valuable time prior to deciding on a proper course of action. Choice C includes an evaluation of the situation and avoidance of a hasty course of action that may lead to unpredictable reactions and is thus the most reasonable step to take first.

14. **The correct answer is B.** The question establishes the definition, nature of, and causes of a fire phenomenon referred to as a "backdraft." This information will be essential in correctly answering the question. From the introductory information, it is clear that a sudden influx of oxygen into an oxygen-depleted environment is the biggest factor in the creation of a backdraft. The scene is displaying signs of the low-oxygen environment that creates a backdraft. Thus, any correct answer will avoid the sudden and significant introduction of oxygen into the mobile home. Choices A and C both would cause a sudden introduction of oxygen into the structure, likely enough to cause a backdraft. Choice D could lower the temperature of the structure but would conflict with the mission of preserving the property in question. Even if it is unclear that choice A reduces the risk of introducing significant oxygen into the environment of the fire, it does address the fuel source in the environment. You can infer that if the unburned matter is removed, the chances of a backdraft occurring are lower.

15. **The correct answer is B.** As in any situational judgment question, here you're being asked to determine the safest and most efficient action to take with the details of the situation. Choice A would risk your safety, that of the potential victim, and those of firefighters tasked with saving those within the structure. Choice C would allow you to confirm what you witnessed but would do little to directly affect the situation. Choice D would effectively communicate information to the command unit on scene but could take valuable time away from rescue operations. Information should be communicated directly for the sake of efficiency. Choice B meets such priorities.

16. **The correct answer is B.** All the information needed to answer correctly is available in the passage. The fire quickly changed course and traveled up the mountain at "rapid speed." Firefighters are unable to get ahead of the fire and are forced to descend. Choices B and C state that fires travel faster uphill. The question is seeking a general rule for the behavior of fires; choice C specifies a greater density of fuel sources on the mountain, which is neither general information about fires nor stated by the passage.

17. **The correct answer is C.** Witness 2's is the only account to state the color of the suspect's eyes. Every other witness described the suspect as wearing sunglasses, which would obscure the suspect's eye color. Witness 2 described the suspect's clothing as a green shirt, as opposed to the jacket described by the other three. Even as Witness 3 misremembers the color of the jacket, the other information provided aligns with the descriptions of witnesses 1 and 4.

18. **The correct answer is D.** Many information ordering questions can be tackled by properly assessing the procedure or by examining the logic of the answer options. To begin advancing the hoseline, a firefighter must first grasp the nozzle and start to remove the hose from its bedding, which eliminates choice B. Then, to obtain proper purchase on the hose, a firefighter places the hose loops over both arms and begins walking away from the hose's storage. Both choices A and D place step two after step five; however, choice A interrupts the procedures by telling the firefighter to advance to the point of attack before placing loops over his or her arms, thus making step five unnecessary in that sequence. This eliminates all answer choices except for D. In examining the procedure, after walking away from the hose bed with loops over one's shoulders, the firefighter advances to the desired location, drops the house, and then begins to "flake out" (meaning "to position the hose so that it uncoils properly with advance") the hose in line with the entry point. Thus, the correct sequence is 3–5–2–4–1.

19. **The correct answer is B.** A firefighter wants to ensure the safety of those at risk, preserve property as possible, and do so as efficiently as possible. Actions taken through strong situational awareness often means delegating tasks and attempting simple solutions before continuing to more extreme measures to meet the duties of the job. Choice A assumes that the door to the vehicle is locked without first attempting to open the door; breaking the window could injure the unresponsive driver due to the woman's proximity to the glass. Choice C will allow the firefighter to address both the potential fire and access the interior of the vehicle should the doors be locked; however, such actions could be completed more efficiently by the other members of the crew with appropriate verbal commands. Choice D seeks to address the source of the fire but potentially endangers the driver of the vehicle; the firefighter's primary concern should be removing the driver from immediate danger.

20. **The correct answer is C.** Strong situational judgment means being able to evaluate the apparent risk of actions and situations quickly and consistently. Prioritizing safety, property, and efficiency means that firefighters will pursue resolution for hazardous situations where the threat is immediate and significant. Choice A describes a collision between two vehicles that often carry multiple vulnerable individuals; however, because of the time and location of the crash, it is safe to infer that the speed and time of the collision (noon on a weekday) resulted in few injuries. Choice B can be easily deferred to a time when no life-threatening circumstances exist. Choice D presents a potentially serious situation, but it pales in comparison with choice C, which represents a very real threat to multiple individuals. The reported fuel spill at the site of the traffic incident must be addressed to allow for safe operation of the road and thus is a high priority in the minds of firefighters.

Chapter 6

Spatial Orientation

OVERVIEW

- **What Do Spatial Orientation Questions Measure?**
- **Two Tips for Answering Spatial Orientation Questions**
- **Guided Practice: Spatial Orientation**
- **Summing It Up**
- **Exercise: Spatial Orientation**
- **Answer Key and Explanations**

6

WHAT DO SPATIAL ORIENTATION QUESTIONS MEASURE?

Spatial orientation questions test your ability to keep a clear idea of where you are in relation to your surroundings. The ability to orient oneself in space is essential to firefighters who must reach a fire as quickly as possible and in the safest and most effective manner. Spatial orientation is also vital to firefighters working in a smoky environment. Knowing in what direction you face after being turned around multiple times with no visual cues is a skill that could save your life—and the lives of others.

Your firefighting training provides clues and instructions to orient yourself in space. You will have plenty of practice before you are put into a position in which you must rely heavily on this skill. The spatial orientation questions on the firefighter exam are meant to test your aptitude in this regard and to measure how carefully you read and how logically you follow through.

Spatial orientation questions on firefighter exams tend to emphasize either where you are (using a diagram) or how to go from one spot to another on a diagram or map. You may be allowed to use your pencil to write on the diagrams or maps as a way of testing your answer choices—if so, be sure to write lightly and erase any of your jottings that do not work out or are no longer needed. If several questions are based on the same diagram or map and you have made pencil markings for them, the diagram can get quite confusing. You may also be asked to look at an image or diagram for an extended time and memorize its prominent features, then answer a set of questions without looking back.

Many diagrams or maps use **legends**, which are lists that explain or identify the symbols used on the map. A dotted line might indicate movement. An arrow might indicate direction. Various icons may represent buildings such as hospitals, airports, and hotels. Another important feature of many diagrams or maps is the **compass**, which indicates cardinal directions.

Examples of Map Legends Icons

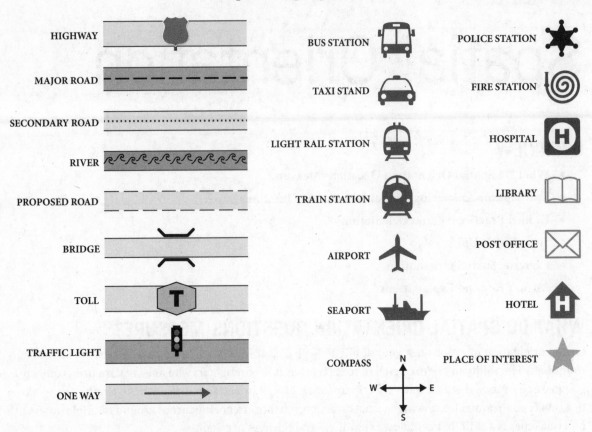

HIGHWAY	BUS STATION	POLICE STATION
MAJOR ROAD	TAXI STAND	FIRE STATION
SECONDARY ROAD	LIGHT RAIL STATION	HOSPITAL
RIVER	TRAIN STATION	LIBRARY
PROPOSED ROAD	AIRPORT	POST OFFICE
BRIDGE	SEAPORT	HOTEL
TOLL	COMPASS	PLACE OF INTEREST
TRAFFIC LIGHT		
ONE WAY		

TWO TIPS FOR ANSWERING SPATIAL ORIENTATION QUESTIONS

1 Questions are often based on phrases such as "turn left," "to the right," or "to the left of the rear entrance." The test maker, however, often approaches a diagram or map from the side or from the top, so "left" and "right" don't correspond to your position in relation to the diagram. For these questions, just turn the test booklet sideways or upside-down to view the map or diagram from the correct standpoint. Turn it so that "left" or "right" on the diagram or map is the same direction as your left or right hand.

2 Occasionally, a question provides information and asks you to relate the information to a map or diagram. For example, the question might say that a fire engine headed north two blocks, then turned east for two blocks, turned south for one block, and then went east one more block. For questions of this sort, it's helpful to draw your own diagram or mark the one in your booklet. If you sketch the problem yourself, you're less likely to get turned around.

With this in mind, let's work through a couple of examples together.

GUIDED PRACTICE: SPATIAL ORIENTATION

Example 1

As indicated by arrows on the street map, Adams and River Streets are one-way going west. Main is one-way going east, and Market is one-way going southwest. Oak and Ash are one-way streets going north, and Elm is one-way going south.

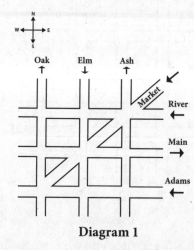

Diagram 1

A fire engine heading west on River Street between Ash and Elm Streets receives a call to proceed to the intersection of Adams and Oak. What turns should the engine take to travel the shortest distance and not break traffic laws?

A. Left on Elm and right on Market.

B. Left on Market and proceed directly to Oak.

C. Left on Elm and right on Adams.

D. Left on Oak and proceed directly to Adams.

Solution

Consider Tip #1 before answering this question. We're told that test makers "often [approach] a diagram or map from the side or from the top," as is the case here. If you work the problem without rotating the diagram, it's going to look something like this:

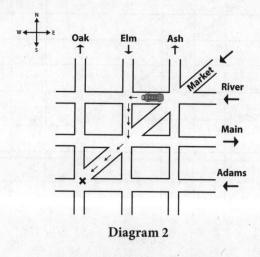

Diagram 2

Note how the turn onto Market Street appears to us as a left turn in Diagram 2. While you may figure the correct route with this method, it would still be easy to get turned around and select the wrong answer. Try rotating the map, so you face the same direction as the "driver." Now left is left, and you won't get mixed up when choosing your answer (just remember to rotate the compass with the diagram):

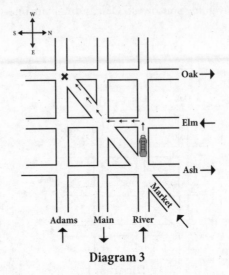

Diagram 3

The correct answer is A. Turning left on Elm and right on Market makes for the shortest possible route to the scene. While choice C might appear equal, taking a diagonal turn onto Market versus a right turn onto Adams cuts out some of the distance. A left turn onto Market—as suggested by choice B—isn't possible given the starting point; turning left on Oak—as suggested by choice D—would point the fire engine the wrong way on a one-way street.

Example 2

This portion of a city street map shows an area that is divided into four fire control sectors as follows:

- **Sector Adam:** Bounded by Tudor Street, Newton Street, Hub Street, Athens Street, and Canal Street
- **Sector Brando:** Bounded by Tudor Street, F Street, West 4th Street, Hub Street, and Newton Street
- **Sector Charles:** Bounded by West 4th Street, F Street, West 2nd Street, C Street, and Hub Street
- **Sector David:** Bounded by Athens Street, C Street, West 2nd Street, and Canal Street

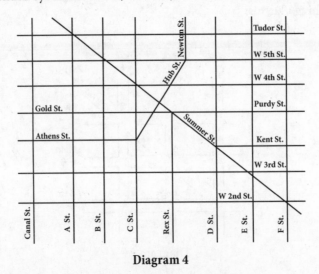

Diagram 4

There is a fire in the block bounded by West 4th Street, Summer Street, and Hub Street. The fire is in what sector?

A. David

B. Charles

C. Brando

D. Adam

Solution

This spatial orientation question appears easy to breeze through on its surface. You can narrow down the region between West 4th, Summer, and Hub Streets and come up with an "X" marking the spot:

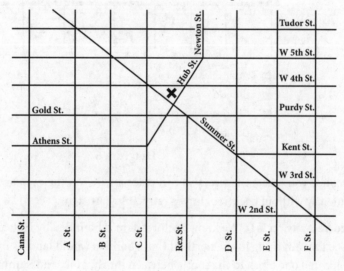

Diagram 5

Remember, however, that time is of the essence. If you race through the test without applying strategy, you might be inclined to ignore this question's preface altogether, in which case you may have identified the location of the fire, but you still have to go back and draw boundaries for each sector. Instead, try identifying the sectors on your diagram first, as shown in the following diagram.

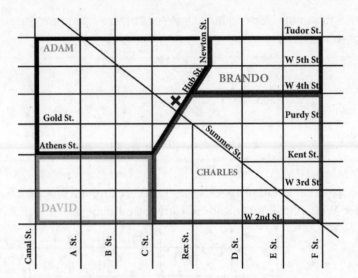

- ■ Adam
- ■ Brando
- ■ Charles
- ■ David

Diagram 6

Now, once you locate the fire, you can place an "X" on the map and answer the question confidently without backtracking or retracing your steps.

The correct answer is D. We know Sector Adam is bounded by Hub and Athens Streets. We can see that anything to the north of those borders would land us in that sector. If the fire were located one block to the south, between Purdy, Hub, and Summer Streets, it would lie within Sector Charles (choice B); one block east would put it in Sector Brando (choice C); and a boundary of Athens instead of West 4th Street would place it in Sector David (choice A).

6

> **NOTE**
>
> The firefighter exam you take might not include a section exclusively about spatial orientation, but the ability to look at a map or diagram of an area and determine your position is invaluable as a firefighter. To preserve the lives of both yourself and others, you should always be able to answer the question, "If my surroundings (be it a single-story or multiple-floor building, a series of buildings, a section of city blocks, or an outdoor area) look like this, what is my current position?"

Summing It Up

- Spatial orientation questions on the firefighter exam test your ability to keep a clear sense of direction in relation to your surroundings. This ability is vital to success as a firefighter. The job requires reaching a fire as quickly, safely, and effectively as possible, as well as working in smoky, dark, and otherwise disorienting environments.

- Spatial orientation questions usually present information in the form of a map or diagram and ask you to navigate from one place to another. Be sure to examine diagrams carefully and make use of the information presented, including legends, compasses, and street directions.

- One way to avoid confusion when reading spatial orientation questions is to rotate the map or diagram so the direction(s) match your own point of view.

- Some spatial orientation questions provide information and ask you to relate it to a map or diagram. For these questions, it's wise to create a sketch of your own or draw directly on the diagram in the book to avoid unnecessary confusion.

6

EXERCISE: SPATIAL ORIENTATION

14 Questions—21 minutes

> **Directions:** The following questions are designed to test your spatial orientation skills. For each question set, study the map or diagram carefully, then choose the best answer to each question.

Questions 1–3 are based on the following map.

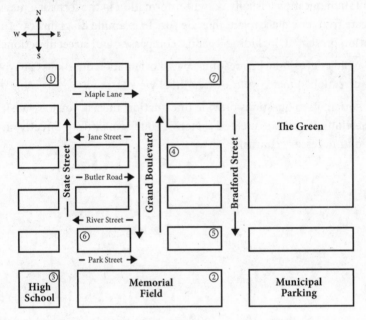

1. If you are located at Point 1 and travel one block east, turn right and travel four blocks, and then turn left and travel one block, to which point will you be closest?

    A. 6

    B. 5

    C. 3

    D. 2

2. You're at the corner of Butler Road and Bradford Street when you receive an alarm for a fire at Butler Road and Grand Boulevard. Which is the best route to take to the scene?

    A. Go one block south on Bradford Street, go two blocks west on River Street, go one block north on State Street, and then go one block east on Butler Road.

    B. Go one block north on Bradford Street, go one block west on Jane Street, and then go one block south on Grand Boulevard.

    C. Go one block south on Bradford Street, go one block west on River Street, and then go one block north on Grand Boulevard.

    D. Go two blocks south on Bradford Street, go one block west on Park Street, and then go two blocks north on Grand Boulevard.

3. You have just checked out and dismissed a false alarm at the high school when you receive word of a trash can fire on The Green near the corner of Bradford Street and Maple Lane. Which is the best route to take to the scene?

   A. Go two blocks east on Park Street and then four blocks north on Bradford Street.

   B. Go two blocks north on State Street, go two blocks east on Butler Road, and then two blocks north on Bradford Street.

   C. Go four blocks north on State Street and then go two blocks east on Maple Lane.

   D. Go one block east on Park Street, go two blocks north on Grand Boulevard, go one block east on Butler Road, and then two blocks north on Bradford Street.

Questions 4–10 are based on the following diagram.

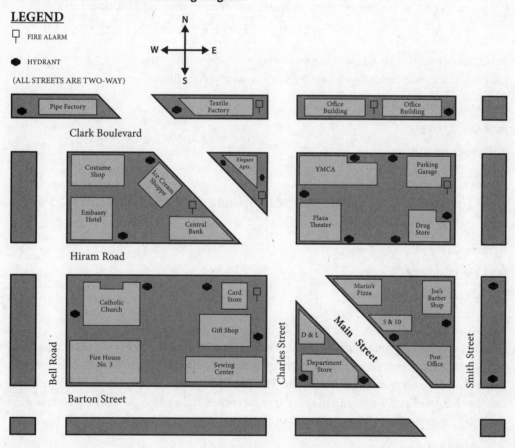

4. A parade down Main Street has cleared Hiram Road and is nearing Barton Street when an alarm is received for a fire at the Post Office. The hydrant to which the firefighters should attach their first hose is located

   A. at the corner of Barton Street and Main Street.

   B. mid-block on the northeast side of Main Street between Smith and Charles.

   C. mid-block on Smith Street between Hiram Road and Barton Street.

   D. at the corner of Hiram Road and Smith Street.

5. The best route for the firefighters to take to the Post Office fire is

   A. straight down Barton Street.

   B. north on Bell Road, right on Clark Boulevard, and then south on Smith Street.

   C. north on Bell Road, right on Hiram Road, and right on Main Street.

   D. east on Barton Street, north onto Charles Street, right onto Hiram Road, and right again onto Smith Street.

6. At 5 p.m., word is received at the firehouse of a fire at the YMCA. The best route to this fire is

   A. east one block on Barton Street and then left onto Charles Street.

   B. north on Bell Road to Clark Boulevard and then right onto Charles Street.

   C. east on Barton Street, left onto Smith Street, and then west onto Clark Boulevard.

   D. north on Bell Road to Hiram Road, east onto Hiram Road, and then north onto Charles Street.

7. While the fire at the YMCA is raging, a strong wind blows from the northeast. Firefighters should properly train their hoses to prevent the fire from spreading to the

   A. Plaza Theater.

   B. Parking Garage.

   C. Elegant Apartments.

   D. Textile Factory.

8. A fire alarm sent from the alarm box on Main Street between Clark Boulevard and Hiram Road is least likely to be reporting a fire

   A. in an Office Building.

   B. at the Pipe Factory.

   C. at the Elegant Apartments.

   D. at the Catholic Church.

9. It's a hot summer evening and a firefighter is sent on a routine check to ensure that no fire hydrants in the area have been opened or lost water pressure. The firefighter leaves the firehouse by way of the Barton Street entrance and heads east. He takes the second left turn, proceeds one block, makes another left, goes one block, and makes three successive right turns. At the next intersection, he turns left, then makes his first right and stops the car. The firefighter is now

   A. back at the firehouse.

   B. at the corner of Hiram Road and Main Street facing southeast on Main Street.

   C. at the corner of Charles Street and Clark Boulevard facing east on Clark Boulevard.

   D. on Bell Road at the side entrance of the Embassy Hotel.

10. The most poorly protected block in terms of a pedestrian's ease for reporting a fire is bounded by

   A. Charles Street, Main Street, and Barton Street.

   B. Hiram Road, Main Street, and Smith Street.

   C. Clark Boulevard, Charles Street, Hiram Road, and Smith Street.

   D. Hiram Road, Bell Road, Barton Street, and Charles Street.

Questions 11–14 are based on the following floor plan and information.

Central Hotel is an elegant, old, five-story structure. The plans of each residential floor, with four floors above the lobby, are identical.

Central Hotel

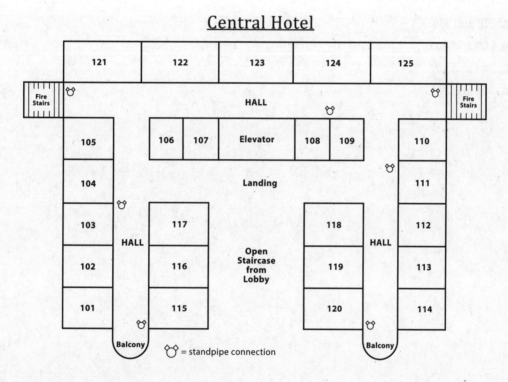

11. If there is a fire in the hotel lobby, the best means by which to evacuate a guest from Room 124 is

   A. via the elevator.

   B. down the fire stairs next to Room 125.

   C. across the hall and down the wide-open staircase.

   D. across the hall and down the corridor to the balcony.

12. During the same lobby fire, the guest in Room 217 should be evacuated by

   A. running down the hall to the balcony.

   B. taking the elevator.

   C. turning the corner and descending the open staircase.

   D. using the fire stairs between Rooms 205 and 221.

13. If there's a fire in Room 406, firefighters should

    A. take the elevator to the roof, enter the fifth floor from the fire stairs, and connect to the standpipe at Room 421.

    B. run up the open staircase and connect hoses to the standpipe between Rooms 403 and 404.

    C. enter the building by way of a ladder placed in front of and up to the balcony, then connect to the standpipe at Rooms 403 and 404.

    D. run up the fire stairs and connect to the standpipe at Room 421.

14. The greatest danger from a fire in Room 309—excluding guests of the room itself—would be posed to the guests of Rooms

    A. 310 and 318.

    B. 209 and 409.

    C. 308 and 409.

    D. 308 and 209.

ANSWER KEY AND EXPLANATIONS

1. D	4. C	7. A	10. B	13. D
2. C	5. B	8. A	11. B	14. C
3. C	6. A	9. C	12. A	

1. **The correct answer is D.** From Point 1: East one block is right on Maple Lane to Grand Boulevard; right four blocks is south on Grand Boulevard to Park Street; left is east onto Park Street; and one block east on Park, while also near Point 5, brings you closest to Point 2.

2. **The correct answer is C.** Bradford Street is one-way southbound, so immediately eliminate choice B. Park Street is one-way eastbound, so eliminate choice D. Choice A is possible, but it's longer than choice C and to no advantage.

3. **The correct answer is C.** The best route is to go four blocks north on State Street and then go two blocks east on Maple Lane. All other choices send you north on Bradford Street, which is one-way southbound.

4. **The correct answer is C.** It would be difficult to position trucks and hoses on either side of the crowd with a parade coming down Main, so choices A and B are incorrect. The hydrant in choice C is closer to the fire than the one in choice D, making choice C the correct answer.

5. **The correct answer is B.** The route straight down Barton Street is the most direct, but don't forget the parade. Under these special circumstances, the smart choice is to skirt the crowd entirely, and go north on Bell Road, right on Clark Boulevard, and then south on Smith Street. The parade route interferes with the routes listed in choices A, C, and D.

6. **The correct answer is A.** Note the time of day. Clark Boulevard is likely clogged with workers from the Pipe and Textile factories on their way home and, if possible, should be avoided. Given the time of day, the route given in choice A is best. The routes in choices B and C are longer, and the route in choice D would interfere with rush-hour traffic.

7. **The correct answer is A.** Wind from the northeast will blow the fire in a southwest direction. While the Elegant Apartments are positioned west of the YMCA fire, they're across the street, and they're not as close as the Plaza Theater.

8. **The correct answer is A.** The fire box on Main between Clark Boulevard and Hiram Road is between the Ice Cream Shoppe and the Central Bank. Direct vision from this box to the office buildings is blocked by the Elegant Apartments; plus, alternate fireboxes exist closer to the office buildings. While the Pipe Factory (choice B), Elegant Apartments (choice C), and Catholic Church (choice D) are all plausible choices, the question is asking about the least likely location, which is in an Office Building.

9. **The correct answer is C.** The firefighter headed east on Barton and made the second left onto Main Street. He went one block and then turned left (west) onto Hiram Road. After one block, he turned right (north) onto Bell Road, right again (east) onto Clark Boulevard, and right once more (southeast) onto Main Street. At the next intersection, he turned left (north) onto Charles Street and then right, placing him on Clark Boulevard facing east. The arrows mark his route:

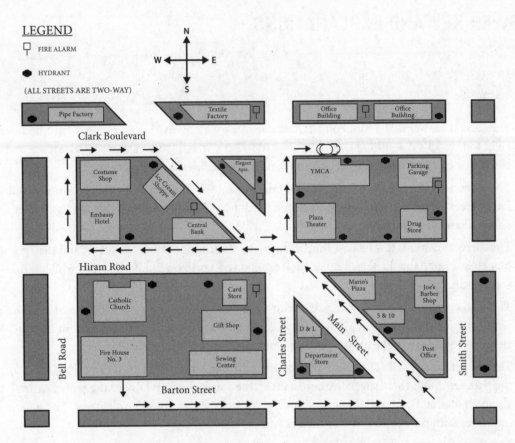

LEGEND

⌐ FIRE ALARM

● HYDRANT

(ALL STREETS ARE TWO-WAY)

N
W ✛ E
S

Pipe Factory

Textile Factory

Office Building

Office Building

Clark Boulevard

Costume Shop

Ice Cream Shoppe

Elegant Apts.

YMCA

Parking Garage

Embassy Hotel

Central Bank

Plaza Theater

Drug Store

Hiram Road

Catholic Church

Card Store

Gift Shop

Mario's Pizza

Joe's Barber Shop

5 & 10

D & L

Main Street

Fire House No. 3

Sewing Center

Department Store

Post Office

Bell Road

Charles Street

Smith Street

Barton Street

10. **The correct answer is B.** There's no fire alarm box on this block. The call box in the block to the north is a good distance away, and a pedestrian would have to cross two major streets to access the box at the corner of Hiram Road and Charles Street. While it is true that there is no call box in choice A, this block is closer to both the firehouse and the call box at Hiram Road and Charles Street.

11. **The correct answer is B.** Fire, heat, and smoke will rise rapidly up the open staircase shaft from the lobby and fill the halls of the floors above. Guests should travel the shortest possible distances in the halls while being evacuated. The fire stairs are close and safe because they're enclosed. Elevators, however, are never safe in a fire. Further, because the fire is in the lobby, patrons should be kept away from that area.

12. **The correct answer is A.** The reasoning is the same as for the answer to the previous question—this guest will reach fresh air and safety fastest and with the least exposure to smoke by running to the balcony for rescue from outside.

13. **The correct answer is D.** You can eliminate choices A and B because, as previously mentioned, the elevator and open staircase present hazards to all people—firefighters, as well as civilians. The safely enclosed fire stairs present a quicker and safer route for carrying hoses to the upper floor than the route given in choice C.

14. **The correct answer is C.** Room 308 shares a common wall with room 309 and is clearly in jeopardy. Common walls tend to be flimsier than floors and ceilings. Because heat and smoke rise, the danger is greater to the room above room 309 than to the room below, though it too should be evacuated.

Chapter 7

Observation and Memory

OVERVIEW

- How Are Observation and Memory Tested?
- Diagrams and Images: Consider the Big Picture
- Five Elements to Look for in Diagrams and Images
- Observation and Memory Guided Practice: Diagrams and Images
- Reading Passages: Focus on the Details
- Observation and Memory Guided Practice: Reading Passages
- Summing It Up
- Observation and Memory Practice: Exercises, Answer Keys, and Explanations

7

HOW ARE OBSERVATION AND MEMORY TESTED?

Firefighters do not work alone. Whatever they're doing—fire inspections, equipment maintenance, firefighting—they always work in pairs, groups, or teams. Much of a firefighter's work is done under direction and supervision. It's important, however, that every firefighter remain alert and not rely solely on the observations and judgments of others.

Fire inspections provide the ideal opportunity for firefighters to learn neighborhood and building layouts, locations of firefighting aids, and possible hazardous situations. It's vital for firefighters out on inspections to observe everything they can about the premises. Observing problem situations during inspections often leads to corrective and preventive measures so that fires never occur on the premises.

Fires, of course, do occur. The firefighter who notices chemicals stored near the site and remembers that they may give off toxic fumes will be better prepared and more effective than one who does not. The firefighter who locates the fire stairs and firehose connectors on-site will be on the scene more quickly and attack the fire with greater efficiency than one who does not. Should firefighters find themselves inside a building engulfed in dense smoke, remembering the layout and points of exit can save lives—including their own.

Because observation and memory are a crucial aspect of effective firefighting, firefighter exams often test applicants on this ability. The usual method is to present a diagram or picture that test takers can study for an allotted time. When time is up, the diagrams are removed, or test takers are asked to cover them up. Applicants must then answer a series of multiple-choice questions based on the information presented.

Pictures and diagrams on firefighter exams are not typically complex; even the shortest amount of time (2-5 minutes) is generally adequate for absorbing the information, provided you use the time systematically. Remember, you can't write anything down during this period—all notes must be mental. It's worthwhile, therefore, to establish categories in advance into which you will later fit information, then approach the diagram as though you'll be asked to fill in the blanks for each category.

DIAGRAMS AND IMAGES: CONSIDER THE BIG PICTURE

A good way to start your observation is to look at the image as a whole—from a wide-screen point of view, so to speak. Determine what you are observing—is it a diagram of a building that requires you to take note of exit routes and potential hazards? Or is it the scene of a car accident? Is it a fire in progress? Look for details that catch your attention at first glance and remember to look for any legends or keys that may aid your interpretation of the scene. Once you have the overview well in mind, try making a mental grid of the image, dividing it into sections, then scanning in a set pattern, either from side to side or top to bottom, taking in as many details as you can. By chunking the image into smaller sections, you will be able to notice details that you may have missed in your initial observation. The following section will discuss how to look effectively for these details.

FIVE ELEMENTS TO LOOK FOR IN DIAGRAMS AND IMAGES

Once you've taken a wide view look at the image, you'll want to start noticing details. As you divide the big picture into smaller portions, pay particular attention to these five elements as you conduct your observation:

1. **People.** Are there any people in the picture or diagram? If so, how many are there? Are they male or female? Adults or children? Where are they? What landmark objects (windows, doors, fire escapes, fire sources) are they near? Are they in danger?

2. **Fire activity.** Is there fire? Is there smoke? Where is the fire located? Where is it located with respect to landmarks? How does it endanger life and property? Is there a predictable direction in which it might spread? Is there a directional indicator, such as a compass? Are there any other potential hazards (e.g., downed electrical wires, flammable liquids, chemicals, or solid materials) that may escalate as a result of the fire?

3. **Layout.** If the picture is an outdoor scene, look for fire equipment such as vehicles, alarm boxes, and hydrants. What are they nearest to and farthest from? Study heights of buildings, natures of buildings, and fire escapes. If you have an indoor scene or floor plan, focus on adjacent rooms, means of entering one room from the next, and locations of doors, windows, and fire escapes. Count and try to remember the exact number of windows and doors.

4. **Special details.** Is there a smoke alarm or a sprinkler system? Where? Is an obstruction noted? Is there any indication that doors are open or closed? If so, which are open, and which are closed? What time of day is it? Are there any street or warning signs visible? How many and what types of vehicles are present? Are there any legible license plate numbers? What about this scene or diagram is unique? What feature would likely lead to a question on an exam?

7

⑤ **Words and symbols.** Another factor to consider when observing an image is any writing that may be presented with it. Like the spatial orientation maps discussed in Chapter 6, the diagrams in the memory and observation section may include legends to identify what special icons and symbols represent. There may also be labels or captions that describe the scene or portions of it. Pay close attention to this information, as it may be key to correctly answering some of the questions presented.

The thought of observing and remembering so much information may seem overwhelming, but by applying these observation strategies, you can improve your observation skills and face this portion of the exam with confidence.

OBSERVATION AND MEMORY GUIDED PRACTICE: DIAGRAMS AND IMAGES

It's time to try a guided set of memory and observation questions. Look at the diagram for the allotted time, making observations based on the five specific elements we've discussed. For this first set, you might want to take notes, since you're training yourself to observe. As you progress through the exercises, rely less on notes and let your memory of your observations go to work.

Directions: Study and memorize the following diagram for five minutes. Then cover the diagram and answer the questions to the best of your ability. Do not refer to the diagram while consulting our guided instruction to check your progress.

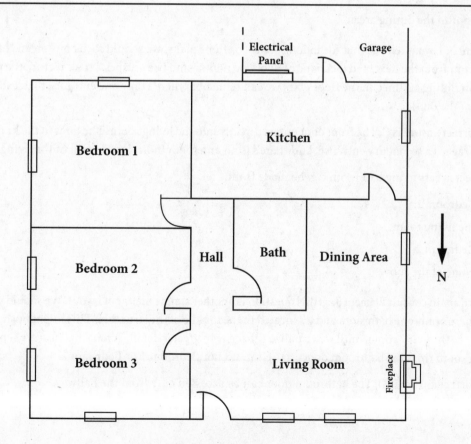

What did you see? In studying this floor plan, you should have noticed the following details:

1 People. None immediately present.

2 Fire activity. None immediately present.

3 Layout. The northern orientation of the house has a front entry to the living room with an L-shaped living-and-dining area. Access to the bathroom is from the hall only. There are three bedrooms in a row that do not connect. Corner bedrooms have two windows each. The hallway does not go through to the kitchen. There is a door from the dining area to the kitchen (as opposed to a possible open doorway without a door). Access to the kitchen is through the garage. The house has a fully interior bathroom.

4 Special details. There is an electrical panel in the garage. A fireplace in the living room. No fire-protective devices.

5 Words and Symbols. Inverted directional indicator.

Now that you have the specific details for the image in mind, answer the questions. The specific element that applies to each question is highlighted before the answer and explanation.

1. The main entry to these premises is the

   A. door to the kitchen.
   B. front vestibule.
   C. door to the living room.
   D. door to the dining area.

Element 3: Layout tells us that for indoor scenes or floor plans, we should focus on "means of entering one room from the next, and locations of doors, windows, and fire escapes." If we picture the perimeter of the building outlined in the floor plan, we can remember there's only one entrance that leads directly in from the outside.

The correct answer is C. The front door enters directly into the living room. The door to the kitchen from the garage is a secondary entrance, and there's is no anteroom indicated in front of the living room.

2. Direct access to the bathroom can be made from

   A. Bedroom 1.
   B. the living room.
   C. Bedroom 2.
   D. None of the above

We can again consult **Element 3**, as this question is another simple matter of layout. We should remember that there's only one bathroom and it's located in the middle of the structure. This might push us toward choice B, the living room, until we visualize the scene in greater detail. What small feature separates the living room from the bathroom doorway? Hint: It's not Bedroom 1 or Bedroom 2.

The correct answer is D. The bathroom door can be accessed only from the hallway.

3. The room with the fewest windows is

   A. Bedroom 2.

   B. the bathroom.

   C. the dining area.

   D. the kitchen.

Element 4: Special details urges us to make mental notes of anything unique about the diagram or picture. As established by our answer to the previous question, the bathroom is in the middle of the layout and not attached to any of the bedrooms, which could be considered unique. With this in mind, it's easier to recall that the bathroom has no windows, and that all windows present border the structure's perimeter.

The correct answer is B. The bathroom has no windows, while all other areas have at least one.

4. The exposure with the greatest possible number of exits is positioned to the

   A. north.

   B. south.

   C. east.

   D. west.

Apply **Element 3: Layout** and **Element 5: Words and symbols** here. Remember that the floor plan tells us there are two main exits to the outside: one through the living room, and one at the opposite end of the structure through the garage. Also recall the number of windows present; while there's only one at the "back" of the structure, we have three windows bordering the "front" side. Once we've determined that the living room-side hosts the greatest number of exits, all we have left to do is remember—according to the diagram—which side is north.

The correct answer is A. Most directional markers indicate north as up. This marker is unusual in that north points down. Reverse the diagram to make north point up and get your bearings. The front of the house is the northern exposure, and there are three windows and a door along the front.

5. Entry to the kitchen is possible from the

   A. dining area only.

   B. dining area and the hall.

   C. dining area and the garage.

   D. dining area, hall, and garage.

Remember that the kitchen runs adjacent to Bedroom 1, the bathroom, the dining room, the garage, and the hallway. Because we studied all doorways in the diagram, as recommended by Element 3, we also remember that there are only two direct paths to the kitchen. And where do those paths lead?

The correct answer is C. While the hall doesn't go through to the kitchen, a direct entry can be made either the dining area or the garage.

6. In the case of an electrical fire, power should be shut off in the

   A. garage.

   B. kitchen.

   C. hall.

   D. bathroom.

Again, recall **Element 4: Special details**. "What about this scene or diagram is unique? What feature would likely lead to a question on the exam?" The only unique features likely to lead to an exam question here are the fireplace and the electrical panel. Therefore, we should have the location of the electrical panel lodged in our memory.

The correct answer is A. The electrical panel is in the garage.

7. If an out-of-control fire were spreading from the fireplace, a person's best course of escape from the bathroom would be

   A. out the bathroom door to the hall, into Bedroom 1, and out the south window.

   B. out the bathroom door to the hall, through the living room and dining area, through the kitchen, and out by way of the garage.

   C. out the bathroom door, down the hall, and out the front door.

   D. across the hall into Bedroom 2 and out the window.

This question requires us to consider **Element 1: People** and **Element 2: Fire activity** before answering. First, are there people present? If so, where are they? We're told there's a person in the bathroom, then asked to chart the most effective path for his or her escape. Second, is fire present? And if so, where? This scenario tells us there's a fire spreading from the fireplace. Now we'll have to visualize the scene to remember a few things: First, the only exit from the bathroom leads to the living room hallway; second, the structure's main exit is located at the end of this hall; and third, the fireplace is located in the northwest corner of the living room. Would it be prudent to bust through a patch of drywall or jump out a window to avoid approaching the path of a fire that's just beginning to spread? Probably not.

The correct answer is C. This question requires memory of the layout and common sense. Exiting by door is always faster and safer than exiting by window, given there's a door that can be reached. The fire in question is spreading from the end of the living room farthest from the door, so a short run out the door makes the most sense.

8. Which of the following are connecting rooms?

   A. Bedrooms 1 and 2

   B. Bedrooms 2 and 3

   C. Bedroom 3 and the dining area

   D. The dining area and the kitchen

We can again apply **Element 3: Layout** to this question. While the dining area, the hall, and the living room as are all connected as part of the same open space, there are no direct connections between bedrooms. We can also recall that the opening of Bedroom 3 leads first to the living room and not the dining area. Having eliminated choices A, B, and C, we're left with the correct answer.

The correct answer is D. Of the options given, only the dining area and kitchen connect directly.

Now that you have a better idea of the type of details to look for, you may want to review the diagram again, perhaps starting with the big picture approach and then making a mental grid of the image to focus and divide your observations using the feature categories as your guide. Find ways that help you to make connections among the details. Those connections will trigger your memory and help you to recall even more of your observations.

READING PASSAGES: FOCUS ON THE DETAILS

Not all observation and memory questions involve images. On some firefighter exams, you may be presented with a reading passage and allotted a certain amount of time to read it. After the time period has expired, you will have to answer questions about the passage without referring to it again. Depending on how the test is administered, you may have an opportunity to jot down some notes after the observation time has ended, but whether or not that is the case, you will want to keep a list of specifics in mind so you can recall the most important points of the passage. Using the **5 *W*'s and an *H*** checklist can help you to accomplish this task.

The 5 *W*'s (and an *H*)	
✓ **Who?**	Determine the people involved (individuals, groups, organizations).
✓ **What?**	Identify the incident.
✓ **Where?**	Identify the location of the incident.
✓ **When?**	Identify the date and time of the incident.
✓ **Why?**	Determine the cause of the incident.
✓ **How?**	Determine by what means or source the incident occurred.

Just as using a mental grid can help you to break down a diagram or image, using this approach can help you break down a passage into manageable chunks and focus on the most important details. You will want to mentally connect these details to help you remember the information without trying to memorize the entire passage. Focusing on the details will help you to identify the main idea of the passage if it isn't stated explicitly. In turn, having the main idea in mind is key to keeping the details fresh in your memory.

OBSERVATION AND MEMORY GUIDED PRACTICE: READING PASSAGES

Let's put the Five *W*'s and an *H* checklist technique to work by analyzing a short paragraph. Take five minutes to read and study this excerpt from a news article.

THEATER PRANK RESULTS IN INJURIES

Two people were critically injured and three suffered minor injuries on Thursday night when a crowd, frightened by a prank, rushed to the exits of a sold-out show at the Cinema Theatre. According to theater manager Nick Watterson, the rush began after an unidentified individual ran into the theater yelling "Fire!" and smoke began to fill the auditorium. "Everyone in the place panicked—it was an instant stampede," Watterson said. Captain Thomas Hickam of the Cabot City Fire Department stated the incident occurred about an hour into the 7:00 p.m. showing of *Sonny and CJ: Too Tough*. Hickham said that that a sweep of the building revealed that there was no fire, but that the individual had tossed several homemade smoke bombs into the auditorium. Cabot City Police Lt. Jeff Hostell is asking anyone with information about the individual responsible for the prank to contact the Cabot City Crime Hotline at 494-578-9933.

Now, without referring to the article, fill in as much information as you can remember about what you just read.

Who?	
What?	
Where?	
When?	
Why?	
How?	

Compare your table with the one below.

Who?	Capt. Thomas Hickam; theater crowd; injured people; Nick Watterson; Lt. Jeff Hostell
What?	Individuals injured during crowd exit—false alarm
Where?	Cabot City; Cinema Theater
When?	Thursday night; 7:00 p.m. showing; hour into show = 8:00
Why?	Someone yelled "Fire!" and threw smoke bombs in the theater auditorium
How?	Rushing crowd exiting caused serious injury to two people, minor to three

Now we will apply the information we've gathered and answer a few questions about the paragraph. The Five *W*'s and an *H* checklist item that applies to each question is highlighted before the answer and explanation.

1. At approximately what time did the incident occur?

   A. 7:00 p.m.

   B. 7:30 p.m.

   C. 8:00 p.m.

   D. 8:15 p.m.

This is a "When" question. Although the actual time of the incident was not stated in the article, it can be determined from the captain's comments.

The correct answer is C. According to the Captain Hickham, the incident occurred "about an hour into the 7:00 showing" of the movie. "An hour into"—in other words, an hour *after* 7:00—would place the time of the incident at approximately 8:00 p.m.

2. Why did the crowd evacuate the auditorium?

   A. Someone yelled "Fire!" and threw smoke bombs into the auditorium.

   B. Someone pulled the fire alarm.

   C. The theater was on fire.

   D. The theater received a bomb threat.

To answer this "Why" question, you might at first have remembered that the crowd left the auditorium as a result of a prank, which would rule out that the theater was truly on fire. Your mental notes should have included that someone yelled "Fire!" and set off the chain of events.

The correct answer is A. An unidentified person ran into the theater yelling "Fire!" and threw smoke bombs in the auditorium, causing the audience to think the threat was real and panic. A fire alarm (choice B) may have been pulled to alert the fire department after the initial rush from the theater, but that is not what caused the crowd to evacuate. The incident was the result of a prank—the theater was not on fire (choice C), and there was no report of a bomb threat (choice D).

3. How many people were injured exiting the theater?

   A. 2

   B. 3

   C. 4

   D. 5

You might have listed the details to answer this question under the "Who" or "How" categories. The "Who" tells us there were people injured; the "How" explains that their injuries were a result of the crowd rushing to the doors to escape what they thought was a fire. The fine detail you needed to remember was the exact number, because the article divided the count between those who were seriously injured and those whose injuries were minor.

The correct answer is D. There were two people critically injured, but three others suffered minor injuries, for a total of five injured people.

4. Where did the incident take place?

   A. City Theater

   B. Cabot City Cinema

   C. Cinema Theater

   D. City Cinema

This simple "Where" question requires you to accurately remember the name of the building. You could keep the initials CT in mind if the entire name is too much, but memorizing the whole name would be better.

The correct answer is C. The name of the movie theater is the Cinema Theater.

5. Who witnessed the incident?

   A. Capt. Robert Hickham

   B. Nick Watterson

   C. Lt. Jeff Hostell

   D. Sonny and CJ

There are quite a few names in this paragraph, so it's important to keep keep track of who's who for this "Who" question. If you can't remember the names outright, consider that the individuals with titles are members of the fire department and police force, and that they would have arrived on the scene after the incident occurred. That will help you narrow your choices.

Chapter 7: Observation and Memory

The correct answer is B. Manager Nick Watterson related the details of what happened inside the theater. Capt. Hickham (choice A) is the firefighter who was involved in the investigation after the incident. Lt. Hostell (choice C) is a member of the police department who is asking for information about the incident. Sonny and CJ (choice D) are the characters in the move title.

Observation and memory passages are approached similarly to "classic" reading comprehension passages, with two notable differences:

1. You don't have to worry about determining inference or themes or recognizing the meaning of vocabulary words—you're looking for just the facts.

2. You are not allowed to refer to the passage once your allotted reading time has expired.

You might consider the first difference a positive and the second a negative, but not having access to the passage doesn't have to be a hardship if you focus on and connect the details to set them firmly in your mind.

7

Summing It Up

- While firefighting requires teamwork, each firefighter must remain alert and avoid relying solely on the observations or judgments of others. For this reason, it's important for firefighters to learn as much as possible about relevant neighborhoods and building layouts, locations of firefighting aids, and possible hazardous situations. The firefighter exam will test your observation and memory skills.

- Observation and memory questions usually take the form of diagrams or pictures that test takers are given to study for an allotted time. The visual aid is removed after the study period, and the test takers are asked to answer a series of multiple-choice questions testing their memory of the diagram and their observation of details.

- For diagrams in observation and memory questions, it's best to focus on four distinct features: the people, potential fire activity, the layout of the scene, and any special details (like smoke alarms, obstructions, and open or closed doors). Try to determine beforehand which of these features might form the basis of an exam question.

- Passage-based observation and memory questions present scenario-based texts that test takers are given to read for an allotted time. The passages are removed after the study period, and test takers must answer a series of multiple-choice questions testing their memory about the details of the passage.

7

OBSERVATION AND MEMORY PRACTICE: EXERCISES, ANSWER KEYS, AND EXPLANATIONS

Exercise 1

Directions: Study and memorize the following diagram for five minutes. Then cover the diagram and answer the questions to the best of your ability. Do not refer to the diagram while answering the questions.

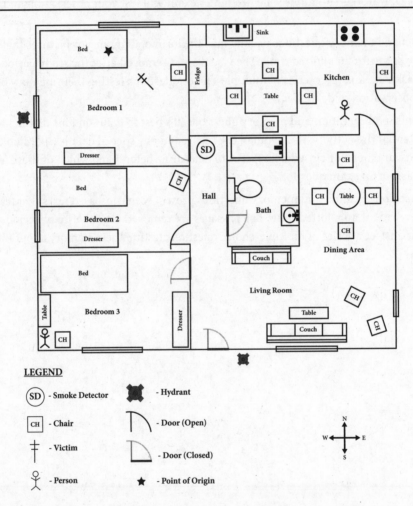

1. What are the number and positions of the fire hydrants in relation to the house?

   A. Two hydrants; one located on the south side of the house, and the other on the west side of the house

   B. Two hydrants; one located on the north side of the house, and the other on the east side of the house

   C. Two hydrants; one located on the south side of the house, and the other on the east side of the house

   D. Three hydrants; one located on the south side of the house, one on the west side, and the other on the east side of the house

2. Where is the point of origin of the fire?

    A. Bathroom

    B. Bedroom 1

    C. Bedroom 3

    D. Kitchen

3. Closed doors retard the spread of fire and smoke. The door that should be closed immediately is the door to

    A. the bathroom.

    B. Bedroom 2.

    C. Bedroom 3.

    D. the kitchen.

4. There are two ways out of every room EXCEPT

    A. Bedroom 2

    B. The dining area

    C. The bathroom

    D. Bedroom 3

5. Smoke detectors are in place

    A. in the hall.

    B. in the hall and the kitchen.

    C. in the hall and the dining area.

    D. nowhere in this unit.

6. Doors to the outside of this unit can be found on the

    A. south and east walls.

    B. north and east walls.

    C. south and west walls.

    D. north, south, and east walls.

7. What is the total number of people in the unit?

    A. 0

    B. 1

    C. 2

    D. 3

8. Which of the following rooms has only one window?

   A. Bedroom 1

   B. Bedroom 3

   C. Living room

   D. Bathroom

Exercise 1: Answer Key and Explanations

1. A	3. B	5. A	7. D
2. B	4. C	6. A	8. B

1. **The correct answer is A.** There are two hydrants—one on the south side of the house outside the front door, and one on the west side, just outside the Bedroom 1 window.

2. **The correct answer is B.** The diagram legend indicates that a star represents the point of origin of the fire. A star is located on the bed in Bedroom 1.

3. **The correct answer is B.** Refer to the legend to determine the status of each door. The bathroom door and the door to Bedroom 3 are already closed. Danger to the immediately adjacent Bedroom 2 is far greater than danger to the remote kitchen.

4. **The correct answer is C.** Only the bathroom has just one exit. Bedrooms 2 and 3 each have a door and a window. The dining area is wide open to the living room and the kitchen, and it has window access as well.

5. **The correct answer is A.** There is one smoke detector at the end of the hall.

6. **The correct answer is A.** Look at the directional marker. The north wall of the unit is at the top of the page, so the doors providing outside access are on the south and east walls.

7. **The correct answer is D.** The three people are the victim in Bedroom 1, the person standing in the kitchen, and the person hiding in Bedroom 3.

8. **The correct answer is B.** Even though it is a corner bedroom, Bedroom 3 has only one window. Bedroom 1 and the living room both have two windows, and the bathroom has none.

In studying this diagram, you should have noticed the following five elements:

1 **People.** Three—one each in Bedroom 1, Bedroom 3, and the kitchen.

2 **Fire activity.** Point of origin in Bedroom 1.

3 **Layout.** Exit doors from the living room and kitchen. Three nonconnecting bedrooms in a row. Fully interior bathroom with exit to the hallway only. L-shaped living-and-dining area. The hallway does not go through to the kitchen. Locations of windows. General volume and placement of furniture. Open and closed doors.

4 **Special details.** Hydrants at the front door and outside the window of Bedroom 1. Smoke detector in the hall. Position of the victims.

5 **Words and symbols.** The legend contains symbols for a smoke detector, chairs, open and closed doors, fire hydrants, fire point of origin, people in the house, and victims of the fire.

Exercise 2

Directions: Study and memorize the following diagram for five minutes. Then cover the diagram and answer the questions to the best of your ability. Do not refer to the diagram while answering the questions.

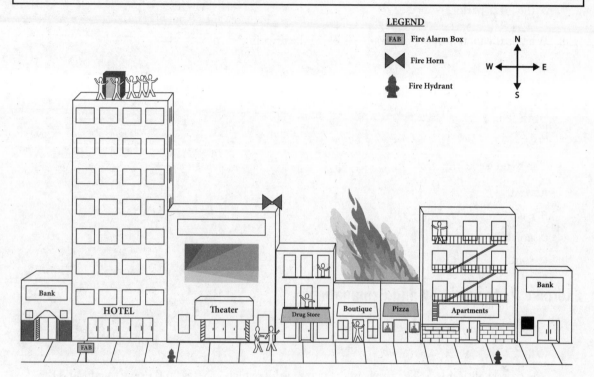

1. The fire is located in

    A. the building between the apartments and the boutique.

    B. the building next to the drug store.

    C. a bank.

    D. the building between the pizza parlor and the apartments.

2. Of the people who can be seen, those in the most immediate danger would be the

    A. people on the roof of the hotel.

    B. residents of the apartment house.

    C. people who live above the drug store.

    D. person in the doorway of the boutique.

3. If the hour were 8 a.m., the least peril to people would occur at the

    A. hotel.

    B. building between the hotel and the drug store.

    C. sidewalk.

    D. building housing the drug store.

4. The building least endangered by this fire is

   A. the apartment house.

   B. a bank.

   C. the theater.

   D. the pizza parlor.

5. What is the total number of people visible in the drawing?

   A. 7

   B. 9

   C. 11

   D. 12

6. The wind is blowing from the

   A. west.

   B. east.

   C. north.

   D. south.

Exercise 2: Answer Key and Explanations

1. A	3. B	5. C
2. C	4. B	6. B

1. **The correct answer is A.** The fire is in the pizza parlor, which is between the apartments and the boutique.

2. **The correct answer is C.** The people who live in the apartments over the drug store are only one building removed from the fire, while the person in the doorway of the boutique is at street level and can simply walk away. With the wind blowing in their direction, the people who live above the drug store are in greater danger than the person in the apartment house next to the fire but upwind of it. The people on the hotel roof are quite a bit removed from the fire as well and in no immediate danger.

3. **The correct answer is B.** The building between the hotel and the drug store is a theater. At 8 a.m., a theater is likely to be deserted, creating peril to property, but not to life.

4. **The correct answer is B.** There are actually two bank buildings (one at each end of the diagram) that are the least endangered by this fire. The bank beside the apartment house is separated from the fire by the apartment house, and it's away from the path of the fire. The bank next to the hotel is the building farthest from the fire and is separated from it by a couple of large, sturdy buildings.

5. **The correct answer is C.** Five people on the hotel roof, plus two pedestrians, plus two residents in the apartments over the drug store, plus one in the doorway of the boutique and one on the apartment house fire escape equals 11 people.

6. **The correct answer is B.** The fire flames and smoke are slanting left, which means that the wind is blowing from east to west. The wind therefore is blowing from the east.

To answer the questions in the exercise correctly, it was important for you to observe the following five elements in the diagram:

1 **People.** Their number (11) and location (hotel, apartments, drug store, boutique) in relation to the fire.

2 **Fire activity.** Note the fire's location with reference to landmarks and buildings. Note the direction of the wind by examining the slant of the smoke and flames. Also remember the extent of the fire's involvement.

3 **Layout.** Note the types of buildings, the sizes of buildings, the arrangement of buildings, and the relationships between buildings in terms of size and types of occupancy.

4 **Special details.** There's a fire horn on top of the theater, and a fire alarm box in front of the hotel. The apartment complex is the only multiple-story building with fire escapes. There's a bank on each end of the block.

5 **Words and symbols.** There is a legend that provides the number and location of hydrants, fire alarm boxes, and fire horns.

Exercise 3

Directions: Take five minutes to read and study this passage. Then, without referring to the passage, choose the best answer for each question that follows.

At 4:00 a.m. on Monday, firefighters responded to a call from Mr. Julius Ogden, an elderly man living at 432 Spurloch Court, a one-story cottage with an unfinished basement. Upon arrival at Mr. Ogden's home, Sgt. Cedar smelled a strong burning odor, but he noticed no flames or smoke. As he escorted Mr. Ogden outside, Sgt. Cedar asked him how long the odor had been present and if Mr. Ogden lived alone in his home. Mr. Ogden said the smell woke him at 3:45 a.m., just before he called the fire department and that, other than his dog Myers, he lived alone. Sgt. Cedar sent Firefighters Huggins and Watt to investigate the source of the odor. As soon as they entered the foyer, dark smoke began to seep up through the heating grates on the floor. Huggins and Watt headed to the basement to investigate and found the source of the fire: some cardboard boxes had fallen against the furnace and caught on fire. Firefighter Watt began to put out the flames with the fire extinguisher he had carried in with him. Firefighter Huggins went outside to get additional help.

1. To what address did the firefighters respond?

A. 422 Spurloch Court

B. 423 Spurlock Circle

C. 432 Spurloch Circle

D. 432 Spurloch Court

2. How long did it take for the firefighters to get to the scene of the emergency call?

   A. 5 minutes

   B. 10 minutes

   C. 15 minutes

   D. 20 minutes

3. What are the names of the three firefighters on the scene?

   A. Spurloch, Ogden, Cedar

   B. Cedar, Huggins, Watt

   C. Huggins, Spurloch, Watt

   D. Cedar, Ogden, Watt

4. What is the name of Mr. Ogden's dog?

   A. Myers

   B. Meyers

   C. Myners

   D. Mylars

5. Where did the fire originate?

   A. In the foyer

   B. In the attic

   C. In the basement

   D. In the living room

Exercise 3: Answer Key and Explanations

1. D	2. C	3. B	4. A	5. C

1. **The correct answer is D.** The correct address is 432 Spurloch Court. It's important to make sure that address numbers don't get transposed, street names don't get misspelled, and street titles don't get confused.

2. **The correct answer is C.** The firefighters responded to the call at 4:00 a.m. Mr. Ogden called the fire department at 3:45 a.m., so it took 15 minutes for the firefighters to arrive.

3. **The correct answer is B.** The firefighters' names are Cedar, Huggins, and Watt. Ogden is the last name of the homeowner; Spurloch is the street name.

4. **The correct answer is A.** The dog's name is Myers.

5. **The correct answer is C.** The fire started in the basement when cardboard boxes fell against the furnace.

Remember: creating a **Five W's and an H** checklist can help answer the questions that follow a passage. In this case, the checklist would look something like this:

Who?	Julius Ogden; Sgt. Cedar; Firefighters Huggins and Watt; Myers the dog
What?	Fire in basement
Where?	432 Spurloch Court; fire in basement
When?	Monday 4:00 a.m. response; 3:45 a.m. call
Why?	Mr. Ogden smelled smoke; smoke came up through heating grates
How?	Cardboard boxes fell against furnace and caught on fire

Exercise 4

Directions: Study and memorize the following diagram for five minutes. Then cover the diagram and answer the questions to the best of your ability. Do not refer to the diagram while answering the questions.

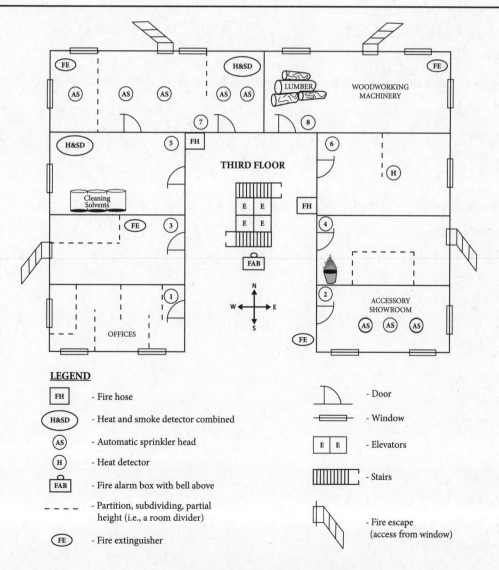

LEGEND

FH	- Fire hose		- Door
H&SD	- Heat and smoke detector combined		- Window
AS	- Automatic sprinkler head	E E	- Elevators
H	- Heat detector		- Stairs
FAB	- Fire alarm box with bell above		
- - - -	- Partition, subdividing, partial height (i.e., a room divider)		- Fire escape (access from window)
FE	- Fire extinguisher		

1. Which room is the most poorly protected in case of fire?

   A. Room 1

   B. Room 4

   C. Room 6

   D. Room 8

2. Which room has the most comprehensive fire protection?

   A. Room 2

   B. Room 5

   C. Room 7

   D. Room 8

3. Fire hoses can be found in

   A. the stairways.

   B. the center hall.

   C. the center hall and Room 6.

   D. Rooms 7 and 8.

4. Which of the following rooms does NOT have access to a fire escape?

   A. Room 2

   B. Room 3

   C. Room 5

   D. Room 8

5. Activities known to be fire hazards occur in

   A. Rooms 1 and 2.

   B. Rooms 5 and 7.

   C. Rooms 2 and 8.

   D. Rooms 5 and 8.

6. In the case of a fire in Room 1, the best exit would be the

   A. fire escape from Room 3.

   B. elevators.

   C. north stairs.

   D. south stairs.

7. In which of the following rooms does a dangerous situation currently exist?

   A. Room 2

   B. Room 4

   C. Room 6

   D. Room 8

8. In the case of a fire, an alert would be sounded from

   A. the east fire escape.

   B. Room 3.

   C. the hall.

   D. the elevators.

9. The intricate pattern of partitions would make a quick exit most difficult from which room?

   A. Room 1

   B. Room 2

   C. Room 6

   D. Room 7

10. What is the total number of windows on this floor?

    A. 14

    B. 16

    C. 18

    D. 20

Exercise 4: Answer Key and Explanations

1. A	3. B	5. D	7. B	9. A
2. C	4. A	6. D	8. C	10. C

1. **The correct answer is A.** Room 1 has no fire-protective device of any kind and has no independent exit to the outside. Room 6 is not much better off, but it has a heat detector. Room 4 has a fire escape but no internal protective device. Room 8 is well protected.

2. **The correct answer is C.** Room 7 has automatic sprinklers, a heat and smoke detector, a fire extinguisher, and a fire escape. Room 2 has only automatic sprinklers, and Room 5 has only a heat and smoke detector. Room 8 has a smoke detector, a fire extinguisher, and a fire escape, but it lacks a sprinkler system.

3. **The correct answer is B.** Fire hoses are only located in the hallway.

4. **The correct answer is A.** Room 2 has no access to a fire escape. Rooms 3 and 8 have fire escapes, and Room 5 has a door connecting it with Room 7, which has a fire escape.

5. **The correct answer is D.** Use and storage of cleaning solvents and woodworking materials can pose fire hazards. The usual activities in offices and accessory showrooms do not present fire hazards. The nature of the business in the other areas is unspecified.

6. **The correct answer is D.** Room 1 is not connected to a fire escape, so its occupants would have to go into the hall to escape the fire. Once in the hall, the quickest way out would be via the nearest stairway (south). Entering Room 3 to go out the window and down the fire escape would be slower and more cumbersome. In addition, Room 3 would be the next room to become involved in the fire due to the cleaning solvents in Room 5. Elevators should be avoided in a fire situation.

7. **The correct answer is B.** A wastebasket in Room 4 is on fire.

8. **The correct answer is C.** There is a fire alarm box topped by a bell in the hall next to the south stair-case. The device in Room 3 is a fire extinguisher, not an alarm.

9. **The correct answer is A.** Room 1 is full of half-partitions that could complicate one's exit.

10. **The correct answer is C.** Be sure to count the windows connected to fire escapes. There are 18 windows in all.

In your initial diagram review, noticing the following information was key to answering the questions correctly:

1 **People.** None.

2 **Fire activity.** The wastebasket fire in Room 4.

3 **Layout.** A center core building with four elevators and two sets of stairs. All rooms have doors to the hallway and at least one window. Corner rooms have multiple windows. Rooms 5 and 7 connect. Rooms 3, 4, 7, and 8 have fire escapes.

4 **Special details.** Two fire hoses, a fire extinguisher, and a fire alarm box with bell in the hall. Fire-hazardous activities in Rooms 5 and 8. Fire extinguishers in Rooms 3, 7, and 8 and in the hall. Sprinkler systems in Rooms 2 and 7. Heat detector in Room 6. Smoke detector in Room 8. Heat and smoke detectors in Rooms 5 and 7. Diagram is of the third floor of the building.

5 **Words and symbols.** Extensive legend.

Exercise 5

Directions: Study and memorize the following diagram for five minutes. Then cover the diagram and answer the questions to the best of your ability. Do not refer to the diagram while answering the questions.

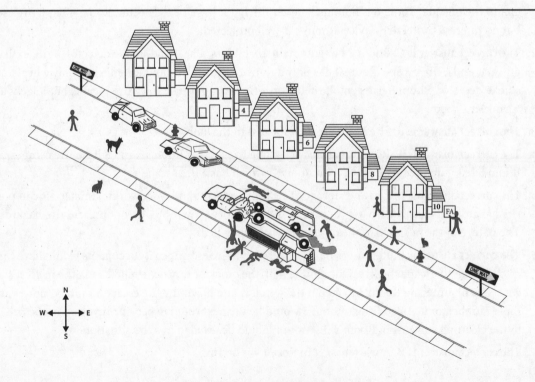

1. How many vehicles are involved in the accident?

   A. 2

   B. 3

   C. 4

   D. 5

2. The number of known victims is

   A. 4.

   B. 5.

   C. 6.

   D. 7.

3. An extra hazard is being created by the

   A. pickup truck.

   B. station wagon.

   C. pedestrian in front of House 10.

   D. person pulling the fire alarm.

4. When firefighters arrive at the scene, they will be hampered by the

   A. situation at the west end of the street.

   B. scarcity of fire hydrants.

   C. absence of witnesses.

   D. crowd of spectators.

5. The house that's missing its house number is

   A. at the east end of the block.

   B. in the middle of the block.

   C. at the west end of the block.

   D. the fourth house from the left.

6. The accident was probably caused by

   A. the station wagon.

   B. the pickup truck.

   C. the car.

   D. a pedestrian.

7. The animals on the scene are

   A. two dogs and a cat.

   B. two cats and a dog.

   C. three cats and a dog.

   D. two cats and two dogs.

8. The vehicle that is still upright is the

    A. station wagon.

    B. sedan.

    C. pickup truck.

    D. convertible.

Exercise 5: Answer Key and Explanations

1. B	3. B	5. C	7. B
2. C	4. A	6. A	8. B

1. **The correct answer is B.** Three vehicles are piled up in the middle of the street. The other two cars are safely parked away from the accident.

2. **The correct answer is C.** There are six victims that we can see (two in the street and four on the side-walk). It's unclear whether any of the cars are still occupied.

3. **The correct answer is B.** The puddle forming at the back of the station wagon is most likely gasoline. If the three vehicles were actively on fire, a gasoline puddle would pose a serious threat of explosion.

4. **The correct answer is A.** Two cars are parked directly in front of the fire hydrant at the west end of the street, completely blocking off access. This is both dangerous and illegal.

5. **The correct answer is C.** House 2, at the far west end of the block, is missing its house number.

6. **The correct answer is A.** Note the one-way signs at each end of the street. It's possible that one or more vehicles spun around on impact, but it appears the station wagon caused the accident by driving the wrong way on a one-way street.

7. **The correct answer is B.** There are two cats and a dog in the scene. The animals have no bearing on the fire problem, but an observant test taker should notice and remember all details.

8. **The correct answer is B.** Two vehicles—the station wagon and the pickup truck—lie on their sides, while the sedan sits upright.

To answer the questions in the exercise correctly, it was important for you to observe the following five elements in the diagram:

1. **People.** Six victims (two lying in the street and four on the sidewalk), one at a fire alarm box near the street, and five approaching the scene.

2. **Fire activity.** A potential gasoline fire threatens all three vehicles involved in the collision.

3. **Layout.** Three cars in a pileup in the middle of street; two are on their sides. Five identical houses in a row. Two parked cars block one hydrant. A second hydrant at the end of the street, and a fire alarm box on the corner.

4. **Special details.** A puddle coming from the rear end of the station wagon. A pickup truck and a station wagon are overturned on their sides. An eastbound one-way street. Two cats and one dog.

5. **Words and symbols.** No legend; compass; one-way street signs pointing east; fire alarm box labeled FA; even-numbered houses with House 2 missing its number sign.

Chapter 8

Mechanical Reasoning

OVERVIEW

- **What Do Mechanical Reasoning Questions Measure?**
- **Guided Practice: Mechanical Reasoning**
- **Summing It Up**
- **Exercise: Mechanical Reasoning**
- **Answer Key and Explanations**

8

WHAT DO MECHANICAL REASONING QUESTIONS MEASURE?

Mechanical reasoning questions evaluate your general understanding of basic physics within the context of mechanics. Some questions ask you to identify a pictured tool or specify the tool's function. Other questions ask you to predict the outcomes of mechanical activities. Others still require you to infer a mechanical connection to a described event. The questions are designed to determine your ability to visualize the movement of objects in three dimensions and assess how well you understand cause-and-effect relationships between mechanical components.

Just as reasoning and judgment questions do not measure intellectual ability, mechanical reasoning questions do not measure innate mechanical aptitude. Rather than assessing your ability to think abstractly, mechanical reasoning questions assume that you have basic knowledge of the following tools and concepts:

- Levers
- Pulleys
- Springs
- Gears
- Electrical Circuits
- Hand Tools
- Shop Arithmetic

Although you are not required to know about specific firefighting equipment, tools, or techniques before taking the exam, firefighters must have a fundamental working knowledge of mechanics. Firefighters rely heavily on machinery, tools, and safety equipment to perform their duties, so it's important to have a baseline understanding of mechanics that allows you to pinpoint the cause or predict the outcome of a mechanical event.

Expect the mechanical reasoning questions you encounter to focus on the principles of mechanics rather than mathematical calculations; the questions may be presented in a firefighting context, but you will not need previous firefighter training to answer them.

Let's walk through some examples of the different types of mechanical reasoning questions.

GUIDED PRACTICE: MECHANICAL REASONING

Some questions, like the following, ask you to identify a pictured tool or specify the tool's function.

Example

The tool shown here is used to

A. set nails.

B. drill holes in concrete.

C. cut a brick accurately.

D. mark a center punch for holes.

Solution

Even if you're not familiar with the item pictured, we can still make logical deductions to narrow it down. First, have you ever heard of a tool used to "set" nails (choice A)? Probably not, because nails do not need to be set before they're hammered in. Next, does the object in question appear sharp enough to cut brick at a precise angle? It looks blunt and solid, not razor sharp, so we can discard choice C. A "center punch for holes" (choice D) doesn't make much sense—if a hole exists, it's already been punched. This leaves us with choice B, a plausible answer; the object resembles a regular drill-bit with a broad spike at the end that could be used to bore through concrete.

The correct answer is B. The tool shown is a star drill. It is hit with a hammer to make a hole in concrete.

Other questions, like the following, ask you to predict the outcomes of mechanical activities.

Example

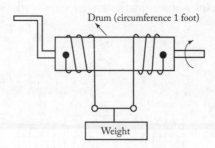

Drum (circumference 1 foot)

Weight

One complete revolution of the windlass drum shown will move the weight up

A. $\frac{1}{2}$ foot.

B. $1\frac{1}{2}$ feet.

C. 1 foot.

D. 2 feet.

Solution

For questions of this nature, it may be helpful to sketch out your own diagram on scratch paper. Also, be particularly aware of direction markers and any measurements provided. The question is asking you to determine the effect of a "complete revolution" around the drum, and the diagram indicates that the circumference of the cylindrical drum is 1 foot.

The correct answer is C. Because the circumference of the drum is 1 foot, one complete revolution of the drum will take up 1 foot of each rope. As each of the separate ropes supporting the weight is shortened by 1 foot, the weight will move up 1 foot.

You may also encounter questions, like the following, that require you to infer a mechanical connection to a described event.

Example

The reason lubricant prevents rubbing surfaces from becoming hot is that the oil

A. is cold and cools off the rubbing metal surfaces.

B. is sticky, preventing the surfaces from moving over each other too rapidly.

C. forms a smooth layer between the two surfaces, preventing them from coming into contact.

D. smooths the surfaces so they move easily over each other.

Solution

If we think through the options provided, we can again make some logical deductions with little prior knowledge here. Intrinsically, oil is neither hot nor cold (choice A); it's a liquid that can be heated or cooled to different temperatures. Stickiness increases friction, which increases heat (choice B), and for choice D to be true, oil would have to actively alter the physical surfaces of the objects it's lubricating.

The correct answer is C. When two pieces of metal rub together, the friction causes a great deal of heat. Oil reduces the friction between the two pieces of metal.

Chapter 8: Mechanical Reasoning   175

Expect questions to focus on principles of mechanics rather than mathematical calculations.

Example

Coupling

Pipe A   Pipe B

8 threads-per-inch

If pipes A and B are free to move back and forth but are held so they cannot turn, and the coupling is turned four revolutions with a wrench, the overall length of the pipes and coupling will

A. decrease $\frac{1}{2}$ inch.

B. remain the same.

C. increase or decrease 1 inch, depending on the direction of turning.

D. increase $\frac{1}{2}$ inch.

Solution

This is a good example of a question for which it's beneficial to review the answer options as soon as you finish reading the problem. The length of the pipes will either increase, decrease, or remain the same. The question tells us pipes A and B "cannot turn," which means only the coupling will be affected. If only the coupling moves, choices A, C, and D are incorrect; regardless of the direction or distance the coupling rotates, the length and position of the pipes will remain the same. You can see that there's little if any math involved here. Instead, this question tests your fundamental understanding of mechanics.

The correct answer is B. If the coupling is turned but the pipes are held firm so they cannot turn, the coupling will move along the length of one or the other of the pipes, but the overall length of the three pieces will remain the same.

To better familiarize yourself with a variety of mechanical reasoning questions, work through the practice exercise following the chapter summary.

Summing It Up

- Mechanical reasoning questions on the firefighter exam assess your understanding of straight-forward mechanical and physical concepts, your ability to visualize the movement of objects through space, and how well you understand cause-and-effect relationships between mechanical components.

- Mechanical reasoning questions assume that you already possess basic knowledge of levers, pulleys, springs, gears, simple electrical circuitry, basic hand tools, and shop arithmetic.

- You are not expected to know about specific firefighting equipment. Remember, however, that fire-fighters rely heavily on machinery, tools, and safety equipment to effectively perform their tasks, so it is important to understand how to predict the outcome of a mechanical activity or determine the mechanical cause of an event.

8

EXERCISE: MECHANICAL REASONING

45 Questions—60 minutes

Directions: Read each question and select the best answer from the choices provided.

---

1. The main reason to use a fiberglass ladder in place of an aluminum ladder is the

   A. length of the ladder.

   B. conductivity of the ladder.

   C. flammability of the ladder.

   D. "rust-resistance" of the ladder.

2. In the figure shown, one complete revolution of the sprocket wheel will bring weight W2 higher than weight W1 by how many inches?

   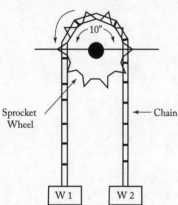

   A. 20

   B. 40

   C. 30

   D. 50

3. Assume all valves in the figure shown are closed.

   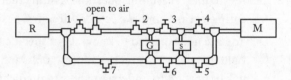

   For air to flow from R through G and then through S to M, which valves must be open?

   A. 1, 2, 6, and 4

   B. 7, 3, and 4

   C. 7, 6, and 4

   D. 7, 3, and 5

4. Nails are galvanized to make

   A. them stronger.

   B. their points sharper.

   C. them smoother.

   D. them rust-resistant.

5. The following figure shows four gears.

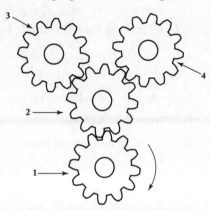

If gear 1 turns as shown, the gears turning in the same direction are

A. 2, 3, and 4.

B. 2 and 4.

C. 2 and 3.

D. 3 and 4.

6. In the figure shown, all four springs are identical.

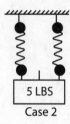

In Case 1, with the springs end to end, the stretch of each spring caused by the 5-pound weight is

A. half as much as in Case 2.

B. the same as in Case 2.

C. twice as much as in Case 2.

D. four times as much as in Case 2.

7. You might use this instrument to complete which of the following tasks?

A. Pitch a tent

B. Poke holes in a fabric

C. Locate studs in a wall

D. Drill multiple holes in a board at equal distance

8. The frequency of oiling and greasing bearings and other moving machine parts depends mainly on the

A. size of the parts requiring lubrication.

B. speed at which the parts move.

C. ability of the operator.

D. amount of use of the equipment.

9.

The tool shown here is a

A. stock screw.

B. screwdriver.

C. drill bit.

D. corkscrew.

10. Why should the plug of a portable tool should be removed from the convenience outlet by grasping the plug, not by pulling on the cord?

A. The plug is easier to grip than the cord.

B. Pulling on the cord might cause the plug to fall on the floor and break.

C. Pulling on the cord might break the wires off the plug terminals.

D. The plug generally is better insulated than the cord.

Chapter 8: Mechanical Reasoning

11. The following figure is a device that attaches to the top of a ladder.

What is the purpose of the device?

A. To allow one to hang the ladder for easier storage

B. To increase the strength of the ladder

C. To give the ladder a greater stability

D. To allow the ladder to function upside down

12. The figure represents an enclosed water chamber that is partially filled with water.

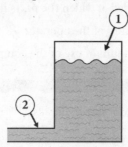

Label 1 indicates air in the chamber, and Label 2 indicates a pipe by which water enters the chamber. If water pressure in the pipe increases, then the

A. water pressure in the chamber will decrease.

B. water level in the chamber will fall.

C. air in the chamber will compress.

D. air in the chamber will expand.

13. When removing the insulation from a wire before making a splice, care should be taken to avoid nicking the wire mainly because

A. its current-carrying capacity will be reduced.

B. its resistance will be increased.

C. its tinning will be injured.

D. it will be more likely to break.

14. Wood screws properly used as compared to nails properly used

A. are easier to install.

B. generally hold better.

C. are easier to drive flush with the surface.

D. are more likely to split the wood.

15. The following figure shows a cutter and a steel block.

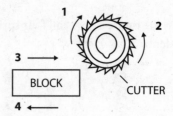

For proper cutting, in which direction should each move?

A. Cutter: 1; Block: 4

B. Cutter: 2; Block: 3

C. Cutter: 1; Block: 3

D. Cutter: 2; Block: 4

16. What is the reading shown on the gauge?

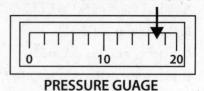

PRESSURE GUAGE

A. 10.35

B. 13.5

C. 10.7

D. 17.0

17. Identify the wrench used principally for pipe work.

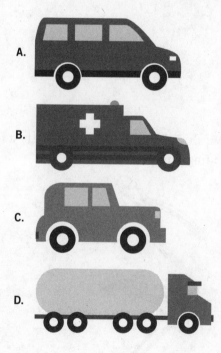

A.

B.

C.

D.

18. Which of the following vehicles is most likely to have difficulty stopping at high speeds?

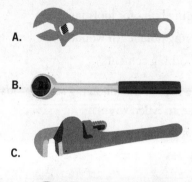

A.

B.

C.

D.

19. To bring the level of the water in the tanks to a height of $2\frac{1}{2}$ feet, what quantity of water needs to be added?

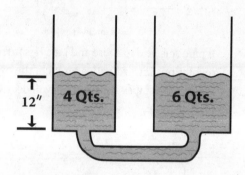

A. 10 quarts

B. 20 quarts

C. 15 quarts

D. 25 quarts

20. Which of the following outlets will accept the plug?

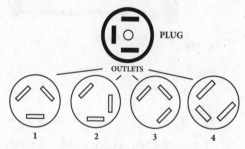

A. 1

B. 2

C. 3

D. 4

21. Identify the tool shown below.

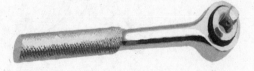

A. A punch

B. A drill holder

C. A Phillips-type screwdriver

D. A socket wrench

Chapter 8: Mechanical Reasoning

8

22.

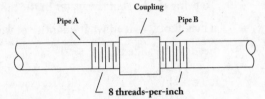

Pipe A   Coupling   Pipe B

8 threads-per-inch

If pipe A is held in a vise and pipe B is turned 10 revolutions inward with a wrench, the overall length of the pipes and coupling will decrease by

A. $\frac{5}{8}$ inch.

B. 2 inches.

C. $1\frac{1}{4}$ inches.

D. $3\frac{3}{4}$ inches.

23. The tool shown here is most often used for cutting which material?

A. Metal

B. Wood

C. Tile

D. Glass

24. Wires are often spliced using a fitting like the one shown below.

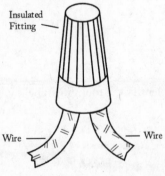

Insulated Fitting

Wire —   — Wire

The use of this fitting does away with the need for

A. skinning.

B. cleaning.

C. twisting.

D. soldering.

25. A trowel is a tool used for

A. clearing out drainpipes.

B. digging holes for footings.

C. carving notches in wood.

D. smoothing cement.

26. With which of the following screw heads do you use an Allen wrench?

A.

B.

C.

D.

27. Which of the tools shown would be best for cutting wire?

A.

B.

C.

D.

28. Which of the following would be best for digging into the ground?

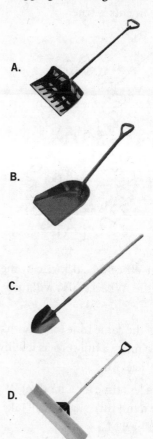

A.

B.

C.

D.

29. Which of the tools shown is used to measure the depth of a hole?

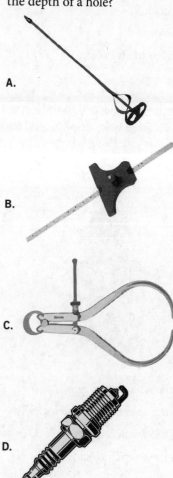

A.

B.

C.

D.

8

Chapter 8: Mechanical Reasoning

30. Neutral wire can quickly be recognized by its

   A. green color.

   B. blue color.

   C. natural or white color.

   D. black color.

31. If a wrench were attached to the top of the hydrant pictured below, how would you turn on the water?

   A. Pull the wrench up.

   B. Turn the wrench counterclockwise.

   C. Push the wrench down.

   D. Turn the wrench clockwise.

32. To exert the greatest force when using a hammer with one hand, you should hold the hammer

   A. near the end of the handle.

   B. in the middle of the handle.

   C. near the head of the hammer.

   D. at the base of the hammerhead.

33. Study the gear wheels in the figure shown here and then determine which of the following statements is true.

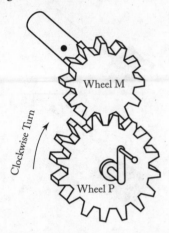

   A. If you turn Wheel M clockwise by means of the handle, Wheel P also will turn clockwise.

   B. It will take the same time for a tooth of Wheel P to make a full turn as it will for a tooth of Wheel M.

   C. It will take less time for a tooth of Wheel P to make a full turn than it will take a tooth of Wheel M.

   D. It will take more time for a tooth of Wheel P to make a full turn than it will for a tooth of Wheel M.

34. Locknuts are frequently used in electrical connections on terminal boards. The purpose of the locknuts is to

   A. eliminate the use of flat washers.

   B. prevent unauthorized personnel from tampering with the connections.

   C. keep the connections from loosening through vibration.

   D. increase the contact area at the connection point.

8

35. For what purpose is the tool shown below designed?

- **A.** To ream holes in wood
- **B.** To countersink holes in soft metals
- **C.** To turn Phillips-head screws
- **D.** To drill holes in concrete

36. For what task is the tool shown below used?

- **A.** Soldering
- **B.** Caulking
- **C.** Shooting
- **D.** Scoring

37. Boxes and fittings intended for outdoor use should be

- **A.** weatherproof.
- **B.** stamped steel no less than No. 16.
- **C.** standard gauge.
- **D.** stamped steel plated with cadmium.

38. The device used to change AC to DC is a

- **A.** frequency changer.
- **B.** regulator.
- **C.** transformer.
- **D.** rectifier.

39. The figure below is a governor on a rotating shaft.

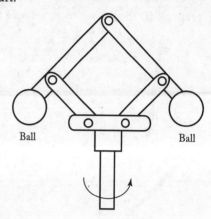

As the shaft speeds up, the governor balls will move

- **A.** down.
- **B.** upward and inward.
- **C.** upward.
- **D.** inward.

40. The purpose of an air valve in a heating system is to

- **A.** prevent pressure from building up in a room due to the heated air.
- **B.** relieve the air from steam radiators.
- **C.** allow excessive steam pressure in the boiler to escape to the atmosphere.
- **D.** control the temperature in the room.

41. If a fuse of higher than the required current rating is used in an electrical circuit,

- **A.** better protection will be afforded.
- **B.** the fuse will blow more often because it carries more current.
- **C.** serious damage might result to the circuit from overload.
- **D.** maintenance of the large fuse will be higher.

8

42. If the following dark lines represent different ways a ladder can be set up, which line represents the safest way to set up a ladder?

A.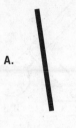

B.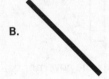

C.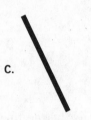

D.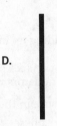

43. Identify the tool shown below.

A. Offset wrench
B. Box wrench
C. Spanner wrench
D. Open-end wrench

44. If gear A makes one clockwise revolution per minute, which one of the following is true?

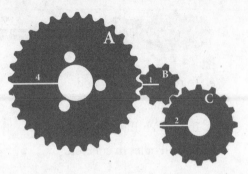

A. Gear B makes one counterclockwise revolution every four minutes.
B. Gear C makes two clockwise revolutions every minute.
C. Gear B makes four clockwise revolutions every minute.
D. Gear C makes one counterclockwise revolution every eight minutes.

45. The sketch here shows a head-on view of a three-pronged plug used with portable electrical power tools.

The function of the U-shaped prong is to

A. ensure that the other two prongs enter the outlet with the proper polarity.
B. provide a half-voltage connection when doing light work.
C. prevent accidental pulling of the plug from the outlet.
D. connect the metallic shell of the tool motor to the ground for grounding.

8

ANSWER KEY AND EXPLANATIONS

1. B	10. C	19. C	28. C	37. A
2. B	11. C	20. C	29. B	38. D
3. D	12. C	21. D	30. C	39. C
4. D	13. D	22. C	31. B	40. B
5. D	14. B	23. A	32. A	41. C
6. C	15. C	24. D	33. D	42. C
7. D	16. D	25. D	34. C	43. D
8. D	17. C	26. C	35. C	44. B
9. C	18. D	27. A	36. B	45. D

1. **The correct answer is B.** The main reason a fiberglass ladder would be used in place of an aluminum ladder is if there were concerns about conductivity or the risk of electrical shock from nearby electrical wires. A fiberglass ladder does not have any advantages in length (choice A) over an aluminum ladder. Fiberglass and aluminum are not flammable (choice C), nor are they susceptible to rusting (choice D).

2. **The correct answer is B.** One half the circumference of the sprocket wheel is 10 inches; therefore, the entire circumference is 20 inches. In one complete revolution of the wheel, the chain will move 20 inches. As weight 2 moves up 20 inches, weight 1 will move down 20 inches. The difference between the heights of the two weights will be 40 inches.

3. **The correct answer is D.** The air from R must follow a route down through valve 7, up through G, through valve 3, down through S, to the right through 5, and then up and over to M. The air could not pass through valves 1 and 2 to G because it would escape through the opening between them (choice A). If either valve 4 or valve 6 were to be opened (choices B and C), the air would be diverted from the appointed route.

4. **The correct answer is D.** A galvanized nail is covered with a protective coating that keeps the nail from rusting.

5. **The correct answer is D.** A turning gear always turns the gear with which it interlocks in the opposite direction. If gear 1 turns clockwise, gear 2 must turn counterclockwise. In turn, gears 3 and 4, because they are both turned by gear 2, must both turn clockwise.

6. **The correct answer is C.** In Case 2, each spring bears half the five-pound weight, or $2\frac{1}{2}$ pounds. In Case 1, each spring bears a full 5 pounds, one after the other. The springs in Case 1 will therefore be stretched twice as much those in Case 2.

7. **The correct answer is D.** The compass shown would be very useful in marking out short, equal distances on a board. The compass would not, of course, be of use in pitching a tent (choice A) or locating studs (choice C). Scissors would be a better option for puncturing fabric (choice B).

8. **The correct answer is D.** Lubrication of machinery is scheduled by time elapsed in accordance with amount of use. Part size (choice A), part movement speed (choice B), and operator ability (choice C) are irrelevant.

9. **The correct answer is C.** The smooth end of the drill bit is inserted into a drill chuck and

tightened for security. When the drill motor starts, the bit turns in rapid motion and drills a hole wherever it is applied.

10. **The correct answer is C.** Yanking at an electric cord can cause hidden damage inside the plug. The force can cause terminals to loosen or bits of wire to break off and fray. Frayed wires can, in turn, contact their opposite poles, causing a fire or short circuit in the plug.

11. **The correct answer is C.** The pictured item is a stabilizer. It attaches to the top of a ladder, giving it greater stability by reducing the likelihood that the ladder will slide to the left or right.

12. **The correct answer is C.** If the water pressure in the pipe increases, more water will flow to the chamber. Because the chamber is closed, air won't be able to escape. Therefore, as more water enters, existing air inside the chamber will be compressed into a smaller space.

13. **The correct answer is D.** A nick in a wire can be dangerous because it weakens the wire at that point and can lead to breakage. If a wire is nicked during stripping, you should cut off the weakened portion and start over. Later breakage from an unnoticed weakness could lead to a short circuit.

14. **The correct answer is B.** Wood screws are usually more difficult to install than nails but are preferable because they tend to hold better and are less likely to split the wood.

15. **The correct answer is C.** For the cutter to cut the block, the two must be in contact; the block must therefore move in direction 3 to establish contact. This eliminates choices A and D. With only choices B and C remaining, consider that for the cutter to cut, it must move in a direction that enables the sharp edge of its teeth to bite into an object. This means that the cutter must move in direction 1. If the cutter were to

move in direction 2, as choice B indicates, the back of the teeth would slide off the block without cutting.

16. **The correct answer is D.** Because there are 10 divisions and 20 units, each division marks two units. The pointer is set at $3\frac{1}{2}$ divisions above the 10-unit mark; $3\frac{1}{2}$ multiplied by 2 is 7, and 10 more is 17.

17. **The correct answer is C.** This is a pipe wrench. Choice A is a crescent or adjustable wrench, choice B is a ratchet wrench, and choice D is an open-end wrench.

18. **The correct answer is D.** A larger vehicle is likely to be heavier and, therefore, is more likely to have difficulty stopping at high speeds.

19. **The correct answer is C.** Ten quarts of water has brought the water level to 1 foot. An additional 15 quarts would raise the water level by $1\frac{1}{2}$ feet to a total height of $2\frac{1}{2}$ feet. Choice A (10 quarts) would bring the level to 2 feet, choice B (20 quarts) to 3 feet, and choice D (25 quarts) to $3\frac{1}{2}$ feet.

20. **The correct answer is C.** Special plug types are compatible only with similarly shaped sockets. This plug has three flat contact pins of identical size, set at right angles to each other. Only outlet 3 has the same characteristics. The other outlets feature inputs that do not correspond to the pins on the plug.

21. **The correct answer is D.** The tool shown is a socket wrench. It is a bar-shaped wrench into which interchangeable sockets can be inserted that are designed to fit nuts and bolts of specific sizes.

22. **The correct answer is C.** The overall length of the pipes and coupling could decrease or increase depending on the direction Pipe B is turned. As stated in this question, however, Pipe B is turned to disappear into

8

the coupling. Because there are eight threads to the inch, eight complete revolutions of the pipe would shorten the pipes and coupling by 1 inch. An additional two turns, for a total of ten, would shorten the pipes and coupling by an additional $\frac{2}{8}$, or $\frac{1}{4}$, of an inch.

23. **The correct answer is A.** The tool shown is a hacksaw, which is used to cut metal.

24. **The correct answer is D.** This is a mechanical or solderless connector. It does away with the need to solder wires and is commonly found in house wiring.

25. **The correct answer is D.** A trowel is a flat-surfaced tool used to smooth cement. A drain snake is used to clear out drainpipes (choice A). Augers are used to dig holes for footings (choice B). A circular saw, router, or a hammer and chisel can be used to cut notches in wood (choice C).

26. **The correct answer is C.** An Allen wrench is used to manipulate a screw with a hexagon-shaped socket in its head. You would use a flat-head screwdriver for a screw with a slotted screw drive (choice A), and a Phillips or Frearson screwdriver for a screw with a cross-slotted screw drive (choice B). Specialized or tamper-resistant screw drives (choice D) require customized bits.

27. **The correct answer is A.** This is a wire cutter. Choice B is a pruning clipper, choice C is a hedge clipper, and choice D is a pair of pliers.

28. **The correct answer is C.** A digging shovel with a pointed tip is best for digging into soft, tilled soil. Choices A and D are used to shovel snow, and choice B is used to shovel grain.

29. **The correct answer is B.** A depth gauge is used to measure the depth of a hole. The flattened part rests at the top of the hole, and the ruler is pushed down into the hole until

it reaches the bottom. The depth of the hole is then read from the ruler. Choice A is a paint mixer attachment for a drill. Choice C is an outside spring caliper, used to measure the diameter or thickness of an object. Choice D is a spark plug.

30. **The correct answer is C.** The neutral wire is white. The hot lead is black (choice D) and the ground wire is green (choice A). A blue wire (choice B) indicates a phase 3 conductor in a three-phase alternating current (AC).

31. **The correct answer is B.** Just as with any water valve, you should turn it counter-clockwise to turn the water on. Pulling the wrench up (choice A) or pushing it down (choice C) will have no effect. Turning the wrench clockwise (choice D) will further tighten the valve.

32. **The correct answer is A.** Holding the hammer near the end of the handle enables you to take full advantage of the hammer's weight with each swing and will result in a more forceful blow.

33. **The correct answer is D.** Wheel P has 16 teeth; Wheel M has 12 teeth. When Wheel M makes a full turn, Wheel P will still have four more teeth to turn. Therefore, Wheel P takes more time to make a full turn.

34. **The correct answer is C.** Locknuts are bent so their metal edges bite into the terminal board to prevent loosening as a result of vibration; they require the use of a wrench to pry them loose.

35. **The correct answer is C.** While this Phillips-head screwdriver *could* be used to create holes in wood (choice A), soft metals (choice B), and concrete (choice C), its proper use is to turn Phillips or cross-slotted screws.

36. **The correct answer is B.** The tool pictured is a caulk gun and is used for caulking.

37. **The correct answer is A.** Outdoor boxes and fittings must be weatherproof to withstand any problems caused by moisture.

38. **The correct answer is D.** A rectifier, or diode, is a device that changes AC to DC.

39. **The correct answer is C.** The centrifugal force acts to pull the balls outward, but, because the two balls are connected to a yolk around the center bar, this outward motion manifests in the balls moving upward.

40. **The correct answer is B.** An air valve on a radiator removes air from the steam pipes. If air is trapped in the pipes, it prevents the steam from going to the radiator, which prevents the radiator from producing heat.

41. **The correct answer is C.** Never use a fuse with a rating higher than the one specifically called for in the circuit. A fuse is a safety device used to protect a circuit from serious damage caused by too high a current.

42. **The correct answer is C.** The best angle for a ladder setup is about 75 degrees. Both choices A and D might cause a person standing at the top to fall over backward. Choice B might cause the bottom of the ladder to slip backward, causing the ladder to fall.

43. **The correct answer is D.** The open face on this tool shows that it is an open-end wrench.

44. **The correct answer is B.** Gear A turns the opposite direction as gear B. A clockwise turn of A results in a counterclockwise revolution of B. Because the distance traversed by A (perimeter = $\pi \times$ diameter = $\pi \times 4$) is twice that of C (perimeter = $\pi \times 2$), the speed of C is doubled.

45. **The correct answer is D.** The third prong in the plug is the grounding wire.

8

Chapter 9

Math

OVERVIEW

- **Common Math Subjects Covered on the Exam**
- **Essential Math Concepts**
- **Fractions**
- **Percentages**
- **Unit Conversions**
- **Algebraic Equations**
- **Geometry**
- **Word Problems**
- **Summing It Up**
- **Formula Sheet**
- **Exercise: Math Practice**
- **Answer Key and Explanations**

While reading comprehension is one of the most important skills necessary to do well on many firefighting exams, knowing basic math is also essential. From calculating how long it takes to get from one place to another, to determining the square footage of a room, to converting liquid measurements from ounces to gallons, firefighters use math every day. Knowing how to do basic math calculations is necessary for every firefighter.

COMMON MATH SUBJECTS COVERED ON THE EXAM

The firefighter's exam requires basic command of the following math skills:

- Addition
- Subtraction
- Multiplication
- Division
- Fractions

- Percentages
- Conversion problems
- Basic algebra
- Geometry
- Word problems

The following sections in this chapter outline some of the basic mathematics rules procedures and formulas that you should be comfortable with as you go into your exam. Rather than working through a series of guided practice questions, you will have an opportunity to practice your skills with some concept reviews in select sections, and you can judge your progress by checking your work against the answer explanations that follow the review exercises. Work through these sections and the exercises carefully and be honest with

9

yourself about your accuracy and speed as you solve these problems. Note which problems are difficult for you as well as those that are easy. After you've completed this section, you'll know exactly which areas you need to strengthen.

ESSENTIAL MATH CONCEPTS

To begin, here is a list of a few basic rules that you must master for speed and accuracy in mathematical computation. These are the rules you should memorize well enough to have at your fingertips when needed:

Any number multiplied by 0 = 0.

$$5 \times 0 = 0$$

If 0 is divided by any number, the answer is 0.

$$0 \div 2 = 0$$

If 0 is added to any number, that number does not change.

$$7 + 0 = 7$$

If 0 is subtracted from any number, that number does not change.

$$4 - 0 = 4$$

If you multiply a number by 1, that number does not change.

$$3 \times 1 = 3$$

If you divide a number by 1, that number does not change.

$$6 \div 1 = 6$$

A number added to itself is doubled.

$$4 + 4 = 8$$

If you subtract a number from itself, the answer is 0.

$$9 - 9 = 0$$

If you divide a number by itself, the answer is 1.

$$8 \div 8 = 1$$

Order of Operations

Always apply the proper **order of operations** to equations that may require you to complete multiple operations to solve them. You can remember the correct order by memorizing the acronym PEMDAS, or by using the related mnemonic device: "Please excuse my dear Aunt Sally."

We'll put PEMDAS to work on the following equation:

$$2 \times 4^2 + 5^2 \div (26 - 1) - 1 =$$

$$2 \times 4^2 + 5^2 \div (26 - 1) - 1 =$$

P	Parentheses	$2 \times 4^2 + 5^2 \div \boxed{(26 - 1)} - 1 =$
E	Exponents	$2 \times \boxed{4^2} + \boxed{5^2} \div 25 - 1 =$
M	Multiplication	$\boxed{2 \times 16} + 25 \div 25 - 1 =$
D	Division	$32 + \boxed{25 \div 25} - 1 =$
A	Addition	$\boxed{32 + 1} - 1 =$
S	Subtraction	$\boxed{33 - 1} = \underline{32} \; (\text{final answer})$

NOTE

PEMDAS lists multiplication before division and addition before subtraction, but these inverse operation pairs should actually be performed from left to right. If in the example the multiplication and division signs were switched, you would work from left to right, completing the division problem first. The same would be true if the addition and subtraction signs were reversed.

9

The Number Line and Signed Numbers

The **number line** exists to both sides of zero. Each positive number on the right of zero has a negative counterpart to the left of zero. The number line below shows the location of some pairs of numbers (+4, –4; +2, –2; +1, –1).

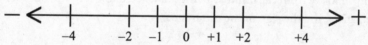

Because each number of a pair is located the same distance from zero (though in different directions), each has the same absolute value. Two vertical bars symbolize absolute value:

$$|+4| = |-4| = 4$$

The absolute value of +4 equals the absolute value of –4. Both are equivalent to 4. If you think of absolute value as the distance from zero, regardless of direction, you will understand it easily. The absolute value of any number, positive or negative, is always expressed as a positive number.

Addition of Signed Numbers

When we add two oppositely signed numbers having the same absolute value, the sum is zero.

$$(+10) + (-10) = 0$$

$$(-1.5) + (+1.5) = 0$$

$$(-0.010) + (+0.010) = 0$$

$$\left(+\frac{3}{4}\right)+\left(-\frac{3}{4}\right)=0$$

If one of the two oppositely signed numbers is greater in absolute value, the sum is equal to the amount of that excess and carries the same sign as the number having the greater absolute value.

$$(+2) + (-1) = +1$$

$$(+8) + (-9) = -1$$

$$(-2.5) + (+2.0) = -0.5$$

$$\left(-\frac{3}{4}\right)+\left(+\frac{1}{2}\right)=-\frac{1}{4}$$

Subtraction of Signed Numbers

Subtraction is the operation that finds the difference between two numbers, including the difference between signed numbers. When subtracting signed numbers, it is helpful to refer to a number line.

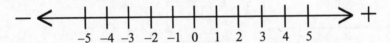

For example, if we wish to subtract +2 from +5, we can use the number line to see that the difference is +3. We give the sign to the difference that represents the direction we are moving along the number line from the number being subtracted to the number from which you are subtracting. In this case, because we are subtracting +2 from +5, we count three units in a positive direction from +2 to +5 on the number line.

When subtracting signed numbers:

- The distance between the two numbers gives you the absolute value of the difference.
- The direction you move from the number being subtracted to get to the number from which you are subtracting gives you the sign of the difference.

Example

Subtract –3 from +5.

Solution

Distance on the number line between –3 and +5 is 8 units.

Direction is from negative to positive—a positive direction.

Answer is +8.

Example

Subtract –6 from –8.

Solution

Distance on number line between –6 and –8 is 2 units.

Direction is from –6 to –8—a negative direction.

Answer is –2.

A quick way to subtract signed numbers accurately involves placing the numbers in columns, reversing the sign of the number being subtracted and then adding the two.

Example

Subtract +26 from +15.

Solution

$$+15 = +15$$
$$+26 = -26$$
$$ = -11$$

Example

Subtract –35 from +10.

Solution

$$+10 = +10$$
$$-35 = +35$$
$$ = +45$$

Notice that in each of the examples, we found the correct answer by reversing the sign of the number being subtracted and then adding.

Multiplication of Signed Numbers

Signed numbers are multiplied as any other numbers would be, with the following exceptions:

The product of two negative numbers is positive.

$$(-3) \times (-6) = +18$$

The product of two positive numbers is positive.

$$(+3.05) \times (+6) = +18.30$$

The product of a negative and positive number is negative.

$$\left(+4\frac{1}{2}\right) \times (-3) = -13\frac{1}{2}$$
$$(+1) \times (-1) \times (+1) = -1$$

Division of Signed Numbers

As with multiplication, the division of signed numbers requires you to observe three simple rules:

When dividing a positive number by a negative number, the result is negative.

$$(+6) \div (-3) = -2$$

When dividing a negative number by a positive number, the result is negative.

$$(-6) \div (+3) = -2$$

> **NOTE**
>
> Change the sign of the number being subtracted and follow the rules for addition.

> **NOTE**
>
> If the signs are the same, the product is positive. If the signs are different, the product is negative.

9

When dividing a negative number by a negative number or a positive number by a positive number, the result is positive.

$$(-6) \div (-3) = +2$$

$$(+6) \div (+3) = +2$$

Concept Review: Signed Numbers

Solve the following signed number addition and subtraction problems. The answer key follows.

1. $(+5) + (+8) =$
2. $(+6) + (-3) =$
3. $(+4) + (-12) =$
4. $(-7) + (+2) =$
5. $\left(-8\frac{1}{2}\right) + \left(+4\frac{1}{4}\right) =$
6. $(+4) - (-58) =$
7. $(+75) - (+27) =$
8. $(-12.6) - (-5.3) =$
9. $(-35) - (+35) =$
10. $(+56.1) - (+56.7) =$

11. $(+5) \times (+8) =$
12. $(+12) \times (-3) =$
13. $(-6) \times (-21) =$
14. $(-4) \times (-10) =$
15. $(+3.3) \times (-5.8) =$
16. $(-75) \div (+3) =$
17. $(+5.6) \div (-0.7) =$
18. $(-3.5) \div (-5) =$
19. $\left(+6\frac{1}{2}\right) \div \left(+3\frac{1}{4}\right) =$
20. $(-8.2) \div (-1) =$

Answer Key

1. +13
2. +3
3. -8
4. -5
5. $-4\frac{1}{4}$
6. +62
7. +48
8. -7.3
9. -70
10. -0.6

11. +40
12. -36
13. +126
14. +40
15. -19.14
16. -25
17. -8
18. +0.7
19. +2
20. 8.2

FRACTIONS

Fractions are used to indicate parts of things. A fraction consists of a **numerator** and a **denominator**.

$$\frac{3}{4} \xleftarrow{} \text{numerator} \xrightarrow{} \frac{7}{8}$$
$$\text{denominator}$$

The denominator tells you how many equal parts the object or number has been divided into, and the numerator tells how many of those parts we are concerned with.

Example

Divide a baseball game, a football game, and a hockey game into convenient numbers of parts. Write a fraction to answer each equation.

1. If a pitcher played two innings, how much of the whole baseball game did he play?

2. If a quarterback played three quarters of a football game, how much of the whole game did he play?

3. If a goalie played two periods of a hockey game, how much of the whole game did he play?

Solution 1

A baseball game is conveniently divided into nine parts (each an inning). The pitcher pitched two innings. Therefore, he played $\frac{2}{9}$ of the game. The denominator represents the nine parts the game is divided into; the numerator, the two parts we are concerned with.

Solution 2

Similarly, there are four quarters in a football game, and a quarterback playing three of those quarters plays in $\frac{3}{4}$ of the game.

Solution 3

There are three periods in hockey, and the goalie played in two of them. Therefore, he played in $\frac{2}{3}$ of the game.

Equivalent Fractions

Fractions having different denominators and numerators may still represent the same amount. Such fractions are called **equivalent fractions**.

For example, the following circle is divided into two equal parts. Write a fraction to indicate how much of the circle is shaded.

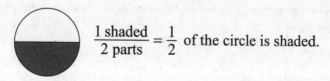

$$\frac{1 \text{ shaded}}{2 \text{ parts}} = \frac{1}{2} \text{ of the circle is shaded.}$$

The circle below is divided into four equal parts. Write a fraction to indicate how much of the circle is shaded.

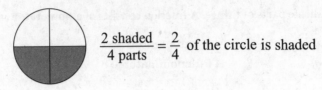

$$\frac{2 \text{ shaded}}{4 \text{ parts}} = \frac{2}{4} \text{ of the circle is shaded}$$

This circle is divided into eight equal parts. Write a fraction to indicate how much of the circle is shaded.

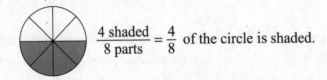

$$\frac{4 \text{ shaded}}{8 \text{ parts}} = \frac{4}{8} \text{ of the circle is shaded.}$$

In each circle, the same amount was shaded. This should show you that there is more than one way to indicate one half of something.

The fractions $\frac{1}{2}$, $\frac{2}{4}$, and $\frac{4}{8}$ that you wrote are equivalent fractions because they all represent the same amount. Notice that the denominator is twice as large as the numerator in every case. Any fraction you write that has a denominator that is exactly twice as large as the numerator will be equivalent to $\frac{1}{2}$.

Example

Write other fractions equivalent to $\frac{1}{2}$.

Solution

Any fraction that has a denominator that is twice as large as the numerator: $\frac{3}{6}$, $\frac{5}{10}$, $\frac{6}{12}$, $\frac{32}{64}$, etc.

Adding and Subtracting Fractions

To add fractions having the same denominators, simply add the numerators.

Example

Add: $\frac{1}{4} + \frac{3}{4} + \frac{3}{4}$

Solution

The denominators are the same, so just add the numerators to arrive at the answer, $\frac{7}{4}$, or $1\frac{3}{4}$.

To find the difference between two fractions having the same denominators, simply subtract the numerators, leaving the denominators alone.

Example

Find the difference between $\frac{7}{8}$ and $\frac{3}{8}$.

Solution

$\frac{7}{8} - \frac{3}{8} = \frac{4}{8}$. Simplified to simplest form, $\frac{4}{8} = \frac{1}{2}$.

To add or subtract fractions having different denominators, you will have to find a **common denominator**. A common denominator is a number that can be divided by the denominators of all the fractions in the problem without a remainder.

Example

Find a common denominator for $\frac{1}{4}$ and $\frac{1}{3}$.

Solution

12 can be divided by both 4 and 3:

$\frac{1}{4}$ is equivalent to $\frac{3}{12}$.

$\frac{1}{3}$ is equivalent to $\frac{4}{12}$.

We can now add the fractions because we have written equivalent fractions with a common denominator.

$$\frac{3}{12} + \frac{4}{12} = \frac{7}{12}$$

Therefore:

$$\frac{1}{4} + \frac{1}{3} = \frac{7}{12}$$

Seven-twelfths is in simplest form because 7 and 12 do not have a whole number (other than 1) by which they are both divisible.

Multiplying and Dividing Fractions

When multiplying fractions, multiply numerators by numerators and denominators by denominators.

$$\frac{3}{5} \times \frac{4}{7} \times \frac{1}{5} = \frac{3 \times 4 \times 1}{5 \times 7 \times 5} = \frac{12}{175}$$

When multiplying fractions, try to work with numbers that are as small as possible. You can make numbers smaller by dividing out common factors. Do this by dividing the numerator of any one fraction and the denominator of any one fraction by the same number.

$$\frac{{}^{1}\cancel{3}}{\cancel{4}_{2}} \times \frac{{}^{1}\cancel{2}}{\cancel{9}_{3}} = \frac{1 \times 1}{2 \times 3} = \frac{1}{6}$$

In this case, the numerator of the first fraction and the denominator of the other fraction were divided by 3, while the denominator of the first fraction and the numerator of the other fraction were divided by 2.

To divide by a fraction, multiply by the reciprocal of the divisor.

$$\frac{3}{16} \div \frac{1}{8} = \frac{3}{\cancel{16}_{2}} \times \frac{{}^{1}\cancel{8}}{1} = \frac{3}{2} = 1\frac{1}{2}$$

Concept Review: Multiplying and Dividing Fractions

Divide out common factors wherever possible and express your answers in simplest form. The answer key follows.

1. $\dfrac{4}{5} \times \dfrac{3}{6} =$

2. $\dfrac{2}{4} \times \dfrac{8}{12} \times \dfrac{7}{1} =$

3. $\dfrac{3}{4} \div \dfrac{3}{8} =$

4. $\dfrac{5}{2} \div \dfrac{3}{6} =$

5. $\dfrac{8}{9} \times \dfrac{3}{4} \times \dfrac{1}{2} =$

6. $\dfrac{7}{8} \div \dfrac{2}{3} =$

7. $\dfrac{4}{16} \times \dfrac{8}{12} \times \dfrac{10}{13} =$

8. $\dfrac{1}{6} \times \dfrac{7}{6} \times \dfrac{12}{3} =$

9. $\dfrac{3}{7} \div \dfrac{9}{4} =$

10. $\dfrac{2}{3} \div \dfrac{2}{3} =$

Answer Key

1. $\dfrac{2}{5}$

2. $2\dfrac{1}{3}$

3. 2

4. $\dfrac{15}{3} = 5$

5. $\dfrac{1}{3}$

6. $\dfrac{21}{16} = 1\dfrac{5}{16}$

7. $\dfrac{5}{39}$

8. $\dfrac{7}{9}$

9. $\dfrac{4}{21}$

10. 1

The fraction bar in a fraction means "divided by." To rename a fraction as a decimal, follow through on the division.

$$\frac{4}{5} = 4 \div 5 = 0.8$$

To rename a decimal as a percent, multiply by 100, move the decimal point two places to the right, and attach a percent sign.

$$0.8 = 80\%$$

PERCENTAGES

Percentage ("hundredths of") is a convenient and widely used way of measuring all sorts of things. By measuring in hundredths, we can be very precise and notice small changes.

There is a relationship between decimals, fractions, and percentages. The following notes will help you to convert numbers from one of these forms to another:

1. To change a percentage to a decimal, remove the percent sign (%) and divide by 100.
2. To change a decimal to a percentage, add the % sign and multiply by 100.
3. To change a percentage to a fraction, remove the % sign and divide by 100.
4. To change a fraction to a percentage, multiply by 100 and add the percent sign (%).

Here are some common percentage and fractional equivalents you should remember:

- Ten percent (10%) is one tenth $\left(\dfrac{1}{10}\right)$, or 0.10.

- Twelve and one-half percent (12.5%) is one eighth $\left(\dfrac{1}{8}\right)$, or 0.125.

- Twenty percent (20%) is one fifth $\left(\dfrac{1}{5}\right)$, or 0.20.

- Twenty-five percent (25%) is one fourth $\left(\dfrac{1}{4}\right)$, or 0.25.

- Thirty-three and one-third percent $\left(33\dfrac{1}{3}\%\right)$ is one third $\left(\dfrac{1}{3}\right)$, or $0.\overline{333}$.

- Fifty percent (50%) is one half $\left(\dfrac{1}{2}\right)$, or 0.50.

- Sixty-six and two-thirds percent $\left(66\dfrac{2}{3}\%\right)$ is two thirds $\left(\dfrac{2}{3}\right)$, or $0.\overline{666}$.

- Seventy-five percent (75%) is three fourths $\left(\dfrac{3}{4}\right)$, or 0.75.

To find a percentage of a number, change the percentage to a decimal and multiply the number by it.

Example

What is 5% of 80?

Solution

5% of 80 = 80 × 0.05 = 4

To find out what a number is when given a percentage of it, change the percentage to a decimal and divide the given number by it.

Example

5 is 10% of what number?

Solution

5 ÷ 0.10 = 50

To find what percentage one number is of another number, create a fraction by placing the part over the whole. Simplify the fraction if possible, then rename it as a decimal (remember the fraction bar means divided by, so divide the numerator by the denominator), and rename the answer as a percentage by multiplying by 100, moving the decimal point two places to the right.

Example

4 is what percent of 80?

Solution

$$\frac{4}{80} = \frac{1}{20} = 0.05 = 5\%$$

Concept Review: Percentages

Solve the following percentage problems in the space provided. The answer key follows.

1. 10% of 32 =
2. 8 is 25% of what number?
3. 12 is what percent of 24?
4. 20% of 360 =
5. 5 is what percent of 60?
6. 12 is 8% of what number?
7. 6% of 36 =
8. 25 is 5% of what number?
9. 70 is what percent of 140?
10. What percent of 100 is 19?

Answer Key

1. $32 \times 0.10 = 3.2$
2. $8 \div 0.25 = 32$
3. $\frac{12}{24} = \frac{1}{2} = 0.5 = 50\%$
4. $360 \times 0.20 = 72$
5. $\frac{5}{60} = \frac{1}{12} = 0.083\overline{3} = 8\frac{1}{3}\%$
6. $12 \div 0.08 = 150$
7. $36 \times 0.06 = 2.16$
8. $25 \div 0.05 = 500$
9. $\frac{70}{140} = \frac{1}{2} = 0.5 = 50\%$
10. $\frac{19}{100} = 0.19 = 19\%$

Percent of Change

Another useful skill to have when working with percentages is calculating the percent of change. A common scenario in which this calculation would be needed is when trying to determine the price of an item after a discount of a certain percent has been applied.

As an example, say you find a kit of smoke detectors on sale. Normally priced at $60, the kit is on sale for 10% off. To find out how much that kit will cost, we need to first set up the percent change formula.

$$\frac{\% \text{ change}}{100} = \frac{\text{difference}}{\text{original\#}}$$

To get the new price, we need two pieces of information. We know the original price was $60, and the discount is ten percent. With that, we can fill the spaces in the formula.

$$\frac{10}{100} = \frac{x}{60}$$

From here, we cross-multiply.

$$\frac{10 \times 60}{100 \times x} = \frac{600}{100x}, \text{ or } 600 = 100x, \text{ which reduces to } 6 = x.$$

Subtract this from the original price to find how much the smoke detector set costs now.

$$\$60 - \$6 = \$54$$

What if you know the old price and the new, but you need to find the percent change between the two? Using the smoke detector kit example again, the original price was $60, and the new price is $54, so plug those figures into the percent change formula.

$$\frac{x}{100} = \frac{6}{60}$$

Cross multiply to obtain $600 = 60x$, which reduces to $10 = x$. The percent change in price is 10%.

Concept Review: Percent of Change

Using the percent change formula, find each requested value. The answer key follows.

1. 25% of 90
2. 33% of 250
3. 10% of 500
4. 15% of 30
5. 45% of 400.5

Convert the following fractions to percentages and solve.

6. $\frac{1}{3}$ of 18

7. $\frac{4}{5}$ of 200

8. $\frac{1}{12}$ of 700

9. $\frac{1}{4}$ of 30

10. $\frac{1}{2}$ of 17.3

9

Answer Key

1.	22.5	6.	6
2.	82.5	7.	160
3.	50	8.	58.3̄33
4.	4.5	9.	7.5
5.	180.225	10.	8.65

UNIT CONVERSIONS

Converting one unit of measurement to another is yet another skill you will need to apply, both on the math portion of the exam and as a firefighter. The following is a glossary of measurement terms and their abbreviations. Below that is a list of common measurement conversions.

Metric System

- Millimeter = mm
- Centimeter = cm
- Meter = m
- Kilometer = km
- Milligram = mg
- Gram = g
- Kilogram = kg
- Milliliter = ml
- Liter = l
- Celsius = °C
- Fahrenheit = °F

Standard (US) System

- Inches = in. or "
- Feet = ft. or '
- Yard = yd.
- Miles = mi.
- Ounce = oz.
- Fluid Ounce = fl. oz.
- Pound = lb. or #
- Cup = c.
- Pint = pt.
- Quart = qt.
- Gallon = gal.

Common Conversions

- 1 km = 1,000 m = 100,000 cm = 1,000,000 mm
- 1 kg = 1,000 g = 1,000,000 mg
- 1 ft. = 12 in.
- 1 yd. = 3 ft. = 36 in.
- 1 mi. = 5,280 ft.
- 1 lb. = 16 oz.
- 1 ton = 2,000 lb.
- 1 gal. = 4 qts. = 16 c.

TIP

You're not expected to memorize all these conversions. But you should know the basics, quarts to gallons, meter to kilometer, ounces to pounds. Remember, the metric system is based on factors of ten; ten millimeters in a centimeter, 1,000 meters in a kilometer, etc.

9

Common Equivalencies

When converting from one system to another, you need to know equivalent values. Here is a list of common equivalencies.

- 1 mi. = 1.96 km = 5,280 ft.
- 1 km = 0.62 mi. = 3,280.8 ft.
- 1 ft. = 30.48 cm = 304.8 mm
- 1 in. = 2.54 cm = 25.4 mm
- 1 m = 3.28 ft. = 39.37 in.
- 1 kg = 2.2 lb. = 35.27 oz.

- 1 lb. = 0.453 kg = 453 g
- 1 gal. = 3.785 l
- 1 l = 0.264 gal. = 1.056 qt. = 4.2 c.
- 1°C = 33.8°F
- 1°F = –17.2°C
- 1°K = –272°C = –457.8°F

Conversion Charts and Formulas

Now let's look at common conversions for length, weight, and volume.

METRIC UNIT CONVERSIONS		
Length and Distance		
when you know:	*multiply by:*	*to find:*
inches	2.5400	centimeters
feet	0.3048	meters
yards	0.9144	meters
miles	1.6093	kilometers
millimeters	0.0394	inches
centimeters	0.3937	inches
meters	3.2808	feet
meters	1.0936	yards
kilometers	0.6214	miles
Weight and Mass		
when you know:	*multiply by:*	*to find:*
ounces	28.3495	grams
pounds	0.4536	kilograms
short tons	0.9072	metric tons
kilograms	2.2046	pounds
metric tons	1.1023	short tons
Volume and Capacity (Liquid)		
when you know:	*multiply by:*	*to find:*
pints (US)	0.4732	liters
quarts (US)	0.9463	liters
gallons (US)	3.7853	liters
liters	2.1134	pints (US)
liters	1.0567	quarts (US)

9

For temperatures, you will have to remember the conversion formulas.

From	To Fahrenheit	To Celsius	To Kelvin
Fahrenheit (F)	F	5/9 (F – 32)	9/5(F – 32) + 273
Celsius (C)	(C • 9 / 5) + 32	C	C + 273.15
Kelvin (K)	9/5(K – 273) + 32	K – 273.15	K

It will be useful to memorize the following specific temperature values as well, as they are most often used as starting points for temperature-related questions:

Temperature Value	Fahrenheit	Celsius	Kelvin
Freezing	32°	0°	273.15K
Boiling	212°	100°	373.15K
Body Temperature	98.6°	37°	310K

Concept Review: Unit Conversions

Solve each conversion problem. The answer key follows.

1. How many feet in a mile?

2. How many kilometers is 3,500 m?

3. How many quarts are in a 2-liter soda bottle?

4. How many inches is 17.78 cm?

5. How warm in Celsius is a 104°F bath?

6. How many feet are in 2 meters?

7. How many liters in one gallon?

8. A 180°C oven is what temperature in Fahrenheit?

Answer Key

1. 5,280 ft.

2. 3.5 km

3. 2.11 qt.

4. 7 in.

5. 40°C

6. 6.56 ft.

7. 3.785 l

8. 356°F

ALGEBRAIC EQUATIONS

Algebra deals with symbols and the rules for working with those symbols, or **variables**, in equations or inequalities. An equation is an equality. The values on either side of the equal sign in an equation must be equal. In order to learn the value of an unknown in an equation, do the same thing to both sides of the equation to leave the unknown on one side of the equal sign and its value on the other side.

Example

$x - 2 = 8$

Solution

Add 2 to both sides of the equation:

$$x - 2 + 2 = 8 + 2$$
$$x = 10$$

Example

$5x = 25$

Solution

Divide both sides of the equation by 5:

$$\left(\frac{^{1}\cancel{5}x}{\cancel{5}_{1}} \right) = \left(\frac{25}{5} \right)$$
$$x = 5$$

Example

$y + 9 = 15$

Solution

Subtract 9 from both sides of the equation:

$$y + 9 - 9 = 15 - 9$$
$$y = 6$$

Example

$a \div 4 = 48$

Solution

Multiply both sides of the equation by 4:

$$\cancel{4}\left(\frac{a}{\cancel{4}_{1}} \right) = 48 \times 4$$
$$a = 192$$

9

Sometimes more than one step is required to solve an equation.

Example

$6a \div 4 = 48$

Solution

First, multiply both sides of the equation by 4:

$$\frac{6a}{4} \times \frac{4}{1} = 48 \times 4$$

$$6a = 192$$

Then divide both sides of the equation by 6:

$$\frac{^1\cancel{6}a}{\cancel{6}_1} = \frac{192}{6}$$

$$a = 32$$

Concept Review: Algebraic Equations

Solve the following equations for x. The answer key follows.

1. $x + 13 = 25$
2. $4x = 84$
3. $x - 5 = 28$
4. $x \div 9 = 4$
5. $3x + 2 = 14$

6. $\frac{x}{4} - 2 - 4 = 0$
7. $10x - 27 = 73$
8. $2x \div 4 = 13$
9. $8x + 9 = 81$
10. $2x \div 11 = 6$

Answer Key

1. $x = 12$
2. $x = 21$
3. $x = 33$
4. $x = 36$
5. $x = 4$

6. $x = 24$
7. $x = 10$
8. $x = 26$
9. $x = 9$
10. $x = 33$

GEOMETRY

Most of the geometry problems you may encounter on the exam will deal with area, perimeter, and volume, which are concepts that you will need to be familiar with when determining the best use of equipment, allocation of resources, and most efficient approaches to a fire scene. to A major component to solving geometry problems is remembering the formulas for the figures involved. The following sections will provide a review of the formulas you should memorize before taking the exam. In addition, a removable list of formulas is included at the end of the chapter for you to study.

Area of Plane Figures

Area is the space enclosed by a plane (flat) figure. Area is always measured in square units. Each basic plane figure has a formula to determine its area, which involves the multiplication of its base and height.

Rectangles and Squares

A rectangle is a plane figure with four right angles. Opposite sides of a rectangle are of equal length and are parallel to each other. To find the area of a rectangle, multiply the length of the base of the rectangle by the length of its height.

9 in.

Area = Base × Height

A = **20 in. × 9 in.**

A = **180 in.²**

20 in.

A square is a rectangle in which all four sides are the same length. You find the area of a square by squaring the length of one side, which is the same as multiplying the square's length by its width.

4 in.

4 in.

$A = s^2$

$A = 4$ in. × 4 in.

$A = 16$ sq. in.

Triangles

A triangle is a three-sided plane figure. You find the area of a triangle by multiplying the base by the altitude (height) and dividing by two.

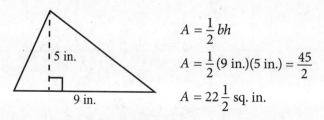

5 in.

9 in.

$A = \dfrac{1}{2} bh$

$A = \dfrac{1}{2} (9 \text{ in.})(5 \text{ in.}) = \dfrac{45}{2}$

$A = 22\dfrac{1}{2}$ sq. in.

Circles

Because circles lack a measurable base and height, we calculate their area by measuring the distance from the center to the edge, also known as a circle's **radius**.

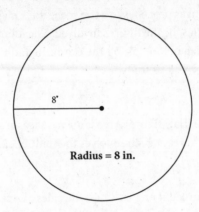

Another common measurement we can use is **diameter**, or the distance from one edge of a circle to the other using a straight line. A circle's diameter is always twice its radius, and its radius always half its diameter.

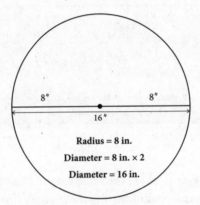

We can now calculate the circle's area by plugging its radius into the following formula, which uses *pi* (π)—a mathematical constant with a value of 3.14.

$$\text{Area} = \pi \times \text{Radius}^2$$

or

$$A = \pi r^2$$

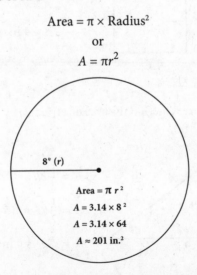

Perimeter of Plane Figures

The **perimeter** of a plane figure is the distance around the outside. To find the perimeter of a polygon (a plane figure bounded by line segments), just add the lengths of the sides.

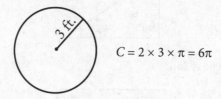

P = 3 in. + 5 in. + 3 in. + 5 in.
P = 16 in.

P = 4 cm + 6 cm + 5 cm
P = 15 cm

The perimeter of a circle is called the **circumference**. The formula for the circumference of a circle is πd or $2\pi r$.

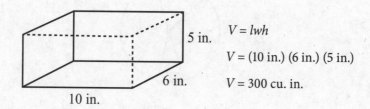

$C = 2 \times 3 \times \pi = 6\pi$

Volume of Solid Figures

The **volume** of a solid figure is the measure of the space within. To find the volume of a solid figure, multiply the area of the base by the height or depth.

The volume of a rectangular solid is length × width × height. Volume is always expressed in cubic units.

$V = lwh$
$V = (10 \text{ in.}) (6 \text{ in.}) (5 \text{ in.})$
$V = 300 \text{ cu. in.}$

The volume of a cube is the cube of one side.

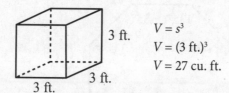

$V = s^3$
$V = (3 \text{ ft.})^3$
$V = 27 \text{ cu. ft.}$

9

The volume of a cylinder is the area of the circular base (πr^2) times the height.

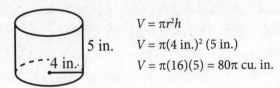

$$V = \pi r^2 h$$
$$V = \pi (4 \text{ in.})^2 (5 \text{ in.})$$
$$V = \pi(16)(5) = 80\pi \text{ cu. in.}$$

Angles

The sum of the angles of a straight line is 180°.

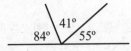

The sum of the angles of a triangle is 180°.

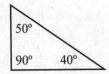

The sum of the angles of a rectangle is 360°.

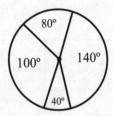

The sum of the angles of a circle is 360°.

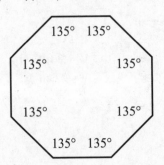

The sum of the angles of a polygon of *n* sides is $(n - 2)180°$.

$$(8 - 2)(180°) = 6 \times 180° = 1{,}080°$$

Two or more angles, shapes, objects, or lines are **congruent** if they're identical in form.

The following triangles not only bear congruent angles—38°, 61°, and 81°—but congruent sides, as well, measuring 71 and 100 inches, respectively. In this case, we can say the triangles themselves are congruent because they have an identical form.

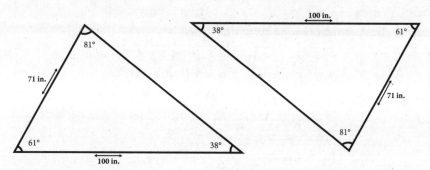

WORD PROBLEMS

While many test takers have no trouble with the basic math on the exam, word problems present a special challenge. For some reason, mixing words with numbers stops many people in their tracks, leading them to make mistakes on even the easiest of math problems. Here are some tips on solving word problems:

1. Read the question carefully. Read it more than once to be sure you understand what it's asking.

2. Determine which mathematical operation is involved in the word problem—addition, subtraction, multiplication, or division—and how to apply it to the situation presented.

3. Translate the problem—rewrite it using numbers, symbols, and variables such as x and y (if necessary).

4. Illustrate the problem by drawing scenes or shapes. Word problems are easier to solve when you can see important elements rather than try to figure out the math in your head.

5. Cross out any unnecessary and distracting information that does not help you solve the problem.

6. Look for similarities to other items on the exam. Does it follow a pattern? Can you use the same formula on the current problem as you used to solve another problem?

7. Solve the problem using the order of operations: complete actions in parentheses first, then exponents (powers and square roots), then multiplication and division (going from left-to-right), then addition and subtraction (left-to-right). The acronym PEMDAS can help you remember the order.

8. Eliminate answers that can't possibly be correct.

9. Confirm that your solution answers the question being asked.

10. Check your work. Once you have the answer, work the problem backwards to make sure you end up with the original question.

> **TIP**
> Most cities will not let you use calculators on the exam, so be prepared.

> **TIP**
> When solving word problems, remember to read the question carefully. The information given to you is important, but also examine the problem for information not given to you. The unknown information can be represented in the problem as x.

9

Translating Word Problems: Basic Terminology

The most effective way to solve word problems is to translate the words into mathematical terms., so it's beneficial to be familiar with terms you will need to translate in word problems. The following is a list of math operations, expressions, and equations and the words that are commonly used to signal them.

Operation/Expression/Equation	Signal Words Used
Addition (+)	*increase, together, total, sum of*
Subtraction (−)	*decrease, take away, less, fewer, minus, the difference of/between*
Multiplication (×)	*times, product of, is doubled/tripled, etc.*
Division (÷)	*per, out of, ratio, divided by, quotient of*
Equals (=)	*is, are, was, adds up to, as much as, the same as, will be*
$x + 5$	Five *more* than x
$x - 5$	Five *fewer* than x
$5x$	Five *times* x
$5x = 25$	The *product* of five times a number is 25.
$0.20x$	Twenty *percent* of x

Two types of questions that are often presented as word problems deal with measures of central tendency and time-rate-and-distance problems. The final section will provide a short review of how to handle these question types.

Measures of Central Tendency

Statistics is all about data. The measures of central tendency help us describe a set of data. There are three measures of central tendency you should be familiar with: mean, median, and mode.

Mean

The first measure of central tendency, **mean**, may be the one you are most familiar with, as it's another word for *average*.

We find the mean by adding the numbers in the set of data, then dividing by the number of terms in that set. For example, given the data set {7, 8, **9**, 10, 11}, we would find the mean by adding the data together (7 + 8 + 9 + 10 + 11) and dividing that sum by the number of data points in the set.

$$\frac{45}{5} = 9$$

The average then, is 9. You can do this with any data set, and the data points do not have to be in numerical order. Just add, then divide. A word problem asking you to identify the mean would be set up something like this:

Example

Five firefighters were stacking sandbags to prevent flooding after a wildfire had razed 10,00 acres of hilly terrain. In a 30-minute period, Firefighter Aldean stacked 75 bags, firefighter Barry stacked 54, Firefighter Carson stacked 62, Firefighter Doane stacked 53, and Firefighter Evans stacked 66. What was the mean number of bags stacked by the firefighters?

Solution

Focus on the important numbers provided in the question: the number of firefighters and the number of bags. Add the number of bags that were stacked by the firefighters:

$$75 + 54 + 62 + 53 + 66 = 310$$

Divide the total by the number of firefighters stacking bags:

$$\frac{310}{5} = 62$$

The mean number of bags stacked is 62.

Median

Median identifies the middle number in a data set. To find the median, put all the data points in order:

In this data set, the median, or the number that is in the middle, is 9. If you have an odd number of digits or data points, put them in order and find the one right in the middle. If the number of data points is even, the median is the mean of the two middle data points:

$$\{6, 7, 8, 9, 10, 11\}$$

$$\frac{8+9}{2} = \frac{17}{2} = 8.5$$

Mode

Mode measures the piece of data that occurs most often in a data set.

$$\{6, 6, 7, 8, 9, 9, 9, 10, 11\}$$

The mode for the set is 9.

Rate, Time, and Distance Problems

The basic formula used in solving problems for distance is $D = RT$ (Distance = Rate × Time). Use this formula when you know rate (speed) and time.

To find rate, use $R = \dfrac{D}{T}$ (Rate = Distance ÷ Time).

To find time, use $T = \dfrac{D}{R}$ (Time = Distance ÷ Rate).

One excellent way to solve distance problems is to organize the data in a chart. Make columns for Rate, Time, and Distance and separate lines for each moving object.

Example

To respond to a large fire several hours away, Engine 4 left Firehouse 7 at 11 a.m. traveling along Route 1 at 30 miles per hour. At 1 p.m., Engine 6 left the firehouse and traveled on the same road at 45 miles per hour. At what **time** did Engine 6 catch up to Engine 4?

Solution

Let x = the time Engine 4 traveled.

Engine 6 left 2 hours later than Engine 4, so it traveled for $x - 2$ hours.

	Rate	× Time	= Distance
Engine 4	30	x	$30x$
Engine 6	45	$x - 2$	$45x - 90$

Since Engine 6 caught up to Engine 4, the distances are equal.

$$30x = 45x - 90$$
$$90 = 15x$$
$$x = 6 \text{ hours}$$

Engine 4 traveled for 6 hours.

$$11 \text{ a.m.} + 6 \text{ hours} = 5 \text{ p.m.}$$

Therefore, Engine 6 caught up with Engine 4 at 5 p.m.

Example

A sailor on leave drove to Yosemite Park from his home at 60 miles per hour. On his trip home, his rate was 10 miles per hour less, and the trip took 1 hour longer. How *far* is his home from the park?

Solution

Let x = time of trip at 60 mph

$x + 1$ = time of trip at 50 mph

	Rate	× Time	= Distance
To Park	60 mph	x	$60x$
From Park	50 mph	$x + 1$	$50x + 50$

The distances are, of course, equal.

$$60x = 50x + 50$$
$$10x = 50$$
$$x = 5$$

$R \times T$ = D; 60 mph × 5 hours = 300 miles

The sailor's home is 300 miles from Yosemite Park.

Example

At 10:30 a.m., a passenger train and a freight train left from stations that were 405 miles apart and traveled toward each other. The rate of the passenger train was 45 miles per hour faster than that of the freight train. If they passed each other at 1:30 p.m., how *fast* was the passenger train traveling?

Solution

Let x = rate of freight train

$x + 45$ = rate of passenger train

Time = 3 hours (10:30 a.m. to 1:30 p.m.)

	Rate $\times$	Time	= Distance
Passenger	$x + 45$	3	$3x + 135$
Freight	x	3	$3x$

Set the distances both trains traveled equal to the point at which they passed each other:

$$3x + 135 + 3x = 405$$
$$6x = 270$$
$$x = 45$$
$$x + 45 = 45 + 45 = 90 \text{ mph}$$

Therefore, the passenger train was traveling at 90 miles per hour.

Remember: When working on time, rate, and distance problems, be sure of what you are solving for so that you can set up the correct formula and solve the problem in as few steps as possible.

9

Summing It Up

- Knowing basic math is essential to doing well on most firefighter exams. Brushing up on basic math skills like addition, subtraction, multiplication, division, fractions, percentages, conversion problems, simple algebra, geometry, and word problems will improve your score.

- Memorizing some simple rules will help you to move through the test more quickly and with less anxiety. Some examples of those rules include: The product of two negative numbers is positive; the product of two positive numbers is positive; and the product of a negative number and a positive number is negative.

- Apply the order of operations when solving a math problem with multiple parts: Parentheses, Exponents, Multiplication, Division, Addition, and Subtraction (PEMDAS), from left to right.

- Remember the number line when subtracting signed numbers.

- The fastest way to find an equivalent fraction is to divide the denominator of the fraction you know by the denominator you want. Take the result and multiply it by the numerator.

- To add fractions having the same denominators, simply add the numerators. To find the difference between two fractions having the same denominators, simply subtract the numerators. To add or subtract fractions having different denominators, you will have to find a common denominator.

- When multiplying fractions, multiply numerators by numerators and denominators by denominators. To divide by a fraction, multiply by the reciprocal of the divisor.

- When solving a percentage problem, be sure to read the notation carefully, read the problem carefully, and use common sense.

  - To change a percentage to a decimal, remove the percent sign (%) and divide by 100.
  - To change a decimal to a percent multiply by 100 and add the % sign.
  - To change a percentage to a fraction, divide by 100 and remove the % sign.
  - To change a fraction to a percentage, multiply by 100 and add the %.

- Memorize the common standard measurements units to metric conversions.

- Memorize the basic formulas of geometry. The formulas are listed on the next page.

- Word problems are prevalent throughout many firefighter exams. Learning to translate word problems into their basic numerical parts is an essential skill for success.

- When working with word problems, make sure you read the problem fully and carefully.

- It's better to sketch a diagram when solving word problems than attempting to do all the math in your head.

FORMULA SHEET

Perimeter

Add the lengths of the sides.

Square

$P = 4s$

Rectangle

$P = 2l + 2w$

Triangle

$P = s_1 + s_2 + s_3$

Circle (circumference)

$C = \pi d$ or $2\pi r$

Area

Always express volume in square units. Multiply the length by the width.

Square

$A = s^2$

Rectangle

$A = bh$

Triangle

Multiply the length by the width and divide by 2.

$A = \frac{1}{2}bh$

Circle

$A = \pi r^2$

Volume

Always express volume in cubic units.

Cube

$V = s^3$

Rectangle

$V = lwh$

Cylinder

$V = \pi r^2 h$

Angles

Straight line = 180°

Triangle = 180°

Rectangle = 180°

Square = 360°

Circle = 360°

Polygon = $(n - 2)180°$ where n = # of sides

Pythagorean Theorem

$a^2 + b^2 = c^2$

Percent Change

$$\frac{\% \text{ change}}{100} = \frac{\text{difference}}{\text{original\#}}$$

Percent to Decimal

$$25\% = \frac{25}{100} = 0.25$$

(Reverse for Decimal to Percent)

Percent to Fraction

$$25\% = \frac{25}{100} = \frac{1}{4}$$

(Reverse for Fraction to Percent)

Distance/Rate/Time

To find distance, use D = RT

(Distance = Rate × Time)

To find rate, use $R = \frac{D}{T}$

(Rate = Distance ÷ Time)

To find time, use $T = \frac{D}{R}$

(Time = Distance ÷ Rate)

9

EXERCISE: MATH PRACTICE

20 Questions—30 minutes

Directions: Solve each problem and select the best answer from the choices provided.

---

1. $\left(\dfrac{1}{4} + \dfrac{1}{3}\right) \times \dfrac{2}{3} =$

   A. $\dfrac{14}{36}$

   B. $\dfrac{1}{21}$

   C. $\dfrac{7}{18}$

   D. $\dfrac{1}{3}$

2. Fireworks are illegal to sell in Adamsville, except around two holidays: the Fourth of July and New Year's Eve. In preparation for New Year's Eve sales, three out-of-town vendors began shipping containers of fireworks to a designated warehouse in Adamsville for their pop-up stores. Each vendor sent 15 containers per week. How many containers were sent to the warehouse in three weeks?

   A. 145

   B. 150

   C. 135

   D. 300

3. $(2 \times 2) \times (2 \times 2) =$

   A. 4

   B. 12

   C. 6

   D. 16

4. Practice for your firehouse's fitness test starts at 3 p.m. You live eight blocks away from the fire station. If it takes you five minutes to walk one block, what is the latest you can leave from your house to get to the firehouse on time for the start of the practice?

   A. 2:15 p.m.

   B. 2:45 p.m.

   C. 2:30 p.m.

   D. 2:20 p.m.

5. What is the third angle in a triangle if the first angle is 65° and the second angle is 100°?

   A. 33°

   B. 30°

   C. 15°

   D. 95°

6. A piece of apparatus equipment just went on sale. It was $350 last week, but it is now $245. What percentage off the original price is the sale price?

   A. 30 percent

   B. 45 percent

   C. 65 percent

   D. 70 percent

9

7. Find the radius of the circle.

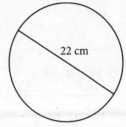

A. 34

B. 11

C. 10

D. 2

8. $9 \times 10 + \dfrac{3}{4} \times 12 =$

A. 200

B. 100

C. 66

D. 99

9. At a local store you find that the prices of six 12-packs of soda are $3.96, $4.55, $5.33, $2.99, $4.50, and $3.33, respectively. What is the average price of a 12-pack of soda?

A. $3.97

B. $4.11

C. $4.66

D. $5.24

10. $\dfrac{1}{6} \times \dfrac{2}{3} =$

A. 0.12

B. 0.11

C. 0.10

D. 13

11. If the radius of Circle B is 6, and Circle A and Circle B are congruent, what is the diameter of Circle A?

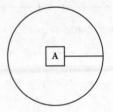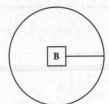

A. 48

B. 36

C. 12

D. 6

12. A fire alarm was called in from a local candle shop. When you arrive on the scene, you see there are exactly 72 candles on display. There are also three dogs and two cats; one of the cats has knocked over a kerosene lamp that started the fire. If there are five other fire-fighters on your crew, how many candles would you each have to remove from the shop if each of you wanted to split the responsibility evenly amongst the entire crew?

A. It cannot be divided evenly.

B. 6

C. 11

D. 12

13. You receive an alarm from a residential neighborhood located five miles south of your firehouse. You realize it will take an extra 10 minutes just to get through downtown because it is rush hour. If you're driving 30 mph, what's the closest estimate of time it will take you to arrive at the alarm destination?

    A. 10 minutes

    B. 20 minutes

    C. 22 minutes

    D. 30 minutes

14. Each firehouse participates in friendly fitness competitions each summer. The winner gets to keep the trophy until their firehouse is unseated. Art from Firehouse B has won the running event seven years in a row, which accounts for 50 percent of the competition's points. Art runs a 7-minute mile. Each year, Firehouse A comes in second; it has never had a runner beat Art's time for a 10K (6.2 miles) run. This year, however, Firehouse A has Ringer, an award-winning triathlete. All things being equal, what is the slowest time Ringer could get while still beating Art in the 10K run?

    A. 50.4 minutes

    B. 43.3 minutes

    C. 40 minutes

    D. 44 minutes

15. Convert 4.75 into a fraction.

    A. $4\dfrac{6}{5}$

    B. $4\dfrac{7}{8}$

    C. $4\dfrac{75}{10}$

    D. $4\dfrac{3}{4}$

16. Your crew is responding to a large woodland fire 30 miles out of town. The fire was started by a camper and has raged nearly unchecked for two weeks. Currently, 18 firefighter crews from around the state are battling the fire, and authorities think they will have the fire 90 percent contained by 6 p.m. this evening. You have just passed the town limits marker and are traveling 15 mph due to all the debris. It is 4:30 p.m.
Keeping your current rate of speed, will you arrive at the fire before it is 90 percent contained?

    A. Yes; the crew will arrive at 5 p.m.

    B. Yes; the crew will arrive at 5:30 p.m.

    C. Yes; the crew will arrive at 6 p.m.

    D. No; the crew will arrive at 6:30 p.m.

17. John lives in Chicago and has to fly home for the holidays. Normally, it takes him an hour to fly the 300 miles home from St. Louis. He needs to get home by 6 p.m. so he can attend his niece's Christmas recital. He booked a flight for 3:05 p.m., but snow has delayed his trip by two hours. He contemplates leaving at noon and driving home. Even with the snow, he estimates he can drive about 50 mph. Should John drive or fly to get to his niece's recital on time?

    A. Drive

    B. Fly

    C. Neither

    D. Either

9

18. Each of the six firehouses in your city has a crew of eighteen firefighters, five operational staff, and three executive officers. At the annual firehouse picnic, firehouses create teams of staff for friendly competitions. All staff are welcome to participate, but normally the executive officers opt out. The teams are evenly split. If two firehouses have 60 percent participation, how many staff must sit out at each of the other firehouses to make the teams even?

    A. 3

    B. 9

    C. 10

    D. 16

19. If the fire department apparatus gets 10 miles to the gallon, and you drive the truck 36 miles to a fire, how many gallons of gas will you have used by the time you return to the firehouse?

    A. 3.6 gallons

    B. 7.2 gallons

    C. 6.0 gallons

    D. 10.2 gallons

20. What is the area of a space measuring 224 feet by 115 feet?

    A. 10,356 sq. ft.

    B. 25,760 sq. ft.

    C. 25,750 sq. ft.

    D. 32,780 sq. ft.

9

ANSWER KEY AND EXPLANATIONS

1. C	**5.** C	**9.** B	**13.** B	**17.** A
2. C	**6.** A	**10.** B	**14.** B	**18.** C
3. D	**7.** B	**11.** C	**15.** D	**19.** B
4. D	**8.** D	**12.** D	**16.** D	**20.** B

1. **The correct answer is C.** Use the order of operations. First, add the fractions in the parentheses: $\frac{1}{4}+\frac{1}{3}=\frac{7}{12}$. Then multiply the result: $\frac{7}{12}\times\frac{2}{3}=\frac{14}{36}$. Finally, reduce the fraction by its greatest common factor: $\frac{14\div2}{36\div2}=\frac{7}{18}$.

2. **The correct answer is C.** There are three vendors, each of which are sending 15 containers a week over a time frame of three weeks:

$$3 \times 15 \times 3 = 135 \text{ containers}$$

3. **The correct answer is D.** $(2\times2)\times(2\times2)=4\times4=16$

4. **The correct answer is D.** Multiply your per-block time by the number of blocks you will walk to determine how long it will take you to get to the firehouse:

$$5 \text{ minutes} \times 8 \text{ blocks} = 40 \text{ minutes}$$

The latest you can leave from your house to get to the firehouse by 3 p.m. is 40 minutes before 3, or 2:20 p.m.

5. **The correct answer is C.** Three angles of a triangle always add up to 180°. To solve, add the two angles you know ($100 + 65 = 165$) and then subtract from 180 to find the third angle. $180 - 165 = 15$.

6. **The correct answer is A.** To find the percentage off an original price, divide the sale price by the original price and multiply the number by 100:

$$\frac{245}{350}=0.7$$

$$0.7\times 100 = 70$$

Subtract that answer from 100 to determine the discount percentage:

$$100 - 70 = 30\%$$

7. **The correct answer is B.** Diameter = $2r$; in other words, the radius is half the length of the diameter, and 22 divided by 2 is 11.

8. **The correct answer is D.** Remember to follow the order of operations and multiply before adding: $9 \times 10 = 90$ and $\frac{3}{4} \times 12 = 9$, so add $90 + 9$ for a total of 99.

9. **The correct answer is B.** To find the average, add up all the values and divide by the number of cans you added.

$$\$3.96 + \$4.55 + \$5.33 + \$2.99 + \$4.50 + \$3.33 = \$24.66$$

$$\$24.66 \div 6 = \$4.11$$

9

10. **The correct answer is B.** Multiply the fractions, then convert the answer to decimals by dividing the numerator by the denominator:

$$\frac{1}{6} \times \frac{4}{6} = \frac{4}{36} = 0.11$$

11. **The correct answer is C.** Both circles are congruent, or equal. Diameter = 2r, so if the radius of Circle B is 6, then the diameter of Circle A is 12.

12. **The correct answer is D.** Remember that you are included, which means six firefighters are available to remove all the candles:

$$72 \div 6 = 12$$

Choice A is incorrect because the number of candles is evenly divisible by the number of firefighters. Choice B is incorrect because it is half the number of candles that each firefighter would have to remove. Choice C is incorrect because it is the total number of individuals (human and nonhuman) mentioned in the problem.

13. **The correct answer is B.** Use the time, speed, and distance formula, $d = st$. Since distance equals time multiplied by speed, divide 5 miles by 30 mph and divide your answer by 60 minutes.

$$5 \text{ miles} \div 30 \text{ mph} = \frac{5}{30} = \frac{1}{6}$$

$$\frac{1}{6} \div 60 \text{ min.} = \frac{1}{6} \times \frac{60}{1} = \frac{1}{{}^1 6} \times \frac{{}^{10} 60}{1} = 10 \text{ minutes}$$

It would normally take 10 minutes to arrive to your destination, but you still must add another 10 minutes to account for rush hour, for a total of 20 minutes.

14. **The correct answer is B.** When you eliminate all the unnecessary details, this is a simple math problem. A 10K is 6.2 miles. Multiply Art's per-mile time by the number of miles in the 10K race to get the time it takes him to run the 10K:

$$7 \text{ min.} \times 6.2 \text{ miles} = 43.4 \text{ minutes}$$

If it takes Art 43.4 minutes to run the 10K, then the slowest time Ringer could run the race and win would be 43.3 minutes. Though 40 minutes (choice C) would beat Art's time, it's not the slowest winning time. Always be sure to answer the question being asked.

15. **The correct answer is D.** You may have recognized right away that the decimal .75 is equal to $\frac{3}{4}$, which makes finding the answer an easy task. If the numbers are not as recognizable, to convert a decimal to a fraction, set up the decimal as a fraction with a denominator of 1 and multiply both the numerator and denominator by 100, then simplify. (You don't have to deal with the whole number in this instance):

$$.75 = \frac{0.75}{1} \times \frac{100}{100} = \frac{75}{100} = \frac{3}{4}$$

Then just add the whole number to the simplified fraction:

$$4 + \frac{3}{4} = 4\frac{3}{4}$$

16. **The correct answer is D.** This is a distance, speed, and time question. Set up the formula and solve:

$$t = \frac{d}{s}$$

$$t = \frac{30 \text{ miles}}{15 \text{ mph}}$$

$$t = 2 \text{ hours}$$

At a rate of 15 mph, it will take 2 hours to travel 30 miles and reach the fire, putting your time of arrival at 6:30 p.m., 30 minutes after authorities predicted the fire would be 90 percent contained.

17. **The correct answer is A.** To arrive at 5 p.m. (choice A), your crew would have to travel at 30 mph, and the fire would have to be 15 miles out of town. To arrive at 5:30 (choice B), your crew would have to travel at 30 miles per hour; 6 p.m. (choice C) is when the fire was predicted to have been 90 percent contained, and your crew would have to travel at 20 mph to arrive at that time.

18. **The correct answer is C.** There's a lot of unnecessary information here. You must pull out the important figures: the most important is that there are 26 staff members at each fire house. Using basic math, we find that 60 percent of 26 is 15.6 (.60 × 26). To make the groups even, at least 10 members from each of the other teams must sit out. Choice A is the number of executive officers on each staff (3); even if all of them were to opt out, it would not be enough to even the teams. Teams with nine members (choice B) sitting out would be larger than the teams with 60 percent-participation. Choice D (16) is 60 percent of 26 rounded to the nearest whole number. Use this number to answer the question being asked.

19. **The correct answer is B.** If the truck gets 10 miles per gallon, then it would use 3.6 gallons to drive 36 miles (36 ÷ 10). Since it is a round trip, multiply 3.6 × 2, which is 7.2 gallons.

20. **The correct answer is B.** Multiply length by width to get the area of a space:

224 ft. × 115 ft. = 25,760 sq. ft.

9

PART IV
THREE PRACTICE TESTS

Practice Tests for the Firefighter Exam

OVERVIEW

- **Preparing to take the Practice Tests**
- **Practice Test 1**
- **Practice Test 2**
- **Practice Test 3**

PREPARING TO TAKE THE PRACTICE TESTS

Actual firefighter exams usually contain between 110 to 120 questions, and last for 3 to 4 hours. We've provided three 100-question practice tests in this section that will take approximately 210 minutes per practice test to complete.

First, assemble all the things you will need to take the test, including the following items:

- No. 2 pencils, at least three
- A timer
- The answer sheet (located before each practice test)

Set a timer for the time specified at the top of the first page of the test. Stick to that time so you are simulating the average per-question time allotted on an actual exam. At this point, it's as important to know how many questions you can answer in the time allotted as it is to answer questions correctly.

Once you have completed a practice test, check your answers against the Answer Key and Explanations that follow each test.

Good luck!

PRACTICE TEST 1 ANSWER SHEET

1. Ⓐ Ⓑ Ⓒ Ⓓ   21. Ⓐ Ⓑ Ⓒ Ⓓ   41. Ⓐ Ⓑ Ⓒ Ⓓ   61. Ⓐ Ⓑ Ⓒ Ⓓ   81. Ⓐ Ⓑ Ⓒ Ⓓ
2. Ⓐ Ⓑ Ⓒ Ⓓ   22. Ⓐ Ⓑ Ⓒ Ⓓ   42. Ⓐ Ⓑ Ⓒ Ⓓ   62. Ⓐ Ⓑ Ⓒ Ⓓ   82. Ⓐ Ⓑ Ⓒ Ⓓ
3. Ⓐ Ⓑ Ⓒ Ⓓ   23. Ⓐ Ⓑ Ⓒ Ⓓ   43. Ⓐ Ⓑ Ⓒ Ⓓ   63. Ⓐ Ⓑ Ⓒ Ⓓ   83. Ⓐ Ⓑ Ⓒ Ⓓ
4. Ⓐ Ⓑ Ⓒ Ⓓ   24. Ⓐ Ⓑ Ⓒ Ⓓ   44. Ⓐ Ⓑ Ⓒ Ⓓ   64. Ⓐ Ⓑ Ⓒ Ⓓ   84. Ⓐ Ⓑ Ⓒ Ⓓ
5. Ⓐ Ⓑ Ⓒ Ⓓ   25. Ⓐ Ⓑ Ⓒ Ⓓ   45. Ⓐ Ⓑ Ⓒ Ⓓ   65. Ⓐ Ⓑ Ⓒ Ⓓ   85. Ⓐ Ⓑ Ⓒ Ⓓ
6. Ⓐ Ⓑ Ⓒ Ⓓ   26. Ⓐ Ⓑ Ⓒ Ⓓ   46. Ⓐ Ⓑ Ⓒ Ⓓ   66. Ⓐ Ⓑ Ⓒ Ⓓ   86. Ⓐ Ⓑ Ⓒ Ⓓ
7. Ⓐ Ⓑ Ⓒ Ⓓ   27. Ⓐ Ⓑ Ⓒ Ⓓ   47. Ⓐ Ⓑ Ⓒ Ⓓ   67. Ⓐ Ⓑ Ⓒ Ⓓ   87. Ⓐ Ⓑ Ⓒ Ⓓ
8. Ⓐ Ⓑ Ⓒ Ⓓ   28. Ⓐ Ⓑ Ⓒ Ⓓ   48. Ⓐ Ⓑ Ⓒ Ⓓ   68. Ⓐ Ⓑ Ⓒ Ⓓ   88. Ⓐ Ⓑ Ⓒ Ⓓ
9. Ⓐ Ⓑ Ⓒ Ⓓ   29. Ⓐ Ⓑ Ⓒ Ⓓ   49. Ⓐ Ⓑ Ⓒ Ⓓ   69. Ⓐ Ⓑ Ⓒ Ⓓ   89. Ⓐ Ⓑ Ⓒ Ⓓ
10. Ⓐ Ⓑ Ⓒ Ⓓ   30. Ⓐ Ⓑ Ⓒ Ⓓ   50. Ⓐ Ⓑ Ⓒ Ⓓ   70. Ⓐ Ⓑ Ⓒ Ⓓ   90. Ⓐ Ⓑ Ⓒ Ⓓ
11. Ⓐ Ⓑ Ⓒ Ⓓ   31. Ⓐ Ⓑ Ⓒ Ⓓ   51. Ⓐ Ⓑ Ⓒ Ⓓ   71. Ⓐ Ⓑ Ⓒ Ⓓ   91. Ⓐ Ⓑ Ⓒ Ⓓ
12. Ⓐ Ⓑ Ⓒ Ⓓ   32. Ⓐ Ⓑ Ⓒ Ⓓ   52. Ⓐ Ⓑ Ⓒ Ⓓ   72. Ⓐ Ⓑ Ⓒ Ⓓ   92. Ⓐ Ⓑ Ⓒ Ⓓ
13. Ⓐ Ⓑ Ⓒ Ⓓ   33. Ⓐ Ⓑ Ⓒ Ⓓ   53. Ⓐ Ⓑ Ⓒ Ⓓ   73. Ⓐ Ⓑ Ⓒ Ⓓ   93. Ⓐ Ⓑ Ⓒ Ⓓ
14. Ⓐ Ⓑ Ⓒ Ⓓ   34. Ⓐ Ⓑ Ⓒ Ⓓ   54. Ⓐ Ⓑ Ⓒ Ⓓ   74. Ⓐ Ⓑ Ⓒ Ⓓ   94. Ⓐ Ⓑ Ⓒ Ⓓ
15. Ⓐ Ⓑ Ⓒ Ⓓ   35. Ⓐ Ⓑ Ⓒ Ⓓ   55. Ⓐ Ⓑ Ⓒ Ⓓ   75. Ⓐ Ⓑ Ⓒ Ⓓ   95. Ⓐ Ⓑ Ⓒ Ⓓ
16. Ⓐ Ⓑ Ⓒ Ⓓ   36. Ⓐ Ⓑ Ⓒ Ⓓ   56. Ⓐ Ⓑ Ⓒ Ⓓ   76. Ⓐ Ⓑ Ⓒ Ⓓ   96. Ⓐ Ⓑ Ⓒ Ⓓ
17. Ⓐ Ⓑ Ⓒ Ⓓ   37. Ⓐ Ⓑ Ⓒ Ⓓ   57. Ⓐ Ⓑ Ⓒ Ⓓ   77. Ⓐ Ⓑ Ⓒ Ⓓ   97. Ⓐ Ⓑ Ⓒ Ⓓ
18. Ⓐ Ⓑ Ⓒ Ⓓ   38. Ⓐ Ⓑ Ⓒ Ⓓ   58. Ⓐ Ⓑ Ⓒ Ⓓ   78. Ⓐ Ⓑ Ⓒ Ⓓ   98. Ⓐ Ⓑ Ⓒ Ⓓ
19. Ⓐ Ⓑ Ⓒ Ⓓ   39. Ⓐ Ⓑ Ⓒ Ⓓ   59. Ⓐ Ⓑ Ⓒ Ⓓ   79. Ⓐ Ⓑ Ⓒ Ⓓ   99. Ⓐ Ⓑ Ⓒ Ⓓ
20. Ⓐ Ⓑ Ⓒ Ⓓ   40. Ⓐ Ⓑ Ⓒ Ⓓ   60. Ⓐ Ⓑ Ⓒ Ⓓ   80. Ⓐ Ⓑ Ⓒ Ⓓ   100. Ⓐ Ⓑ Ⓒ Ⓓ

Answer Sheet

Practice Test 1

PRACTICE TEST 1

100 Questions—210 minutes

Directions: The following questions are similar to those you will find on an actual firefighter exam. Be sure to read the questions carefully and follow any specific instructions that precede them. Choose the best answer to each question and fill in the corresponding circle on the answer sheet. The Answer Key and Explanations follow.

Questions 1–8 are based on the following diagram. Study and memorize the diagram for five minutes. Then cover the diagram and answer the questions, without referring back to the diagram.

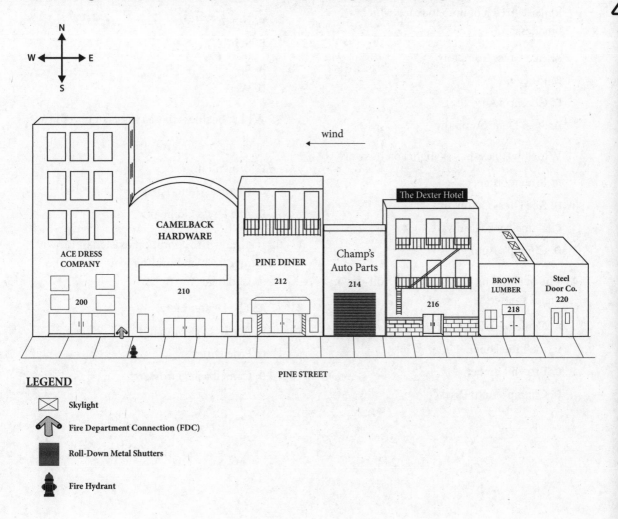

1. The building that would require the longest ladder to enable you to climb to the top floor would most likely be
   A. 212 Pine Street.
   B. 216 Pine Street.
   C. 200 Pine Street.
   D. 220 Pine Street.

2. For a building fire on Pine Street, if the fire department pumper is connected to the hydrant, the firefighter would need the longest stretch of hose to reach which business?
   A. Ace Dress Company
   B. Pine Diner
   C. Champ's Auto Parts
   D. Steel Door Company

3. Which business has skylights on its roof?
   A. Brown Lumber
   B. Ace Dress Company
   C. Camelback Hardware
   D. Champ's Auto Parts

4. The business on this block with roll-down metal shutters is
   A. Camelback Hardware.
   B. the Pine Diner.
   C. Brown Lumber.
   D. Champ's Auto Parts.

5. Buildings with automatic wet sprinkler systems are required to have a Fire Department Connection (FDC) on the wall of the address side of the building. Which business on Pine Street has an automatic wet sprinkler system?
   A. The Steel Door Company
   B. The Ace Dress Company
   C. Brown Lumber
   D. The Dexter Hotel

6. From which direction is the wind blowing?
   A. North
   B. South
   C. East
   D. West

7. Which business has a trussed (curved) roof?
   A. Camelback Hardware
   B. Brown Lumber
   C. Champ's Auto Parts
   D. Ace Dress Company

8. If a heavy fire condition existed in Brown Lumber, which building would be in the most danger?
   A. The Dexter Hotel
   B. Ace Dress Company
   C. Pine Diner
   D. Camelback Hardware

9. Hotels represent significant obstacles for efficient firefighting practice. There are numerous rooms which may or may not be occupied as well as individuals who are likely unfamiliar with a hotel's layout. In responding to a fire alarm at a multi-story hotel, your fire company finds groups of guests scattered throughout the parking lot and some frantic hotel staff. A staff member reveals that after a quick headcount many guests are unaccounted for. The fire company then proceeds to the location of the fire and extinguishes it without any guests suffering harm. What would be the most logical recommendation to hotels in general to prevent such situations in the future?

A. Remove all obstructions from hallways and other passageways.

B. Limit the number of persons per room.

C. Provide clear instructions as to the locations of exits throughout the building.

D. Check the proper functioning of fire alarms on the premises.

10. While driving to work, a firefighter notices a high-tension wire that has been blown down and is now lying across the sidewalk and one lane of the road and occasionally whipping about. The firefighter exits her vehicle and evaluates the situation. It is unclear if the wire is energized. Unfortunately, the firefighter's cellphone battery is dead. In this situation, the most appropriate course of action for the firefighter to take would be to

A. move the wire out of the road using a stick or branch and continue to the firehouse to report the situation.

B. continue on her way to the firehouse and report the situation to the officer on duty.

C. locate a public telephone and call the public utility company.

D. park the vehicle in the road to warn passersby and ask the first individual to call the public utility company.

11. Locals reported an explosion at a family owned sporting goods store. As a first responder to the sporting goods store fire, your company has followed proper protocols for fire attack. However, after beginning fire attack, your commander receives and transmits further eyewitness accounts that a man was seen placing objects around the perimeter of the store shortly before the explosion. You learn as well that several similar incidents have been reported across town, though only your location appears to have resulted in a fire. Because suspicious packages have been reported at multiple sites, the local police force is spread thin. No officers have arrived, and no police line has been created. Onlookers have started to encroach upon the scene, some even standing on hoselines and others resting on the fire engines as firefighters combat the flames inside. In this scenario, you or another member of your company should

A. locate and contain any suspicious packages on the fireground.

B. immediately direct all civilians to clear the area and retreat to an appropriate safe distance.

C. avoid all further action until police units arrive on scene.

D. request additional fire companies to contain the situation.

Questions 12–15 are based on the following passage and floor plan.

Because many children might need to be rescued in the event of a school fire, New York City firefighters must become familiar with the floor layouts of public schools. Firefighters can develop this familiarity by conducting training drills at the schools.

A ladder company and an engine company recently conducted a drill at Pierce High School. The firefighters determined that the room layout is the same on all floors.

Several days after the drill, the ladder and engine companies report to a fire at Pierce High School in classroom 304, which is on the third floor. The fire has spread into the hallway in front of Room 304, blocking the hallway.

Summit High School

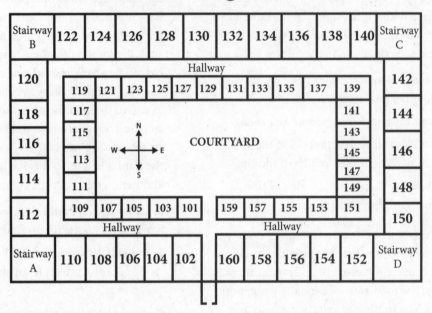

12. A firefighter is instructed to search for victims in the southwest area of the third floor. He wants to search as many rooms as possible and begins as close to the fire as possible without passing through the flames. From the street, the firefighter should use his ladder to enter

   A. Room 302.
   B. Room 306.
   C. Room 312.
   D. Room 352.

13. A firefighter goes to the third floor by way of the southwest building stairway. In Room 317, he finds a child who has been overcome by smoke. Upon returning to the hallway, he finds that the stairway he came up is now blocked by fire hoses. The closest stairway the firefighter can use to bring the child to the street level is

   A. stairway A.
   B. stairway B.
   C. stairway C.
   D. stairway D.

14. The fire is in Rooms 303 and 305. Fire-fighters are told to go to the rooms in the north corridor facing the courtyard that are directly opposite 303 and 305. Which rooms should the firefighters go to?

    A. Rooms 323 and 325

    B. Rooms 326 and 328

    C. Rooms 333 and 335

    D. Rooms 355 and 357

15. Another fire breaks out in Room 336, block-ing the entire hallway. Firefighters have brought a hose up the northeast stairway to fight this fire. Another hose must be brought up another stairway so that firefighters can approach the fire from the same direction. What is the closest stairway the firefighters could use?

    A. Stairway A

    B. Stairway B

    C. Stairway C

    D. Stairway D

16. The leverage system in the following sketch is used to raise a weight.

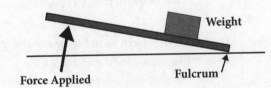

    To reduce the amount of force required to raise the weight, it is necessary to

    A. decrease the length of the lever.

    B. place the weight closer to the fulcrum.

    C. move the weight closer to the person applying the force.

    D. move the fulcrum farther from the weight.

17. Wooden ladders should not be painted because

    A. the paint will wear off rapidly due to conditions under which ladders are used.

    B. paint can weaken the wood.

    C. the paint will rub off on surfaces the ladder touches.

    D. paint hides potential defects in the ladder.

18. What is the sum of $\frac{2}{3} + \frac{2}{3}$?

    A. $1\frac{1}{3}$

    B. $3\frac{1}{3}$

    C. 7

    D. $9\frac{1}{3}$

19. Your station is ordering new equipment. Extrication equipment costs $28,000, uniforms $17,250, and radio repair $7,025. What will the total cost be?

    A. $37,525

    B. $52,275

    C. $54,425

    D. $42,250

20. A fire engine is required to carry six hoses. The lengths of the hoses are 100 feet, 100 feet, 150 feet, 150 feet, 250 feet, and 300 feet. What is the average hose length?

    A. 300 feet

    B. 275 feet

    C. 200 feet

    D. 175 feet

21. A firefighter needs to crawl through a win-dow that is 5 feet high and 2 feet wide. What is the area of the opening?

    A. 30 sq. ft.

    B. 25 sq. ft.

    C. 15 sq. ft.

    D. 10 sq. ft.

Practice Test 1

Questions 22 and 23 are based on the following table.

Four different categories of fire engines carry ladders or platforms. Each of these has a specific range when the ladder or platform is extended.

Category	Common Range
Straight single-roof ladder	14 ft.
Extension ladder	14–35 ft.
Aerial ladder	50–135 ft.
Aerial ladder platform	85–110 ft.
Telescoping aerial platform	50–100 ft.
Articulating aerial platform	55–102 ft.

22. For many buildings, floors are 10 vertical feet apart, and windows are positioned three feet from the floor. Thus, a window on the second floor of a standard building has approximately 13 feet between its sill and the ground. Firefighters use those estimates to decide which ladder is appropriate for reaching windows to attack fires or rescue victims. If firefighters needed to conduct a search of the tenth story of a tenement and stairway access was blocked, which ladder or platform would be most appropriate for the situation?

    A. Extension ladder

    B. Articulating aerial platform

    C. Straight single-roof ladder

    D. Telescoping aerial platform

23. If the articulating aerial platform were extended to 75 feet, what percentage of its range would be in use?

    A. 42.5 percent

    B. 43.5 percent

    C. 45.3 percent

    D. 46.2 percent

24. Firefighters respond to an alarm at a retirement community to find that a lit cigarette has set fire to a bench. The fire started in close proximity to community members using oxygen tanks. A firefighter would most likely provide the following advice to residents:

    A. Oxygen provides an essential component of combustion and in high concentrations can cause embers to flare.

    B. Smoking tobacco is a severe irritant to persons with respiratory conditions and should occur only at designated locations.

    C. Improper disposal of cigarette buds is a major cause of fires in residential structures.

    D. Tobacco has been found to be the cause of numerous ailments and diseases, and elderly populations are particularly vulnerable.

25. An engine company arrives at a large blaze at a residential compound that is producing significant smoke, limiting visibility. A perimeter has already been established by police, so the four firefighters immediately begin their search of the structure with each member of the company choosing a different point of entry. Of the options listed, which choice presents the greatest potential problem for safe and efficient firefighting?

A. The firefighters entered the structure individually rather than in pairs.

B. The firefighters did not secure a zone around the fire to keep civilians at a safe distance.

C. The firefighters do not know the source of the blaze.

D. The firefighters are unfamiliar with the layout of the building.

26. The following steps constitute basic firefighting procedure. Place them in their most logical order.

Step 1. Suppress the fire using hoselines and other extinguishing methods.

Step 2. Search the structure for victims that are unaccounted for.

Step 3. Perform a rapid search to locate victims.

Step 4. Determine the main source and area of the fire.

Step 5. Secure property.

A. 3–4–2–1–5

B. 5–4–3–2–1

C. 4–2–3–1–5

D. 1–3–2–4–5

27. At the first sign of a fire, the manager of a movie theater turned on the lights of the theater and made the following announcement: "Ladies and gentlemen, we've discovered a fire in one of our stock rooms. We've contacted the fire department. We're dismissing you. Please, remain seated until it is time for your aisle to file out. Follow the directions of the ushers to reach an appropriate exit." In meeting with the manager after the fire had been extinguished, firefighters indicated what action could have been performed differently in the situation?

A. State that the audience will all receive refunds for their ticket purchase prices.

B. Avoid discussion of the cause of the evacuation as it may incite unnecessary panic.

C. Change the method of evacuation, allowing all members of the audience to evacuate simultaneously.

D. Provide more details as to the nature of the fire (size, location, intensity, etc.).

28. Which of the following is used to make curved cuts?

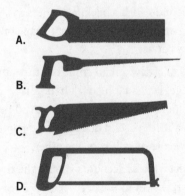

29. After a fire in a condominium had been brought under control, firefighters engaged in extinguishing the last traces of the fire and checking for extension. Activities were concentrated in one room in the condo. A firefighter who noticed an expensive vase in the space decided to move it from harm's way into the kitchen of the residence before putting it back when firefighting was completed. As the firefighters were later preparing to leave the scene, the owner of the condo approached and asked what firefighters had done with the vase and several other objects from the room. Firefighters returned to the residence to search but found nothing. They began questioning civilians present at the scene and learned the following:

Witness 1: "I saw a man with long brown hair and a dark sweater exit through the garage. He was carrying a small box in one hand and a vase in the other."

Witness 2: "I saw a woman enter the building through the garage. When she came out, she had a vase with her and something else. She went that way."

Witness 3: "I saw a man with brown hair exit the condo with a backpack on. He wasn't carrying anything. But he went to the condo two doors down."

Witness 4: "I saw a man come out through the garage. He had long dark hair. His sweater looked dark, even stained. And he had a beautiful vase in one hand and something like a jewelry box in the other."

Which eyewitness accounts should the firefighters transmit to police?

A. 1, 2, 3
B. 1, 2, 4
C. 1, 3, 4
D. 2, 3, 4

30. Firefighter Stephanie Martin has just completed some of her daily maintenance activities on the fire engine when she is approached by a woman with a baby carriage. The woman asks Stephanie if she could watch her baby while she visits a doctor in a nearby office complex. In this situation, the best course of action for Stephanie to take is

A. agree to the woman's request but warn her that it might be necessary to leave to answer an alarm.

B. refuse politely after explaining that she is on duty and cannot become involved in other activities.

C. refer the woman to the officer on duty for possible solutions.

D. speak with the officer on duty to receive permission to grant the favor.

31. When driving a nail into a piece of wood, the most effective way to prevent the wood from splitting is to

A. use a carpenter's hammer.

B. first drill a small hole in the wood.

C. drive the nail into the wood slowly.

D. drive the nail into the wood quickly.

32. Fire department permits are required for persons to create public events that include certain hazardous activities. Most special events require such permits due to the number of people involved as well as the presence of certain fire risks or dangers to crowds (i.e., fireworks, canopies, compressed gases, motorized vehicles). Obtaining such a permit requires offering in-depth information describing the event as well as payment of a fee. From the fire department's perspective, the most likely justification for requiring permits or certificates for such events is to

    A. generate revenue for the city government.

    B. prevent the creation of dangerous events by unqualified persons.

    C. obtain information from such activities to plan for fire emergencies.

    D. warn the public of the hazardous nature of these activities.

33. On his way into the firehouse, a firefighter is stopped by a man who complains that the employees of a nearby store frequently pile empty crates and boxes blocking one of the doorways while they stock shelves. This man claims that this violates fire codes and creates a potential danger for customers and employees inside the store. In this situation, the most appropriate action for the firefighter to take would be to

    A. assure the citizen that the fire department's inspection activities will eventually come to the store to issue a citation.

    B. obtain the address of the store and immediately investigate to determine whether the citizen's complaint is justified.

    C. obtain the address of the store and report the complaint to a superior officer.

    D. ask the citizen for specific dates on which the practice occurred to determine the truthfulness of the complaint.

34. Arson is the willful and malicious burning of property. The crime can refer to a variety of property types: public lands, vehicles, buildings. Which of the following constitutes arson according to the given definition?

    A. Mobile home fire started by a woman smoking in bed that spreads to nearby properties.

    B. Garage fire started after a man leaves oily rags near electrical wiring exposed by pests.

    C. Home fire started after the owner pours gasoline on the flooring within the home and sets it alight.

    D. Wildfire spread from an untended campfire started by multiple homeless individuals

Practice Test 1

Questions 35–37 are based on the following floor plan and refer to a fire in Room 111.

This floor plan represents a typical high-rise office building. Numbers shown indicate room numbers. The pipe connections for the water supply system are outside the building at street level. Firefighters attach hoses to these connections to send water into the pipes in the building.

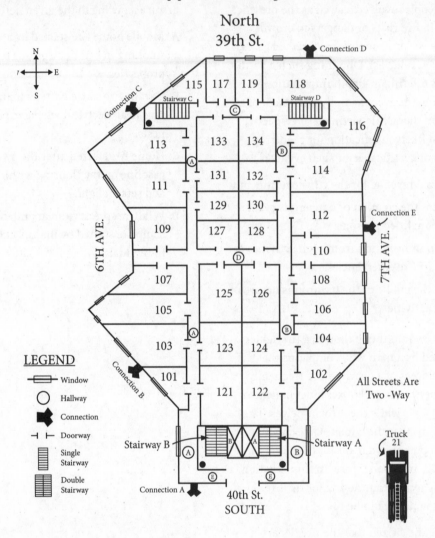

35. After fighting a fire in Room 111, firefighters are instructed to go immediately to the east-west hallway in the center of the building and search for victims. Which one of the following lists all the rooms the firefighters should search?

A. 115, 117, 118, 119, 133, and 134

B. 125, 126, 127, 128, and 129

C. 107, 109, 125, 126, 127, and 128

D. 121, 122, 123, 124, 125, and 126

36. Firefighters in Truck 21 have been ordered to attach a hose to a connection outside the building. The firefighters cannot use Connection A because 40th Street is blocked by traffic. What is the first connection to which the firefighters can drive?

A. Connection B

B. Connection C

C. Connection D

D. Connection E

37. Firefighters are told to search Room 134. They enter the building from 40th Street. The shortest route for the firefighters to take to reach this room is to go

   A. west in Hallway E, north in Hallway A, and then east in Hallway C.

   B. west in Hallway E, north in Hallway A, east in Hallway D, north in Hallway B, and then west in Hallway C.

   C. east in Hallway E, north in Hallway B, and then west in Hallway C.

   D. east in Hallway E, north in Hallway B, west in Hallway D, north in Hallway A, and then east in Hallway C.

Questions 38–40 are based on the following table.

The following is a list of firefighters and their respective ages and years served.

Name	Age	Years Served
Firefighter Algren	28	6
Firefighter Amari	46	16
Firefighter McNamara	25	3
Firefighter Rill	37	14
Firefighter Stephens	39	11

38. What is the mean age of the firefighters?

   A. 25

   B. 31

   C. 35

   D. 37

39. What is the median number of years served by the firefighters?

   A. 3

   B. 11

   C. 14

   D. 16

40. Which of the following statements regarding the mean, median, and mode of the information in the table is true?

   A. The median number of years served by the firefighters is greater than the mean number of years served.

   B. The mean age of the firefighters is greater than the median age.

   C. The mode of the firefighters' ages is greater than their mean age.

   D. The mean age of the firefighters is less than the mean number of years served by the firefighters.

Practice Test 1

41. In the case of suspected arson, firefighters engaged in fighting the fire need to pay attention to the conditions that existed at the time of arrival. Particular attention should be paid to doors and windows to detect potential points of entry for suspected arsonists as broken windows and doors can signal intrusion. Upon arriving on site of a potential case of arson, Firefighter Sultana sees multiple broken windows, but one ground floor window has most of the glass on the floor inside of the structure. A fire investigator would likely conclude that

    A. the window has been broken for a long time.

    B. a resident used this window as an exit point to escape the flames.

    C. the window must have been broken after the fire started.

    D. this was the point of entry for the suspected arsonist.

42. A firefighter inspecting buildings in a commercial district arrives at a building whose outside surface appears to be made of natural stone. The owner of the structure assures the firefighter that an inspection is unnecessary as the building is fireproof. Despite this claim, however, the firefighter insists on completing the inspection. The firefighter should say which of the following to explain his decision to the owner?

    A. "You're wrong, sir. Stone buildings catch fire just as readily as wooden buildings."

    B. "Step back now, sir. The fire department cannot make exceptions in its inspection procedures."

    C. "This is imitation stone and is combustible."

    D. "While certain materials may be fireproof or fire-resistant, the interiors and contents of any building can catch fire."

43. To properly conduct an investigation into the causes of a fire, a fire investigator will complete a specific procedure upon arriving at the scene of a fire. (The following steps are not in order.)

    Step 1. Remove evidence from the scene

    Step 2. Document the location of evidence at the scene

    Step 3. Preserve transient evidence, such as shoe prints and tire impressions, with tarpaulin or containers

    Step 4. Mark evidence with flags, cones, or other markers

    Step 5. Determine the origin of the fire

    Step 6. Generate a conclusion for the cause of the fire

    Place the steps into the most logical order for properly preserving the evidence at a fire scene and coming to a conclusion.

    A. 3–4–2–1–5–6

    B. 3–5–6–1–4–2

    C. 3–1–2–5–6–4

    D. 4–1–5–3–2–6

44. A liquefied petroleum gas installation can present a severe risk in a firefighting situation. Firefighters can limit the risk of such an installation by using the following steps (steps are not in order).

    Step 1. Spray the fuel cylinder or tank with water to control the temperature.

    Step 2. Open the valve enclosure to access the gas shutoff.

    Step 3. If risk persists, flatten the supply line with a hammer.

    Step 4. Close the valve by turning it to the right.

    Step 5. Determine the location of the control valve.

    What is the most logical order for the steps listed?

    A. 2–5–4–3–1
    B. 4–5–2–3–1
    C. 5–2–4–3–1
    D. 5–3–2–4–1

45. While on duty at a fire, a probationary firefighter receives a direct order from his lieutenant that appears to conflict with the principles of firefighting the firefighter learned during training. Of the following options, the best course of action for the firefighter is to follow the order and, at a convenient time after the fire,

    A. address the apparent inconsistency with the lieutenant.
    B. discuss the inconsistency with another senior officer.
    C. mention the inconsistency with other fire crew members during daily activities.
    D. ask a more experienced firefighter whether the lieutenant is prone to such orders.

46. While on a boating trip near a coastal town, you observe a fire break out at the end of a pier due to some illegal fireworks use. Firefighters arrive and begin controlling the scene. You see firefighters direct civilians present at the scene away from the pier and begin setting up equipment. One firefighter lowers a device off the side of the pier into the water. It appears to be pumping seawater to a hose junction on the pier itself. After watching the firefighters extinguish the blaze, you conclude that firefighters use the water from the harbor because

    A. it is less likely to cause water damage in such an area.
    B. the harbor water is available in near limitless quantities compared to a fire engine's water tank.
    C. the salinity of the water is more effective when extinguishing fires.
    D. it is less likely to freeze in low temperatures due to its salt content.

Practice Test 1

Questions 47–50 are based on the following passage.

A gas mask with a canister consists of a tight-fitting facepiece connected to a canister containing chemicals that filter toxic gases and smoke from otherwise breathable air. These masks do not provide oxygen necessary to support life and absorbs only two or three percent of toxic substances in the air. In general, if flame is visible, there is sufficient oxygen for firefighters although toxic gases (such as carbon monoxide) might still be present. Where there is heavy smoke and no flame, an oxygen deficiency might exist. Fatalities have occurred when filter-type canister masks have been used in attempting rescue from manholes, wells, basements, or other locations deficient in oxygen.

47. If the mask described in the passage is used in an atmosphere containing oxygen, nitrogen, and carbon monoxide, we would expect the mask to remove which of the following from the air breathed?

   A. Nitrogen only
   B. Carbon monoxide only
   C. Nitrogen and carbon monoxide
   D. None of the above

48. According to the passage, when firefighters are wearing these masks at a fire in which flame is visible, the firefighters generally can feel that, as far as breathing is concerned, they are

   A. safe because a visible flame is an indicator that there is sufficient oxygen to support life.
   B. unsafe if the toxic gas concentration is below 2 or 3 percent.
   C. safe, provided the toxic gas concentration is above 2 or 3 percent.
   D. unsafe because the mask will not provide them with sufficient oxygen to live.

49. According to this passage, persons using this type of gas mask in manholes, wells, and basements have died because

   A. the supply of oxygen provided by the mask ran out.
   B. the air in those places did not contain enough oxygen to support life.
   C. heavy smoke interfered with the operation of the mask.
   D. the chemicals in the canister did not function properly.

50. The following formula can be used to show, in general, the operation of the gas mask described in the passage:

   (Chemicals in canister) → (air + gases)
   = breathable air

   The arrow in the formula, when expressed in words, most nearly means

   A. replace.
   B. are changed into.
   C. act upon.
   D. give off.

Questions 51–53 are based on the following passage.

The only openings permitted in fire partitions, except openings for ventilating ducts, shall be those required for doors. There shall be but one such door opening unless the provision of additional openings would not exceed in total width of all doorways 25 percent of the length of the wall. The minimum distance between openings shall be 3 feet. The maximum area for such a door opening shall be 80 square feet, except that such openings for the passage of trucks may be a maximum of 140 square feet.

51. According to the passage, openings in fire partitions are permitted only for

A. doors.

B. doors and windows.

C. doors and ventilation ducts.

D. doors, windows, and ventilation ducts.

52. In a fire partition 22 ft. long and 10 ft. high, the maximum number of doors 3 ft. wide and 7 ft. high is

A. 1.

B. 2.

C. 3.

D. 4.

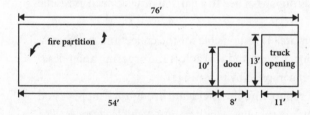

53. The most accurate statement about the diagram shown above is that the

A. total width of the openings is too large.

B. truck opening is too large.

C. truck and door openings are too close together.

D. layout is acceptable.

54. When conducting a fire inspection, firefighters try to determine ways in which fires could start, the functioning of safety systems (including smoke alarms, fire extinguishers, sprinkler systems), assistance for egress (exits signs and exit doors), as well as ease of access and exit for civilians and emergency personnel. Which of the following scenarios would present the most troubling combination of issues during a fire inspection?

A. Multiple fire extinguisher types and an externally locked exit door

B. Storage of highly combustible materials in common areas and broken smoke alarms

C. A broken elevator and exposed wiring in the ceiling

D. A lack of sprinkler systems and illuminated exit signs

55. Of the following items commonly found in a household, the one that uses the most electric current is a(n)

A. 150-watt light bulb.

B. toaster.

C. door buzzer.

D. 8-inch electric fan.

56. What is the sum of −6 and 8?

A. −14

B. 14

C. −2

D. 2

Practice Test 1

57. A fax machine listed at $360 and was purchased for $288. What was the rate of discount?

A. 18 percent

B. 20 percent

C. 22 percent

D. 24 percent

58. Zain's gas tank is $\frac{1}{8}$ full. After she adds 8 gallons of gas to the tank, it is then $\frac{5}{6}$ full. Approximately how many gallons of gas can her tank hold?

A. 9

B. 11

C. 13

D. 17

Questions 59–62 are based on the following passage.

Most accidents that lead to firefighter injuries or fatalities occur at the scene of an emergency. To avoid accidents, it is important to have a system that clarifies the roles and responsibilities of personnel.

The Incident Command System (ICS) was adopted by the National Fire Academy (NFA) to coordinate resources during a variety of emergency situations. The ICS assists different agencies in coordinating their efforts by using common terminology and operating procedures. The five major functional areas of the ICS are command, operations, planning, logistics, and finance.

Command—For a large-scale operation to run safely and effectively, it is necessary to have people in charge. Individuals occupying positions such as safety officer, liaison, and public information officer are responsible for the ordering and releasing of resources.

Operations—Once command has established the strategic goals, operations is responsible for managing all the operations that directly affect the primary mission. Operations is divided into branches that can be divided again into groups assigned to a particular task, such as rescue or ventilation.

Planning—As the incident develops, this area is responsible for the collection, evaluation, dissemination, and use of relevant information. Command will adjust the ordering and releasing of resources according to the information compiled by planning.

Logistics—This area is responsible for supporting the incident through its support and service branches. The support branch maintains supplies, facilities, and vehicle services. The service branch maintains medical, communications, and food services.

Finance—This section takes care of all costs and financial aspects of the incident. Finance is usually only a concern, however, during large-scale incidents that last for a particularly long period of time.

59. The title that best describes the content of this passage is

   A. "The Purpose and Origin of the National Fire Academy (NFA)"

   B. "Why Most Injuries and Fatalities Occur at the Scene of an Emergency"

   C. "The Purpose and Functions of the Incident Command System (ICS)"

   D. "Why Command Is the Most Important Functional Area of the ICS"

60. According to the passage, which of the following is necessary for a large-scale operation to run safely and effectively?

   A. People in charge

   B. Adequate ventilation

   C. Sufficient funds

   D. Food services

61. If an operation does not turn out to take much time to resolve, which functional area of the ICS is least likely to be necessary?

   A. Command

   B. Operations

   C. Logistics

   D. Finance

62. The Planning section is responsible for all but which one of the following?

   A. Dissemination of material about resources

   B. Evaluation of status of resources

   C. Collecting information on resources

   D. Determining what resources can be released

63. What is the area of the following rectangle?

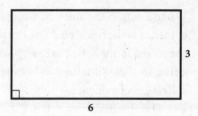

   A. 9

   B. 12

   C. 15

   D. 18

64. If water travels through a fire hose at a rate of 5 feet per second, how long will it take a hose that is 125 feet long to fill with water?

   A. 50 seconds

   B. 35 seconds

   C. 25 seconds

   D. 12 seconds

65. If a salary of $20,000 is subject to a 20% deduction, what is the net salary?

   A. $14,000

   B. $15,500

   C. $16,000

   D. $18,000

Practice Test 1

Questions 66–69 are based on the following passage.

When arson is the suspected cause of a fire, it is important to ensure the proper collection of evidence at the fire scene. The fire investigator typically is responsible for collecting evidence at the scene. It might be the case, however, that an investigator is not available immediately after a fire. In these situations, it is important for the firefighters on the scene to ensure the proper collection of evidence.

The fire department has the authority to control a fire scene for as long after a fire as is necessary. As soon as the last firefighter leaves the scene, however, the department's control of it is limited. Often, a search warrant or written consent is necessary to make later visits to the scene. It is therefore important that all the evidence be tagged, marked, and photographed as soon as possible. If it is necessary to remove any evidence from the scene, firefighters should be careful not to damage any of the evidence in the process.

Until the investigation of the fire is complete, no one should be allowed to enter the scene unless accompanied by a fire officer. Any entry, even by the owner of the premises, should be carefully logged. The person's name, time of entry, time of departure, and descriptions of any items taken from the premises should be recorded.

If it is deemed necessary, fire scenes can be guarded to ensure the safety of anyone near the scene and to ensure that no one tampers with the evidence. Depending on the number of possible entrances to the scene and the severity of safety concerns, a fire scene could be watched by one person or a full-time guard force.

66. If an investigator is not available immediately after a fire, firefighters should

   A. destroy the evidence at the scene.

   B. tag, mark, and photograph the evidence.

   C. allow the owner to find the evidence alone.

   D. leave the fire scene unguarded.

67. All the following should be logged when someone enters the fire scene EXCEPT

   A. a description of the person.

   B. the person's name.

   C. time of entry.

   D. time of departure.

68. The fire department has the authority to control a fire scene

   A. for about two weeks.

   B. after proper collection of evidence.

   C. for as long after a fire as is necessary.

   D. when the last firefighter leaves.

69. To ensure that the fire scene is not contaminated by the activity of the firefighters, they should NOT

   A. secure the fire scene.

   B. call the fire investigator.

   C. damage any evidence.

   D. tag any evidence.

70. You're sitting in your car after having exited a general merchandise big-box store when you see multiple fire engines enter the parking lot. You can see smoke rising from the rear of the store and you hear word that a large fire was found in the rear stockrooms. Soon, you can hear many of the firefighters' radios announcing the presence of foodstuffs in the area of fire attack. Firefighters will conduct an inspection after the fire has been fully extinguished. The most logical reason for completing a thorough inspection is to

A. observe whether foodstuffs increased temperatures enough to weaken the surrounding structure.

B. provide insight to police for what to protect to prevent looting.

C. ensure retrieval of all firefighting equipment.

D. determine which items may have been contaminated by the fire or firefighting procedures.

71. Why is it safer to to use the ladder positioned as shown in Diagram 1 than positioned as shown in Diagram 2?

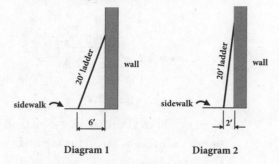

Diagram 1   Diagram 2

A. Less strain is placed on the center rungs of the ladder in Diagram 1.

B. It is easier to grip and stand on the ladder in Diagram 1.

C. The ladder in Diagram 1 reaches a lower height.

D. The ladder in Diagram 1 is less likely to tip over backward than the ladder in Diagram 2.

72. In order to determine the cause of a fire at a gas station, firefighters began interviewing witnesses present at the scene. They received the following eyewitness accounts:

Witness 1: "The fire started after a woman got out of her car and touched the nozzle. There was a flash and she ran away screaming."

Witness 2: "This red truck pulled up and started fueling. The driver then returned to the cab for a phone call, exited again, withdrew the nozzle, and that's when the fire started."

Witness 3: "A woman was talking on her phone next to that truck at pump #4. She was leaning against the tailgate and talking when the fire started."

Witness 4: "It was whoever was driving that red one over there. They got in and out of their car multiple times. I saw them walk over to the far side of the vehicle where the tank was, and that's when the fire started."

Which account should the firefighters ignore?

A. Witness 1

B. Witness 2

C. Witness 3

D. Witness 4

73. Which of the following siphon arrangements would most quickly transfer a solution from the container on the left side to the one on the right side?

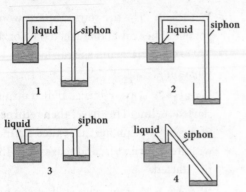

A. 1

B. 2

C. 3

D. 4

74. The following diagrams show flywheels made of the same material, with the same dimensions, and attached to similar engines. The solid areas represent equal weights attached to the flywheel.

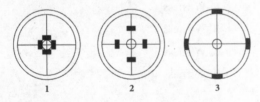

If all three engines are running at the same speed for the same length of time and the power to the engines is shut off simultaneously,

A. wheel 1 will continue turning longest.

B. wheel 2 will continue turning longest.

C. wheel 3 will continue turning longest.

D. all three wheels will continue turning for the same time.

75. In the following diagram, it is easier to get the load onto the platform by using the ramp than by lifting it directly onto the platform.

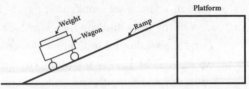

This is true because the effect of the ramp is to

A. reduce the amount of friction so that less force is required.

B. distribute the weight over a larger area.

C. support part of the load so that less force is needed to move the wagon.

D. increase the effect of the moving weight.

76.

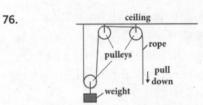

DIAGRAM 1

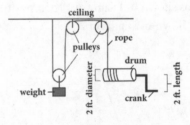

DIAGRAM 2

More weight can be lifted by the method shown in Diagram 2 than the method in Diagram 1 because

A. it takes less force to turn a crank than it does to pull in a straight line.

B. the drum will prevent the weight from falling by itself.

C. the length of the crank is larger than the radius of the drum.

D. the drum has more rope on it, easing the pull.

77. If the head of a hammer has become loose on the handle, it should be properly tightened by

A. driving the handle further into the head.

B. driving a nail alongside the present wedge.

C. using a slightly larger wedge.

D. soaking the handle in water.

78. Which of the following pairs is NOT a set of equivalents?

A. $\frac{1}{5}\%$, 0.002

B. 3.5%, $\frac{7}{200}$

C. 35%, $\frac{35}{100}$

D. 125%, 0.125

79. Amanda is paid double-time for each hour she works beyond 30 hours during the weekdays. Last week, she worked h hours overtime and earned $785 for the week. Which of the following equations can be used to determine her normal hourly rate, r?

A. $30r + 2hr = 785$

B. $30hr = 785$

C. $785r = 30 + h$

D. $(30 + h)r = 785$

80. Firefighters Gonzaga and Morris respond to a report of a multi-car incident on the nearby highway leading into the higher passes of the mountains. Subzero temperatures and snow have created treacherous conditions both for motorists and firefighters alike. The firefighters quickly extract drivers and passengers from the vehicles involved. But a fire breaks out, and the firefighters begin fire suppression using their engine's water tank. The fire is quickly extinguished, and firefighters stop the flow of water and cease fire attack. Paramedics and police are on scene to tend to the victims and direct existing traffic. Meanwhile, state authorities have closed off access to the highway until the storm has passed. The firefighters begin clearing the scene and storing gear but discover a problem. The firefighters neglected to

A. fully extinguish the fires in the vehicles and have created a hazard for other responders on scene.

B. control the flow of water so as to prevent unnecessary pooling on the roadway.

C. maintain a warm area for victims of the incident to wait in.

D. let their hoselines keep flowing so as to prevent freezing within the nozzle and hoses.

Questions 81 and 82 are based on the following table.

FIRE CLASSIFICATION SYSTEM		
Type of Fire	**Combustible Materials**	**Extinguishing Process**
Class A	paper, cloth, wood, rubber, plastics	water, foam
Class B	paints, oil, gasoline, mineral spirits	oxygen exclusion (the blanketing effect)
Class C	energized electrical equipment	dry chemicals, carbon dioxide
Class D	combustible metals (aluminum, titanium)	depends on the type of metal

81. Firefighters use dry chemicals and carbon dioxide extinguishers on fires caused by energized electrical equipment because

    A. water might cause the fire to spread to Class A materials in the space.

    B. there is a risk of electrical shock or further shorts when using water.

    C. water is only for Class B fires of combustible liquids.

    D. all the metals used in the equipment are best treated as though they were Class C.

82. If a painter is working near an open flame and the paint catches fire, the extinguishing process he or she should use

    A. depends on the type of paint.

    B. is dry chemicals or carbon dioxide.

    C. is water or a noncombustible foam.

    D. is a fire blanket.

83. When using a life net, firefighters are told to watch the person jumping rather than focus on the other firefighters, their surroundings, or a fire. The best justification for this statement is that

    A. a person jumping might over- or underestimate the distance to the net from the building and need to be caught.

    B. some people need firefighters' attention to generate the confidence to be able to jump.

    C. firefighters should be prepared to let the net give slightly upon the jumper's impact.

    D. firefighters need to be evenly spaced around the perimeter of the net to distribute the force of a jumper.

84. Two balls of the same size but different weights are dropped from a 10-foot height. The most accurate statement is that

    A. both balls will reach the ground at the same time because they are the same size.

    B. both balls will reach the ground at the same time because the effect of gravity is the same on both balls.

    C. the heavier ball will reach the ground first because it weighs more.

    D. the lighter ball will reach the ground first because air resistance is greater on the heavier ball.

85. If boiling water is poured into a drinking glass, the glass is likely to crack. If a metal spoon is first placed in the glass, however, the glass is much less likely to crack. The reason that the glass with the spoon is less likely to crack is that the spoon

A. distributes the water over a larger surface of the glass.

B. quickly absorbs heat from the water.

C. reinforces the glass.

D. reduces the amount of water that can be poured into the glass.

86. It takes more energy to force water through a long pipe than through a short pipe of the same diameter. The principal reason for this is

A. gravity.

B. friction.

C. inertia.

D. cohesion.

87. A pump discharging at 300 pounds psi pressure delivers water through 100 feet of pipe laid horizontally. If the valve at the end of the pipe is shut so that no water can flow, the pressure at the valve is, for practical purposes,

A. greater than the pressure at the pump.

B. equal to the pressure at the pump.

C. less than the pressure at the pump.

D. greater or less than the pressure at the pump, depending on the type of pump used.

Questions 88–92 are based on the following image. Study and memorize the image for five minutes, then cover the image and answer the questions. Do not refer to the image while answering the questions.

Practice Test 1

88. How many firefighters are actively engaged in training a hose on the fire?

   A. 1

   B. 2

   C. 3

   D. 4

89. How many wood pallets are visible?

   A. 0

   B. 1

   C. 2

   D. 3

90. How many of the upper-story windows are obstructed by fire?

   A. 1

   B. 2

   C. 3

   D. 4

91. How many of the firefighters are wearing a self-contained breathing apparatus (SCBA)?

   A. 1

   B. 2

   C. 3

   D. 4

92. How many doorways are visible?

   A. 0

   B. 1

   C. 2

   D. 3

93. Firefighters need to be prepared to handle all manner of emergency situations. First-aid methods are particularly helpful for many circumstances. Firefighters should be well-versed in first aid in order to

   A. save victims the expense of having to visit a doctor for simple injuries.

   B. prevent lawsuits against the fire department by tending to manageable injuries.

   C. respond quickly in an emergency to save a life.

   D. fulfill the role of paramedics should none be available for an emergency.

94. While observing emergency responders at the scene of a fire, you see paramedics seat a man who was just removed from the fire on the rear bumper of a nearby vehicle. Paramedics begin administering oxygen and place blankets over his shoulders and torso. As you watch the firefighting activities, you notice the paramedics checking in with the state of the man every few minutes. You overhear that this man was going into shock. From these observations, you can conclude that victims of shock should be

   A. placed in a horizontal position to maximize blood flow.

   B. given oxygen to counter the effects of the shock condition.

   C. kept at a cooler temperature than the surrounding environment.

   D. allowed to recover without disturbance while attending to other victims.

95. Tourniquets offer a stop-gap measure for stopping bleeding in cases of extreme limb trauma. It is only a temporary measure while waiting for expert medical personnel to arrive and can be dangerous when used improperly. The following steps outline the necessary actions when applying a tourniquet (steps are not in the correct order):

Step 1. Mark the duration of tourniquet application.

Step 2. Call 911 for the aid of emergency responders.

Step 3. Use a stick as a windlass to twist and tighten the tourniquet.

Step 4. Apply pressure to the wound and position the tourniquet above the injury.

Step 5. Find the source of the bleeding.

What is the most logical order for the steps above?

A. 2–1–4–3–5

B. 5–3–4–1–2

C. 4–5–1–2–3

D. 2–5–4–3–1

96. Firefighter Jemisin and Nguyen arrive at the scene of a hit-and-run traffic incident involving two cars and a cyclist. One driver fled the scene. The other driver is currently pinned inside her vehicle but is responsive to questions and appears uninjured; however, she is completely unable to move. Upon inspecting the vehicle, fuel and oil can be seen leaking onto the street. Meanwhile, the cyclist has an open fracture in his lower leg and is bleeding. The first action firefighters should take is to

A. seek eyewitness accounts to aid with the apprehension of the other driver.

B. remove the pinned driver from the vehicle and move both victims a safe distance from the wreck.

C. ensure that paramedics are on their way to the scene to aid the cyclist.

D. provide medical care to the cyclist and wait with him until paramedics arrive.

Practice Test 1

Questions 97–99 are based on the following passage and diagram. Assume there is a fire in an apartment on the west side of the sixth floor.

An eight-story apartment building has scissor stairs beginning on the first floor and going to the roof. Scissor stairs are two separate stairways (stairway A and stairway B) that crisscross each other and lead to opposite sides of the building on each floor. Once a person has entered either stairway, the only way to cross over to the other stairway on any floor is to leave the stairway and use the hallway on that floor. A person entering stairway A, which starts on the east side of the building on the first floor, would end up on the west side of the building on the second floor and back on the east side on the third floor. Similarly, a person entering stairway B, which starts on the west side of the building on the first floor, would end up on the east side of the building on the second floor and back on the west side on the third floor.

The apartment building has one water pipe for fighting fires. The pipe runs in a straight line near the stairway on the east side of the building from the first floor to the roof. There are water outlets for this pipe on each floor.

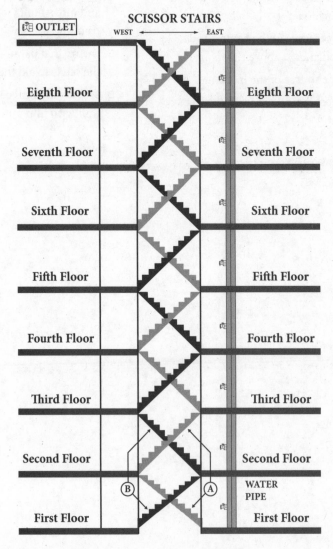

Practice Test 1

97. Firefighters are ordered to connect a hose to the nearest outlet below the fire. Upon reaching this outlet, they find that it is not usable. The next available outlet is on the

    A. fifth floor near stairway B.
    B. third floor near stairway A.
    C. fourth floor near stairway B.
    D. fourth floor near stairway A.

98. A firefighter working on the west side of the seventh floor is ordered to search for victims on the west side of the eighth floor. The door leading to the stairway on the west side of the seventh floor is jammed shut. To reach the victims, the firefighter should take

    A. stairway A to the eighth floor and then go across the hallway to the west side of the floor.
    B. stairway B to the eighth floor and then go across the hallway to the west side of the floor.
    C. the hallway to the east side of the seventh floor and go up stairway A.
    D. the hallway to the east side of the seventh floor and go up stairway B.

99. A firefighter entered stairway B from the roof and needs to hook up a hoseline to the seventh-floor outlet to assist in extinguishing the apartment fire. Which action would be the most effective and safe?

    A. Proceed down stairway B to the seventh floor. Carry the hose through the seventh-floor hallway from the west side of the building, attach the hose, and run it down stairway A to the sixth floor.
    B. Carry the hose through the eighth-floor hallway from the east side. Go down stairway A to the seventh floor, attach the hose, then run the hose down stairway A to the sixth floor.
    C. Proceed down stairway B to the seventh floor. Walk through the seventh-floor hallway from the west side of the building, attach the hose, then run the hose back to the west side of the seventh floor and down stairway B to the sixth floor.
    D. Carry the hose through the eighth-floor hallway from the east side. Return to the roof and cross over to stairway A, go down to the seventh floor, attach the hose, then run the hose down stairway A to the sixth floor.

Practice Test 1

100. When attempting to rescue a person trapped at a window, firefighters frequently use an aerial ladder with a rotating base. The rotating base enables the ladder to move up and down and from side to side. In a rescue situation, the ladder should be placed so that both sides rest fully on the windowsill after it has been raised into position. Which one of the engines' rotating bases is best positioned in relation to the window to provide safe ladder assistance to the person in the building?

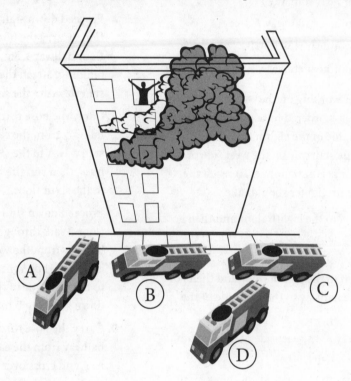

A. Engine A

B. Engine B

C. Engine C

D. Engine D

ANSWER KEY AND EXPLANATIONS

1. C	21. D	41. D	61. D	81. B
2. D	22. B	42. D	62. D	82. D
3. A	23. A	43. A	63. D	83. A
4. D	24. A	44. C	64. C	84. B
5. B	25. A	45. A	65. C	85. B
6. C	26. A	46. B	66. B	86. B
7. A	27. B	47. B	67. A	87. B
8. A	28. B	48. A	68. C	88. B
9. C	29. B	49. B	69. C	89. C
10. D	30. B	50. C	70. D	90. C
11. B	31. B	51. C	71. D	91. A
12. B	32. B	52. A	72. C	92. B
13. B	33. C	53. B	73. D	93. C
14. A	34. C	54. B	74. C	94. B
15. D	35. C	55. B	75. C	95. D
16. B	36. D	56. D	76. C	96. B
17. D	37. C	57. B	77. C	97. C
18. A	38. C	58. B	78. D	98. C
19. B	39. B	59. C	79. A	99. B
20. D	40. A	60. A	80. D	100. B

1. **The correct answer is C.** 200 Pine Street is the tallest building on the block.

2. **The correct answer is D.** The Steel Door Company is the building farthest from the hydrant.

3. **The correct answer is A.** The diagram shows that Brown Lumber has skylights on the roof of the building.

4. **The correct answer is D.** The legend and the diagram show that Champ's Auto Parts has roll-down shutters.

5. **The correct answer is B.** The FDC connection on the front wall of the Ace Dress Company building indicates that the building has an automatic wet sprinkler system.

6. **The correct answer is C.** The wind is blowing from the east as indicated by the arrow and compass points at the top of the diagram.

7. **The correct answer is A.** Refer to the diagram and the definition of a trussed roof in the first sentence of the question.

8. **The correct answer is A.** The Dexter Hotel is immediately adjacent to the building afire. Fire burning through the roof of Brown Lumber would expose the hotel to flames, especially with the wind blowing from the east.

9. **The correct answer is C.** A hotel's guests are likely unfamiliar with the area and the layout of the building, thus in an emergency situation unaccounted for guests are likely still in their rooms, having ignored the alarms,

or somewhere within the hotel itself. To aid hotel guests, hotel staff need to explicitly inform guests of the location of fire exits. All other answer options would be true if hotels did not follow proper fire codes. There is no implication in this situation or general that they do not.

10. **The correct answer is D.** A fallen high-tension wire constitutes an active emergency. The firefighter needs to take action to ensure the safety of passing civilians. Moving the wire (choice A) risks electric shock if it is energized. Continuing to the firehouse (choice B) creates a significant delay in response, potentially endangering civilians. While contacting a public utility company can address the issue, as was the case with choice B, it creates the possibility of injury while the firefighter is away from the scene. As such, the firefighter should guide civilians around the danger and request that a passerby contact the utility company.

11. **The correct answer is B.** Firefighters must prioritize the safety of emergency victims as well as those at the scene should the situation change. With the news from command and the incursion of civilians onto the fireground, firefighters must clear them immediately for both safety and to ensure efficient firefighting. No other answer choice addresses the civilian interference with firefighting equipment and techniques.

12. **The correct answer is B.** Room 304 is on the south side of the building. Room 306 is the nearest room to the west of Room 304. If the firefighter entered through Room 302 (choice A), he would need to pass through the flames. Room 312 (choice C) and Room 352 (choice D) are farther away from the fire than Room 306.

13. **The correct answer is B.** Stairway B, as shown in the diagram, is the closest. The stairway used by the firefighter to gain access to the third floor was stairway A.

14. **The correct answer is A.** By checking the compass points in the center of the diagram, we know that Rooms 303 and 305 are on the south side of the courtyard. Rooms 323 and 325 are on the opposite side of the courtyard, which is the north side of the building.

15. **The correct answer is D.** The northeast stair is stairway C, and the firefighters have already brought a hose up this stairway. Stairway D is the next closest stairway where both hose-lines can operate from the same direction to extinguish the fire.

16. **The correct answer is B.** This is an example of a second-class lever. (The weight is between the fulcrum and the lift.) By moving the weight closer to the fulcrum, an increase in distance between the load and the lift point is achieved. This increases the mechanical advantage of the lever, and less effort is necessary to lift the load.

17. **The correct answer is D.** You cannot see a defect such as a knot or a split in the wood in a painted ladder. A wooden ladder should never be painted.

18. **The correct answer is A.** Add $\frac{2}{3} + \frac{2}{3} = 1\frac{1}{3}$.

19. **The correct answer is B.** Add the cost of each piece of equipment to find the total cost. $28,000 + $17,2502 + $7,025 = $52,275.

20. **The correct answer is D.** To find the average of a list of numbers, first add them up (100 + 100 + 150 + 150 + 250 + 300 = 1,050), and then divide the sum of the numbers by the number of lengths listed (1,050 ÷ 6 = 175). The average hose length is 175 feet.

21. **The correct answer is D.** To find the area of a flat surface, multiply the length times the width. 5 × 2 = 10 sq. ft.

22. **The correct answer is B.** The window on the tenth story of a building would have 103 ft. from the ground to the windowsill. The articulating aerial platform is likely closest to reaching such a height.

23. **The correct answer is A.** First, find the full range of the articulating aerial ladder. 102 ft. – 55 ft. = 47 ft. The range of the ladder if it were extended 75 feet then is 75 ft. – 55 ft. = 20 ft. To find the percentage of its range, divide 20 by 47. Hence, $20 \div 47 = .42.5$, or 42.5 percent.

24. **The correct answer is A.** A firefighter's expertise and priorities would allow him or her to offer insight into conditions that create fires. For this situation and given the presence of oxygen tanks, a firefighter would direct residents to avoid mixing compressed oxygen and open flames because of the danger of combustion.

25. **The correct answer is A.** With the limited visibility created by the smoke and the fact that all firefighters began their primary search of the building separately, it is possible for firefighters either to become disoriented and lost in the blaze, or to have difficulty searching the building for victims. Working in pairs could preempt those issues.

26. **The correct answer is A.** The most logical order is 3–4–2–1–5. Firefighters' first responsibility is to conduct a search for victims (3), then determine the source of the fire (4). If victims are unaccounted for, firefighters must perform a thorough search (2). Once victims have been extracted, firefighters can begin fire suppression (1). Finally, firefighters should secure any property damaged or otherwise (5).

27. **The correct answer is B.** Providing the specific reason for the evacuation (in this case a fire in one of the stock rooms) may cause panic in the situation, making safe and efficient evacuation more difficult. While some audience members may be reluctant to leave if they're uncertain of a refund (choice A), other choices take priority. Evacuations can quickly turn to chaos when not conducted in an orderly fashion (choice C), thus trying to evacuate everyone at the same time would

not be recommended. Choice D runs counter to the correct response as further details about the nature of the emergency waste valuable time and can cause greater panic.

28. **The correct answer is B.** This is a keyhole saw used to make curved cuts. Choice A is a backsaw, often used in woodworking. Choice C is a rip or crosscut saw, also used for woodworking but effective on larger pieces of material as well. Choice D is a hacksaw, which is typically used on metal.

29. **The correct answer is B.** Witness 3's account has the greatest number of inconsistencies with the other accounts and should be eliminated. Even as Witness 2 states that he or she saw a woman exiting the condo, this is a reasonable mistake because of the long hair described by Witnesses 1 and 4. Witness 3 does not specifically describe the vase, stating that the suspect had on a backpack, while also neglecting to mention the suspect's hair length, a key feature as described by the other witnesses.

30. **The correct answer is B.** While Stephanie Martin is on duty, her chief responsibility is to be available for alarms received by the fire department. Any other task beyond activities in her daily routine while on duty are detriments to her firefighting ability. The same can be said of other firefighters and officers on duty at the firehouse. Stephanie should politely refuse the request and explain her reasoning to the woman.

31. **The correct answer is B.** By first drilling a small hole into the wood, you can reduce the amount of stress the nail places on the wood and therefore reduce the likelihood that the wood will split.

32. **The correct answer is B.** By requiring individuals and groups to provide in-depth information about the nature of events, fire departments can prevent fire emergencies from occurring. While a fee is required for the permit process (choice A), revenue

Answers | Practice Test 1

Answers

Practice Test 1

generation is an effect rather than a primary reason for the process. Information gleaned from the paperwork can provide insight for future firefighting (choice C), but this is also secondary to the primary task of preventing emergencies from happening to begin with. The fire department aims to minimize active hazards to the public, not simply providing warning; thus, choice D would constitute poor reasoning.

33. **The correct answer is C.** By reporting the complaint to a superior officer, the firefighter is ensuring that information will be recorded and properly communicated to those who can take direct action to investigate the complaint. If the complaint is found to be true, a citation will be issued. Other answer choices do little to address the situation and affect effective firefighting practice.

34. **The correct answer is C.** While many of the answer choices represent negligent behavior that is likely to result in property damage, only the individual in choice C can be said to have committed arson due to the willful destruction of property in a situation in which no other result was likely.

35. **The correct answer is C.** The directional compass in the upper-left corner of the diagram indicates that north is pointing up, so east-west is from right to left. Since Corridor D is the east-west hallway in the center of the building, the firefighters should search Rooms 107, 109, 125, 126, 127, and 128.

36. **The correct answer is D.** We can see from the diagram that Truck 21 is facing north on 7th Avenue. The nearest hose connection is Connection E, about midway between 39th and 40th Streets.

37. **The correct answer is C.** The firefighters enter the building on 40th Street, which is the south side of the building. Upon entering the lobby, they would have to turn east in Hallway E, north in Hallway B, and west in Hallway C.

38. **The correct answer is C.** To find the mean, or average, add the ages of all the firefighters:

$$28 + 46 + 25 + 37 + 39 = 175$$

Then divide the total by the number of firefighters:

$$175 \div 5 = 35$$

39. **The correct answer is B.** To find the median, arrange the years served data in numerical order: 3, 6, 11, 14, 17. The median is the middle value, or 11.

40. **The correct answer is A.** The median number of years served is 11; the mean number of years served is 10. Choice B is not true because the mean age of the firefighters is 35 which is less than the median age of 37. The mode is the number that occurs most frequently in a data set, but there are no repeating numbers in the table. Since there is no mode, choice C cannot be true. Choice D is inaccurate because the mean age of the firefighters is 35, which is greater than the mean number of years served (10).

41. **The correct answer is D.** The presence of a significant amount of glass on the inside of the window indicates that the window was broken from the outside. As such, a fire investigator would conclude this was the point of entry. Little could be gleaned regarding how long ago the window was broken (choice A) or that the window must have been broken after the fire started (choice C) without further evidence. If a resident used the window to escape the fire (choice B), then the glass would most likely be located outside the structure.

42. **The correct answer is D.** The firefighter needs to communicate the necessity of a proper building inspection while maintaining an appropriate demeanor. The only answer option to provide adequate reasoning and avoid introducing emotion into the situation is choice D.

43. **The correct answer is A.** The preservation of transient evidence at the scene (3) should occur as early on as possible as it is likely to be changed or contaminated as emergency responders work their way through the scene, thus eliminating choice D. It's important then for an investigator to clearly mark evidence (4) to avoid damage or changes to the scene. This would be followed by clear documentation of said evidence (2), to be followed by its removal for preservation and further inspection (1). Both choices B and C attempt to remove evidence before its proper documentation and mapping, thus conflicting with logical order presented in choice A.

44. **The correct answer is C.** Prior to any action being taken, the control valve first must be located. This eliminates choices A and B. Before any action can be taken to close the valve or alter the supply line, the enclosure must be opened. This eliminates choice D. Therefore, the most logical order is 5–2–4–3–1, as listed in choice C.

45. **The correct answer is A.** To efficiently address the issue, the probationary firefighter should discuss the issue with the officer in question. Any other actions do not serve to directly address the issue and waste the time not only of the probationary firefighter but also others at the fire house.

46. **The correct answer is B.** With the available information, little can be known regarding the increased effectiveness of saltwater in firefighting (choice C) or the importance of its lower freezing temperature (choice D). Similarly, little is revealed by the situation that illuminates whether using saltwater would limit water damage (choice A) in the situation. While the pier is logically exposed to saltwater with greater frequency, nothing is known about how freshwater and saltwater affect the materials involved differently. It is then reasonable to conclude that the quantity of water available is a sound choice for firefighting in the situation.

47. **The correct answer is B.** Carbon monoxide is a toxic gas. Since the atmospheric air we breathe is composed of 84 percent nitrogen and 16 percent oxygen, choices A and C cannot be correct.

48. **The correct answer is A.** The flame indicates that there is sufficient oxygen for the firefighter to breathe while wearing this type of mask. A toxic gas concentration of 2 to 3 percent is low enough to be handled by the mask, so in the presence of a fire, the firefighter should not feel unsafe *unless* the toxic gas concentration is *above* 2 or 3 percent.

49. **The correct answer is B.** According to the last sentence of the paragraph, there is not enough oxygen to sustain life.

50. **The correct answer is C.** The canister-type gas mask contains chemicals that filter toxic gases and smoke, resulting in breathable air.

51. **The correct answer is C.** The first sentence states that doors are the only openings that are permitted in fire partitions.

52. **The correct answer is A.** The correct answer can be found in the second sentence. Doorway openings permitted in the wall are a maximum of 25 percent of 22 feet, or 5.5 feet. One opening would be 3 feet, and two openings would be a total of 6 feet. Therefore, there can be only 1 door.

53. **The correct answer is B.** According to the last sentence of the passage, the maximum opening for a motor vehicle is 140 square feet. The truck opening in the diagram is 13 feet × 11 feet, or 143 square feet, and is therefore too large.

54. **The correct answer is B.** When evaluating the potential risks in each answer choice, the most likely factors to directly contribute to fires and subsequent harm would be combustible materials and malfunctioning alert systems. That combination could result in a fire that then proceeds without alerting tenants or emergency responders. Other choices

represent clear code violations; however, none are as likely to contribute to a volatile situation as those in choice B.

55. **The correct answer is B.** The average household toaster uses 1,400 watts of energy, much more than a 150-watt light bulb (choice A), a door buzzer (choice C), and an 8-inch electric fan (choice D).

56. **The correct answer is D.** The larger of the two whole number parts determines the sign. Thus $8 + (-6) = 2$.

57. **The correct answer is B.** $360 - $288 = $72 discount.

$$\frac{72}{360} = \frac{1}{5} = 20\%$$

58. **The correct answer is B.** Let x be the number of gallons of gas the tank can hold. Then, $\frac{1}{8}x + 8 = \frac{5}{6}x$. Solve for x:

$$\frac{1}{8}x + 8 = \frac{5}{6}x$$
$$24 \cdot \left(\frac{1}{8}x + 8\right) = 24 \cdot \left(\frac{5}{6}x\right)$$
$$3x + 192 = 20x$$
$$192 = 17x$$
$$x = \frac{192}{17} = 11\frac{5}{17}$$

The tank holds approximately 11 gallons of gas.

59. **The correct answer is C.** This entire passage discusses the purpose and functions of the Incident Command System (ICS). Of the options listed, the title that best reflects the content of the passage is "The Purpose and Functions of the Incident Command System (ICS)."

60. **The correct answer is A.** Under the heading of Command, the passage states that, for a large-scale operation to run safely and effectively, it is necessary to have people in charge.

61. **The correct answer is D.** Under the heading of Finance, the passage states that collecting money is usually a concern only during large-scale incidents that last for a particularly long period of time.

62. **The correct answer is D.** Planning is responsible for collecting, evaluating, disseminating, and using relevant information. Command determines which resources can be released based on the information provided by the Planning section.

63. **The correct answer is D.** Area is calculated by multiplying the width of a shape by its height. In this case, $6 \times 3 = 18$.

64. **The correct answer is C.** It takes the water one second to travel through five feet of hose. Therefore, $125 \div 5 = 25$.

65. **The correct answer is C.** If 20% is deducted, the net salary is 80%. $20,000 \times 80\% = $20,000 \times .80 = $16,000$.

66. **The correct answer is B.** The first paragraph states that, if an investigator is not available immediately after a fire, it is important for the firefighters on the scene to ensure proper collection of the evidence. The second paragraph then states that the firefighters should tag, mark, and photograph the evidence as soon as possible.

67. **The correct answer is A.** The third paragraph indicates that only the person's name, time of entry, time of departure, and a description of the items taken should be logged.

68. **The correct answer is C.** The first sentence of the second paragraph states that the fire department has the authority to control a fire scene for as long after a fire as is necessary.

69. **The correct answer is C.** The last sentence of the second paragraph states that it is important for firefighters to not damage any evidence.

70. **The correct answer is D.** You can conclude that because of the nature of foodstuffs firefighters need to determine whether they are still edible. Other answer choices represent standard procedures common in any

firefighting scenario as firefighters work to preserve life and property.

71. **The correct answer is D.** The ladder with the gentler grade is more stable and is less likely to tip over. The horizontal distance between the wall and the base of the ladder is determined by dividing the length of the ladder by 5 and adding 2. For example, for a 20-foot ladder, dividing by 5 equals 4; 4 plus 2 equals 6; 6 feet is the proper distance from the wall for the 20-foot ladder.

72. **The correct answer is C.** Witnesses 1, 2, and 4 describe how the driver of the vehicle near where the fire started was doing something near the gas tank itself, likely handling the nozzle. These accounts appear to indicate that it was a static charge that provided the spark for combustion. Witness 3 does not mention the driver handling the nozzle but instead speaks to the driver using her cellphone when the fire started. The driver's placement and apparent cause of the fire differ and should thus be discarded.

73. **The correct answer is B.** Notice that siphon 2 is longer than siphons 1, 3, and 4. The liquid flowing down siphon 2 will be moving faster as it travels to the bottom and will generate greater pressure, which in turn will produce greater velocity to increase the height of the liquid in the second container. Therefore, of the options given, siphon 2 will most quickly transfer a solution from the container on the left side to the one on the right side.

74. **The correct answer is C.** Because of the placement of the weights on the outer rim in wheel 3, centrifugal force will cause it to continue turning the longest.

75. **The correct answer is C.** The inclined ramp (or plane) is simply a sloping platform that enables a person to raise an object without having to lift it vertically. It is a simple machine that helps you perform work. The ramp and wagon allow the force to be distributed across the length of the plane rather than concentrated over a shorter vertical distance.

76. **The correct answer is C.** A distinct mechanical advantage is gained by using a large lever (the crank) to move a small object (the drum).

77. **The correct answer is C.** If you look at the top of a hammer where it is joined to the handle, you will see the top of either a wooden or metal wedge. Driving another wedge into the handle will tighten the hammerhead.

78. **The correct answer is D.** 125% = 1.25, not 0.125 (12.5%).

79. **The correct answer is A.** The amount Amanda earns for the first 30 hours of work is $30r$. For the h hours she works beyond these initial hours, she earns $h(2r) = 2hr$. The sum of these amounts, $30r + 2hr$ is the amount she earns in the week, $785.

80. **The correct answer is D.** The details of the situation reveal that temperatures are well below freezing, the firefighters are located on an inclined road, the fire is fully extinguished, and victims are being assisted. By stopping the flow on their hoses, the water in the lines could stagnate and possibly freeze, depending upon how long the lines sit inactive. This can potentially damage equipment and extend the firefighters' time on scene. Choice A is untrue according to the passage. Choice B is irrelevant as the road is on an incline and the highway has been closed for further access. Choice C is being addressed by paramedics and police on scene.

81. **The correct answer is B.** Water conducts electricity, and its usage on energized electronics could lead to further shocks or shorts. Even without that information, it is clear from the available chart that choices C and D are false. Similarly, if the fire were to spread to Class A materials (choice A), then water would appear to adequately stifle those flames as well.

82. **The correct answer is D.** By locating paints in the fire classification system table, the only suggested extinguishing process is "oxygen exclusion (the blanketing effect)." From this, you can conclude that a fire blanket would be the only appropriate choice from the options offered.

83. **The correct answer is A.** Logically, the purpose of watching an object as it falls is to best predict and travel to its point of impact. That reasoning is no different for a person. While other answer choices may have logical merit, little else speaks to the utility of the safety net itself—that in order to function properly, the person must be caught in the first place.

84. **The correct answer is B.** Both balls will reach the ground at the same time because the gravitational force on objects with the same surface size varies with the distance of the objects from the center of the earth. The weight of the objects does not matter.

85. **The correct answer is B.** The metal spoon is a good conductor and will rapidly conduct heat away from the water. This reduces the amount of heat absorbed by the glass and prevents it from breaking.

86. **The correct answer is B.** Friction in a pipe or a hose varies directly with the length. The longer the pipe or hose, the greater the friction. The immediate result of friction in a hose is to cut down the available pressure at the nozzle.

87. **The correct answer is B.** This is a principle of pressure in fluids. Pressure applied to a confined fluid from within is transmitted in all directions without differentiation. Therefore, all points in the 100-foot pipe would have the same pressure.

88. **The correct answer is B.** While there's only one visible hose in action, it takes one firefighter to steady the hose and one to train the nozzle on the fire. We can see this by looking closely at the left side of the picture.

89. **The correct answer is C.** There are two pallets positioned on the forward-facing side of the house—one on the ground in front the door and the other leaned against the far right window.

90. **The correct answer is C.** There are three upper-story windows visible in the photograph, and all three are obstructed by a wall of flame.

91. **The correct answer is A.** Only one of the firefighters is wearing a SCBA.

92. **The correct answer is B.** There is one doorway that is visible.

93. **The correct answer is C.** A firefighter's primary goal is to ensure the safety of victims in an emergency. Thus, a firefighter who is well-versed in first aid will be able to tend to a victim's needs should their injuries require immediate attention.

94. **The correct answer is B.** The man is not placed in a horizontal position (choice A), he is given blankets, not kept cool (choice C), and paramedics repeatedly monitor the man's condition (choice D). Sentence 2 states that the paramedics began to administer oxygen. Thus, you can conclude that victims of shock should be given oxygen to counter the effects of the shock condition.

95. **The correct answer is D.** Because a tourniquet is a triage procedure and not a permanent medical solution to an injury, it is imperative that in the event of serious injury emergency responders be contacted (2). The necessity of that step as early in the process as possible eliminates choices B and C. The individual then needs to determine the source of the bleeding (5) to apply the tourniquet effectively. This eliminates choice A, which completes that step last. As a result, choice D places the steps in the most logical order.

96. **The correct answer is B.** While multiple victims are present on scene and one suffers from a serious injury, the vehicle leaking

flammable liquids represents a serious hazard. Should the liquids ignite, both the driver inside the vehicle, the cyclist, and the firefighters would be at risk of injury or death. Firefighters can stabilize the cyclist until paramedics arrive after freeing the driver.

97. **The correct answer is C.** Stairway B is the dark-colored stairway. It enters the fourth floor on the east side. With the fifth-floor outlet not usable, this is the nearest usable outlet below the fire.

98. **The correct answer is C.** By using stairway A on the east side of the seventh floor, he would come out on the eighth floor on the west side.

99. **The correct answer is B.** The firefighter should carry the hose through the eighth-floor hallway from the east side. Go down stairway A to the seventh floor, attach the hose, then run the hose down stairway A to the sixth floor. This is the most direct route that won't put the firefighter on the side of the building directly above where the fire is burning.

100. **The correct answer is B.** The rotating base of Engine B is directly in front of the victim at the window. Ladders generally are positioned with both beams on the sill to prevent twisting of the ladder under the weight of individuals using them.

Answers | Practice Test 1

PRACTICE TEST 2 ANSWER SHEET

1. Ⓐ Ⓑ Ⓒ Ⓓ   21. Ⓐ Ⓑ Ⓒ Ⓓ   41. Ⓐ Ⓑ Ⓒ Ⓓ   61. Ⓐ Ⓑ Ⓒ Ⓓ   81. Ⓐ Ⓑ Ⓒ Ⓓ

2. Ⓐ Ⓑ Ⓒ Ⓓ   22. Ⓐ Ⓑ Ⓒ Ⓓ   42. Ⓐ Ⓑ Ⓒ Ⓓ   62. Ⓐ Ⓑ Ⓒ Ⓓ   82. Ⓐ Ⓑ Ⓒ Ⓓ

3. Ⓐ Ⓑ Ⓒ Ⓓ   23. Ⓐ Ⓑ Ⓒ Ⓓ   43. Ⓐ Ⓑ Ⓒ Ⓓ   63. Ⓐ Ⓑ Ⓒ Ⓓ   83. Ⓐ Ⓑ Ⓒ Ⓓ

4. Ⓐ Ⓑ Ⓒ Ⓓ   24. Ⓐ Ⓑ Ⓒ Ⓓ   44. Ⓐ Ⓑ Ⓒ Ⓓ   64. Ⓐ Ⓑ Ⓒ Ⓓ   84. Ⓐ Ⓑ Ⓒ Ⓓ

5. Ⓐ Ⓑ Ⓒ Ⓓ   25. Ⓐ Ⓑ Ⓒ Ⓓ   45. Ⓐ Ⓑ Ⓒ Ⓓ   65. Ⓐ Ⓑ Ⓒ Ⓓ   85. Ⓐ Ⓑ Ⓒ Ⓓ

6. Ⓐ Ⓑ Ⓒ Ⓓ   26. Ⓐ Ⓑ Ⓒ Ⓓ   46. Ⓐ Ⓑ Ⓒ Ⓓ   66. Ⓐ Ⓑ Ⓒ Ⓓ   86. Ⓐ Ⓑ Ⓒ Ⓓ

7. Ⓐ Ⓑ Ⓒ Ⓓ   27. Ⓐ Ⓑ Ⓒ Ⓓ   47. Ⓐ Ⓑ Ⓒ Ⓓ   67. Ⓐ Ⓑ Ⓒ Ⓓ   87. Ⓐ Ⓑ Ⓒ Ⓓ

8. Ⓐ Ⓑ Ⓒ Ⓓ   28. Ⓐ Ⓑ Ⓒ Ⓓ   48. Ⓐ Ⓑ Ⓒ Ⓓ   68. Ⓐ Ⓑ Ⓒ Ⓓ   88. Ⓐ Ⓑ Ⓒ Ⓓ

9. Ⓐ Ⓑ Ⓒ Ⓓ   29. Ⓐ Ⓑ Ⓒ Ⓓ   49. Ⓐ Ⓑ Ⓒ Ⓓ   69. Ⓐ Ⓑ Ⓒ Ⓓ   89. Ⓐ Ⓑ Ⓒ Ⓓ

10. Ⓐ Ⓑ Ⓒ Ⓓ   30. Ⓐ Ⓑ Ⓒ Ⓓ   50. Ⓐ Ⓑ Ⓒ Ⓓ   70. Ⓐ Ⓑ Ⓒ Ⓓ   90. Ⓐ Ⓑ Ⓒ Ⓓ

11. Ⓐ Ⓑ Ⓒ Ⓓ   31. Ⓐ Ⓑ Ⓒ Ⓓ   51. Ⓐ Ⓑ Ⓒ Ⓓ   71. Ⓐ Ⓑ Ⓒ Ⓓ   91. Ⓐ Ⓑ Ⓒ Ⓓ

12. Ⓐ Ⓑ Ⓒ Ⓓ   32. Ⓐ Ⓑ Ⓒ Ⓓ   52. Ⓐ Ⓑ Ⓒ Ⓓ   72. Ⓐ Ⓑ Ⓒ Ⓓ   92. Ⓐ Ⓑ Ⓒ Ⓓ

13. Ⓐ Ⓑ Ⓒ Ⓓ   33. Ⓐ Ⓑ Ⓒ Ⓓ   53. Ⓐ Ⓑ Ⓒ Ⓓ   73. Ⓐ Ⓑ Ⓒ Ⓓ   93. Ⓐ Ⓑ Ⓒ Ⓓ

14. Ⓐ Ⓑ Ⓒ Ⓓ   34. Ⓐ Ⓑ Ⓒ Ⓓ   54. Ⓐ Ⓑ Ⓒ Ⓓ   74. Ⓐ Ⓑ Ⓒ Ⓓ   94. Ⓐ Ⓑ Ⓒ Ⓓ

15. Ⓐ Ⓑ Ⓒ Ⓓ   35. Ⓐ Ⓑ Ⓒ Ⓓ   55. Ⓐ Ⓑ Ⓒ Ⓓ   75. Ⓐ Ⓑ Ⓒ Ⓓ   95. Ⓐ Ⓑ Ⓒ Ⓓ

16. Ⓐ Ⓑ Ⓒ Ⓓ   36. Ⓐ Ⓑ Ⓒ Ⓓ   56. Ⓐ Ⓑ Ⓒ Ⓓ   76. Ⓐ Ⓑ Ⓒ Ⓓ   96. Ⓐ Ⓑ Ⓒ Ⓓ

17. Ⓐ Ⓑ Ⓒ Ⓓ   37. Ⓐ Ⓑ Ⓒ Ⓓ   57. Ⓐ Ⓑ Ⓒ Ⓓ   77. Ⓐ Ⓑ Ⓒ Ⓓ   97. Ⓐ Ⓑ Ⓒ Ⓓ

18. Ⓐ Ⓑ Ⓒ Ⓓ   38. Ⓐ Ⓑ Ⓒ Ⓓ   58. Ⓐ Ⓑ Ⓒ Ⓓ   78. Ⓐ Ⓑ Ⓒ Ⓓ   98. Ⓐ Ⓑ Ⓒ Ⓓ

19. Ⓐ Ⓑ Ⓒ Ⓓ   39. Ⓐ Ⓑ Ⓒ Ⓓ   59. Ⓐ Ⓑ Ⓒ Ⓓ   79. Ⓐ Ⓑ Ⓒ Ⓓ   99. Ⓐ Ⓑ Ⓒ Ⓓ

20. Ⓐ Ⓑ Ⓒ Ⓓ   40. Ⓐ Ⓑ Ⓒ Ⓓ   60. Ⓐ Ⓑ Ⓒ Ⓓ   80. Ⓐ Ⓑ Ⓒ Ⓓ   100. Ⓐ Ⓑ Ⓒ Ⓓ

Answer Sheet

Practice Test 2

PRACTICE TEST 2

100 Questions—210 Minutes

> **Directions:** The following 100 questions are similar to those you will find on an actual firefighter exam. Be sure to read the questions carefully and follow any specific instructions that precede them. Choose the best answer to each question and fill in the corresponding circle on the answer sheet. The Answer Key and Explanations follow this practice test.

Questions 1–6 are based on the following passage. Take five minutes to read and study this passage. Then, without referring to the passage, choose the best answer for each question that follows.

As a result of drought and an extended heat wave, a water shortage occurred last summer. When citizens opened hydrants in an attempt to find relief from the high temperatures, water resources were rapidly depleted, forcing the city to take emergency measures to conserve water.

Fire department personnel conducted a survey that revealed that 600 hydrants were opened daily by citizens, and an average of 1,100 gallons of water per minute was wasted at each open hydrant. Hydrant patrols were implemented using 75 engine companies on 2-hour shifts to close down open hydrants.

One day, while on hydrant patrol, Engine 299 stopped to shut down an open hydrant that was being used by area residents to gain relief from the summer heat. While the firefighters were in the act of closing the hydrant, they were subjected to severe verbal abuse by the crowd that quickly formed around them. A potentially explosive situation developed rapidly. The firefighters closed the hydrant and promptly left the scene to return to the firehouse.

They were in the firehouse for a brief time when an alarm was received to return to the same street for a reported fire in an occupied multiple-dwelling building. Engine 299 responded to the alarm. As the trucks turned into the street, the firefighters were greeted with a barrage of rocks and bottles thrown from doorways and rooftops. The officer in command ordered the firefighters to take cover immediately and transmitted a radio message requesting police assistance. Police officers arrived and dispersed the crowd. The firefighters then checked the location of the reported fire and learned that there was no actual fire; it was a false alarm. They returned to the firehouse, and a report of the incident was forwarded to the fire commissioner.

The following day, the deputy chief requested that a meeting be arranged between fire department officials and community leaders to discuss and resolve the problem. At the meeting, fire department representatives informed community leaders of the importance of having adequate water pressure available to extinguish fires and attempted to convince residents that firefighters were there to help them. Residents also were informed that sprinkler caps for fire hydrants were available at the firehouse. The use of sprinkler caps will allow residents to cool off while maintaining sufficient water pressure necessary for fighting fires.

Community leaders must be convinced that responding to false alarms can result in the destruction of property and the deaths of citizens because firefighters are not able to respond to an actual fire if they are responding to a false alarm.

1. According to the passage, a severe water shortage in the city last summer was due to

   A. broken water mains.

   B. open hydrants.

   C. an extended heat wave and drought.

   D. misuse of water by industry.

2. What was the average number of hydrants shut down each day by each engine company?

   A. 4

   B. 6

   C. 8

   D. 10

3. The firefighters of Engine 299 stopped to shut down the open hydrant while

   A. returning to quarters.

   B. responding to an alarm.

   C. on alarm box inspection duty.

   D. on hydrant patrol duty.

4. The firefighters shut down the hydrant and hastily left the scene in order to

   A. respond to an alarm for a fire in a multiple dwelling.

   B. respond to a false alarm.

   C. obtain police assistance.

   D. avoid a physical confrontation with the crowd.

5. Engine 299 was dispatched from the station to a fire in a

   A. multiple-use building

   B. single-family residence

   C. multiple-dwelling building

   D. multiple-store building

6. The officer in command of Engine 299 forwarded a report of the rock-and bottle-throwing incident to the

   A. fire commissioner.

   B. deputy chief.

   C. community leaders.

   D. police department.

7. When −4 and −5 are added, what is the sum?

   A. −9

   B. 9

   C. −1

   D. 1

8. What is the product of $(-6)\left(+\dfrac{1}{2}\right)(-10)$?

   A. $-15\dfrac{1}{2}$

   B. $15\dfrac{1}{2}$

   C. −30

   D. 30

9. A firefighter is searching through rubble in the wake of an explosion when he finds a man wailing in pain. Upon inspection, the firefighter can see that the man has a leg injury that is bleeding severely. The firefighter knows that in situations like this, shock—a condition in which the body is not receiving enough oxygen—is common. Shock can be treated by warming the body and providing a source of oxygen. Under these circumstances, the first action the firefighter should take is attempt to

   A. cover the man with a blanket or coat.

   B. provide the man with oxygen from available protective gear.

   C. stop the bleeding.

   D. immobilize the leg.

10. Spontaneous combustion is the self-ignition of a material that occurs through chemical, biological, or physical means. Common culprits include piles of dirty rags, round hay bales in a field, and compost piles. This process can be accelerated by the presence of other heat sources. Consider the following situation: a firefighter responds to an alarm for a garage that has caught fire. The garage has no electrical wiring and after the fire is extinguished there are no clear signs of arson. The most likely cause of the fire is

A. cool, damp compost in the shade beside the garage.

B. a full canister of gasoline kept in a cabinet.

C. piles of oily rags sitting in the midafternoon sun.

D. an oil spot beneath a parked car in the garage.

11. A fire marshal when questioning firefighters at the scene of a suspected arson at a rural farmstead obtained some conflicting statements about details of the situation present upon their arrival. Firefighters gave the following accounts:

Firefighter 1: Multiple windows were broken on the farmhouse, and muddy footprints were present all over the porch, at least two different sizes.

Firefighter 2: The fire was concentrated on the first floor with significant charring on the outside of the building as if someone used some sort of improvised explosive.

Firefighter 3: When we pulled up, we could see flames on both the exterior and interior of the house. The dry conditions allowed the flames to spread pretty quickly.

Firefighter 4: The wind had kicked up a lot of dust, but it was clear that the flames started on the outside of the house and penetrated inside through an open window near the entry.

Which account should the fire marshal ignore?

A. Firefighter 1

B. Firefighter 2

C. Firefighter 3

D. Firefighter 4

Practice Test 2

Questions 12–15 are based on the following map.

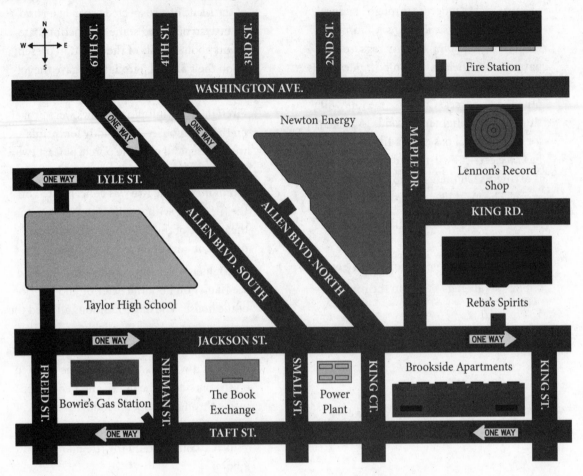

12. Exiting the gas station at the intersection of Neiman and Taft Streets, you travel one block west, one block north, three blocks east, and one block northwest. You're in front of which establishment?

    A. Taylor High School

    B. The Book Exchange

    C. Newton Energy

    D. Lennon's Record Shop

13. A fire is called into the station from Taylor High School. What is the most direct route to the scene?

    A. West on Washington, South on Maple, West on Jackson, Northwest on Allen, and West on Lyle.

    B. West on Washington, Southeast on Allen Blvd N., and West on Lyle.

    C. West on Washington, South on Maple, East on Jackson, South on King, West on Taft, and North on Freed.

    D. West on Washington, Southeast on Allen Blvd. S., and West on Lyle.

14. There's a fire burning on the far east side of the Power Plant with a slight breeze blowing from the east. Which of the following actions should be taken first?

    A. Evacuate the high school to ensure safety for all children.

    B. Evacuate the Brookside Apartments.

    C. Evacuate the Book Exchange to prevent a large-scale paper fire.

    D. Protect the gas station at all costs to prevent an explosion.

15. How many blocks must one drive to get from the southwest corner of the Book Exchange to the Fire Station at Washington and Maple?

    A. 5

    B. 8

    C. 10

    D. 11

16. The highest point in California is Mt. Whitney with an elevation of 14,505 feet above sea level. The lowest point is Death Valley with an elevation of 282 feet below sea level. How much higher is a rock on the top of Mt. Whitney than a person standing at the lowest point in Death Valley?

    A. 282 feet

    B. 14,223 feet

    C. 14,505 feet

    D. 14,787 feet

17. A fire consumed portions of three floors of a building. On the first floor, 1,300 square feet was damaged; on the second floor, 12,000 square feet was damaged; on the third floor, 7,500 square feet was damaged. What is the total damaged area of the building?

    A. 13,300 square feet

    B. 19,500 square feet

    C. 20,800 square feet

    D. 23,500 square feet

18. If a water tanker can pump out water at 10,000 gallons per hour, how long will it take to pump out 1,000 gallons of water?

    A. 6 minutes

    B. 9 minutes

    C. 10 minutes

    D. 12 minutes

19. In an enclosed room, a house fire can create temperatures of 900°F. How many times hotter is this than an average room temperature of 75°F?

    A. 10

    B. 12

    C. 13

    D. 15

20. If a fully extended 24-foot ladder is needed to reach a second-story window, how long should a ladder be to reach a fifth-story window?

    A. 35 feet

    B. 40 feet

    C. 50 feet

    D. 60 feet

21. In any city or suburb with a population of at least 20,000 people, there should be two fire hydrants for every square city block. If there are 75 square city blocks in one mile, how many fire hydrants should there be in two square miles?

A. 200

B. 225

C. 250

D. 300

22.

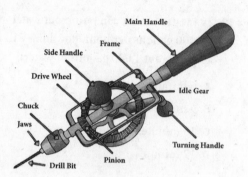

The function of the pinion gear in the hand drill shown in the diagram is to

A. increase the speed of the chuck.

B. keep the speed gear from wobbling.

C. double the turning force on the chuck.

D. allow reverse rotation of the speed gear.

23. Assume that two identical insulated jugs are filled with equal quantities of water from a water tap. A block of ice is placed in one jug and the same quantity of ice, chopped into small cubes, is placed in the other jug. The most accurate statement is that the water in the jug containing the chopped ice, compared to the water in the other jug, will be chilled

A. faster but to a substantially higher temperature.

B. faster and to approximately the same temperature.

C. slower but to a substantially higher temperature.

D. slower and to approximately the same temperature.

24. The long pole and hook shown is called a pike pole.

Firefighters sometimes push the point and hook through plaster ceilings and then pull the ceiling down. Of the following, the most likely reason for this practice is to

A. allow heat and smoke to enter the room.

B. trace defective electric wiring through the house.

C. see if a hidden fire is burning above the ceiling.

D. remove combustible material that will provide fuel for the fire.

25. The following sketches show four objects that have the same weight but different shapes.

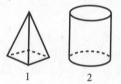

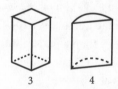

Which object would be the most difficult to tip over?

A. Object 1

B. Object 2

C. Object 3

D. Object 4

26. When dragging a slightly leaky, cloth-covered hose filled with water across a gravel surface, the element most likely to make the task difficult is the

    A. cloth hose covering.

    B. gravel surface.

    C. leaking water.

    D. weight of the water.

27. School administrators must regularly conduct fire drills throughout the year with more drills conducted in the first half of the school year to train students. Administrators will follow the steps listed below to execute a proper fire drill (steps are not in the correct order):

    Step 1. Have teachers take attendance once they've reached the safe zone.

    Step 2. Trigger the fire alarm.

    Step 3. Inspect classrooms for closed doors and missing students.

    Step 4. Give teachers possible times when the fire drill will occur.

    Step 5. Contact the fire department to notify them of the impending drill.

    Step 6. Provide teachers with evacuation routes and waiting areas.

    What would be the most logical order for the steps above?

    A. 5–4–6–2–1–3

    B. 6–2–1–3–4–5

    C. 5–4–2–6–3–1

    D. 4–5–2–1–3–6

28. Following a severely smoky fire in the lobby of a hotel, a man was found unconscious in a room on the fourth floor. The paramedics who examined the man concluded that the victim suffered from respiratory issues related to the inhalation of smoke and toxic gases. From this scenario, it can be concluded that

    A. paramedics regularly make mistakes in their assessments.

    B. the victims of fires commonly seek higher ground to escape the fire.

    C. gases and smoke can travel through vertical openings and impact the upper stories of buildings.

    D. fires on ground floors are often accompanied by fires on higher floors.

29. Fires can quickly devolve into a web of serious hazards: smoke plumes, extreme heat, structural collapse, etc. From those hazards emerge many dangers, including smoke inhalation, suffocation, burns, blunt force trauma, and poor visibility. Poor visibility is not itself a health risk; however, it can create circumstances that regularly lead to severe injury and even death. Firefighters are trained to ventilate spaces to improve visibility, thus making the task of searching easier.

    After responding to a fire in a two-story residence, two probationary firefighters, Homer and Awad, became disoriented and trapped, struggling to navigate the interior of the first floor of the structure. In this situation, the firefighters should

    A. request additional support over their radios to effect a rescue.

    B. puncture holes in the walls around them to try to remove smoke.

    C. follow a wall until it leads them to a window they may break for ventilation or exit through.

    D. hold their position until they encounter other firefighters searching the structure.

Practice Test 2

30. While operating at a five-alarm fire, a firefighter is approached by an obviously intoxicated man claiming to be a former firefighter. The man offers to help extinguish the blaze. In this situation, the best course of action for the firefighter to take is to

A. allow the man to perform a simple task and then send him on his way.

B. refer the man to the officer in command of the fire to whom he can volunteer his services.

C. decline the offer of help and ask the man to remain outside the perimeter of the fire ground.

D. ask to see the man's credentials and allow him to assist if he is who he says he is.

Questions 31–36 are based on the following diagram. Study and memorize the details of the buildings on Salt Street for five minutes, cover the diagram, and answer the questions. Do not refer to the diagram while answering the questions.

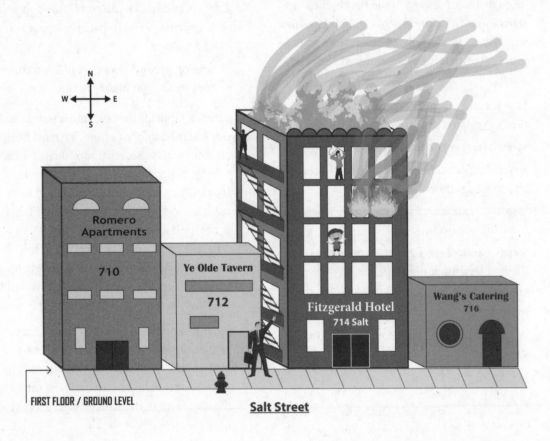

31. Flames are visible on the

A. first and fourth floor.

B. second and fifth floor.

C. fourth floor.

D. third and fifth floor.

32. The smoke and flames are blowing toward

A. Romero Apartments.

B. Ye Olde Tavern.

C. Wang's Catering.

D. straight up; there is no wind.

33. There is someone on the fire escape on the

    A. fourth floor.

    B. second floor.

    C. third floor.

    D. fifth floor.

34. People are visible in windows at the front of the Fitzgerald Hotel on the

    A. first and second floors.

    B. first and fifth floors.

    C. second and fifth floors.

    D. third and fifth floors.

35. How many people require immediate rescue?

    A. 4

    B. 3

    C. 2

    D. 1

36. The fire hydrant is stationed in front of

    A. the Fitzgerald Hotel.

    B. the Romero Apartments.

    C. Ye Olde Tavern.

    D. Wang's Catering.

Questions 37–40 are based on the following passage.

The sizes of living rooms shall meet the following requirements:

1. In each apartment, there shall be at least one living room containing at least 120 sq. ft. of clear floor area; every other living room, except a kitchen, shall contain at least 70 sq. ft. of clear floor area.

2. Every living room that contains less than 80 sq. ft. of clear floor area or that is located in the cellar or basement shall be at least 9 feet high; every other living room shall be at least 8 feet tall.

3. Apartments containing three or more rooms can have dining bays, which shall not exceed 55 sq. ft. in floor surface area and shall not be deemed separate rooms or subject to the requirements for separate rooms. Every such dining bay shall be provided with at least one window containing an area at least one-eighth of the floor surface area of such dining bay.

37. A builder proposes to construct an apartment house containing an apartment consisting of a kitchen that measures 10 feet by 6 feet, a room that measures 12 feet by 12 feet, and a room that measures 11 feet by 7 feet. This apartment

    A. does not comply with the requirements listed in the passage.

    B. complies with the requirements listed in the passage, provided that it is not located in the cellar or basement.

    C. complies with the requirements listed in the passage provided that the height of the smaller rooms is at least 9 feet.

    D. may or may not comply with the requirements listed in the passage depending on the clear floor area of the kitchen.

38. The definition of the term "living room" that is most in accord with its meaning in the passage is

    A. a sitting room or parlor.

    B. the largest room in an apartment.

    C. a room used for living purposes.

    D. any room in an apartment containing 120 square feet of clear floor area.

Practice Test 2

39. Assume that one room in a four-room apartment measures 20 feet × 10 feet and contains a dining bay of 8 feet × 6 feet. According to the passage, the dining bay must be provided with a window measuring at least

   A. 6 square feet.

   B. 7 square feet.

   C. 25 square feet.

   D. 55 square feet.

40. According to the passage, kitchens are

   A. not considered "living rooms."

   B. considered "living rooms" and must, therefore, meet the height and area requirements of the passage.

   C. considered "living rooms" but need meet only the height or area requirements of the passage, not both.

   D. considered "living rooms" but need not meet area requirements.

41. If a fire truck is 55 feet away from a hydrant, it is how many feet nearer to the hydrant than a truck that is 105 feet away?

   A. 40 feet

   B. 50 feet

   C. 55 feet

   D. 60 feet

42. A truck going at a rate of 20 miles an hour will reach a town 40 miles away in how many hours?

   A. 3 hours

   B. 4 hours

   C. 1 hour

   D. 2 hours

43. A folding chair regularly sells for $29.50. How much money is saved if the chair is bought at a 20% discount?

   A. $4.80

   B. $5.90

   C. $6.20

   D. $7.40

44. Fire escape platforms are attached to buildings so as to be flush with the windowsills that lead onto them. Placing the fire escape platforms flush makes them clearly visible from the interior and prevents tripping in the event of egress.

A newly renovated hotel also had its fire escape modernized; however, during the course of an evacuation, several guests who used the fire escape were found to have injuries to their legs and hands when tended to by paramedics. With the information provided, the most likely cause of such injuries would be that

   A. the railings of the fire escape were improperly maintained and resulted in cuts.

   B. guests tripped on platforms that were either too high or too low in relation to their windowsills.

   C. the fire was burning at waist height inside the hotel.

   D. the windows of the hotel room have sharp edges that are abrasive on hands when opened.

Practice Test 2

45. You watch as fire apparatus arrive on scene at a traffic incident at a busy intersection. You see the firefighters secure the scene and aid victims. The incident and the emergency response have generated a significant traffic jam. But you notice that as the fire company drives away, they do not use their sirens to navigate the traffic more quickly. For situations like this one, you infer that

A. the chances of being involved in a traffic incident are severely reduced when obeying traffic laws and following the flow of traffic.

B. firefighters are restricted from using sirens to return to the firehouse as haste is unnecessary after a fire has been extinguished.

C. returning to the firehouse occurs on less crowded stress than when responding to alarms.

D. commanding officers are better able to exchange radio messages with the fire alarm dispatcher.

46. A man enters a firehouse to report that a hydrant has been turned on and is spewing water in his neighborhood. Firefighter Baldwin, who is on housewatch at the time, records the location of the hydrant and sends the man on his way. Firefighter Baldwin realizes he forgot to do something. The firefighter should have

A. given the man an approximate time when the fire department would arrive to turn off the hydrant.

B. inquired as to who activated the hydrant so proper police action could be taken.

C. provided the man with a sprinkler head to attach to the hydrant.

D. asked for the man's name, phone number, and address.

47. A man on his way home from work one evening hears an alarm ringing inside a building and sees water running out of a sprinkler discharge pipe on the side of a building. No smoke or other indications of fire can be seen. The front entrance of the building has a padlock, no fire alarm box is within sight, the man's cellphone battery is dead, and there is a firehouse located one block away. In this situation, the most appropriate action would be to

A. break a window to provide ventilation to the building and determine the source of the fire.

B. attempt to find the name and contact details of the building's owner to notify him or her of the situation.

C. find a fire alarm box and use it to send an alarm.

D. travel to the firehouse and inform a firefighter of the situation.

48. What is the function of the flat surface machined into the shaft shown below?

A. To prevent slippage of a pulley positioned at this end on the shaft

B. To provide a nonskid surface to hold the shaft steady as it is machined

C. To prevent the shaft from rolling about when it is placed on a flat workbench

D. To reveal subsurface defects in the shaft

Practice Test 2

49. You're a firefighter on housewatch when a woman rushes into the firehouse and reports that several gang members appear to be assaulting a man on the street nearby. In this situation, the best course of action for you to take is to

    A. notify your fellow firefighters of the incident and rush to the aid of the man.

    B. suggest to the woman that she report the matter to the police department.

    C. travel to the scene of the disturbance and verify the woman's report before passing it to police.

    D. notify the police department of the reported event.

50. You see a woman collapse on the sidewalk while you're on your way to work. As a crowd gathers around the woman, a man pushes his way through the crowd claiming to be a firefighter. The firefighter assesses the victim and determines she is not breathing. In these kinds of situations, firefighters seek to

    A. explain to someone else how to do CPR while the firefighter uses a cellphone to call an ambulance.

    B. try to find first-aid equipment such as an automatic external defibrillator at a nearby business.

    C. take the appropriate steps to restore respiration and notify paramedics.

    D. perform CPR until the victim is revived.

51. Which of the following wrenches is also known as an adjustable wrench?

    A.

    B.

    C.

    D.

52. Which of the following is used to make precise cuts in woodworking, such as mitres and dovetails?

    A.

    B.

    C.

    D.

Practice Test 2

53. As a firefighter, one of your duties is to conduct safety inspections for businesses. On this day, you are assigned to inspect a local fireworks factory. When you attempt to discuss minor violations with the owner, he becomes upset and tells you that he has friends in high places, including the fire department. In this situation, the appropriate action would be to

    A. inform the factory owner that it is illegal to intimidate firefighters while they perform their duties.

    B. continue the inspection until you find a major infraction and then confront the owner.

    C. disregard the owner's comments and complete the inspection.

    D. attempt to uncover the names of the owner's acquaintances by asking him questions.

54. Certain procedures should be followed when evacuating a large public space such as a theater. To evacuate a theater, the following steps should be followed (steps are not in the correct order):

    Step 1. Provide instructions to the audience for evacuation.

    Step 2. Call the fire department.

    Step 3. Inform the audience of the situation.

    Step 4. Perform a sweep of audience restrooms.

    Step 5. Check the indicator panel to determine the location of the fire alarm.

    Step 6. Take a headcount of audience members and compare it to ticket sales.

    The correct order for the above steps is

    A. 2–3–1–4–5–6

    B. 5–2–3–1–4–6

    C. 5–3–1–2–6–4

    D. 6–5–2–4–1–3

55. At a fire on the fourth floor of an apartment building, the first engine company that arrived advanced a hoseline up the stairwell to the third floor of the building before charging the hose with water. In these kinds of situations, the primary reason that firefighters delay charging that line is that such a decision

    A. limits property damage as hoses are known to leak water.

    B. makes it easier to carry the hose and maneuver it up narrow stairwells.

    C. will prevent whipping of the hoseline and thus injury to firefighters.

    D. prevents damage to the hose itself as firefighters carry it up the stairs.

56. Before entering a burning building, firefighters will often try to ventilate the structure to improve visibility and reduce heat. Suppose the owner of a burning tenement building complains that although the fire is located on the first floor, firefighters are puncturing holes in the roof of the structure. Of the following reasons, you can conclude that firefighters took this action in order to

    A. allow smoke and hot gases to escape the structure.

    B. help other firefighters attack the fire from above.

    C. gain access to upper floors through the created holes.

    D. inspect the upper stories for extension of the fire.

Practice Test 2

57. Firefighters Hunt and Ashberry are assigned to clean the fire engine and protective equipment after returning from a fire. Firefighter Ashberry wants to attend to other duties, but Hunt convinces Ashberry to help by saying the following:

   A. A firefighter who disobeys direct orders will be subject to disciplinary action.

   B. Cleaning the engine and other equipment is a simple task compared to other activities at the firehouse.

   C. Skipping assigned duties is bad for the company's morale.

   D. Over time, accumulation of dirt and grime can lead to wear on the equipment, perhaps leading to malfunction.

58. A team played 30 games, of which it won 24. What part of the games played did the team lose?

   A. $\frac{4}{5}$

   B. $\frac{1}{4}$

   C. $\frac{1}{5}$

   D. $\frac{3}{4}$

59. What is the area of the following square?

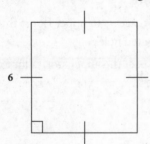

   A. 32 square units

   B. 36 square units

   C. 38 square units

   D. 60 square units

60. Fire Station 35 received a call at 4:20 p.m., and the firefighters arrived at the scene at 4:25 p.m. The fire was extinguished at 5:15 p.m., and the firefighters arrived back at the station at 5:30 p.m. How much time (in minutes) elapsed from the time of the call to the firefighters' arrival back at the station?

   A. 60 minutes

   B. 70 minutes

   C. 75 minutes

   D. 80 minutes

61. The following is a sketch of a block and fall.

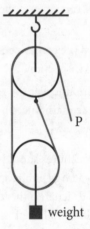

weight

If the end of the rope P is pulled so that it moves one foot, the distance the weight will rise is

   A. $\frac{1}{2}$ foot.

   B. 1 foot.

   C. $1\frac{1}{2}$ feet.

   D. 2 feet.

Practice Test 2

62. You're a firefighter in uniform on your way home from your shift when you enter the subway and are greeted by several frantic individuals. The civilians provide the following information:

    Witness 1: A man was pushed onto the tracks and electrocuted. We pulled him off and back onto the platform, but he's not breathing.

    Witness 2: A man fell onto the tracks and got shocked. I saw the smoke come off him. He's moaning and gripping his chest.

    Witness 3: He came flying off the platform and hit that third rail. There was this loud pop, and his phone's stuck to his hand. He's not moving.

    Witness 4: He won't wake up. I saw him talking on his phone, but then he tumbled over the edge. We got him off the tracks, but he looks really hurt.

    Of the information available, what accounts would you communicate to the fire department?

    A. 1, 2, 3

    B. 1, 2, 4

    C. 1, 3, 4

    D. 2, 3, 4

63. Rescue operations in confined spaces require specialized signaling methods. One method firefighters use is OATH, which connects the number of tugs on a safety line to specific actions. **O** (one tug) stands for "okay." **A** (two tugs) means "advance." **T** (three tugs) indicates the rescuer wants to be "taken up." And **H** (four tugs) means the individual needs "help."

    A firefighter is attempting to rescue a child from an abandoned well. How many tugs will she use to indicate she wants to return to the surface?

    A. 5

    B. 4

    C. 3

    D. 2

Questions 64–68 are based on the following diagram.

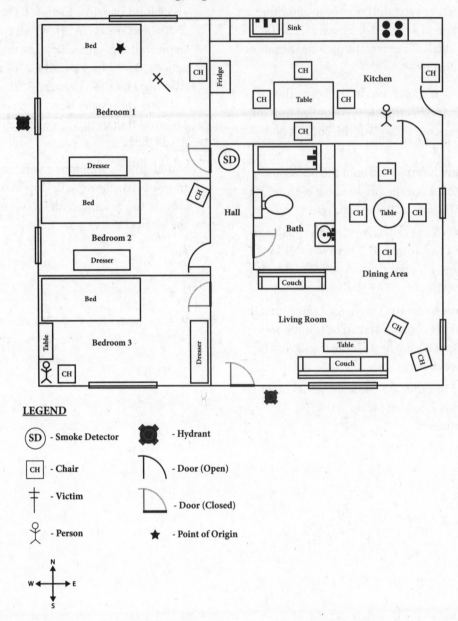

LEGEND

SD - Smoke Detector
CH - Chair
✝ - Victim
☺ - Person

- Hydrant
- Door (Open)
- Door (Closed)
★ - Point of Origin

N S E W

64. The fire started in what quadrant of the apartment?

A. Southwest
B. Southeast
C. Northwest
D. Northeast

65. The people on scene who haven't yet fallen victim to the fire should be evacuated

A. out the front door and the kitchen door.
B. out the Bedroom 3 window and the dining area window.
C. both out the front door.
D. out the Bedroom 3 window and the kitchen door.

66. Once they've arrived on scene, what is the fastest way for firefighters to reach the victim?

A. Through the front door and down the hall

B. Through the kitchen door, passing the dining area and living room

C. Through the Bedroom 1 window on the west side of the unit

D. Through the Bedroom 1 window on the north side of the unit

67. It would be most efficient for firefighters to connect their hoses to the

A. hydrant on the south side of the unit.

B. hydrant on the west side of the unit.

C. waterline that feeds into the sink faucet.

D. hydrant on the north side of the unit.

68. How many chairs are there in the southeast quadrant of the apartment?

A. 2

B. 5

C. 6

D. 7

Questions 69–73 are based on the following passage.

EMPLOYEE-LEAVE REGULATIONS

"As a full-time, permanent city employee under the Career and Salary Plan, firefighter Peter Smith earns an annual leave allowance. This consists of a certain number of days off a year with pay and can be used for vacation, personal business, or observing religious holidays. As a newly appointed employee, during his first eight years of city service, he will earn an annual leave allowance of 20 days off a year (an average of $1\frac{2}{3}$ days off a month). After he has finished eight full years of working for the city, he will begin earning an additional five days off a year. His annual leave allowance will then be 25 days a year and will remain at this amount for seven full years. He will begin earning an additional two days off a year after he has completed a total of 15 years of city employment. Therefore, in his sixteenth year of working for the city, Smith will be earning 27 days off a year as his annual leave allowance (an average of $2\frac{1}{4}$ days off a month).

A sick leave allowance of one day a month also is given to firefighter Smith, but it can be used only in the case of actual illness. He will be required to have a doctor's note if he is absent for more than three days. However, Smith could be asked to provide a doctor's note for a one, two, or three day absence.

69. Peter Smith's annual leave allowance consists of a certain number of days off each year that he

A. does not get paid for.

B. gets paid at time and a half.

C. can use for personal business.

D. cannot use for observing religious holidays.

70. After Peter Smith has been working for the city for nine years, his annual leave allowance will be

A. 20 days a year.

B. 25 days a year.

C. 27 days a year.

D. 37 days a year.

71. According to the passage, Peter Smith will begin earning an average of $2\frac{1}{4}$ days off a month as his annual leave allowance after he has worked for the city for

   A. 7 full years.
   B. 8 full years.
   C. 15 full years.
   D. 17 full years.

72. Peter Smith is given a sick leave allowance of

   A. 1 day every 2 months.
   B. 1 day per month.
   C. $1\frac{2}{3}$ days per month.
   D. $2\frac{1}{4}$ days a month.

73. According to the passage, when Peter Smith uses sick leave allowance, he might be required to show a doctor's note

   A. even if his absence is for only one day.
   B. only if his absence is for more than two days.
   C. only if his absence is for more than three days.
   D. only if his absence is for three days or more.

Questions 74–77 are based on the following list of warnings concerning electricity.

Firefighting procedures provide the following strict guidelines for handling situations involving energized wires:

- Firefighters never should attempt to cut any wires. They should wait until trained utility workers are available to do any necessary cutting.

- When downed electrical wires are encountered, a danger zone should be established around the downed wire to ensure the safety of firefighters.

- All wires should be treated as though they are charged with a high voltage electrical current.

- Firefighters are in danger of not only shock and burns from electrical equipment but also eye injuries from electrical flashing. A firefighter should never look directly at flashing electrical lines.

- Specific attention must be paid to electrical dangers when raising or lowering hoselines, ladders, or equipment near overhead lines.

- Firefighters should be aware of any tingling sensation felt in the feet when working in an area where wires are down. This sensation might indicate that the ground is charged.

- Full protective clothing should always be worn in areas where electrical hazards might exist. Only approved insulated tools that are regularly tested should be used.

74. When a firefighter is a safe distance away from a downed wire, but the wire is sparking and flashing as the current jumps from the wire to a nearby car, the firefighter should

    A. cut the wire near the power source.

    B. avoid looking directly at the flashing.

    C. watch the flashing closely for flames.

    D. ignore any tingling felt in the feet.

75. When in an area in which an electrical hazard might exist, firefighters should wear

    A. street clothes.

    B. full protective clothing.

    C. only protective gloves.

    D. only protective boots.

76. Raising a ladder near an overhead power line

    A. should never be done when there are possible electrical dangers.

    B. is a job that should be conducted only by trained utility workers.

    C. is not a serious concern if a safety zone has been established.

    D. should be done with specific attention to electrical dangers.

77. When working around a downed wire, a firefighter notices a tingling sensation in her feet. This sensation might indicate that

    A. the ground is charged.

    B. the wire is not charged.

    C. the wire should be cut.

    D. there is no electrical danger.

Questions 78–81 are based on the following passage.

Whenever a social group has become so efficiently organized that it has gained access to an adequate supply of food and has learned to distribute it among its members so well that wealth considerably exceeds immediate demands, it can be depended on to utilize its surplus energy in an attempt to enlarge the sphere in which it is active. The structure of ant colonies renders them particularly prone to this sort of expansionist policy. With very few exceptions, ants of any given colony are hostile to those of any other colony, even of the same species. This condition is bound to produce preliminary bickering among colonies that are closely associated.

78. According to the passage, a social group is wealthy when it

    A. is efficiently organized.

    B. controls large territories.

    C. contains energetic members.

    D. produces and distributes food reserves.

79. According to the passage, the structure of an ant colony is its

    A. social organization.

    B. nest arrangement.

    C. territorial extent.

    D. food-gathering activities.

80. The society considered the least expansionist could be described as

    A. having widespread poverty throughout the society.

    B. a functioning society with more wealth than members.

    C. a social structure where all members receive more resources than they need.

    D. unequal distribution of wealth between the rich and the poor society members.

81. According to the passage, an ant generally is hostile EXCEPT to other

    A. insects.

    B. ants.

    C. ants of the same species.

    D. ants of the same colony.

Questions 82–85 are based on the following information and table.

Carbon monoxide (CO) is a lethal gas that causes more deaths than any other product of combustion. Very small concentrations of carbon monoxide readily combine with chemicals in the blood and quickly cause damage to the brain and other body tissues by blocking the blood's ability to carry oxygen.

TOXIC EFFECTS OF CARBON MONOXIDE	
Carbon Monoxide in Air (%)	**Symptoms**
1.23	Instant unconsciousness; death likely in one to three minutes
0.32	Dizziness, headache, nausea after 5–10 minutes; unconsciousness after 30 minutes
0.04	Headache after 1–2 hours of exposure
0.01	No damage—no symptoms

On a very cold day in January, Anthony starts up his car in the garage. Due to the frigid temperatures outside, he decides to stay in the car and to leave the garage door closed until the car warms up. After about 10 minutes, Anthony has a headache and starts to feel dizzy and nauseous.

82. According to the information and table presented, the likely cause of Anthony's symptoms is

    A. the extremely cold temperature.

    B. the lack of carbon monoxide in his blood.

    C. the lack of oxygen in his blood.

    D. carbon monoxide levels of 0.04 percent.

83. According to the information and table, Anthony could become unconscious if he

    A. has no symptoms.

    B. has a headache three hours later.

    C. gets any more oxygen.

    D. stays in the car for another twenty minutes.

84. Two firefighters enter a room that contains a smoldering fire. Against the advice of his partner, one of the firefighters takes off his breathing apparatus to clear some debris from the inside of his mask. He instantly falls to the floor unconscious. The likely reason for the firefighter's unconsciousness is

   A. carbon monoxide levels of 0.01 percent.

   B. carbon monoxide levels of 0.04 percent.

   C. carbon monoxide levels of 0.32 percent.

   D. carbon monoxide levels of 1.23 percent.

85. A fire started in a large apartment building and took several hours to extinguish. Evacuation of the building took over an hour to complete. Some of the last people to leave the building were complaining of headaches. What was the likely concentration of carbon monoxide in the apartment building?

   A. 1.5 percent

   B. 1.23 percent

   C. 0.32 percent

   D. 0.04 percent

Questions 86–88 are based on the following image. Study and memorize the details of the image for five minutes, cover the image, and answer the questions. Do not refer to the image while answering the questions.

86. How many cars can be confirmed as involved in the accident?

   A. 1

   B. 2

   C. 3

   D. Unclear

87. What is the crew number on the firefighter's helmet?

   A. 119

   B. 191

   C. 911

   D. 991

88. What source of lighting is being used on the scene?

   A. Natural light from outside the tunnel

   B. Lighting emitted from the tunnel

   C. Headlights from the emergency vehicles

   D. Floodlights set up by the firefighters

89. Firefighters Jones and Smith were recently called to a traumatic fire involving a crashed passenger jet. Jones was assigned to a crew responsible for containing and putting out the fire. Smith was assigned to a crew responsible for rescuing victims from the plane. Many of the victims Smith attempted to rescue were younger, and some did not survive. In the weeks that followed the plane crash, Jones noticed Smith shrugging off duties around the firehouse, acting belliger-ent toward the crew, and arriving late for work. Considering recent events, the cause for Smith's behavior is most likely

   A. job stress.

   B. boredom.

   C. drugs and alcohol.

   D. laziness.

90. As your company arrives at the scene of a fire in a large rooming house, a man is visible at the third-story fire escape. It appears that he has fashioned a torn and knotted sheet into a rope. He has attached the crudely fashioned rope to an object inside the structure. Two women and a young boy are observed below him descending to the streets using the fire escape. Flames and smoke are issuing from the fourth-floor windows. In this situation, firefighters would likely advise the man to

   A. continue using the improvised rope as it will lower him to the ground quickly.

   B. attempt to use the stairways within the boarding house.

   C. tie the rope to the fire escape rather than an anchor inside the building.

   D. abandon the rope and use the fire escape to descend the structure.

91. Suppose the same quantity of water is placed in the cup and bowl pictured below and both are left on a table.

The time required for the water to evaporate completely from the cup, as compared to the bowl, would be

   A. longer.

   B. shorter.

   C. equal.

   D. longer or shorter depending on the tem-perature and humidity in the room.

92. Some tools are known as all-purpose tools because they can be used for a great variety of purposes. Others are called special-purpose tools because they are suitable only for a particular purpose. In general, an all-purpose tool, as compared to a special tool for the same use, is

    A. cheaper.
    B. less efficient.
    C. safer to use.
    D. simpler to operate.

93. During a snowstorm, a passenger car with rear-wheel drive gets stuck in the snow. It is observed that the rear wheels are spinning in the snow, and the front wheels are not turning. The statement that best explains why the car is not moving is that

    A. moving parts of the motor are frozen or blocked by the ice and snow.
    B. the front wheels are not receiving power because of a defective or malfunctioning transmission.
    C. the rear wheels are not obtaining sufficient traction because of the snow.
    D. the distribution of the power to the front and rear wheels is not balanced.

94. When the inside face of a rubber suction cup is pressed against a smooth wall, it usually remains in place because of the

    A. force of molecular attraction between the rubber and the wall.
    B. pressure of the air on the rubber cup.
    C. suction caused by the elasticity of the rubber.
    D. static electricity generated by the friction between the rubber and the wall.

Questions 95 and 96 are based on the following information and diagram.

Gear A is the driver. Gears A and D each have twice as many teeth as gear B, and gear C has four times as many teeth as gear B.

95. Two gears that turn in the same direction are

    A. A and B.
    B. B and C.
    C. C and D.
    D. B and D.

96. The two gears that revolve at the same speed are gears

    A. A and C.
    B. A and D.
    C. B and C.
    D. B and D.

97. If water travels through a fire hose at a rate of 5 feet per second, how long will it take a hose that is 125 feet long to fill with water?

    A. 25 seconds
    B. 35 seconds
    C. 50 seconds
    D. 125 seconds

Practice Test 2

98. What is the volume of the following rectangle?

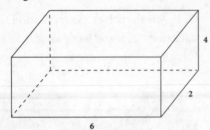

A. 12 cubic units

B. 24 cubic units

C. 42 cubic units

D. 48 cubic units

99. Mick starts walking on a trail at a rate of 4 miles per hour. Ninety minutes later, Rebecca starts jogging at 6 miles per hour on the same trail from where Mick started. In total, how far has Mick walked by the time Rebecca catches up with him?

A. 4 miles

B. 12 miles

C. 14 miles

D. 18 miles

100. An employee's weekly salary is increased from \$350 to \$380. What is the approximate percent of increase?

A. 6%

B. $8\frac{1}{2}\%$

C. 10%

D. $12\frac{1}{2}\%$

ANSWER KEY AND EXPLANATIONS

1. C	21. D	41. B	61. A	81. D
2. C	22. B	42. D	62. C	82. C
3. D	23. B	43. B	63. C	83. D
4. D	24. C	44. B	64. C	84. D
5. C	25. A	45. A	65. A	85. D
6. A	26. D	46. D	66. C	86. B
7. A	27. A	47. D	67. B	87. B
8. D	28. C	48. A	68. B	88. D
9. C	29. C	49. D	69. C	89. A
10. C	30. C	50. C	70. B	90. D
11. A	31. C	51. A	71. C	91. A
12. C	32. C	52. A	72. B	92. B
13. D	33. D	53. C	73. A	93. C
14. B	34. D	54. B	74. B	94. B
15. B	35. B	55. B	75. B	95. D
16. D	36. C	56. A	76. D	96. B
17. C	37. C	57. D	77. A	97. A
18. A	38. C	58. C	78. D	98. D
19. B	39. A	59. B	79. A	99. D
20. D	40. D	60. B	80. A	100. B

1. **The correct answer is C.** The first sentence of paragraph 1 states that the severe water shortage in the city last summer was the result of "drought and an extended heat wave."

2. **The correct answer is C.** Paragraph 2 states that there were 600 hydrants opened daily by citizens and 75 engine companies employed daily to close down the hydrants. The average number of hydrants shut down each day by each company is computed as follows: 600 hydrants ÷ 75 companies = 8 hydrants.

3. **The correct answer is D.** As stated in the first sentence of paragraph 3, Engine 299 was on hydrant patrol.

4. **The correct answer is D.** Paragraph 3 details that a verbally abusive crowd formed and a

"potentially explosive situation developed." The firefighters shut down the hydrant and left the scene quickly to avoid a physical confrontation with the crowd.

5. **The correct answer is C.** The beginning of paragraph 4 states that there was an alarm for a reported fire in a multiple-dwelling building.

6. **The correct answer is A.** The officer in command called the police, but he forwarded the report of the incident to the fire commissioner. This information is stated in the last sentence of paragraph 4.

7. **The correct answer is A.** When adding numbers with the same sign, add their magnitudes (4 + 5 = 9) and keep the same sign.

8. **The correct answer is D.** Multiplying an even number of negative terms makes the product positive.

$$(-6)\left(+\frac{1}{2}\right)(-10) = (6)\left(\frac{1}{2}\right)(10)$$

Reduce the numbers with the greatest common divisor 2, then multiply to solve:

$$(\cancel{6})\left(\frac{1}{\cancel{2}}\right)(10) = 3(10) = 30$$

9. **The correct answer is C.** While shock may be a concern in situations such as this, the clear danger to the man's well-being is the severe blood flow from the man's leg. By addressing the bleeding first, the firefighter will be able to address the other concerns facing the injured civilian.

10. **The correct answer is C.** Given the situation, the oily rags represent a known source for spontaneous combustion, and with the aid of heat from the afternoon sun, they are the most likely cause of the fire. The other options would likely lack the internal or added heat that would push them to combust.

11. **The correct answer is A.** The testimony of Firefighter 1 indicates the presence of mud near the front of the house, which conflicts with the accounts of Firefighters 3 and 4 who both speak to the dry conditions present. It is likely that Firefighter 1 was recalling the state of the house after his fire company began fire suppression by breaking windows for ventilation and turning the dust present into mud with their fire suppression techniques.

12. **The correct answer is C.** Traveling a block west of Neiman and Taft brings you to Freed Street. A block north of that puts you on Jackson Street, and three blocks east puts you at the crossing between Allen Boulevard North and King Court. Since Allen Blvd. North is the only road that runs northwest, going one

block northwest places you directly in front of the Newton Energy building.

13. **The correct answer is D.** The most direct route from the fire station to the high school is west on Washington Ave., southeast on Allen Blvd. South, and west on Lyle Street. Choices A and B would involve an illegal turn onto a one-way street, and the route for choice C is longer than that of choice D.

14. **The correct answer is B.** The high school (choice A) is far enough away that it's out of immediate danger, but all life must be considered, regardless, not just that of children. If the fire were to spread to Brookside Apartments, it could result in multiple fatalities. Therefore, the firefighters first action should be to evacuate the Brookside Apartments. A slight easterly wind isn't enough to pose an imminent threat to the Book Exchange (choice C), especially with the fire on the east side of the Power Plant, nor would the gas station be endangered (choice D).

15. **The correct answer is B.** The southwest corner of the Book Exchange is at the intersection of Neiman and Taft Streets. From there, travel a block north on Neiman to Jackson (1), two blocks east to Maple (3), and two blocks north to Washington (5). Even if the drive down Jackson is counted as three blocks, it would only bring the total to 6, which is closer to 5 than 8.

16. **The correct answer is D.** This question is really asking about distance between two things, so the answer will be positive. To solve, figure it is 14,505 feet from the top of Mt. Whitney to sea level, and then another 282 feet to get to the lowest point of Death Valley. Add the two numbers:

$$14,505 + 282 = 14,787.$$

17. **The correct answer is C.** The total area of the building that was damaged is the sum of the square feet consumed on the three floors. Thus, $1,300 + 12,000 + 7,500 = 20,800$ square feet.

18. The correct answer is A. 1,000 gallons is one-tenth of 10,000 gallons. If 10,000 gallons are pumped per hour, we want to know what one-tenth of one hour is. Because there are 60 minutes in 1 hour:

$$60 \times \frac{1}{10} = 6 \ \text{min}$$

19. The correct answer is B. $900 \div 75 = 12$. Check your answer: $75 \times 12 = 900$.

20. The correct answer is D. If it takes a 24-foot ladder to reach the second story, it takes 12 feet of ladder for each story ($24 \div 2 = 12$). Because there are five stories, $12 \times 5 = 60$.

21. The correct answer is D. Because there are two hydrants for every block and 75 blocks for every square mile, there are $75 \times 2 = 150$ hydrants for every square mile. Because we are looking at 2 square miles, $150 \times 2 = 300$ hydrants for two square miles.

22. The correct answer is B. The pinion gear is a small bevel or spur gear that meshes with the speed gear. The pinions "bind" the large gear to prevent it from wobbling.

23. The correct answer is B. The small cubes of chopped ice have a greater surface area than the large block of ice. Therefore, more water will be exposed to the area of the chopped ice, and it will chill faster to the same temperature.

24. The correct answer is C. In a fire, flame and hot gases can enter cracks or holes in a ceiling or wall and can burn undetected. If the ceilings are not opened, the fire can remain undetected and continue to burn and spread throughout the structure. The pike pole is used to create the openings.

25. The correct answer is A. With all the objects equal in weight, the pyramid is the most difficult to tip over. This is because the bulk of the volume and weight is at its base.

26. The correct answer is D. The weight of the water is most likely to make the task difficult because it makes the hose extremely heavy and hard to drag. The cloth hose covering (choice A) will have little effect, and the gravel surface (choice B) may make the task easier by providing a movable surface over which to drag the hose. The water leakage (choice C) will have little consequence.

27. The correct answer is A. The most logical order is 5–4–6–2–1–3. Prior to beginning a fire drill, school officials should notify their local fire department to prevent unnecessary emergency response. The greater the notice the better. Choice B erroneously places this step last, so this choice can be eliminated. It is reasonable that teachers be informed of the impending drill before the fire department, but the ordering of actions in choice D incorrectly provides teachers with the evacuation plan after the drill has begun. This same mistake is made in choice C.

28. The correct answer is C. If the fire was on the ground floor of the structure but a victim suffering from respiratory issues, but no burns, was found on a higher floor, then it is likely that gases and smoke rose through the structure. Little can be inferred from the abilities of paramedics from the information provided (choice A). The situation also provides little insight into the nature of human behavior in a fire scenario (choice B). No mention is made of a fire on the upper floors (choice D).

29. The correct answer is C. The information given in the question tells you that in order to improve visibility within a structure, firefighters will try to ventilate the space. Ventilation may take place in multiple ways. This often means breaking windows or puncturing holes in the ceiling. Making holes in the surrounding walls would do little good to disperse the smoke (choice B). Choices A and D jeopardize the lives of both firefighters by having them wait for rescue rather than taking immediate action that may save their lives.

30. The correct answer is C. While the man may be adamant in offering his assistance in the situation, it is best for the safety of the man as well as other firefighters that his offer for help be declined. Firefighters need to be certified and assigned to a fire department in order to serve. This prevents obvious safety issues and legal issues in emergencies. In addition, the man's obvious intoxication further disqualifies him from service.

31. The correct answer is C. The note at the bottom of the drawing states that the ground floor is the first floor. Flames are coming out of the windows three stories up, on the fourth floor.

32. The correct answer is C. The smoke and flames are blowing to the right, which is toward Wang's Catering.

33. The correct answer is D. The fire escapes are on the west side of the Fitzgerald Hotel. There is a person on the fire escape on the fifth floor.

34. The correct answer is D. There is a child in a window on the third floor. There is a man waving a white flag in a window on the fifth floor of the building.

35. The correct answer is B. The child next to the flames, as well as the man with the flag and the man on the fire escape—both of whom are above the flames—would require immediate rescue.

36. The correct answer is C. The fire hydrant is directly in front of Ye Olde Tavern.

37. The correct answer is C. The second requirement states that every living room with less than 80 square feet of floor area shall be 9 feet high. As long as the height of the smaller rooms is at least 9 feet, this room would comply with the requirements listed.

38. The correct answer is C. According to the passage, "living rooms" are rooms used for living purposes.

39. The correct answer is A. The floor space of the dining bay is $6 \times 8 = 48$ square feet. So:

$$\left(\frac{1}{8}\right)48 = 6 \text{ sq. ft.}$$

40. The correct answer is D. The words "every other living room except a kitchen" imply that a kitchen is a living room but that it is not subject to the size requirements of other living rooms.

41. The correct answer is B. 105 feet – 55 feet = 50 feet

42. The correct answer is D. 40 miles ÷ 20 mph = 2 hrs.

43. The correct answer is B. $29.50 × 20% = $29.50 × 0.20 = $5.90 saved.

44. The correct answer is B. As the passage describes that fire escapes are commonly placed at window height, you can deduce that injuries of the sort described would result from tripping on the fire escape during use. No mention is made of the victims being near a fire (choice C), nor is there reason to suspect jaggedness on the fire escape railings (choice A)—at least none that would result in leg injuries—or poor construction of the windows (choice D).

45. The correct answer is A. Emergency response is a balancing act between safety and efficiency; however, when no emergency is present, firefighters prioritize the safety of themselves and those around them. Choice B approximates this reasoning but incorrectly states that haste is unnecessary after an emergency. While firefighters have no need to use their sirens and further disrupt traffic patterns, they will look for ways to return to the firehouse safely yet efficiently to be prepared for their next alarm. The firefighters will thus avoid impacting the driving of others to reduce the chances of accident and further delay.

46. The correct answer is D. When taking a report, it is vital to acquire as much information about the scene as well as the identity of the point of contact. This allows the fire department to contact the individual for follow-up questions or to inform them that the situation has been remedied.

47. **The correct answer is D.** The civilian should recognize that the most efficient means of addressing the situation is to operate upon information that he is certain of (the location of the firehouse) and involve those who can resolve the situation safely and efficiently. While the actions listed in choices A and B are logical, they reflect actions that would have the greatest effect when completed by firefighters. The fire alarm box (choice C) would be an effective method of sending an alarm, but the uncertainty of its location versus the known location of the firehouse makes it a secondary choice.

48. **The correct answer is A.** The flat surface of the shaft is called a keyway. A corresponding opening in a gear or pulley accommodates the keyway and prevents slippage of the gear or pulley on the shaft.

49. **The correct answer is D.** While the firefighter has a responsibility to aid those in need, he or she will want to ensure that any action taken can lead to the safe and efficient resolution of a situation. There is no guarantee that a firefighter's training will be able to resolve the assault. Emergencies of this nature are within the purview of the police, and thus they should be contacted to resolve the situation so that the firefighter is available to respond to alarms.

50. **The correct answer is C.** Firefighters will want to complete two tasks as efficiently as possible: (1) notify emergency medical personnel and (2) attempt to resuscitate the woman. They will seek to employ their training rather than focus on actions that could be completed by bystanders (choice A). Firefighters would elect to employ skills they know they have rather than expend time

searching businesses for medical equipment (choice B) that may or may not be present. At the same time, firefighters understand that they can provide immediate emergency aid (choice D), but they cannot know whether that will address the woman's condition fully.

51. **The correct answer is A.** The wrench commonly known as a crescent wrench is officially classified as an adjustable wrench. Choice B is a ratchet wrench, choice C is a pipe wrench, and choice D is an open-end wrench.

52. **The correct answer is A.** This is a backsaw, able to make precise cuts because of its stiffening rib on the edge opposite its cutting edge. Choice B is a keyhole saw, used to make curved cuts. Choice C is a crosscut saw, used for cutting wood across the grain. Choice D is a hacksaw, used for cutting metal, plastic and wood.

53. **The correct answer is C.** Knowing a firefighter's priorities on and off the job, the owner's comments are irrelevant to the completion of your duties. No exceptions can be made during a fire inspection.

54. **The correct answer is B.** It's vital that in the event of an apparent emergency, managers have insight into the nature of the issue (location and severity) and then communicate this to proper authorities. As such, the manager of a theater would need to determine the location of the fire alarm first (Step 5), thus eliminating choices A and D. Next, the fire department needs to be called (Step 2) so that emergency response can begin. This eliminates choice C, which notifies the fire department only after evacuation procedures have begun. The correct order of the steps is 5-2-3-1-4-6, as shown in choice B.

55. **The correct answer is B.** With water flowing through a hose at the pressures necessary to suppress fires, the hose will stiffen. To gain access to the fire, firefighters will first have

to maneuver to its location. As such, charging the hose should occur only once the hose is in position for fire attack. Limiting property damage is important (choice A) but ultimately unavoidable given the situation. A charged hoseline can be difficult to handle (choice C) but firefighters are well-trained in their use, and this concern would come second to efficient handling of the hose itself. Certain hose types are prone to damage (choice D), but equipment used by firefighters is designed to handle rough conditions and would not be the primary concern when safety of residents and property is at risk.

56. **The correct answer is A.** The passage informs you that ventilation is a standard step in fire attack. With firefighters creating holes in the roof of the structure, their aim must be to release trapped smoke and gases, which will serve to reduce hazards within the structure and improve the effectiveness of search procedures.

57. **The correct answer is D.** Firefighters have three priorities: save lives, control fires, and protect property. The first item listed will come before all others. Proper maintenance of protective gear and firefighting apparatus can have a direct impact on the safety of firefighters as well as the ability of a firefighter to bring about effective rescue and fire suppression.

58. **The correct answer is C.** The team lost 6 games out of 30 or one-fifth of the games.

$$\frac{6}{30} = \frac{1}{5}$$

59. **The correct answer is B.** Area = 6^2 = 36 square units

60. **The correct answer is B.** There are 60 minutes in every hour. 5:30 p.m. is 1 hour and 10 minutes after 4:20 p.m. Therefore, 60 minutes + 10 minutes = 70 minutes.

61. **The correct answer is A.** The sketch is of a fixed pulley and a moveable pulley. With this arrangement, the effort to move the weight will be one half. The effort distance (the length of the pull), however, will be twice the distance the weight travels. Therefore, a 1-foot pull raised the weight $\frac{1}{2}$ foot.

62. **The correct answer is C.** Witnesses 1, 3, and 4 claim that the man is in some state of unresponsiveness while Witness 2 states the man is making sounds and moving. That contradiction is the most significant as it will impact the actions of emergency responders coming to the scene. As such, Witness 2's account should be dismissed.

63. **The correct answer is C.** The passage indicates that "taken up" is signaled by the T in the OATH acronym. Thus, the firefighter will signal with three tugs of the safety line.

64. **The correct answer is C.** The legend indicates that a star marks the fire's point of origin. In the diagram, the star is located on the bed in the northwest corner of the apartment.

65. **The correct answer is A.** If the fire were located between the occupants and the front and/or kitchen door, evacuating through the windows (choices B and D) would be a plausible option. In this scenario, however, the fire is at the far end of the apartment. Thus, it makes the most sense to evacuate using the nearest natural exits, which would be the front door and the kitchen door, respectively.

66. **The correct answer is C.** While the front door/ main entrance directs people to enter on the south side of the unit, the fire is already burning at the opposite end of the apartment with a victim in unknown condition. While it's best to avoid any damage to property if possible, this scenario would justify breaking a window to enter and check on the victim because it could reduce loss of life. It's not the safest option in the face of a fire, but it's the most direct. Because of the origin of the fire,

firefighters would need to use the window on the west side of the room.

67. **The correct answer is B.** Attaching a firehose to a sink fixture isn't possible (choice C). The hydrant on the south side (choice A) is farthest from the fire, and while a hydrant on the north side (choice D) of the building would be relatively close, it is not present on the diagram.

68. **The correct answer is B.** If we look closely, we can see that one of the four chairs set around the dinner table falls above the apartment's centerline. Just because an object is in the same room or general space as other objects doesn't mean they all belong to the same quadrant. The three chairs on the south side of the dinner table, plus the two in the living room, make five.

69. **The correct answer is C.** The second sentence of the passage indicates that Peter can use a certain number of days for personal business, as well as for vacation or observing religious holidays.

70. **The correct answer is B.** For eight to fifteen years of service, the annual leave is 25 days.

71. **The correct answer is C.** The sixteenth year, in which leave is earned at the rate of $2\frac{1}{4}$ days per month, comes after 15 full years.

72. **The correct answer is B.** The first sentence of the paragraph 2 indicates that Peter is given a sick leave allowance of one day per month.

73. **The correct answer is A.** The last sentence of the passage indicates that Peter could be asked to provide a doctor's note for a one-, two-, or three-day absence.

74. **The correct answer is B.** The fourth warning on the list states that firefighters should never look directly at flashing electrical lines.

75. **The correct answer is B.** The last warning on the list states that full protective clothing should always be worn in areas in which electrical hazards might exist.

76. **The correct answer is D.** The fifth warning on the list states that specific attention must be paid to electrical dangers when raising a ladder near an overhead power line.

77. **The correct answer is A.** The sixth warning on the list states that any tingling sensation felt in the feet might indicate that the ground is charged.

78. **The correct answer is D.** When supply exceeds current needs, the society is wealthy and can distribute its surplus.

79. **The correct answer is A.** It can be inferred from the first and second sentences that the structure of an ant colony is in its social organization.

80. **The correct answer is A.** Poverty is the opposite of wealth. If there is poverty, there is no surplus and no expansionism.

81. **The correct answer is D.** The third sentence states that, "With very few exceptions, ants of any given colony are hostile to those of any other colony, even of the same species."

82. **The correct answer is C.** The table lists headache, dizziness, and nausea as signs that someone has been exposed to an atmosphere with carbon monoxide levels of 0.32 percent for 5 to 10 minutes. The paragraph indicates that carbon monoxide causes damage by blocking the blood's ability to carry oxygen.

83. **The correct answer is D.** The table lists unconsciousness as a symptom of remaining in an atmosphere with carbon monoxide levels of 0.32 percent for more than 30 minutes. Because Anthony already exhibits the symptoms of headache, dizziness, and nausea after 10 minutes, he could become unconscious if he remains in the car for an additional 20 minutes.

84. **The correct answer is D.** The table lists instant unconsciousness as a symptom of breathing air with carbon monoxide levels of 1.23 percent.

85. **The correct answer is D.** The table lists headache as a symptom of exposure to carbon monoxide levels of 0.04 percent for 1 to 2 hours. Because the last people to leave the building were in the building for over an hour and were complaining of headaches, choice D is the correct response.

86. **The correct answer is B.** There are two cars—one in the left foreground and one in the right midground—that are clearly involved in the accident. While it's unclear whether additional vehicles were involved without being pictured or included in the scene, your task is to remember what you observe, not what may or may not be.

87. **The correct answer is B.** The number on the firefighter's helmet is 191.

88. **The correct answer is D.** Firefighters have set up at least two of their own floodlights in order to better survey the scene and attend to victims. If the tunnel provides its own electric lighting, there's no indication from the photo that any of those lights are turned on.

89. **The correct answer is A.** The nature of firefighting can lead to significant stress for firefighters. Given the recent events for Smith, it likely that he is coping with what he witnessed at the plane crash. The irregularities with Smith appear to be isolated to his behavior and not physical condition, which would eliminate drugs and alcohol (choice C). While the shirking of duties and tardiness may indicate boredom (choice B) or laziness (choice D), his aggressiveness with other firefighters does not follow from those conditions.

90. **The correct answer is D.** It is clear from the presence of the two women and child on the fire escape below the man that he has a clear exit from the structure that does not require reliance on the quality of his anchor or his ability to rappel using the improvised rope. Firefighters should advise the man to take the safest and most efficient route possible to escape the structure. In this case, that solution is still the fire escape.

91. **The correct answer is A.** Evaporation occurs when the molecules near the surface of a liquid escape into the air. The water in the bowl has a greater surface area exposed to the air, causing it to evaporate faster than the water in the cup.

92. **The correct answer is B.** The special-purpose tool generally is more efficient because it is designed for one specific purpose. The all-purpose tool can accomplish the intended job, but it usually requires more time and works less effectively. In firefighting, time and efficiency are essential.

93. **The correct answer is C.** For the rear wheels (which are the driving wheels) to drive or push the car, friction or resistance must be present between the tires and the road surface. The ice and snow create a slippery road condition, causing the tires to lose traction. The front wheels do not turn because power from the engine is transmitted to the rear wheels only.

94. **The correct answer is B.** When the suction cup is pressed against the wall, the air in the cup is forced out, and a vacuum or negative pressure remains. Atmospheric air with a pressure of 14.7 psi (pounds per square inch) pushes against the rubber cup and holds it against the wall.

95. **The correct answer is D.** Adjacent gears turn in opposite directions. Gear A turns in a clockwise direction; therefore, gear B, which is adjacent to it, will turn in a counterclockwise direction. Continuing, gear C, which is adjacent to gear B, will turn in a clockwise direction; gear D, which is adjacent to gear C, will turn counterclockwise—the same as gear B.

96. **The correct answer is B.** Gears of the same size connected into the same system will turn at the same speed. In this case, gears A and D revolve at the same speed.

97. The correct answer is A. It takes the water one second to travel through 5 feet of hose. Therefore, $125 \div 5 = 25$.

98. The correct answer is D. The volume of a right rectangular prism is equal to the product of its length, width, and height. The formula is $V = lwh$. Therefore, $V = (6)(2)(4) = 48$ cubic units.

99. The correct answer is D. Let x equal the time Mick walks (in hours). His 90-minute head start equals 1.5 hours. Using the formula of distance = rate × time, the distance Mick walks is $4(x + 1.5)$, and the distance Rebecca jogs is $6x$. Equate these expressions and solve for x:

$$4(x + 1.5) = 6x$$
$$4x + 6 = 6x$$
$$2x = 6$$
$$x = 3$$

So, Mick has walked for an additional 3 hours by the time Rebecca catches up with him. Substitute the value of x back into the original equation and calculate. Since Mick walks at 4 miles per hour, he has walked 12 miles in three hours, plus an additional 6 miles from the 90 minutes he walked before Rebecca started jogging. This totals 18 miles.

100. The correct answer is B. To find percent of increase, subtract the original figure from the new figure. Then divide the amount of change by the original figure.

$$\$380 - \$350 = \$30; \$30 \div \$350 = .0857$$
(which is approximately $8\frac{1}{2}\%$).

PRACTICE TEST 3 ANSWER SHEET

1. Ⓐ Ⓑ Ⓒ Ⓓ	21. Ⓐ Ⓑ Ⓒ Ⓓ	41. Ⓐ Ⓑ Ⓒ Ⓓ	61. Ⓐ Ⓑ Ⓒ Ⓓ	81. Ⓐ Ⓑ Ⓒ Ⓓ
2. Ⓐ Ⓑ Ⓒ Ⓓ	22. Ⓐ Ⓑ Ⓒ Ⓓ	42. Ⓐ Ⓑ Ⓒ Ⓓ	62. Ⓐ Ⓑ Ⓒ Ⓓ	82. Ⓐ Ⓑ Ⓒ Ⓓ
3. Ⓐ Ⓑ Ⓒ Ⓓ	23. Ⓐ Ⓑ Ⓒ Ⓓ	43. Ⓐ Ⓑ Ⓒ Ⓓ	63. Ⓐ Ⓑ Ⓒ Ⓓ	83. Ⓐ Ⓑ Ⓒ Ⓓ
4. Ⓐ Ⓑ Ⓒ Ⓓ	24. Ⓐ Ⓑ Ⓒ Ⓓ	44. Ⓐ Ⓑ Ⓒ Ⓓ	64. Ⓐ Ⓑ Ⓒ Ⓓ	84. Ⓐ Ⓑ Ⓒ Ⓓ
5. Ⓐ Ⓑ Ⓒ Ⓓ	25. Ⓐ Ⓑ Ⓒ Ⓓ	45. Ⓐ Ⓑ Ⓒ Ⓓ	65. Ⓐ Ⓑ Ⓒ Ⓓ	85. Ⓐ Ⓑ Ⓒ Ⓓ
6. Ⓐ Ⓑ Ⓒ Ⓓ	26. Ⓐ Ⓑ Ⓒ Ⓓ	46. Ⓐ Ⓑ Ⓒ Ⓓ	66. Ⓐ Ⓑ Ⓒ Ⓓ	86. Ⓐ Ⓑ Ⓒ Ⓓ
7. Ⓐ Ⓑ Ⓒ Ⓓ	27. Ⓐ Ⓑ Ⓒ Ⓓ	47. Ⓐ Ⓑ Ⓒ Ⓓ	67. Ⓐ Ⓑ Ⓒ Ⓓ	87. Ⓐ Ⓑ Ⓒ Ⓓ
8. Ⓐ Ⓑ Ⓒ Ⓓ	28. Ⓐ Ⓑ Ⓒ Ⓓ	48. Ⓐ Ⓑ Ⓒ Ⓓ	68. Ⓐ Ⓑ Ⓒ Ⓓ	88. Ⓐ Ⓑ Ⓒ Ⓓ
9. Ⓐ Ⓑ Ⓒ Ⓓ	29. Ⓐ Ⓑ Ⓒ Ⓓ	49. Ⓐ Ⓑ Ⓒ Ⓓ	69. Ⓐ Ⓑ Ⓒ Ⓓ	89. Ⓐ Ⓑ Ⓒ Ⓓ
10. Ⓐ Ⓑ Ⓒ Ⓓ	30. Ⓐ Ⓑ Ⓒ Ⓓ	50. Ⓐ Ⓑ Ⓒ Ⓓ	70. Ⓐ Ⓑ Ⓒ Ⓓ	90. Ⓐ Ⓑ Ⓒ Ⓓ
11. Ⓐ Ⓑ Ⓒ Ⓓ	31. Ⓐ Ⓑ Ⓒ Ⓓ	51. Ⓐ Ⓑ Ⓒ Ⓓ	71. Ⓐ Ⓑ Ⓒ Ⓓ	91. Ⓐ Ⓑ Ⓒ Ⓓ
12. Ⓐ Ⓑ Ⓒ Ⓓ	32. Ⓐ Ⓑ Ⓒ Ⓓ	52. Ⓐ Ⓑ Ⓒ Ⓓ	72. Ⓐ Ⓑ Ⓒ Ⓓ	92. Ⓐ Ⓑ Ⓒ Ⓓ
13. Ⓐ Ⓑ Ⓒ Ⓓ	33. Ⓐ Ⓑ Ⓒ Ⓓ	53. Ⓐ Ⓑ Ⓒ Ⓓ	73. Ⓐ Ⓑ Ⓒ Ⓓ	93. Ⓐ Ⓑ Ⓒ Ⓓ
14. Ⓐ Ⓑ Ⓒ Ⓓ	34. Ⓐ Ⓑ Ⓒ Ⓓ	54. Ⓐ Ⓑ Ⓒ Ⓓ	74. Ⓐ Ⓑ Ⓒ Ⓓ	94. Ⓐ Ⓑ Ⓒ Ⓓ
15. Ⓐ Ⓑ Ⓒ Ⓓ	35. Ⓐ Ⓑ Ⓒ Ⓓ	55. Ⓐ Ⓑ Ⓒ Ⓓ	75. Ⓐ Ⓑ Ⓒ Ⓓ	95. Ⓐ Ⓑ Ⓒ Ⓓ
16. Ⓐ Ⓑ Ⓒ Ⓓ	36. Ⓐ Ⓑ Ⓒ Ⓓ	56. Ⓐ Ⓑ Ⓒ Ⓓ	76. Ⓐ Ⓑ Ⓒ Ⓓ	96. Ⓐ Ⓑ Ⓒ Ⓓ
17. Ⓐ Ⓑ Ⓒ Ⓓ	37. Ⓐ Ⓑ Ⓒ Ⓓ	57. Ⓐ Ⓑ Ⓒ Ⓓ	77. Ⓐ Ⓑ Ⓒ Ⓓ	97. Ⓐ Ⓑ Ⓒ Ⓓ
18. Ⓐ Ⓑ Ⓒ Ⓓ	38. Ⓐ Ⓑ Ⓒ Ⓓ	58. Ⓐ Ⓑ Ⓒ Ⓓ	78. Ⓐ Ⓑ Ⓒ Ⓓ	98. Ⓐ Ⓑ Ⓒ Ⓓ
19. Ⓐ Ⓑ Ⓒ Ⓓ	39. Ⓐ Ⓑ Ⓒ Ⓓ	59. Ⓐ Ⓑ Ⓒ Ⓓ	79. Ⓐ Ⓑ Ⓒ Ⓓ	99. Ⓐ Ⓑ Ⓒ Ⓓ
20. Ⓐ Ⓑ Ⓒ Ⓓ	40. Ⓐ Ⓑ Ⓒ Ⓓ	60. Ⓐ Ⓑ Ⓒ Ⓓ	80. Ⓐ Ⓑ Ⓒ Ⓓ	100. Ⓐ Ⓑ Ⓒ Ⓓ

PRACTICE TEST 3

100 Questions—210 minutes

Directions: The following questions are similar to those you will find on an actual firefighter exam. Be sure to read the questions carefully and follow any specific instructions that precede them. Choose the best answer to each question and fill in the corresponding circle on the answer sheet. The Answer Key and Explanations follow.

---

1. While performing a routine inspection of a factory building, a firefighter is asked a question by the plant manager about a matter under the control of the health department and about which the firefighter has little knowledge. In this situation, the best course of action for the firefighter to take is to

   A. answer the question to the best of his or her knowledge.

   B. tell the manager that he or she is not permitted to answer the question because it is irrelevant to firefighting.

   C. tell the manager that a referral will be made to the health department.

   D. suggest to the manager that he communicate with the health department about the matter.

2. Last winter, the coldest recorded temperature was −37 degrees Fahrenheit, and the warmest was 38 degrees Fahrenheit. How many degrees warmer was the warmest day than the coldest day?

   A. −75

   B. −1

   C. 1

   D. 75

3. At a five-alarm fire in the West End, several companies from a neighboring district are temporarily reassigned to occupy the West End station and take over duties of companies engaged in fighting the fire. The most logical reason for making such a decision is to

   A. protect firehouses from robbery or vandalism while firefighters are on a call.

   B. have additional units on standby should they be required to fight the fire.

   C. develop knowledge of a neighboring district among multiple fire companies.

   D. provide coverage for the district should other emergencies occur while the blaze continues.

4. While working structure protection in the vicinity of a large fire sweeping through a wildland-urban interface, Firefighter Alvarez sees the situation suddenly worsen, and officers request additional firefighters. A former firefighter approaches Alvarez and offers his assistance. Firefighter Alvarez should tell the man

   A. that the offer is appreciated, but he will need protective gear before he can assist with fire suppression.

   B. he must be currently certified and active in a department to assist and that the man should retreat to safety.

   C. the location of extra protective equipment and assigns him tasks.

   D. to give him his personal information and report to command for assignment.

5. In the aftermath of a building collapse, a member of the construction crew assigned for cleanup found an official fire department badge. Knowing that his son is fascinated by firefighters, the man gave it to him as gift after returning home later that evening. The fire department would suggest that the

   A. man frame the badge out of respect for the fire department.

   B. badge be disposed of as its design can lead to injury.

   C. man should make an effort to locate the owner of the badge before giving it to his son.

   D. badge be returned to the nearest firehouse.

6. You've heard reports of multiple drop-off mailboxes being set on fire across town. One day while walking home from work, you see firefighters responding to such an incident. You observe a probationary firefighter unfurling a hoseline when he is stopped by a more senior member of the company. You conclude that firefighters avoid using hose-lines in these situations as

   A. water is not effective on fires in small enclosed spaces.

   B. chemicals may be present in the materials that could create a volatile reaction after contact with water.

   C. mail untouched by the fire could be ruined by the extinguishing effort.

   D. another smothering agent could extin-guish the fire faster than water.

7. The news has reported multiple suspected arsons on the east side of your town within the past few days. The chief of the fire department has announced that they are unsure of the precise cause of the fires and physical evidence is scarce, though authorities have a sketch of the suspect from eyewitness reports. From this information, you can conclude that

   A. firefighters are often more concerned with extinguishing fires than investigating their causes.

   B. few people have knowledge of the variety of fire hazards.

   C. fires destroy much of the evidence that would provide insight into their causes.

   D. fire departments are more interested in future fire prevention than investigation.

8. You hear of a spat of false alarms from fire boxes in your neighborhood. You've recently seen firefighters modifying the alarms in response. One afternoon, you hear sirens approach the end of your street then stop. When you leave your house, you see a fire engine and police cruiser parked at the end of the block near a fire box. A large crowd has gathered and both police and firefighters are examining the hands of those gathered with specialized flashlights. You can con-clude from your observations that

   A. firefighters and police perform regular community outreach.

   B. the emergency responders are checking hands for injuries that would result from using the alarm box.

   C. the flashlights are ultraviolet and can reveal dye that was added to the handles of the fire boxes.

   D. firefighters quickly extinguished a fire in a nearby property.

9. Which of the following statements about the boiling point of water is correct?

   A. Water always boils at the same temperature, regardless of pressure.

   B. Water heated slowly by a low flame will boil at a higher temperature than water heated quickly by a high flame.

   C. A large quantity of water will boil at a higher temperature than a small quantity.

   D. Water heated at sea level will boil at a higher temperature than water heated on the top of a mountain.

Questions 10–14 are based on the following passage.

When several victims are involved in a motor vehicle incident, it is essential that firefighters quickly assess the extent of each victim's injuries so the people can be treated and removed from their vehicles in a logical sequence. Uninjured victims able to exit the vehicle on their own should be quickly removed to make room for firefighters to attend to the most seriously injured individuals. After the most seriously injured individuals have been stabilized, firefighters should give priority to victims trapped in their vehicles.

Last week, firefighters Warren and Mauro were the first to arrive at the scene of a multi-car incident that occurred in a rural area. Realizing that the next emergency vehicle would not be able to reach the location for another 20 minutes, the firefighters had to quickly assess which victims should be treated and moved or removed from their vehicles.

Three vehicles were involved in the incident. Each vehicle had a driver and one passenger. The first vehicle was severely damaged with the driver trapped inside. The driver of the car was unconscious and did not appear to be breathing. The passenger did not appear to have any life-threatening injuries.

The second car was not damaged as severely. The driver of the car appeared to have a broken leg that was trapped by the steering column but had no other serious injuries. The passenger of the car appeared to be quite shaken from the accident but had no serious injuries.

The third car was the least damaged of the three cars involved in the incident. The driver, however, was not wearing a seat belt and hit the windshield with her head. She had some minor cuts on her forehead and was extremely disoriented. The passenger in her car had a life-threatening compound fracture of his leg that was bleeding profusely.

10. Which two victims should be quickly removed from the cars to make room for rescue operations?

    A. Driver 1 and Passenger 1

    B. Passenger 1 and Passenger 2

    C. Driver 2 and Driver 3

    D. Driver 3 and Passenger 3

11. If Firefighter Mauro is treating Driver 1 and no other victims have been treated, who should Firefighter Warren attend to first?

    A. Passenger 1

    B. Passenger 3

    C. Driver 2

    D. Driver 3

12. After the most seriously injured individuals have been stabilized, who should firefighters Warren and Mauro attend to next?

    A. Driver 1 and Driver 2

    B. Passenger 1 and Passenger 2

    C. Driver 1 and Passenger 1

    D. Driver 2 and Passenger 2

13. A clear sign that Driver 3 might have suffered a major head injury is that

    A. she had cuts on her forehead.

    B. her car had the least damage.

    C. she did not appear to be breathing.

    D. she was extremely disoriented.

14. Passenger 1 should be quickly removed from the car because he or she

    A. was seriously injured.

    B. was bleeding profusely.

    C. was not injured.

    D. had a broken leg.

15. If there should be two fire hydrants for every square city block and there are seventy-five square city blocks in a mile, what percentage of a mile would be covered by 120 fire hydrants?

    A. 60 percent

    B. 70 percent

    C. 80 percent

    D. 90 percent

16. A fire has started 3.2 miles from the firehouse. How long will it take the firefighters to arrive at the fire if they travel at an average speed of 30 mph?

    A. 6.6 minutes

    B. 7.1 minutes

    C. 8.3 minutes

    D. 8.5 minutes

17. $17 \times 17 + (7.4 - 2.4) =$

    A. 278

    B. 269

    C. 199

    D. 294

18. What is the solution to the equation $P \div A - 2(W)$, if water pressure (P) is 500, water temperature (W) is 45, and the spray angle (A) is 3.2?

    A. 23.4

    B. 42

    C. 56.32

    D. 66.25

19. In Hewson County, Missouri, last year, there were calls for 21 house fires, 17 industrial fires, 2 industrial accidents, and 46 car accidents. Fire station A received 34 of these calls. What percentage of the total number of calls did station A receive?

    A. 23 percent

    B. 35 percent

    C. 40 percent

    D. 42 percent

20. One half of the employees of Acme Co. earn salaries above $18,000 annually. One third of the remainder earn salaries between $15,000 and $18,000. What part of the staff earns below $15,000?

A. $\frac{1}{6}$

B. $\frac{2}{3}$

C. $\frac{1}{2}$

D. $\frac{1}{3}$

21. The following figure represents a water tank. The number 1 indicates an intake pipe, and the number 2 indicates a discharge pipe.

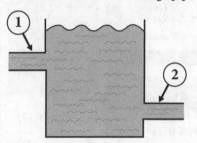

Of the following, the least accurate statement is that the

A. tank will eventually overflow if water flows through the intake pipe at a faster rate than it flows through the discharge pipe.

B. tank will empty completely if the intake pipe is closed and the discharge pipe remains open.

C. water in the tank will remain at a constant level if the rate of intake is equal to the rate of discharge.

D. water in the tank will rise if the intake pipe is operating when the discharge pipe is closed.

22.

The tool shown above is a(n)

A. Allen-head wrench.

B. double scraper.

C. offset screwdriver.

D. nail puller.

23. You're a firefighter on house watch duty when a civilian enters the firehouse. The man introduces himself as a British fire-fighter on vacation. He explains that while in the country he wishes to learn more about American firefighting methods. He asks you for permission to ride on the fire apparatus when it responds to alarms so that he can observe operations firsthand. In this situation, you should

A. refuse the request but suggest that he follow the apparatus in his own vehicle when there is an alarm.

B. call headquarters and request permission to permit the visitor to ride the apparatus.

C. direct the man to apply for permission at headquarters.

D. refuse the request and suggest the man return when next the fire department holds an open house.

Practice Test 3

Master the™ Firefighter Exam

24. While on vacation at a coastal town, you observe firefighters combating a fire at the end of a pier. You find it strange to see the firefighters carry their equipment down the length of the pier from the waterline, but when you think about it further, you realize they did not drive onto the pier in order to

A. build stamina among the firefighters.

B. give time for the fire to burn itself out naturally.

C. prevent damage or destruction of fire department equipment should the fire rapidly spread.

D. create more space for emergency first-aid.

Questions 25–27 are based on the following street map.

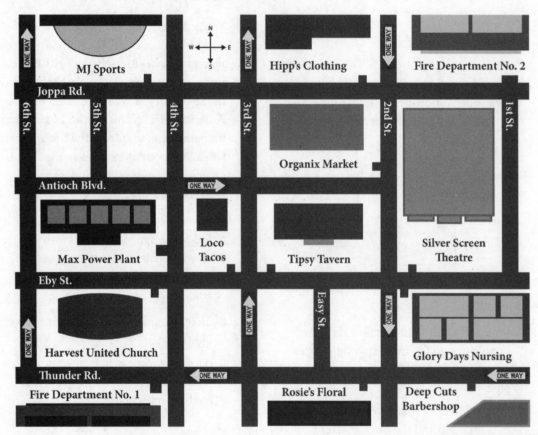

25. What is the shortest drive in terms of blocks from Fire Dept. No. 1 to Fire Dept. No 2?

A. 7

B. 8

C. 9

D. 10

26. You're heading east on Joppa Road between 3rd and 4th Streets when you take five consecutive right-hand turns, then stop. What is your new location?

A. Between Organix Market and the Silver Screen Theatre

B. At the intersection of 2nd and Eby Streets

C. Between the Silver Screen Theatre and Tipsy Tavern

D. At the intersection of 3rd Street and Joppa Road

27. On the map, the black squares adjacent to the street in front of each building indicate the entryways to each location. Which of the following trips can be made from entryway to entryway without traveling on a one-way street (crossing an intersection is allowed)?

    A. MJ Sports to Organix Market

    B. Hipp's Clothing to Loco Tacos

    C. Deep Cuts Barbershop to Tipsy Tavern

    D. Fire Department No. 1 to Silver Screen Theatre

28. The hypotenuse of a right triangle whose legs are 6 feet and 8 feet is

    A. 6 feet

    B. 7 feet

    C. 9 feet

    D. 10 feet

29. For every mile-per-hour a fire engine is traveling, it takes $\frac{3}{4}$ of a foot to come to a complete stop. How many feet will it take a fire engine traveling 60 mph to come to a full stop?

    A. 60 feet

    B. 50 feet

    C. 45 feet

    D. 30 feet

30. When firefighters remove a cornice from a building façade or roof, they make every effort to pull it back onto the rooftop. Responding to reports of a loose cornice on a six-story office building, firefighters are observed on the rooftop securing the loose piece and preparing to lift it with an aerial platform. You can conclude that firefighters in this situation primarily are

    A. trying to save time in the removal process.

    B. considering the safety of people on the street.

    C. making it possible to reuse the cornice after maintenance.

    D. protecting the safety of firefighters on the rooftop.

31. Emergency vehicle drivers have been trained to navigate traffic with specific protocols in mind. The same can be said of civilian drivers who must react in a particular way to emergency vehicles operating with their lights on. You would use the following steps to yield right-of-way to an emergency vehicle approaching from behind near the center of the roadway (these steps are not in order):

    Step 1. Use your right turn signal to indicate a lane change or maneuver.

    Step 2. Remain stopped until the emergency vehicle has passed and rejoin the flow of traffic.

    Step 3. Decelerate your vehicle until arriving at a complete stop.

    Step 4. Determine the position of the emergency vehicle relative to your vehicle.

    Step 5. Travel as close as possible to the right-hand curb or roadside.

    What is the most logical order for the listed steps?

    A. 4–5–1–2–3

    B. 4–1–5–3–2

    C. 4–3–2–5–1

    D. 5–4–1–3–2

Practice Test 3

Questions 32–35 are based on the following passage. Take five minutes to read and study this passage. Then, without referring to the passage, choose the best answer for each question that follows.

Three firefighters, Frederick Wright, Maria Moretti, and Nicholas Freeman, were slightly injured while fighting a fire at a local two-story residence at 2:45 a.m. The home belongs to the Lewis family. Mr. Harrison Lewis and his wife, Jennifer, have three children: Ethan (age 17), Michael (age 13), and Nicole (age 9). Mrs. Lewis remembers waking up at 1:55 a.m. to hear a window break and the curtains catching on fire. The smoke alarm went off, the family dog began barking, and the rest of the family was awakened. The living room had caught on fire, and the fire was rapidly spreading throughout the lower level. The Lewis's next-door neighbors, the Rodriguez family, called the fire department.

Jennifer, Ethan, and Michael Lewis all exited the home (along with the family dog) according to the escape plan the family had agreed upon earlier. Harrison Lewis and his daughter, Nicole, remained upstairs; Nicole was too frightened to leave her room, and her father remained with her to try to coax her down the stairs. Eventually, the fire blocked their escape, and they had to be rescued by firefighters. After the remaining family members were rescued, firefighters spent the next few hours extinguishing the blaze. It was at this time that Firefighters Wright, Moretti, and Freeman were injured. The firefighters (along with Mr. Lewis and his daughter) were transported to St. Mary Magdalene Hospital to be treated for their injuries and smoke inhalation.

While looking into a possible cause for the fire, police officers interviewed the family and neighbors. Mr. and Mrs. Pryce, neighbors who live across the street from the Lewis family, reported seeing teenagers sitting in a car outside of the house before the fire. They noted that shortly afterward, they heard the car's tires squealing as it drove away. They did not think anything of this fact until police and firefighters were summoned to the scene. Police officers asked Michael and Ethan Lewis if they knew anyone who had a grudge against them. Ethan looked uncomfortable and was unwilling to speak with the authorities.

32. Which pair of people were transported to St. Mary Magdalene Hospital to be treated for their injuries?

   A. Harrison and Jennifer Lewis

   B. Firefighter Moretti and Michael Lewis

   C. Firefighter Freeman and Jennifer Lewis

   D. Firefighter Wright and Nicole Lewis

33. Who summoned the firefighters to the scene?

   A. The Rodriguez family

   B. Mr. and Mrs. Pryce

   C. Teenagers outside of the Lewis home

   D. Ethan Lewis

34. Why didn't Harrison and Nicole Lewis initially leave the house according to the family escape plan?

   A. Harrison was trying to coax Nicole out of her bedroom because she was too frightened to leave.

   B. The fire was located in Nicole's bedroom.

   C. The fire blocked Harrison's escape, and Nicole did not want to leave him by himself.

   D. They were asleep and did not know that there was a fire in the living room.

35. When were the firefighters injured?

    A. As they tried to rescue Nicole Lewis
    B. As they tried to rescue Harrison Lewis
    C. As they attempted to extinguish the blaze
    D. As they arrived on the scene

Questions 36–39 are based on the following passage.

Plastic does not consist of a single substance; it is a blended combination of several substances. In addition to the resin, it may contain various fillers, plasticizers, lubricants, and coloring material. Depending on the type and quantity of substances added to the binder, its properties, including combustibility, might be altered considerably. The flammability of plastic depends on its composition and, as with other materials, on its physical size and condition. Thin sections, sharp edges, or powdered plastic ignite and burn more readily than the same amount of identical material in heavy sections with smooth surfaces.

36. According to the passage, all plastics contain a

    A. resin.
    B. resin and a filler.
    C. resin, filler, and plasticizer.
    D. resin, filler, plasticizer, lubricant, and coloring material.

37. The conclusion best supported by the passage is that the flammability of plastic

    A. generally is high.
    B. generally is moderate.
    C. generally is low.
    D. varies considerably.

38. Based on the information given in the passage, plastic can best be described as

    A. a trade name.
    B. the name of a specific product.
    C. the name of a group of products that have some similar and some dissimilar properties.
    D. the name of any substance that can be shaped or molded during the production process.

39. In a manufacturing process, large thick sheets of a particular plastic are cut, buffed, and formed into small tools. The statement most in accord with the information in the passage is that

    A. the dust particles of the plastics are more flammable than the tools or the sheets.
    B. the plastic tools are more flammable than the dust particles or the sheets.
    C. the sheets of plastic are more flammable than the dust particles or the tools.
    D. there is insufficient information to determine the relative flammability of sheets, tools, and dust particles.

Questions 40–42 are based on the following passage.

An overcurrent protective device is provided for each circuit to guard against overheating of electrical conductors in buildings. This device is designed to open the circuit and to cut off the flow of current whenever the current exceeds a predetermined limit. The fuse, which is a common form of overcurrent protection, consists of a fusible metal element that, when heated by the current to a specific temperature, melts and opens the circuit.

40. According to the passage, an overcurrent protective device is designed to

A. open the circuit and cut the flow of current.

B. open the circuit and establish the flow of current.

C. close the circuit and cut the flow of current.

D. close the circuit and establish the flow of current.

41. As used in the passage, the best example of a conductor is a(n)

A. metal table that comes in contact with a source of electricity.

B. storage battery generating electricity.

C. electrical wire carrying an electrical current.

D. dynamo converting mechanical energy into electrical energy.

42. According to the passage, the maximum number of circuits that can be handled by a fuse box containing six fuses is

A. 3.

B. 6.

C. 12.

D. Cannot be determined from the information given in the passage.

Questions 43–45 are based on the following passage.

Essentially, unlined linen hose is a fabric tube made of closely woven linen yarn. Due to the natural characteristics of linen, very shortly after water is introduced, the wet threads swell, closing the minute spaces between them and making the tube practically watertight. This type of hose tends to deteriorate rapidly if not thoroughly dried after use or if installed where it will be exposed to dampness or weather conditions. It is not ordinarily built to withstand frequent service or use in which the fabric will be subjected to chafing from rough or sharp surfaces.

43. Seepage of water through an unlined linen hose is observed when the water is first turned on. We can conclude that the seepage

   A. indicates that the hose is defective.

   B. will be in direct proportion to the water pressures within the hose.

   C. is likely the result of improper storage or drying.

   D. is expected as long as seepage ceases after the threads have been thoroughly soaked.

44. Unlined linen hose is most suitable for use

   A. as a garden hose.

   B. on fire department apparatus.

   C. as emergency fire equipment in buildings.

   D. in fire department training schools.

45. The use of unlined linen hose would be least appropriate in a(n)

   A. outdoor lumberyard.

   B. nonfireproof office building.

   C. department store.

   D. cosmetic manufacturing plant.

Questions 46 and 47 are based on the following passage.

One of the most common emergency situations that a firefighter might face is a motor vehicle incident. Victims in these situations are commonly trapped in a vehicle, making it difficult for a rescuer to administer proper first aid. It is common for injuries incurred during a motor vehicle incident to be very serious and even life-threatening. Therefore, it is critical to quickly gain access to the vehicle so that at least one rescuer can be placed inside to begin stabilizing the victim. After a rescuer gains access to the vehicle, he or she should conduct an initial survey to assess any life-threatening injuries. While conducting the initial survey, the rescuer should keep the victim's airway open, perform CPR if necessary, and treat any uncontrolled bleeding. These procedures are listed in terms of importance and always should be conducted in that order.

46. It might be difficult for a rescuer to administer first aid to the victim of a motor vehicle incident because the victim often is

   A. stubborn.

   B. trapped.

   C. breathing.

   D. young.

47. After gaining access to the vehicle, the first thing a rescuer should assess is whether

   A. there is uncontrolled bleeding.

   B. CPR is necessary.

   C. the victim is trapped.

   D. the victim's airway is open.

Practice Test 3

Questions 48 and 49 are based on the following passage.

Fire Chief Williams has prepared the following list of procedures, which are not in sequence, for rescuing victims from burning buildings:

1. From the time of entrance, an internal building search always should be conducted on hands and knees. Visibility in a burning building often is poor, making it dangerous to walk upright.
2. Firefighters involved in rescue operations always should enter a burning building in groups of at least two.
3. Victims removed from a building always should be placed in the custody of an individual who can ensure that the victim will not attempt to re-enter the building.
4. Full protective clothing and a protective breathing apparatus always should be donned and double-checked for malfunctions prior to any rescue operation.
5. After a room has been searched, a firefighter should always leave a sign to notify other firefighters that the search has been completed. Hang tags should be left on door handles to indicate that the room has been searched.
6. An internal search always should begin with an outside wall. Windows typically are located on an outside wall and can be opened for ventilation.

48. The logical order for the procedures listed is

A. 1, 5, 3, 6, 2, 4

B. 6, 5, 4, 2, 3, 1

C. 6, 5, 1, 3, 4, 2

D. 4, 2, 1, 6, 5, 3

49. According to the procedures listed, a firefighter who walks inside of a burning building is violating which procedural rule?

A. Firefighters should enter a burning building in groups of at least two.

B. Full protective clothing and breathing apparatus should be worn.

C. Firefighters should leave tags on doors to indicate that the room has been searched.

D. Searches should be conducted on hands and knees when visibility is poor.

50. The easiest way to chop through wood with an axe is to align the blade

A. with the grain.

B. across the grain at 90°.

C. across the grain at 45°.

D. around the grain.

51. The diagram below shows four convenience outlets.

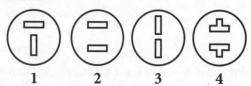

1   2   3   4

Which of the convenience outlets shown is known as a polarized outlet?

A. Outlet 1

B. Outlet 2

C. Outlet 3

D. Outlet 4

52. As a firefighter, you receive a call during the night while off duty from a neighbor who says his house is on fire. The most appropriate action for you to take first is to

A. call for fire department assistance if it has not been contacted.

B. go to the neighbor's home to evaluate the extent of the fire.

C. call other off-duty firefighters who live close by to help fight the fire.

D. inform the neighbor to wait to take further action until you arrive.

Questions 53–60 are based on the following diagram. Study and memorize the diagram for five minutes, cover the diagram, and answer the questions. Do not refer to the diagram while answering the questions.

Doors:

Windows:

Doorways:

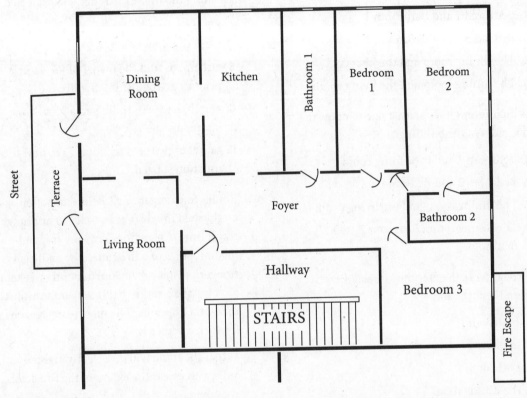

53. The fire escape is farthest from which room?

A. Bedroom 2

B. Bedroom 3

C. Kitchen

D. Dining room

54. Which one of the following rooms has only one door or doorway?

A. Living room

B. Bedroom 1

C. Kitchen

D. Dining room

55. Which room can firefighters reach directly from the fire escape?

A. Dining room

B. Living room

C. Bedroom 1

D. Bedroom 3

56. Which room does not have a door or doorway leading directly to the foyer?

A. Bathroom 1

B. Bathroom 2

C. Bedroom 1

D. Dining room

Practice Test 3

57. A firefighter leaving Bathroom 1 would be in

   A. Bedroom 1.

   B. Bedroom 2.

   C. Bedroom 3.

   D. the foyer.

58. Firefighters on the terrace would be able to enter directly into which rooms?

   A. Bedroom 1 and Bathroom 1

   B. Bedroom 2 and Bathroom 2

   C. The dining room and the kitchen

   D. The dining room and the living room

59. Which rooms have at least one window on two sides of the building?

   A. Bedroom 2 and the dining room

   B. Bedroom 2 and Bedroom 3

   C. The dining room and the living room

   D. The dining room, Bedroom 2, and Bedroom 3

60. Firefighters can enter the kitchen directly from the foyer and

   A. Bedroom 1.

   B. the living room.

   C. Bathroom 1.

   D. the dining room.

61. Firefighters Hernandez and Delany have responded to a fire in an empty vehicle abandoned on the sidewalk at an intersection near the entrance to a subway station. After extinguishing the fire with a hoseline, the firefighters hear a call for help from the stairs leading to the train platform. A man has fallen and injured his neck. Prior to extinguishing the fire, the firefighters neglected to

   A. place a tarpaulin to direct water away from the subway entrance.

   B. attempt to find the owner of the vehicle prior to extinguishing the fire.

   C. search the surrounding area for anyone injured by the vehicle.

   D. gather eyewitness accounts as to how the situation started.

62. Routes to emergency situations are often established in advance in order to minimize travel time. An engine company responding to reports of a fire caused by an illegal firework display on a Fourth of July weekend elect to take a route that is longer in distance than other options. The most likely reason for such a choice is

   A. that the route will give the firefighters a view to assess the extent of the fire before arriving.

   B. doing so will allow the engine to avoid holiday traffic jams.

   C. the report of the fire indicates that it is minor and does not require haste.

   D. the selected route will allow firefighters to stop at another call on the way to the fire.

63. From a distance, an off-duty firefighter sees a group of teenage boys set fire to a newspaper and then toss the flaming pages into the open window of a building being torn down. The firefighter's cell phone battery is dead. In this situation, the first action that should be taken by the firefighter is to

    A. send a fire alarm from the closest street alarm box.

    B. chase the boys and attempt to catch one of them.

    C. investigate whether a fire has been started.

    D. call the police from the closest police alarm box or telephone.

64. When responding to an alarm, officers are not to talk to the company driver except to give orders or directions. While responding to a large fire at an apartment complex, which of the following would be appropriate for an officer to communicate to the driver?

    A. Concerns over whether the alerted companies will be adequate to combat the fire

    B. Indications that the driver missed the appropriate turn

    C. Suggestions that the driver change lanes to increase pace

    D. Commands to turn to avoid a certain stretch of road because of known construction

65. Late one night, you're walking to a nearby subway station after leaving a party when you see flames raging through the windows of a shoe store. You're not very familiar with the part of town you're in. You know that you need to try to alert emergency responders in the most efficient way possible, so you decide to

    A. begin knocking on doors until someone answers and ask them to report the fire.

    B. seek out the closest fire alarm box.

    C. call 911 and describe your surroundings.

    D. search on foot for the nearest firehouse.

Practice Test 3

Questions 66–70 are based on the following image. Study and memorize the image for five minutes, cover the image, and answer the questions. Do not refer to the image while answering the questions.

66. How many ladders have been deployed to deal with the situation?

    A. 1

    B. 2

    C. 3

    D. 4

67. The waterline from the firehose currently being used to fight the fire is trained

    A. up toward the roof from below.

    B. onto the roof from above.

    C. toward the side of the house.

    D. toward the upstairs window.

68. The firefighters pictured are currently

    A. extinguishing the flames so they can enter and search for victims.

    B. extinguishing the flames to minimize property damage.

    C. monitoring the fire and waiting for it to burn out.

    D. waiting for direction from their senior officer.

69. Which of the following tools is one of the firemen carrying?

    A. A flat-head axe

    B. A pike pole

    C. A chainsaw

    D. A Halligan tool

70. How many trees are visible?

A. 1

B. 2

C. 3

D. 4

71. The following diagram shows various types of ramps leading to a loading platform.

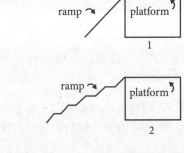

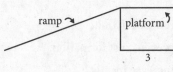

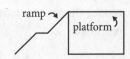

Which ramp would permit the load to be moved up to the platform with the least amount of force?

A. Ramp 1

B. Ramp 2

C. Ramp 3

D. Ramp 4

72. A substance that is a good conductor of heat is most likely to be a poor

A. conductor of electricity.

B. insulator of heat.

C. vibrator of sound.

D. reflector of light.

73. In the diagram below, what will result from crossing the V-belt as shown by the dotted lines?

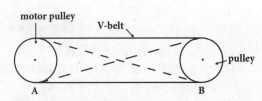

A. Pulley A will reverse direction.

B. There will be no change in the direction of either pulley.

C. Pulley B will reverse direction.

D. The motor will stop.

Practice Test 3

Questions 74–76 are based on the following diagram.

Assume that the teeth of the gears are continuous around each gear.

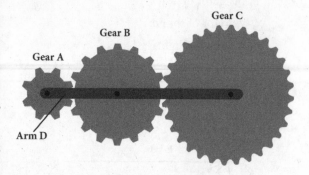

Gear C

Gear B

Gear A

Arm D

74. Fastening Gear A to Arm D at another point in addition to its shaft results in

   A. Gear B rotating on its shaft in a direction opposite to Gear A.

   B. Gear C rotating on its shaft in a direction opposite to Gear A.

   C. Arm D rotating around the shaft of Gear C.

   D. the locking of all gears.

75. If Gear C is fastened to a supporting frame (not shown) so that it cannot rotate, and if Gear A turns clockwise on its shaft, then Gear B will turn

   A. counterclockwise and Arm D will turn clockwise around the shaft of Gear C.

   B. counterclockwise and Arm D will turn counterclockwise around the shaft of Gear C.

   C. clockwise and Arm D will turn clockwise around the shaft of Gear C.

   D. clockwise and Arm D will turn counterclockwise around the shaft of Gear C.

76. If Gear B is fastened to a supporting frame (not shown) so that it cannot rotate, and if Arm D rotates clockwise around the shaft of Gear B, then for each complete revolution Arm D makes, Gear A will make

   A. more than one turn clockwise about its shaft.

   B. less than one turn clockwise about its shaft.

   C. more than one turn counterclockwise about its shaft.

   D. less than one turn counterclockwise about its shaft.

77. Of the following, the most important reason for lubricating moving parts of machinery is to

   A. reduce friction.

   B. prevent rust formation.

   C. increase inertia.

   D. reduce the accumulation of dust and dirt on the parts.

78. Public education in how to prevent fires has been shown to decrease the rate at which loss of property due to fires occurs. At a meeting concerned with fire prevention, it was stated that the rate of fire loss has been maintained near its previous levels as efforts to educate the public in fire prevention have increased. From this statement, it can be inferred that

   A. further public education in fire prevention will result in reduction in the fire loss rate.

   B. fire loss has an inverse relationship with the amount of public education related to fire prevention.

   C. the steady rate of fire loss may be due to the success of public education but also increases in potential fire hazards and fire-prone conditions.

   D. recent years have seen a decrease in the number of arson cases.

Practice Test 3

79. The local fire department has been trying to pioneer safer and more effective firefighting techniques. The department has been piloting a new program that stations additional firefighters at several locations around the city without any firefighting apparatus. You infer that positioning firefighters in this way will

   A. satisfy the demands of larger fires as the primary need is often not supplies or equipment but firefighters.

   B. help firefighters respond to emergencies faster.

   C. allow the fire department to rotate firefighters to different areas of the city.

   D. impart specialized knowledge of certain parts of the city to firefighters.

Questions 80–85 are based on the following diagram and information.

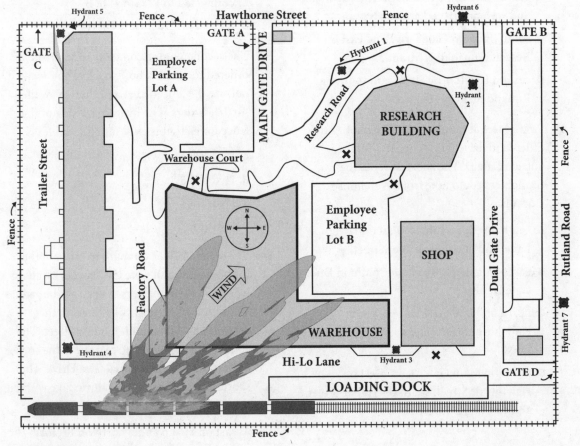

LEGEND

✖ = Building Entrance

▓ = Fire Hydrant

At 3 a.m., a fire alarm is received for the area shown in the diagram. A train loaded with highly flammable material is on fire. The entire area is surrounded by a 10-foot high fence. At the time of the fire, Gate A is open, but Gates B, C, and D are locked.

80. The first engine company arrives at the fire scene. The security guard at Gate A informs the firefighters of the location of the fire. Firefighter Jensen knows the area. He should inform the lieutenant that the best route to take to reach the hydrant closest to the fire while avoiding smoke and flames is

    A. south on Main Gate Drive, northeast on Research Road, south on Dual Gate Drive, and west on Hi-Lo Lane to Hydrant 3.

    B. south on Main Gate Drive, west on Warehouse Court, south on Factory Road, and west on Hi-Lo Lane to Hydrant 4.

    C. south on Main Gate Drive and east on Research Road to Hydrant 1.

    D. east on Hawthorne Street and south on Rutland Road to Hydrant 7.

81. Firefighters at Employee Parking Lot A are ordered to drive their truck to the fence outside Gate D. The shortest route the firefighters could take from Warehouse Court is

    A. south on Factory Road, west on Hi-Lo Lane, and north on Trailer Street.

    B. east on Research Road and south on Dual Gate Drive.

    C. north on Main Gate Drive, east on Hawthorne Street, and south on Rutland Road.

    D. north on Main Gate Drive, west on Hawthorne Street, south on Trailer Street, and east on Hi-Lo Lane.

82. The first ladder company arrives at the fire scene. As they are driving north on Rutland Road, firefighters see the fire through Gate D. They cut the locks and enter Gate D. The lieutenant orders a firefighter to go on foot from Gate D to the Research Building to search the building for occupants. The entrance to the Research Building that is closest to the firefighter is

    A. connected to the Visitor Parking Lot.

    B. located on Research Road.

    C. connected to Parking Lot B.

    D. located on Dual Gate Drive.

83. The second engine company to arrive is ordered to attach a hose to a hydrant located outside the fenced area and then to await further orders. The hydrant outside of the fenced area that is closest to the flames is

    A. Hydrant 6.

    B. Hydrant 3.

    C. Hydrant 4.

    D. Hydrant 7.

84. The second ladder company to arrive at the fire scene is met at Gate C by a security guard who gives them the keys to open all the gates. They drive south on Trailer Street to the corner of Hi-Lo Lane and Trailer Street. The company is then ordered to drive to the corner of Research Road and Dual Gate Drive. The shortest route for the company to take without being exposed to the smoke and flames is

    A. east on Hi-Lo Lane, north on Factory Road, and east on Warehouse Court to Research Road.

    B. east on Hi-Lo Lane and north on Dual Gate Drive.

    C. north on Trailer Street, east on Hawthorne Street, and south on Dual Gate Drive.

    D. north on Trailer Street, east on Hawthorne Street, south on Main Gate Drive, and east on Research Road.

85. The heat from the fire in the railroad cars ignites the warehouse on the other side of Hi-Lo Lane. The officer of the first ladder company orders two firefighters on the west end of the loading dock to break the windows on the north side of the warehouse. Of the following, the shortest way for the firefighters to reach the northwest corner of the warehouse without passing through the smoke and flames is to go

A. east on Hi-Lo Lane, north on Dual Gate Drive, and then west on Research Road to the entrance on Warehouse Court.

B. west on Hi-Lo Lane, north on Factory Road, and then east on Warehouse Court to the Visitor Parking Lot on Warehouse Court.

C. east on Hi-Lo Lane, north on Rutland Road, west on Hawthorne Street, and then south on Main Gate Drive to the Visitor Parking Lot on Warehouse Court.

D. east on Hi-Lo Lane, north on Dual Gate Drive, west on Hawthorne Street, and then south on Main Gate Drive to the entrance on Warehouse Court.

86. During a four-plex apartment fire, a firefighter catches a frantic woman attempting to re-enter the burning building. The woman is crying and screaming that she must save her family photographs. She insists the photos are in an area the fire has not yet reached and continuously tries to run back into the structure. The appropriate response from the firefighter is to

A. allow the woman to re-enter the building briefly with a firefighter in front of her to assess the conditions.

B. call a police officer to remove the woman from the scene.

C. send the woman to the incident commander for permission to go back inside.

D. alert the other firefighters so someone can retrieve the photos before they burn.

87. While walking past a firehouse one day, you can see firefighters washing the fire engine, mopping floors, inspecting gear, and preparing food—tasks not entirely related to firefighting and emergency response. You induce that the primary reason for these assignments is to

A. occupy firefighters when they're not responding to alarms.

B. keep department equipment and quarters in good condition.

C. limit costs by having firefighters perform maintenance activities.

D. develop internal competition for the best daily activities.

88. Dense smoke can cause severe eye and lung issues, so firefighters try to avoid exposure as much as possible with protective gear and respirators. If a firefighter lacked proper protective gear and had to run through an area of dense smoke, it would be best for the firefighter to

A. take deep, slow breaths of air while running.

B. breathe deeply before entering the area then slowly while passing through.

C. take a shallow breath before starting and a deep breath while passing through the area.

D. refrain from breathing while passing through the area.

Questions 89–91 are based on the following map.

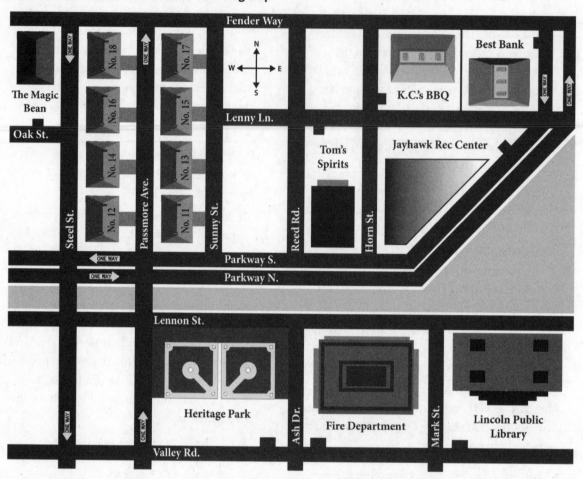

89. What is the most direct route from the Fire Department to Best Bank?

  A. Valley to Ash to Lennon to Passmore to Fender to Parkway South

  B. Valley to Passmore to Parkway South

  C. Valley to Passmore to Fender to Parkway South

  D. Valley to Passmore to Parkway North to Fender to Parkway South

90. It's spring and there's a fire in House No. 11 at noon on a Saturday with a southward breeze in the air. Of the following, who is most likely to notice the fire first and call it in?

  A. A teller at Best Bank

  B. Someone on staff at the Fire Department

  C. An instructor exiting Jayhawk Rec Center

  D. A father in the stands at Heritage Park watching his son play baseball

91. You're traveling east on Lenny Lane between Sunny Street and Reed Road when you take three consecutive right-hand turns, followed by two lefts, and a right. Where are you located?

    A. In front of the Magic Bean

    B. Near Heritage Park

    C. Near Tom's Spirits

    D. At House No. 11

92. Firefighters Robinson and Chiang are dispatched to a business that sells a variety of gases and tanks for medical, welding, and industrial purposes. The fire is in a storage building full of CO_2 cylinders. The firefighters enter the building and realize they have taken an extreme risk. The firefighters are concerned with

    A. a sudden release of toxic gases.

    B. the expansion of the fire due to the presence of the CO_2.

    C. the CO_2 cylinders expanding and exploding.

    D. a sudden structural collapse.

93. During extended periods of hot weather, firefighters can expect to add hydrant patrol to their daily routines. Hydrant patrol aims to curb uncontrolled use of the hydrants in order to prevent wasteful water usage and drops in water pressure that can affect firefighting. Of the following actions, which should not be taken during these patrols?

    A. Dedicating time to learning the location and condition of hydrants in a district

    B. Threatening residents who frequently open fire hydrants

    C. Making opportunities for community outreach

    D. Closing open fire hydrants to maintain adequate water pressure.

94. An alarm was received to go to Blount Street for a reported fire in an occupied multiple-dwelling building. Engine 299 responded to the alarm. As the trucks turned into the street, the firefighters were greeted with a barrage of rocks and bottles thrown from doorways and rooftops.

    Lieutenant Peters, the officer in command, ordered the firefighters to take shelter from the barrage of rocks and bottles being thrown by civilians at the scene of the false alarm. The lieutenant's action were

    A. improper; the lieutenant should have first ordered a search for the fire.

    B. proper; however, the lieutenant should have tried to calm the crowd first.

    C. improper; the lieutenant should have requested more fire department units to respond to the scene.

    D. proper; the lieutenant's immediate responsibility was the safety of the firefighters under attack.

95. A canvas tarpaulin measures 6 feet × 9 feet. The largest circular area that can be covered completely by this tarpaulin is a circle with a diameter of

    A. 9 feet.

    B. 8 feet.

    C. 7 feet.

    D. 6 feet.

Practice Test 3

Questions 96–100 are based on the following table and information.

A homeowner who recently lost many of her possessions in a fire is trying to estimate the value of the lost items. Below is a list of some of the lost items and their approximated values.

Item	Approximate Value
Computer	$3,000
Wardrobe	$2,200
Jewelry	???
Stereo system	$1,500
Oriental rug	$500

96. If the total value of the lost items was equal to $10,378, what was the approximate value of the lost jewelry?

A. $6,178

B. $6,678

C. $3,178

D. $2,678

97. If the jewelry was worth one-third of the value of the wardrobe, how much would the jewelry be worth?

A. $763.66

B. $733.33

C. $933.33

D. $1,113.13

98. As she replaces the items in her home, the homeowner buys a dining room table that is four times as expensive as the oriental rug. How much does the dining room table cost?

A. $1,000

B. $1,500

C. $2,000

D. $2,500

99. If the homeowner were to buy a stereo system that is six percent more expensive than the original, how much would it cost?

A. $900

B. $1,410

C. $1,590

D. $2,400

100. Assuming that the jewelry was worth $1,600, what is the average value of the lost items?

A. $880

B. $1,760

C. $2,200

D. $2,760

ANSWER KEY AND EXPLANATIONS

1. D	21. B	41. C	61. A	81. C
2. D	22. C	42. D	62. B	82. C
3. D	23. C	43. D	63. C	83. D
4. B	24. C	44. C	64. D	84. C
5. D	25. B	45. A	65. C	85. A
6. C	26. C	46. B	66. C	86. B
7. C	27. B	47. D	67. A	87. B
8. C	28. D	48. D	68. B	88. D
9. D	29. C	49. D	69. C	89. D
10. B	30. B	50. A	70. A	90. D
11. B	31. B	51. A	71. C	91. A
12. A	32. D	52. A	72. B	92. C
13. D	33. A	53. D	73. C	93. B
14. C	34. A	54. B	74. D	94. D
15. C	35. C	55. D	75. B	95. D
16. A	36. A	56. B	76. A	96. C
17. D	37. D	57. D	77. A	97. B
18. D	38. C	58. D	78. C	98. C
19. C	39. A	59. A	79. A	99. C
20. D	40. A	60. D	80. A	100. B

1. **The correct answer is D.** A firefighter should act to bring about the most efficient solution to a problem. In this case, that means referring the plant manager to the proper authority on matters of health regulations. It is unlikely that any knowledge the firefighter has on the matter would exceed that which could be offered by the health department.

2. **The correct answer is D.** Approach this problem like a distance question. The question is really asking what the distance is on the number line from −37 to +38. Add the magnitudes:

$$-37 - 38 = -75$$

Remember, when subtracting a positive number from a negative number, add the magnitude and make the difference positive. The difference is 75 degrees.

3. **The correct answer is D.** With large fires the concern is that other emergencies may be overshadowed or neglected. As such, requesting that available companies be temporarily reassigned from a neighboring district is reasonable as it would allow efficient response to alarms that occur while the other firefighters battle the five-alarm fire.

4. **The correct answer is B.** Firefighter Alvarez understands that his first responsibility is to protect the public from harm. Regardless of who the civilian claims to be, it is improper for anyone to participate in firefighting activities who is not a certified emergency responder.

5. **The correct answer is D.** A firefighter's badge is an official emblem of the bearer's status. It should be treated as such and returned to a firehouse regardless of whether it has been replaced or its owner is still an active firefighter.

6. **The correct answer is C.** Firefighters will make every effort once the safety of the public has been assured to preserve property. As such, firefighters would attempt to use an alternative extinguishing method to suppress a fire in a mailbox to, if at all possible, preserve packages and letters present. From the details of the situation, none of the other answer choices can be said to be reasonable.

7. **The correct answer is C.** From the fire chief's announcement, there is a lack of clear physical evidence at the scenes to provide insight into the cause of the fires. To consider that piece of information then leads you to the conclusion that the arsonist has found a method of starting fires that limits physical evidence (not among the answer choices) or that fires often destroy much of the evidence that elucidates their causes.

8. **The correct answer is C.** You know from the question that a series of false alarms has occurred and that firefighters modified alarm boxes in response. The presence of the "specialized flashlights" is also significant. You can conclude that police or fire crews are attempting to identify the culprit of the false alarms. While the method may not be completely clear, choice C is the only answer that addresses the circumstances of the situation in question.

9. **The correct answer is D.** Water boils at 212°F at sea level, a higher temperature at higher air pressure. Cooking and baking instructions often vary for certain altitudes above sea level.

10. **The correct answer is B.** The first paragraph states that victims who are not injured or

who can leave the vehicle on their own should be quickly removed from the vehicle to make room for the rescuers. Passenger 1 and Passenger 2 did not have any serious injuries and therefore should be quickly removed from the cars to make room for the rescuers.

11. **The correct answer is B.** The first paragraph states that the most seriously injured individuals should be stabilized first. If Firefighter Mauro is treating Driver 1, then Passenger 3 is the most seriously injured individual left and should be treated next.

12. **The correct answer is A.** The first paragraph states that, once the most seriously injured individuals have been stabilized, priority should be given to victims trapped in their vehicles. Driver 1 and Driver 2 both are trapped in their cars and should be attended to next.

13. **The correct answer is D.** Disorientation is often a sign that head trauma has occurred. While it is true that Driver 3 had cuts on her forehead, choice A is not the best answer because cuts do not necessarily indicate that she suffered a major head injury.

14. **The correct answer is C.** The first paragraph states that individuals who are not injured should be quickly removed from their cars. Since Passenger 1 did not appear to have any life-threatening injuries, he or she should be quickly removed from the car.

15. **The correct answer is C.** There are 150 hydrants for every square mile. To figure out what percentage of 150 fire hydrants 120 hydrants is, take $120 \div 150 = 0.80$. To convert this to a percent, take $100\% \times 0.80 = 80\%$.

16. **The correct answer is A.** In one hour, the firefighters would have traveled 30 miles by traveling 30 mph. It will take them a fraction of that time to travel 3.2 miles. Thus, take $3.2 \div 30 = 0.11$. Because there are 60 minutes in an hour, $60 \times 0.11 = 6.6$ minutes.

17. **The correct answer is D.** When solving the equation, first solve the numbers in the parentheses: 7.4 − 2.4 = 5. Then add 5 to 17 × 17, which equals 294.

18. **The correct answer is D.** To figure out the equation, replace the letters with the corresponding numbers: 500 ÷ 3.2 − 2(45). To solve, first multiply 2 by what is in the parentheses: 2 × 45 = 90. Then divide 500 by 3.2 to get 156.25. Now solve: 156.25 − 90 = 66.25.

19. **The correct answer is C.** The total number of calls was 21 + 17 + 2 + 46 = 86. Since station A received 34 calls, the percentage can be calculated as follows: 34 ÷ 86 ≈ 0.40. Therefore, station A received 40 percent of the calls.

20. **The correct answer is D.** One-half earn over $18,000. One-third of the other half, or one-sixth, earn between $15,000 and $18,000. This accounts for $\frac{1}{2} + \frac{1}{6}$, or $\frac{3}{6} + \frac{1}{6} = \frac{4}{6} = \frac{2}{3}$ of the staff. Therefore, $\frac{1}{3}$ of the staff earn below $15,000.

21. **The correct answer is B.** If pipe 2 is open while pipe 1 is closed, the level will drop to the lowest level of pipe 2. This leaves the volume below pipe 2 still filled, having no course for discharge. All other statements are true.

22. **The correct answer is C.** This tool is an offset screwdriver, used for tightening screws in hard-to-reach places where a regular screwdriver can't make a complete rotation.

23. **The correct answer is C.** Civilian participation in firefighting activities is restricted for the safety of both civilians and firefighters. Any requests that seek to circumvent that policy should be referred to individuals higher in the chain of command.

24. **The correct answer is C.** During fire attack, firefighters will try to limit damage to department property and equipment as such damage hampers departmental capabilities and goes against firefighters' ethos of being efficient emergency responders. In the case of a pier fire, driving onto the pier itself while a fire burns creates the possibility of firefighting equipment being lost in the event of a structural collapse.

25. **The correct answer is B.** At first it may appear that the fastest route would be to proceed from Fire Dept. No. 1 west on Thunder Rd. (1 block), north on 6th Street (3 blocks), and east on Joppa Rd. (5 blocks) to Fire Dept. No. 2. But that route is 9 blocks due to the extra stop for Antioch Blvd. A better route is to go west on Thunder Rd. (1 block), north on 6th Street (1 block), east on Eby St. (5 blocks), and north on 1st Street for 1 block to Fire Dept No. 2. This route is 8 blocks.

26. **The correct answer is C.** The five right turns are as follows: right on 2nd, right on Eby, right on 3rd, right on Antioch, and right again on 2nd. This puts you just south of Antioch on 2nd Street, right between Tipsy Tavern and the Silver Screen Theatre.

27. **The correct answer is B.** To get from Hipp's Clothing to Loco Tacos, turn right out of the entryway onto Joppa Rd, left on 4th Street, left on Eby St., and left into the Loco Tacos entryway. The other choices include at least one location with an entryway on a one-way street.

28. **The correct answer is D.** The Pythagorean theorem states that for any right triangle the sum of the squares of the legs is equal to the square of the length of the hypotenuse.

$$6^2 + 8^2 = h^2$$
$$36 + 64 = h^2$$
$$h^2 = 100$$
$$h = 10$$

29. **The correct answer is C.** For every mile per hour that a fire engine is traveling, it takes $\frac{3}{4}$ of a foot to come to a complete stop. If an engine is traveling 60 mph, the answer is found by multiplying 60 by $\frac{3}{4}$. In other words, 60 × 3 = 180; 180 ÷ 4 = 45.

30. **The correct answer is B.** Since firefighters not only are concerned with the preservation of property but also care for public safety, you can conclude that they reposition the cornice on the rooftop as it then represents the smallest threat to other firefighters and civilians on the street and sidewalks below.

31. **The correct answer is B.** Before beginning the process of pulling over and stopping for an emergency vehicle, it is important to determine the emergency vehicle's relative position in order to reduce the risk of unnecessary traffic incidents (Step 4). In this case, the question indicates that the emergency vehicle is near the center of the roadway. The next logical step is for you to use your right turn signal (Step 1), and then begin changing to the right-hand lane, travelling as close as possible to the right-hand curb or roadside (Step 5). Decelerate your vehicle and come to a complete stop (Step 3). Remain stopped until the emergency vehicle has passed and rejoin the flow of traffic (Step 2).

32. **The correct answer is D.** According to the second paragraph, all three firefighters were taken to the hospital for treatment, along with Harrison Lewis and his daughter Nicole. The only correct combination of individuals taken to the hospital is Firefighter Wright and Nicole Lewis.

33. **The correct answer is A.** According to the first paragraph, the Rodriguez family summoned firefighters to the scene.

34. **The correct answer is A.** According to the second paragraph, Harrison and Nicole Lewis were unable to escape according to the preplanned family escape plan because Nicole Lewis was too frightened to leave her bedroom and Harrison Lewis was attempting to persuade her to escape.

35. **The correct answer is C.** According to the second paragraph, the firefighters were injured as they attempted to extinguish the blaze.

36. **The correct answer is A.** The second sentence indicates that all plastics contain resin.

37. **The correct answer is D.** The third and fourth sentences of the passage indicate that the flammability of plastic varies based on substances added, its composition, and its physical size and condition.

38. **The correct answer is C.** The information given in the first, second, and third sentences best describes plastic as a group of products that have some similar and some dissimilar properties.

39. **The correct answer is A.** The last sentence of the passage states that powdered plastic ignites and burns more readily than heavy sections with smooth surfaces. The statements in choices B and C contradict the information given in the passage. Choice D is inaccurate because the passage gives enough information to conclude relative flammability.

40. **The correct answer is A.** According to the second sentence in the passage, an overcurrent protective device is designed to open the circuit and cut the flow of electrical current.

41. **The correct answer is C.** An electrical wire carrying electrical current is a common example of a conductor.

42. **The correct answer is D.** There is no information about the ratio of circuits to fuses in the passage.

43. **The correct answer is D.** The second sentence indicates that the introduction of water will cause the threads to swell, thus reducing the space between threads and making the hose practically watertight.

44. **The correct answer is C.** Unlined linen hose cannot withstand very hard wear; thus, it is best suited for use as onsite emergency equipment. Since the passage states that outdoor storage is likely to increase the speed of deterioration, this type of hose is not suitable for use as a garden hose (choice A). The

passage indicates that this type of hose is not built to withstand frequent service or use, which means that it would not be suitable for use on a fire department apparatus (choice B) nor in fire department training schools (choice D).

45. **The correct answer is A.** Unlined linen hose could withstand neither the punishment of being dragged over rough lumber nor the exposure to weather conditions. While use in an office building (choice B), department store (choice C), or cosmetics plant (choice D) may prevent proper drying, the hose will have a higher chance of proper functioning in the event of one fire, if not for repeated use.

46. **The correct answer is B.** The second sentence indicates that victims often are trapped in a vehicle, making it difficult for a rescuer to administer proper first aid.

47. **The correct answer is D.** The passage indicates that keeping the victim's airway open, performing CPR if necessary, and treating any uncontrolled bleeding are listed in terms of importance. Therefore, a rescuer should first assess whether the victim's airway is open.

48. **The correct answer is D.** Full protective clothing must be put on before any other action is taken (4). The next step is to enter the building in groups of at least two (2). After you have entered the building, the search should be conducted on hands and knees (1) and begin on an outside wall (6). After a room has been searched, the door should be tagged (5). Then, victims who have been removed should be placed in someone's custody to prevent incident (3).

49. **The correct answer is D.** Walking inside a burning building is a violation of Procedure 1. An internal building search always should be conducted on hands and knees to limit injuries to the head and torso.

50. **The correct answer is A.** Wood is weakest when a cut is made with the grain. Any angle that cuts across the grain (choices B and C) won't be as effective. Choice D doesn't make sense as there's no way to cut around the grain.

51. **The correct answer is A.** The plug can go into the outlet in only one way in a polarized outlet. In the outlets illustrated in choices B, C, and D, the plug can be reversed.

52. **The correct answer is A.** The sooner the fire department arrives at the scene of a fire the more likely it is that damage to life and property will be kept to a minimum. A single firefighter would not be able to combat the fire alone without the assistance of other firefighters and the use of firefighting apparatus.

53. **The correct answer is D.** The fire escape is in the lower right corner of the diagram. The dining room is in the upper left corner. The dining room is the greatest distance from the fire escape.

54. **The correct answer is B.** Bedroom 1 has only one door. The living room (choice A) has two door openings and a doorway, the kitchen (choice C) has two doorways, and the dining room (choice D) has one door and three doorways.

55. **The correct answer is D.** As indicated in the diagram, the fire escape is directly outside Bedroom 3.

56. **The correct answer is B.** Bathroom 2 does not have a door or doorway leading into the foyer. It has only a door that leads directly to Bedroom 2.

57. **The correct answer is D.** Bathroom 1 has a door that leads directly into the foyer.

58. **The correct answer is D.** The terrace is on the left side of the building. It has two door symbols to indicate access to the living room and the dining room.

59. The correct answer is A. The window symbols are visible in the black outline of the floor plan. The diagram shows that there are two windows in the dining room and three windows in Bedroom 2.

60. The correct answer is D. Doorways are shown by the break in the solid lines within the floor plan. The kitchen can be entered using the doorway in the dining room as well as the doorway from the foyer.

61. The correct answer is A. When conducting firefighting operations, firefighters need to account for the impact of fire attack on the surrounding environment. In situations where water can pool or be deposited in areas of high civilian traffic, firefighters need to plan their approach to suppression. In this case, with the subway entrance so near to the scene of the incident, the firefighters should have directed water away from the subway entrance. Choice B has the firefighters complete an action that does not enable successful fire suppression and can be performed after the immediate danger is addressed. Choices C and D both represent important procedural steps but not those to be taken before attending to the most obvious source of danger: the enflamed vehicle.

62. The correct answer is B. Since firefighters wish to minimize time between the reception of a call and their arrival on scene, you can infer that despite the longer distance involved the route is likely to result in shorter travel time. This is likely due to the presence of holiday traffic. A route with a faster traffic pattern means higher speeds of travel for the emergency vehicles.

63. The correct answer is C. The first action to be taken by an experienced firefighter in this situation is to determine whether a fire has been started. If a fire has occurred, then the firefighter should seek out an alarm box to notify the local fire department. The sooner a fire is discovered the easier it will be to extinguish. This generally is true for all fires.

64. The correct answer is D. As stated in the question, only orders or directions should be given to drivers while on route to an alarm. A driver will make a variety of decisions to reach the source of the alarm and should only be provided commands to change his or her route.

65. The correct answer is C. Even though you are unfamiliar with your current location and may be unable to provide a specific address or intersection, firefighters can prepare for the alarm while dispatch helps you explain your surroundings to locate the fire. Numerous visual details—such as store names, block numbers, and building styles—will be available in the surrounding area to pinpoint your location. Other answer choices create possible delays for emergency response.

66. The correct answer is C. While only two standard ladders have been set up for roof access, the fire truck ladder has also been deployed, which brings the count to three ladders total.

67. The correct answer is A. While the hose itself isn't visible, we can see the water stream spraying up from underneath the balcony and exiting through a damaged corner of the house.

68. The correct answer is B. Firefighters search for victims and attend to their needs before extinguishing the flames of a fire. Property damage is taken into consideration only after all potential loss of life has been addressed and dealt with. Therefore, we can reasonably assume victims have already been searched for (choice A) and that the firefighters are currently extinguishing the flames to minimize property damage. Letting the fire burn would result in preventable damage (choice C), as would sitting around and waiting for direction (choice D).

69. **The correct answer is C.** The fireman descending the ladder is carrying a chainsaw.

70. **The correct answer is A.** There is one tree visible on the left side of the image.

71. **The correct answer is C.** The incline of ramp 3 is not nearly so steep as that of ramp 1. Ramps 2 and 4 have irregularities in their inclines that would make it even more difficult to move a heavy load to the top of the platform.

72. **The correct answer is B.** It follows that a substance that carries heat well cannot be used as an insulator of heat.

73. **The correct answer is C.** When it is desired that one pulley be turned in the opposite direction from its connecting pulley, drive belts must be crossed as shown in the diagram.

74. **The correct answer is D.** With the center of Gear A fastened at one point on the shaft, the gear can rotate at that point. If Gear A is fastened at an additional point on the shaft, the gear becomes rigid and unable to rotate. Therefore, Gear A cannot turn Gear B, and all gears will lock.

75. **The correct answer is B.** Anchoring Gear C makes it the pivoting point. The remaining gears will then rotate around the pivot. Gear A will cause Gear B to turn counterclockwise, which will then cause Gear B to travel counterclockwise around the pivot (the shaft of Gear C).

76. **The correct answer is A.** Gear A, being smaller than Gears B and C, must revolve at a greater rate of speed to travel the same distance. Therefore, Gear A will make more than one rotation on its shaft for every revolution that Arm D makes.

77. **The correct answer is A.** Lubrication with oil, grease, or any other suitable substance reduces friction between moveable parts of machinery. In the absence of lubrication, the machinery would wear out quickly due to increased friction.

78. **The correct answer is C.** It is revealed through the meeting that investment in educating the public in fire prevention has coincided with a steady rate of fire loss. Assuming that public education can reduce fire loss rates, something else must account for the steady rate of fire loss. There is no guarantee that increased education alone will be sufficient to reduce the fire loss rate (choice A). There is also no evidence that increased public education leads to an increase in fire loss rate as education has increased while the loss rate has remained nearly constant (choice B). There is no evidence presented that the number of arson cases has decreased (choice D); however, if it did, one might expect to see a noticeable decrease in the overall fire loss rate. As such, if public education can decrease fire loss rate, there must exist another factor, such as an increase in potential fire hazards, that is compensating for the reduction.

79. **The correct answer is A.** The information in the question specifies that these are "additional firefighters" and will not receive any firefighting apparatus. The primary goal, then, must be to increase the number of firefighters at each station. The most likely result of increasing the number of firefighters alone would not be to increase response speed (choice B) or act as a form of training (choices C and D)—without specifying the level of firefighter being assigned—but to meet the needs of larger fires, which often demand more personnel, not equipment.

80. **The correct answer is A.** Hydrants 3 and 4 are both considerably closer to the fire than Hydrants 1 and 7. Hydrant 4 cannot be reached without passing through smoke and fire. Hydrant 3 is in the best position for protecting the warehouse from the fire, so Firefighter Jensen should direct the lieutenant to go south on Main Gate Drive, northeast/east on Research Road, south on Dual Gate Drive, and west on Hi-Lo Lane to Hydrant 3.

81. **The correct answer is C.** Of the routes given, the shortest route is for the firefighters to go north on Main Gate Drive, east on Hawthorne Street, and south on Rutland Road. This route gets them out of the complex and away from danger.

82. **The correct answer is C.** As the diagram shows, the entrance to the Research Building that is closest to the firefighter is connected to Parking Lot B.

83. **The correct answer is D.** Of the choices offered, only Hydrants 6 and 7 are outside the fence. Hydrant 7 is closer to the fire.

84. **The correct answer is C.** You can eliminate the routes given in choices A and B because Hi-Lo Lane is engulfed in smoke and flame. The firefighters must double back on Trailer Street so that they can go east on Hawthorne Street. The route given in choice C is shorter than the route given in choice D.

85. **The correct answer is A.** Try each route. Of the answer choices given, the shortest way for the firefighters to reach the northwest corner of the warehouse without passing through smoke and flames is to go east on Hi-Lo Lane, north on Dual Gate Drive, and then west on Research Road to the entrance on Warehouse Court.

86. **The correct answer is B.** The woman is behaving in an unsafe manner and will be injured or killed if she continues. Therefore, the appropriate action is to call a police officer to remove the woman from danger. The firefighter is needed to fight the fire, and someone must keep the woman from being injured.

87. **The correct answer is B.** The primary reason for these assignments is to ensure proper maintenance of departmental equipment. This equates to longer, better functioning in the field. While these tasks could be assigned to occupy firefighters when they aren't responding to alarms, choice A is not a primary reason why these duties are performed. Choice C is not the best answer because there are other methods available to cut costs. While competition can lead to better morale in some cases, choice D is not the best answer because competition may result in unwanted aggression in team dynamics.

88. **The correct answer is D.** The best way to limit damage is to limit exposure, as stated by the question itself. As such, the firefighter should refrain from inhaling the smoke while passing through.

89. **The correct answer is D.** The most direct route is to take Valley to Passmore to Parkway North to Fender to Parkway South. The route given in choice A is longer. Taking Valley to Passmore to Parkway South (choice B) would be the fastest if it didn't require driving down the wrong side of the road. And while taking Valley to Passmore to Fender to Parkway South (choice C) requires the fewest number of legitimate turns, it fails to take advantage of the diagonal stretch on Parkway North.

90. **The correct answer is D.** The orientation of the baseball fields south of House No. 11 would mean that someone sitting in the stands behind home plate would be looking toward the house. The distances of the bank, the fire department, and the rec center from House No. 11, as well as their orientations away from the houses, would make it unlikely that someone at any one of those locations would see the fire first.

91. **The correct answer is A.** Make the first right from Lenny Lane onto Reed Road, then right onto Parkway S., and right onto Sunny Street. The first left you can take is at Fender Way. The next left you can take is at Steel Street because of the one-way traffic on Passmore Avenue. Continue south to make a right onto Oak Street. This places you in front of the Magic Bean.

92. **The correct answer is C.** With the tanks of CO_2, it is possible that the fire could cause the metal to expand and explode. CO_2 is not a toxic gas (choice A), nor will it accelerate a fire (choice B). And too little is known about the situation to suspect a sudden structural collapse (choice D).

93. **The correct answer is B.** At all times, firefighters focus on maintaining the safety and wellbeing of their communities, whether by providing inspection services, offering community education, or creating conditions that will allow for safe and efficient firefighting. Any acts that violate the trust of that relationship can make future emergencies worse. Choices A, C, and D represent actions that would benefit the fire department. As the question is seeking what would "not" be acceptable, choice B is correct.

94. **The correct answer is D.** In a situation where no victims are present, an officer's first consideration will then be the safety of his firefighters. The barrage of rocks and bottles represented a clear physical threat to the responders' physical well-being, and so the lieutenant took proper action.

95. **The correct answer is D.** Because the tarpaulin measures 6 feet (wide) by 9 feet (long), it is not possible to completely cover any circular area that exceeds 6 feet in diameter.

96. **The correct answer is C.** To determine the value of the jewelry, add together the values of the computer, wardrobe, stereo system, and oriental rug. Then subtract this total ($7,200) from $10,378. The answer is $3,178.

97. **The correct answer is B.** To calculate the value of the jewelry, divide the value of the wardrobe ($2,200) by 3. The jewelry is worth $733.33.

98. **The correct answer is C.** To calculate the value of the dining room table, multiply the value of the oriental rug ($500) by 4. The dining room table costs $2,000.

99. **The correct answer is C.** To determine the value of the new stereo system, multiply the value of the old stereo system by 6 percent, or 0.06. $1,500 × 0.06 = $90. Add $90 to $1,500 to obtain the cost of the stereo system. The new stereo system is $1,590.

100. **The correct answer is B.** To determine the average value of the lost items, add together the total value of the items, assuming that the jewelry was worth $1,600. The total is $8,800. Then divide the total by 5. The average value is $1,760.

PART V
APPENDIXES

Fire Terminology

The following is a list of common fire terms that firefighter candidates should be familiar with. Study the terms so that you are familiar with their applicable usage in a firefighting setting. Keep in mind that it's more important to understand the terms and the concepts associated with them than to spend study time memorizing the definitions word-for-word.

Accelerant: A substance (usually a liquid) used to aid the spread of fire.

Aerial Ladder: A mechanically operated extensible ladder usually mounted on a fire truck.

Air Pack: A protective device that uses a face piece, compressed air tank, and air flow regulator to provide compressed air to the wearer (see **SCBA**).

Air Chisel: Also known as an air hammer; a pneumatic hand tool used to carve in stone and to break or cut metal objects apart; an air hammer operates on compressed air and is used for cutting sheet metal and commonly used for extrication from autos.

Apparatus: Commonly refers to fire service vehicles (engines, ladders, rescue truck, water tenders, etc.).

Appliance: A device (ball valve, gate valve, wye, water thief, Siamese) connected to a hoseline or hydrant used to control, augment, divide, or discharge a water stream or fire extinguishing agent.

Arson: A crime involving starting a fire with the intent to kill, injure, defraud, or destroy property.

Attack Hose: A small-diameter hose stretched off engine apparatus by firefighters to extinguish fires inside structures.

Automated External Defibrillator (AED): A device designed to analyze the cardiac rhythm of a patient and determine if defibrillation is needed and to apply a measured dose of electrical current to restore normal rhythm of the heart.

Backdraft: A phenomenon in which a fire that has consumed all available oxygen suddenly explodes when more oxygen is made available, typically because a door or window has been opened; the sudden influx of air mixes with flammable gases (carbon monoxide, hydrogen, methane) already above their ignition temperature to create an explosion.

Basic Life Support (BLS): A basic level of emergency care and nonemergency medical care that includes airway management, cardiopulmonary resuscitation (CPR), control of shock and bleeding, and splinting of fractures.

Boiling Liquid Expanding Vapor Explosion (BLEVE): Generally relating to the failure of a pressure vessel containing liquefied gas as a result of fire impinging on the container or structural damage from impact.

Booster Hose: A small-diameter rubberized hose carried on a reel of an engine apparatus and used to fight small fires.

Booster Tank: An internal water container found within engine apparatus.

British Thermal Unit (BTU): The amount of heat energy required to raise the temperature of a pound of water—measuring 60 degrees Fahrenheit at sea level—one-degree Fahrenheit. One BTU equals 1.055 kilojoules(kJ).

Bunker Gear: Firefighter protective clothing consisting of coat jacket and pants. The term can also refer to the entire firefighter ensemble (helmet, gloves, hood, and boots).

A

Calorie: A heat energy unit. The amount of heat energy required to raise the temperature of one gram of water (measured at 15 degrees Celsius at sea level) one degree Celsius.

Carbon Dioxide: Extinguishing agent (gas) used to smother and cool a fire.

Carbon Monoxide: A flammable gas that is a deadly by-product of combustion.

Cardiopulmonary Resuscitation (CPR): Application of ventilations and external cardiac compressions used on patients in cardiac arrest.

Chief Officer: Superior officer, generally taking on the role of incident commander at a firefighting incident or emergency.

Clean Agent: An electrically nonconductive, volatile, or gaseous fireextinguishing agent that does not leave a residue upon evaporation.

Community Emergency Response Team (CERT): Citizen corps program designed to train civilians to be better prepared to respond to emergency situations and assist first responders.

Company Officer: Company leader, generally having the rank of lieutenant or captain.

Conduction: The transfer of heat through a medium (solid, liquid, or gas).

Confined Space: An area (tunnel, trench, storage tank, sewer pipe) not designed for human habitation due to physical dimensions and lack of natural ventilation.

Confinement: Operations designed to control a fire to a manageable area.

Convection: The transfer of heat through a circulating medium (air).

Decay Stage: When a fire's heat release rate begins to decline due to lack of fuel (fuel limited) or lack of oxygen (ventilation limited).

Decontamination: Removal of harmful substances from victims. It usually consists of removing outer clothing and washing down the victim.

Defibrillation: Delivery of a measured dose of electrical current in order to regain normal rhythm of the heart.

Deflagration: An explosion that propagates at a speed less than the speed of sound.

Demobilization: Removal of personnel and equipment from working at a fire or emergency operation.

Detonation: An explosion that propagates at a speed greater than the speed of sound.

Dilution: Extinguishing method using water on a water-soluble material to lower its concentration and raise its flash point.

Drafting: Use of suction hose and engine apparatus pump to lift water from below the level of the pump.

Dry Chemical: A fire-extinguishing agent that interferes with the chemical chain reaction of combustion.

Dry Powder: A fire-extinguishing agent used on combustible metals.

Dry Standpipe: A standpipe fire protection system that is not filled with water until needed in firefighting.

Emulsification: Extinguishment method using water to cause agitation of insoluble liquids to produce a vapor-inhibiting froth.

Endothermic Reaction: A chemical reaction that absorbs heat.

Engine Apparatus (Pumper): A fire service vehicle consisting of a water pump, portable water tank, various lengths and sizes of hose and applicable appliances, nozzles, tips, and fittings.

Exothermic Reaction: A chemical reaction that gives off heat.

Explosion: Rapid expansion of gases that have premixed prior to ignition.

Extension Ladder: A portable ladder with one or more movable sections that can be extended to a desired height.

Extinguisher: A firefighting device consisting of a metal container containing extinguishing agent under pressure.

Fire (Combustion): Rapid, self-sustaining oxidation reaction with the emission of heat and light.

Fire Department Connection (FDC): Device that a pumper connects to in order to supply and augment the water flow in a standpipe and/or sprinkler fire protection system. Combines two hoselines into one. Also referred to as a Siamese sprinkler.

Fireground: Area in and around the operational jurisdiction of firefighters.

Firehouse: Where firefighters work and where fire apparatus are stored. Also known as a fire station.

Fire Hydrant: A source of water supply to firefighters consisting of one or more valves and outlets usually connected to a municipal water supply.

Fire Inspector: A person employed to enforce the Fire Code.

Fire Marshal: A person designated to prevent and investigate fires.

Fire Tetrahedron: Model used to represent the growth of ignition to fire. It expands on the fire triangle by adding a fourth factor (chemical chain reaction).

Fire Triangle: Model used to represent the three factors—oxygen, fuel, and heat—necessary for ignition. Connectors and adapters are used in conjunction with hoseline couplings to solve hose connection problems.

Fittings: Devices (increasers, reducers, double male/female connections, adapters) used in conjunction with hoseline couplings to solve hose connection problems.

Flammable Range: The percentage mixture of vapors in air that will sustain combustion.

Flashover: Fire phenomenon that occurs when all the contents of a room or compartment reach their ignition temperature and simultaneously burst into flames.

Flashpoint: Lowest temperature at which a substance/material will emit a vapor that is ignitable in air.

Flow Path: A path within a structure where heat and smoke flows, from an area of higher pressure to area of lower pressure. It must be composed of at least one intake vent, one exhaust vent and the connecting volume between the vents.

Foam: An extinguishing agent created by introducing air into a mixture of water and foam concentrate.

Fog Stream: A hoseline stream characterized by a wide pattern of small droplets of water.

Free Burning Phase (Fully Developed): The second phase of fire development.

Friction Loss: Reduction in the amount of water flowing through hose or piping as a result of inner lining resistance.

Fuel: Material that will burn.

Fuel-Limited Fire: A fire in which the heat release rate of growth is controlled by the amount of fuel available to the fire.

Fulcrum: A pivot point or support on which a lever turns.

Ground Ladder: Portable ladder designed to be utilized manually on the fireground.

Halligan: Forcible entry tool with a pointed pick and adze at right angles at one end of the shaft and a fork at the other end.

Halyard: A rope attached to extension ladders for use in raising and lowering the fly ladder.

Hard Suction Hose: A noncollapsible hose used for drafting water.

Hazardous Material (Hazmat): Substance (solid, liquid, or gas) that because of its physical and chemical characteristics is dangerous to life and the environment.

Heat Release Rate: The rate at which heat energy is generated.

Heat Transfer: The process by which energy is transferred from a body at high temperature to a body at low temperature. There are three forms of heat transfer: convection, conduction, and radiation.

A

Hose Bed: Part of engine apparatus designed to hold various types of hose for ready use at firefighting operations.

Hose Bridge: A ramp used to allow vehicles to pass over hose without damaging it.

Hose Couplings: Ends of fire hose used to connect to other lengths of hose or to hydrants, engine apparatus pumps, and appliances.

Hose Roller: Device designed to be attached to the roof or windowsill to facilitate hoisting and lowering of hoseline.

Hose Spanner: Tool used to loosen and tighten hoseline couplings.

Hose Strap: A tool (rope with an eye-loop at one end and a metal hook at the other end) used to support the weight of hose couplings when hose is stretched vertically up stairwells and fire escapes.

Hydrant Wrench: A tool used to operate and open and shut down a hydrant.

Hydraulics: The study of water pressure, flow, friction loss, and water supply systems.

Hydraulic Spreader (Jaws of Life): Mechanical levering tool powered by a hydraulic pump engine. It is used by firefighters to extricate trapped victims inside motor vehicles.

Ignition Temperature: Minimum temperature a material must be heated to for it to ignite and be self-sustaining without an external input of heat.

Incendiary Device: Item used by arsonists to start fires.

Incendiary Fire: A fire that is deliberately set.

Incipient Phase (Growth): The first phase of fire development.

Inert Gas: Nonflammable gas that will not support combustion.

Joule: An International System of Units (SI) heat energy unit, it represents the amount of heat energy provided by one watt flowing for one second.

K-Tool: Steel block with a sharp K-shaped notch on one side designed to be slipped over cylinder locks for their removal.

Ladder Apparatus (Truck): Fire service vehicle having a motorpowered ladder and tools and equipment designed for search and rescue, access to upper floors, forcible entry, ventilation, and overhaul operations.

Ladder Company: Firefighters assigned to work on a ladder truck apparatus.

Large Caliber Stream: A water flow of greater than 300 gpm.

Lever: A device or bar turning about a fulcrum.

Master Nozzle (Deluge): Devices used to direct large water streams of greater than 300 gpm.

Nozzle: A device attached to a hoseline or appliance designed to close, open, and regulate a water stream.

Overhaul: Operations designed to find hidden fire and provide complete extinguishment.

Oxidation: Chemical reaction between an oxidizer (an oxygen-containing substance) and fuel.

Oxidizer: A substance containing oxygen that will chemically react with fuel to start and/or feed a fire.

Personal Alert Safety System (PASS): An alarm device that emits a signal when a firefighter is disabled, lost, or in distress.

Personal Protective Equipment (PPE): Equipment worn by firefighters to protect themselves from fire, heat, smoke, toxic gases, contamination, and many other dangers associated with firefighting and medical emergencies. It includes bunker gear, helmet, hood, gloves, boots, self-contained breathing apparatus, safety goggles/glasses, latex gloves, etc.

Pike Pole: Long-handled tools with hooks on the end that are used to pull apart ceilings, open walls, lift roofing material, and break windows in emergencies.

Positive Pressure Ventilation (PPV) Fans: Fans designed to provide forced, uncontaminated air into a room or building to displace the by-products of fire.

Pyrolysis: Decomposition reaction within a solid fuel brought about by the introduction of heat that is not fast enough to be self-sustaining.

Radiation: The transfer of heat through space in straight lines via electromagnetic waves.

Rescue Company: An elite group of firefighters specially trained to work on a rescue apparatus.

Residual Pressure: Pressure remaining in a water supply when water is flowing, measured in psi.

Respirator: A full-face or half-face respiratory protection device having replaceable cartridges.

Salvage: Operations designed to conserve property and minimize damage following a fire.

Self-Contained Breathing Apparatus (SCBA): Positive pressure breathing equipment worn by firefighters during structural firefighting operations. It consists of an air cylinder, high- and low-pressure hoses, pressure regulator, and facepiece.

Smoke Ejectors: Fans primarily designed to eject smoke and toxic gases from a space, room, or area.

Smoldering Phase (Decay): The third phase of fire development.

Specific Gravity: The ratio of the weight of a liquid to the weight of an equal volume of water.

Spontaneous Combustion: Endothermic chemical reaction causing self-ignition.

Standpipe System: A fire extinguishment system utilizing water that is distributed through piping to floor outlets that permit firefighters to connect and operate attack hoselines on a fire.

Static Pressure: Water at rest; potential energy measured in psi (head pressure).

Suction Hose: A noncollapsible hose used to draw water up vertically into an engine apparatus during drafting operations.

Supply Hose: A large-diameter hoseline used to provide large amounts of water to fire apparatus, appliances, and building fire extinguishing systems.

Suspicious Fire: A fire that has not conclusively been determined incendiary.

Temperature: A measure of how fast molecules are vibrating inside a substance.

Thermal Conductivity: A material's ability to conduct heat.

Tips: Devices attached to hoselines and appliances designed to shape and project a water stream.

Vapor Density: The relative density of a gas/vapor as compared to air.

Ventilation: Operations designed to remove heat, smoke, and toxic gases from a building or structure.

Viscosity: A measure of a liquid's flow in relation to time.

Volunteer Fire Department: A fire department generally organized and manned by unpaid personnel.

Water Hammer: Force created by the rapid deceleration of water, generally resulting from closing a hose nozzle or hydrant valve too quickly.

Wet Chemical: An extinguishing agent for use on kitchen fires involving unsaturated fat and vegetable cooking oils.

Wet Standpipe: A standpipe fire protection system that is always filled with pressurized water.

Wildland Firefighting: Operations conducted to extinguish fires in forests, nature sanctuaries, and grasslands that generally do not involve structures.

A

Wildland Firefighting

OVERVIEW

- **Requirements for Wildland Firefighting**
- **Jobs for Wildland Firefighters**
- **How to Apply for a Wildland Firefighter Position**
- **Sources of Additional Information**
- **Wildland Firefighting Terminology**
- **Summing It Up**

All firefighters must work in situations involving heavy smoke and intense heat, and all are required to carry heavy packs and equipment. But a specialized firefighting career—wildland firefighting—elevates these situations to another level.

A wildland fire is defined as any nonstructure fire that occurs in the wild. In a building, you would never set a fire to control a fire—but you sometimes do in wildland firefighting. In traditional firefighting, climbing ladders and stairs is common; in wildland firefighting, climbing hills and mountains is part of the job. A helicopter does not drop water onto a house or other building to suppress a fire, but this practice is common in wildland firefighting. Structural firefighters return to a fire station after extinguishing a fire; wildland firefighters may return to a temporary camp in the forest or near the site of the fire. Structural firefighters are trained to handle brush fires and supplement forestry units when structures are involved, but wildland firefighters are trained specifically to handle forest fires.

Although small-scale wildland fires are necessary to preserve and regenerate forest ecosystems, larger fires have the potential to be dangerous and catastrophically destructive, especially if they threaten lives, property, and valuable natural resources. Some wildland fires are started by natural processes such as lightning strikes, but most originate from human carelessness or inattention. Smoldering cigarette butts; sparks from machinery, unattended or improperly dampened campfires, arcing electrical wires, and arson are some of the ways in which humans generate forest fires.

According to the NOAA National Climate Data Center, in 2019, there were 49,786 such fires, which consumed more than 4.6 million acres of land in the United States. These numbers were reduced in comparison to those earlier in the decade; for example, in 2015, 61,922 fires consumed more than 10 million acres. In 2003, 15 people (including one firefighter), 2,820 structures, and 273,246 acres were lost in a single wildfire started by a man in southern California.

As you can see, wildland firefighters are vital frontline defenders of our forests, homes, and lives. As difficult as firefighting itself is, wildland firefighting is an even more challenging and demanding occupation—one

B

in which nature and the environment rule the workday. In addition to facing the same physiological challenges common to all firefighters, wildland firefighters are expected to function in steep and rugged terrain, and endure high temperatures and unpredictable weather patterns for long and irregular hours.

REQUIREMENTS FOR WILDLAND FIREFIGHTING

Wildland firefighting requires both a high level of physical fitness to safely perform all duties, especially under very stressful or arduous conditions, as well as basic education or experience with firefighting practice.

Physical Requirements: The Work Capacity Test

Working in heavy smoke and intense heat, and climbing steep, rugged terrain carrying heavy equipment on minimal sleep is extremely demanding work. Naturally, there are stringent physical fitness requirements for all wildland firefighters.

All federal wildland firefighters must pass a work capacity test (WCT) to legally qualify to fight forest fires. The WCT measures fitness, acclimatization, nutrition, skill, experience, motivation, and intelligence. Passing the WCT ensures that wildland firefighters can perform their work without undue fatigue and without becoming a hazard to themselves or their coworkers. Testing wildland firefighters for work capacity is vital to ensuring health and safety and improving operations.

Before taking the WCT, prospective candidates must complete a healthcare screening questionnaire (HSQ), available online from the US Forestry Service of the Department of the Interior. The form must be submitted before a candidate trains for or takes the WCT. The agency then determines whether further medical evaluation is needed and may require a physician to medically clear a candidate before he or she takes the WCT. The agency pays for applicants' medical exams and provides instructions to examining physicians. Applicants, their appointing officer, and a physician must then complete an additional medical exam form.

The WCT has three different levels, and each firefighter takes on a level appropriate to their respective job.

1. The **Arduous** fitness level test is required for all wildland firefighters. Arduous work involves lifting more than 50 pounds, having above-average aerobic fitness, and being able to perform extremely strenuous activities. This version is also called a **pack test**—it consists of carrying a 45-pound pack on a 3-mile hike that must be completed within 45 minutes.

2. Safety officers and fire behavior officers fall into the **Moderate** level. At this level, you must be able to lift between 25 and 50 pounds and complete moderately strenuous activities. This version is a field test in which you must complete a 2-mile hike wearing a 25-pound pack and finish within 30 minutes.

3. The **Light** level is for those who generally work in an office environment and rarely go out into the field. This version consists of a 1-mile walk without a pack that must be completed in 16 minutes.

Jogging or running is not allowed during any of the WCT tests. It is not a competition, and the tests are graded on a pass/fail basis. Times for all tests may be adjusted depending on the altitude where the test is conducted.

A proper training and conditioning program benefits all wildland firefighters. Once you've been medically cleared to take the WCT, you should begin training and conditioning at least four to six weeks before taking the exam. Find a safe place to train, a comfortable and well-fitted pack, and comfortable boots or shoes that provide ankle support. Know what level of test you'll need to take to meet your position's requirements (Light, Moderate, or Arduous) and vary your distance and pack weight appropriately.

Training in wildland fire boots is a good idea if they are the equipment that you will be using once hired, but do not run in them. Start off by walking the specified distance for your level of the test but do so on flat terrain. Once you're able to complete the course in the exam's time frame, add some weight to the pack, and then gradually increase it until you can complete the hike in less than the allowed time with a fully weighted pack. If you want to take your training a step further, add even more weight than required for the test. This will make the pack seem light on test day.

Adding hills to your training course helps you build strength, endurance, and stamina. Cross-train with weights, run, go mountain biking, swim, or take on other regular activities that interest you; they'll improve your overall fitness level. The FireFit Program from the National Interagency Fire Center (is an excellent and easy-to-follow fitness program designed specifically for wildland firefighters. You can find more information about FireFit and other fire programs at **www.nifc.gov/programs/programs_main.html**.

Education and Experience Requirements: Earning Your Red Card

You can earn wildfire experience in positions such as Helitack operations, smokejumping, engine crew, and hotshot or hand crew. Experience consists of on-the-line wildland firefighting, including containment, control, suppression, and/or use of wildland fire. In addition to finding a federal position, you can also gain the required experience serving in a temporary, seasonal, or equivalent private-sector fire position. Or you can work with a rural or militia fire department. To get wildfire experience, however, you must find a sponsoring agency such as the Bureau of Land Management or the National Park Service.

The **Incident Qualification Card** or **Red Card** is part of the fire qualifications management system used by many state and all federal wildland fire management agencies. This card is similar to a driver's license; without a driver's license you are not legally permitted to drive, and without a Red Card you are not permitted to fight forest fires. The WCT represents one step in the process but past levels of experience and/or education may be required. The NWCG Standards for Wildland Fire Position Qualifications (online at **www.nwcg.gov/publications/310-1**) list steps necessary to acquire a Red Card and advance through the wildland firefighting system to higher positions.

JOBS FOR WILDLAND FIREFIGHTERS

Most wildland firefighter jobs are temporary, seasonal, or part-time. Although full-time positions are available, it may take several years of seasonal employment before you are hired full-time, and you must have plenty of wildland firefighting experience before you can be hired for a permanent position.

Federal Government Jobs

Wildland firefighters are often called forestry or range technicians by the federal government and by forestry agencies. Federal agencies such as the US Forest Service, the Bureau of Land Management, the National Park Service, the US Fish and Wildlife Service, and the Bureau of Indian Affairs employ many forestry technicians.

State agencies, private companies, and local municipalities may also employ wildland firefighters. For the most part, wildland firefighter jobs are concentrated in western states: Alaska, Arizona, California, Colorado, Montana, Nevada, New Mexico, Oregon, Washington, and Wyoming.

The application process for Forest Service jobs is handled through the USAJOBS website (**www.usajobs.gov**).

Multiple levels of forestry technicians are employed by the federal government. The most common system for determining federal job grade levels is the **General Schedule (GS)**. The GS assigns every federal job a grade level from 1 to 15, according to the minimum level of education and experience required to perform the job. For example, positions for which an applicant needs no experience or education are graded a GS-01; positions for which an applicant must have a bachelor's degree but not necessarily any experience are graded a GS-05 or GS-07, depending on the applicant's academic credentials and the hiring agency's policies. In addition to the minimum qualification standards, selective factors, such as an applicant having certain abilities and knowledge of basic skills that are required for the position, are also involved in hiring at each level.

Common firefighting positions include the following:

- Range/Forestry Aid GS-02/03—fire crew member who suppresses fires, sets prescribed fires, use wildland fires for resource benefits; higher levels aid with backfires and burnouts, engine attack, helispots, Helitack operations, and hover hookups.
- Range/Forestry Technician GS-04—crew member of an engine, Helitack, hand or fuel crew who completes assignments related to tree felling, backfire, and burnout through a variety of specialized tools and techniques.
- Range/Forestry Technician GS-05—a senior firefighter who may lead a hand, prescribed fire, engine, or Helitack crew and gather and act on weather, topographic, fuel, and fire behavior data.

HOW TO APPLY FOR A WILDLAND FIREFIGHTER POSITION

As we've mentioned, most entry-level wildland firefighting jobs in the United States are seasonal or part-time, and you must be 18 years or older to apply. Standardized written tests, such as those administered to structural firefighters, typically are not required. However, you must meet the education and/or experience requirements dictated by the hiring department before also completing the WCT and requirements for a Red Card (if not already attained). Some forestry units recruit workers from state employment offices, and most federal employers hire directly.

Beginning the Job Search

Start searching for job opportunities in October or November before the fire season when you would like to begin your wildland firefighting career. Some areas may not have information on open positions until January or February of the next year because personnel numbers and funding vary from year to year.

Decide in which area of the country you would most like to work and for which agency you'd like to work. You can raise your chances of being hired by applying to many agencies at once. Because the application process can be confusing and stressful, keep in mind that persistence and patience throughout the hiring process will often pay off.

Application procedures and deadlines vary widely among and within agencies. Some agencies allow you to apply for positions online; others must be completed by hand and faxed or mailed to the agencies' human resource departments. You can search for full-time, part-time, seasonal, and permanent federal wildland firefighting jobs online at **www.usajobs.gov**. Use the key terms "wildland + fire" to find related job postings.

Increasing Your Chances

Another way to raise the odds of your being hired as a wildland firefighter is to learn new skills. If you haven't already learned basic emergency medical procedures such as CPR, take a course and learn them now—or better yet, sign up for a wilderness EMT course. Core wildland firefighting classes are available at many community colleges throughout the country. Plan to earn a commercial driver's license (CDL), which could give you the opportunity to drive water tankers, engines, and other large vehicles used in wildland firefighting. Learn to operate a chain saw, navigate with a compass, tie basic knots, build trails, and perform other outdoor survival skills. The more you know, the more you will be perceived as a knowledgeable, well-rounded candidate for wildland firefighting, and you'll have an edge over the competition in the application process. Likewise, if you've already tried to get a wildland firefighting position and haven't been successful, don't give up: Plan to volunteer for various hiring agencies. This will give you an insider's edge when a position does become available. Some employers also offer internships to college students who are interested in becoming wildland firefighters.

Submitting Your Application

Remember that first impressions count. Carefully follow all application instructions and adhere to all deadlines. Check your spelling and accuracy, then make sure you've completed the full application prior to submission—especially if you're submitting it online. You can't fix the information once it's submitted, and you don't want to give the impression that you are careless or lack attention to detail.

Some applications require that you include a recent resume. If so, be sure you do so, and check your resume again to be sure all the information is up to date. Be truthful: If you have prior wildland firefighting experience, include this information on your resume, but don't invent experience you don't have. For positions requiring prior education, arrange to have your college transcripts sent to the agency. If you already have a Red Card or position task book, be sure you have copies available if needed.

To apply for most federal jobs, you will have to fill out the following forms:

- OF-612 (the Optional Application for Federal Employment)
- OPM-1170, on which you list your college courses, or a college transcript
- Forms DD-214 (Report of Separation) and SF-15 (Application for 10-Point Veteran Preference), if you are a US veteran
- You may also need to fill out supplemental applications required by individual national forests, such as the SF-177 (Statement of Physical Ability for Work)

It is extremely important to adhere to all deadlines in the application process. Once your application is received and reviewed, you will be notified if you are eligible for an available position. Follow the instructions for the position and submit any other requested paperwork. Other paperwork may include the health care screening (HSQ) form and medical clearance.

Once you are medically cleared, start training for the WCT and for your career. If you already have a Red Card, then prepare yourself for the upcoming season by refreshing your firefighting knowledge and skills. Once you've cleared all these hurdles and landed a wildland firefighter job, you can look forward to a highly rewarding and satisfying career.

B

SOURCES OF ADDITIONAL INFORMATION

Remember that hiring procedures vary greatly, so contact your chosen agency's local human resources division for the most accurate and up-to-date hiring information. Your state forestry division, environmental protection agency, local fire department, or college can also provide resources regarding wildland firefighting employment in your area. Several wildland fire academies are in western states, especially in the Rocky Mountain area. You might also search for private wildland fire suppression companies, which offer education and career opportunities.

The Fire Integrated Recruitment Employment Systems (FIRES) is integrated with USAJOBS, the official job search website of the federal government. FIRES allows you to apply for temporary positions with the Bureau of Indian Affairs (BIA), the Bureau of Land Management, the US Fish and Wildlife Service, and the National Park Service in seven locations with just one application.

Bureau of Land Management
(Department of the Interior)
Fire and Aviation
www.blm.gov/programs/fire-and-aviation

National Park Service
Fire and Aviation Management
3833 S. Development Avenue
Boise, ID 83705-5354
Phone: 208-387-5200
Fax: 208-387-5250
www.nps.gov/fire/

US Department of the Interior
FIRES Program Office
1849 C Street, NW
Washington, DC 20240
Phone: 888-364-6432
Email: fa_fires@nifc.blm.gov
www.firejobs.doi.gov

US Fish and Wildlife Service
Fire Management
3833 S. Development Avenue
Boise, ID 83705-5354
Phone: 208-387-5583
Email: fire_webmaster@fws.gov
www.fws.gov/fire

US Forest Service
Fire and Aviation Management
3833 S. Development Avenue
Boise, ID 83705-5354
Phone: 208-387-5092
www.fs.fed.us/fire

National Interagency Fire Center
Phone: 208-387-5512
Email: nifc_comments@nifc.blm.gov
www.nifc.gov

WILDLAND FIREFIGHTING TERMINOLOGY

It's helpful to learn and understand the terminology and basic concepts that are part of the trade. Some fundamental facts:

- To support combustion, the three sides of what is called the **fire triangle** —fuel, oxygen, and heat— must exist. If you remove any one ingredient from the fire triangle, the fire cannot sustain itself and will extinguish.
- Wildland fires involve weeds, grass, field crops, brush, forests, and vegetation.

There are three factors that affect forest fire behavior:

1. **Organic fuel:** Fuel size, compactness, continuity, volume, and moisture content affect a fuel's burning characteristics
2. **Weather:** Relative humidity, temperature, wind, and precipitation contribute to a wildfire's movement
3. **Topography:** Aspect, local terrain, and drainages affect fire behavior

Fuels for wildfires fall into three general categories:

1. **Subsurface fuels:** Roots, peat, duff, and decomposing organic matter
2. **Surface fuels:** Conifer needles, twigs, grass field crops, brush up to 6 feet tall, and small trees
3. **Aerial fuels:** Trees taller than 6 feet, limbs, leaves, and conifer needles

WILDFIRE NOMENCLATURE

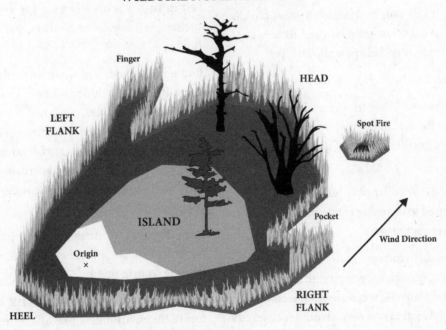

Common terms you should be familiar with are as follows:

- **Origin:** Where the fire started
- **Head:** The part of the fire that moves most rapidly
- **Finger:** Long, narrow strips of fire extending from the main fire; has the potential to form new heads

- **Perimeter:** The outer boundary of the burning/burned area
- **Heel:** Opposite of the head; this section burns slower and burns downhill or against the wind
- **Flanks:** The sides of the fire, parallel to the main spread
- **Island:** An unburned area in the fire perimeter
- **Spot fire:** A smaller fire outside the main fire caused by embers
- **Pocket:** Unburned indentations at the fire's edge formed by fingers or slow-burning areas

The following is a list of terms specific to wildland firefighting. Knowing these terms will help you establish a working knowledge of wildland firefighting nomenclature. A comprehensive list can be found on the National Wildfire Coordinating Groups website at **www.nwcg.gov/glossary/a-z.**

Aerial Fuels: All live and dead vegetation in the forest canopy or above surface fuels, including tree branches, twigs and cones, snags, moss, and high brush.

Aerial Ignition: Ignition of fuels by dropping incendiary devices or materials from aircraft.

Air Tanker: A fixed-wing aircraft equipped to drop fire retardants or suppressants.

Anchor Point: An advantageous location, usually a barrier to fire spread, from which to start building a fire line. An anchor point is used to reduce the chance of firefighters being flanked by fire.

Aspect: The direction a slope is facing.

Backfire: A fire set along the inner edge of a fire line to consume the fuel in the path of a wildfire and/or change the direction of force of the fire's convection column.

Bambi Bucket: A collapsible bucket slung below a helicopter used to dip water from a variety of sources for aerial fire suppression.

Blowup: A sudden increase in fire intensity or rate of spread strong enough to prevent direct control or to upset control plans. Blowups are often accompanied by violent convection and may have other characteristics of a **Fire Storm** (see also **Flareup**).

Brush: A collective term that refers to stands of vegetation dominated by shrubby, woody plants, or low-growing trees, usually of a type undesirable for livestock or timber management.

Brush Fire: A fire burning in vegetation that is predominantly composed of shrubs, brush, and scrub growth.

Bucket Drops: The dropping of fire retardants or suppressants from specially designed buckets slung below a helicopter.

Buffer Zones: An area of reduced vegetation that separates wildlands from vulnerable residential or business developments. This barrier is like a greenbelt in that it is usually used for another purpose such as agriculture, recreation, park land, or golf course.

Bump-up Method: A progressive method of building a fire line on a wildfire without changing relative positions in the line. Work begins with a suitable space between workers. Whenever one worker overtakes another, all workers ahead move one space forward and resume work on the uncompleted part of the line. The last worker does not move ahead until completing his or her space.

Burn Out: Setting fire inside a control line to widen the line or consume fuel between the edge of the fire and the control line.

Burning Conditions: The state of the combined factors of the environment that affect fire behavior in a specified fuel type.

Burning Index: An estimate of the potential difficulty of fire containment as it relates to the flame length at the most rapidly spreading portion of a fire's perimeter.

Burning Period: That part of each 24-hour period when fires spread most rapidly, typically from 10 a.m. to sundown.

Campfire: When used to classify the cause of a wildland fire, the term describes a fire that was started for cooking or warming that spreads sufficiently from its source to require action by a fire control agency.

Candle (Candling): A single tree or a very small clump of trees that is burning from the bottom up.

Cold Front: The leading edge of a relatively cold air mass that displaces warmer air. The heavier cold air may cause some of the warm air to lift. If the lifted air contains enough moisture, it may result in cloudiness, precipitation, and thunderstorms. If both air masses are dry, no clouds should form. Following the passage of a cold front in the northern hemisphere, westerly or northwesterly winds of 15 to 30 or more miles per hour often continue for 12 to 24 hours.

Cold Trailing: A method of controlling a partly dead fire edge by carefully inspecting and feeling with the hand for heat to detect any fire, digging out every live spot, and trenching any live edge.

Contain (a fire): To complete a fuel break around a fire. This break may include natural barriers or manually and/or mechanically constructed lines.

Control (a fire): The complete extinguishment of a fire, including spot fires. The fire line has been strengthened so that flare-ups from within the perimeter of the fire will not break through this line.

Control Line: All built or natural fire barriers and treated fire edge used to control a fire.

Coyote Tactics: A progressive-line construction duty involving self-sufficient crews that build firelines until the end of the operational period, remain at or near the point while off duty, and begin building firelines where they left off in the next operational period.

Creeping Fire: Fire burning with a low flame and spreading slowly.

Crown Fire (Crowning): The movement of fire through the crowns of trees or shrubs, more-or-less independent of the surface fire.

Curing: Drying and browning of herbaceous vegetation or slash.

Dead Fuels: Fuels with no living tissue, in which moisture content is governed almost entirely by atmospheric moisture (relative humidity and precipitation), dry-bulb temperature, and solar radiation.

Debris Burning: A fire spreading from any fire originally set for the purpose of clearing land or for burning rubbish, garbage, range, stubble, or meadow.

Defensible Space: A natural or manmade area in which material capable of causing a fire to spread has been treated, cleared, reduced, or changed to act as a barrier between an advancing wildland fire and the loss to life, property, or resources. In practice, defensible space is defined as an area measuring at least 30 feet around a structure that is cleared of flammable brush or vegetation.

Direct Attack: Any treatment of burning fuel, such as by wetting, smothering, or chemically quenching the fire, or by physically separating burning from unburned fuel.

Dozer: Any tracked vehicle with a front-mounted blade used for exposing mineral soil.

Dozer Line: Fire line constructed by the front blade of a dozer.

Drip Torch: Handheld device for igniting fires by dripping flaming liquid fuel on the materials to be burned; consists of a fuel fount, burner arm, and igniter. Fuel used is generally a mixture of diesel and gasoline.

Drop Zone: Target area for air tankers, helitankers, and cargo dropping.

Dry Lightning Storm: A thunderstorm in which negligible precipitation reaches the ground. Also called a **Dry Storm**.

Duff: A layer of decomposing organic materials lying below the litter layer of freshly fallen twigs, needles, and leaves and immediately above the mineral soil.

B

Escape Route: A preplanned and understood route firefighters take to move to a safety zone or other low-risk area, such as an already burned area, a previously constructed safety area, a meadow that won't burn, or a natural rocky area that is large enough to take refuge without being burned. When escape routes deviate from a defined physical path, they should be clearly marked (flagged).

Escaped Fire: A fire that has exceeded or is expected to exceed initial attack capabilities or prescription.

Extreme Fire Behavior: Implies a level of fire behavior characteristics that ordinarily precludes methods of direct control action. One or more of the following is usually involved: a high rate of spread, prolific crowning and/or spotting, presence of fire whirls, and a strong convection column. Predictability is difficult because such fires often exercise some degree of influence on their environment and behave erratically, sometimes dangerously.

Fine (Light) Fuels: Fast-drying fuels, generally with comparatively high surface area-to-volume ratios, which are less than a quarter inch in diameter and have a timelag of one hour or less. These fuels readily ignite and are rapidly consumed by fire when dry.

Fire Behavior: The manner in which a fire reacts to the influences of fuel, weather, and topography.

Fire Behavior Forecast: Prediction of probable fire behavior, usually prepared by a Fire Behavior Officer, in support of fire suppression or prescribed burning operations.

Fire Break: A natural or constructed barrier used to stop or check fires that may occur or to provide a control line from which to work.

Fire Front: The part of a fire within which continuous flaming combustion is taking place. Unless otherwise specified, the fire front is assumed to be the leading edge of the fire perimeter. In ground fires, the fire front may be mainly smoldering combustion.

Fire Line (Fireline): A linear fire barrier that is scraped or dug to mineral soil.

Fire Load: The number and size of fires historically experienced on a specified unit over a specified period (usually one day) at a specified index of fire danger.

Fire Management Plan (FMP): A strategic plan that defines a program to manage wildland and prescribed fires and that documents the Fire Management Program in the approved land use plan. The plan is supplemented by operational plans such as preparedness plans, preplanned dispatch plans, prescribed fire plans, and prevention plans.

Fire Season: 1) Period(s) of the year during which wildland fires are likely to occur, spread, and affect resource values sufficient to warrant organized fire management activities. 2) A legally enacted time during which burning activities are regulated by state or local authority.

Fire Shelter: An aluminized tent offering protection by means of reflecting radiant heat and providing a volume of breathable air in a fire entrapment situation. A fire shelter should be used only in a life-threatening situation as a last resort.

Fire Storm: Violent convection caused by a large, continuous area of intense fire. Often characterized by destructively violent surface in-drafts near and beyond the perimeter, and sometimes by tornado-like whirls.

Fire Use Module (Prescribed Fire Module): A team of skilled and mobile personnel dedicated primarily to prescribed fire management. These are national and interagency resources, available throughout the prescribed fire season, who are permitted to ignite, hold, and monitor prescribed fires.

Fire Weather: Weather conditions that influence fire ignition, behavior, and suppression.

Fire Weather Watch: A term used by fire weather forecasters to notify agencies, usually 24 to 72 hours ahead of the event, that current and developing meteorological conditions may evolve into dangerous fire weather.

Fire Whirl: A spinning column of ascending hot air and gases rising from a fire and carrying aloft smoke, debris, and flame. Fire whirls range from less than 1 foot to more than 500 feet in diameter. Large fire whirls have the intensity of a small tornado.

Flaming Front: The zone of a moving fire where the combustion is primarily flaming. Behind this flaming zone combustion is primarily glowing. Light fuels typically have a shallow flaming front, whereas heavy fuels have a deeper front. Also called **Fire Front.**

Flareup: Any sudden acceleration of fire spread or intensification of a fire. Unlike a blowup, a flareup lasts a relatively short time and does not radically change control plans.

Flash Fuels: Fuels such as grass, leaves, draped pine needles, fern, tree moss, and some kinds of slash that ignite readily and are consumed rapidly when dry. Also called **Fine (Light) Fuels.**

Fuel Reduction: Manipulation (including combustion) or removal of fuels to reduce the likelihood of ignition and/or to lessen potential damage and resistance to control.

Fuel Type: An identifiable association of fuel elements of a distinctive plant species, form, size, arrangement, or other characteristic that will cause a predictable rate of fire spread or difficulty of control under specified weather conditions.

Fusee: A colored flare designed as a railway warning device and widely used to ignite suppression and prescription fires.

Ground Fuel: All combustible materials below surface litter, including duff, tree, or shrub roots; punchy wood; peat; and sawdust, which normally support a glowing combustion without flame.

Haines Index: Atmospheric index used to indicate the potential for wildfire growth by measuring the stability and dryness of the air over a fire.

Hand Line: A fire line built with hand tools.

Heavy Fuels: Fuels of large diameter, such as snags, logs, and large limb wood, which ignite and are consumed more slowly than flash fuels.

Helibase: The main location within the general incident area for parking, fueling, maintaining, and loading helicopters. The helibase is usually located at or near the incident base.

Helispot: A temporary landing spot for helicopters.

Helitack: The use of helicopters to transport crews, equipment, and fire retardants or suppressants to the fire line during the initial stages of a fire.

Helitack Crew: A group of firefighters trained in the technical and logistical use of helicopters for fire suppression.

Holding Actions: Planned actions required to achieve wildland-prescribed fire management objectives. These actions have specific implementation timeframes for fire use actions, but they can have less sensitive implementation demands for suppression actions.

Holding Resources: Firefighting personnel and equipment assigned to do all required fire suppression work following fire line construction, but generally not including extensive mop-up.

Hose Lay: Arrangement of connected lengths of fire hose and accessories on the ground beginning at the first pumping unit and ending at the point of water delivery.

Hotshot Crew: A highly trained fire crew used mainly to build fire lines by hand.

Hotspot: A particularly active part of a fire.

Hotspotting: Reducing or stopping the spread of fire at points of particularly rapid rate of spread or at points of special threat; generally the first step in prompt control, with emphasis on first priorities.

Incident: A human-caused or natural occurrence, such as a wildland fire, which requires emergency service action to prevent or reduce the loss of life or damage to property or natural resources.

Incident Action Plan (IAP): An oral or written series of objectives reflecting the overall incident strategy and specific tactical actions and supporting information for the next operational period. When written,

B

the plan may include attachments such as incident objectives, organization assignment lists, division assignments, an incident radio communication plan, a medical plan, a traffic plan, a safety plan, and an incident map.

Incident Command Post (ICP): Location at which primary command functions are executed. The ICP may be co-located with the incident base or other incident facilities.

Incident Command System (ICS): The combination of facilities, equipment, personnel, procedure, and communications operating within a common organizational structure; responsible for managing assigned resources to effectively accomplish stated objectives pertaining to an incident.

Infrared Detection: Use of heat sensing equipment, known as **Infrared Scanners**, for detecting heat sources that are not visually evident using normal surveillance methods of either ground or air patrols.

Jump Spot: Selected landing area for smokejumpers.

Jump Suit: Approved protection suit used by smokejumpers.

Keech-Byram Drought Index (KBDI): Commonly used drought index adapted for fire management applications, with a numerical range of 0 (no moisture deficiency) to 800 (maximum drought).

Knock Down: To reduce the flame or heat on more vigorously burning parts of a fire edge.

Ladder Fuels: Fuels that provide vertical continuity between strata, thereby allowing fire to carry from surface fuels into the crowns of trees or shrubs with relative ease. They help initiate and assure the continuation of crowning.

Lead Plane: Aircraft with pilot used to make dry runs over a target area, to check wing and smoke conditions and topography, and to lead air tankers to targets and supervise their drops.

Light (Fine) Fuels: Fast-drying fuels, generally with comparatively high surface area–to-volume ratios, which are less than one quarter inch in diameter and with a timelag of one hour or less. These fuels readily ignite and are rapidly consumed by fire when dry.

Lightning Activity Level (LAL): A number, on a scale of 1 to 6, reflecting frequency and character of cloud-to-ground lightning. The scale is exponential, based on powers of 2 (e.g., LAL 3 indicates twice the lightning of LAL 2).

Litter: Top layer of the forest, scrubland, or grassland floor directly above the fermentation layer, composed of loose debris of dead sticks, branches, twigs, and recently fallen leaves or needles that are little altered in structure by decomposition.

Live Fuels: Living plants such as trees, grasses, and shrubs, in which the seasonal moisture content cycle is controlled largely by internal physiological mechanisms rather than by external weather influences.

Micro-Remote Environmental Monitoring System (Micro-REMS): Mobile weather monitoring station that usually accompanies an incident meteorologist and the Advanced Technology Meteorological Unit (ATMU) to an incident.

Mobilization: The process and procedures used by all organizations (federal, state, and local) for activating, assembling, and transporting all resources requested to respond to or support an incident.

Modular Airborne Firefighting System (MAFFS): A manufactured unit with a capacity of 3,000 gallons, consisting of five interconnecting tanks, a control pallet, and a nozzle pallet; designed to be rapidly mounted inside an unmodified C-130 (Hercules) cargo aircraft for use in dropping retardant on wildland fires.

Mop Up: Make a fire safe or reduce residual smoke after the fire has been controlled by extinguishing or removing burning material along or near the control line, felling snags, or moving logs so they won't roll downhill.

National Fire Danger Rating System (NFDRS): A uniform fire danger rating system focusing on the environmental factors that control the moisture content of fuels.

National Wildfire Coordinating Group (NWCG): Formed under the direction of the Secretaries of Agriculture and the Interior and comprised of representatives of the US Forest Service, Bureau of Land Management, Bureau of Indian Affairs, National Park Service, US Fish and Wildlife Service, and Association of State Foresters. The group's purposes are to facilitate coordination and effectiveness of wildland fire activities and provide a forum to discuss, recommend action, or resolve issues and problems of substantive nature. NWCG is the certifying body for all courses in the National Fire Curriculum.

Normal Fire Season: 1) A season in which weather, fire danger, and number and distribution of fires are about average. 2) Period of the year that normally comprises the fire season.

Paracargo: Anything dropped or intended for dropping from an aircraft by parachute, by other retarding devices, or by free fall.

Peak Fire Season: Period of the fire season during which fires are expected to ignite most readily, burn with greater than average intensity, and create damages at an unacceptable level.

Prescribed Fire: Fire ignited by management actions under certain predetermined conditions to meet specific objectives related to hazardous fuels or habitat improvement. A written, approved prescribed fire plan must exist, and NEPA requirements must be met prior to ignition.

Prescribed Fire Plan (Burn Plan): Provides the prescribed fire burn supervisor with information needed to implement an individual prescribed fire project.

Prescription: Measurable criteria that define conditions under which a prescribed fire may be ignited, that guide selection of appropriate management responses, and that indicate other required actions. Prescription criteria may include safety, economic, public health, environmental, geographic, administrative, social, or legal considerations.

Project Fire: A fire of such size or complexity that a large organization and prolonged activity is required to suppress it.

Pulaski: A combination chopping and trenching tool that combines a single-bitted axe-blade with a narrow adze-like trenching blade fitted to a straight handle. Useful for grubbing or trenching in duff and matted roots, and well-balanced for chopping.

Rappelling: Technique of landing specifically trained firefighters from hovering helicopters; it involves sliding down ropes with the aid of friction-producing devices.

Rate of Spread: The relative activity of a fire in extending its horizontal dimensions, expressed as a rate of increase of the total perimeter of the fire, as a rate of forward spread of the fire front, or as rate of increase in area, depending on the intended use of the information. Usually, it is expressed in chains or acres per hour for a specific period in the fire's history.

Reburn: Burning an area that has been previously burned but that contains flammable fuel that ignites when burning conditions are more favorable; an area that has reburned.

Red Card: Fire qualification card issued to fire-rated persons showing their training needs and their qualifications for filling specified fire-suppression and support positions in a large fire suppression or incident organization.

Red Flag Warning: Used by fire weather forecasters to alert forecast users to an ongoing or imminent critical fire weather pattern.

Rehabilitation: Activities necessary to repair damage or disturbance caused by wildland fires or fire suppression activity.

Relative Humidity (RH): The ratio of the amount of moisture in the air to the maximum amount of moisture the air would contain if saturated; the ratio of the actual vapor pressure to the saturated vapor pressure.

Remote Automatic Weather Station (RAWS): An apparatus that automatically acquires, processes, and stores local weather data for later transmission to the GOES Satellite, from which the data is retransmitted to an earth-receiving station for use in the National Fire Danger Rating System.

B

Run (of a fire): The rapid advance of the head of a fire with a marked change in fire line intensity and rate of spread from what was noted before and after the advance.

Running: Describes a rapidly spreading surface fire with a well-defined head.

Safety Zone: An area cleared of flammable materials and used for escape in the event that the line is outflanked or in case a spot fire causes fuels outside the control line to render the line unsafe. In firing operations, crews progress so as to maintain a safety zone close at hand, allowing the fuels inside the control line to be consumed before proceeding. Safety zones may also be constructed as integral parts of fuel breaks; these are greatly enlarged areas that can be used with relative safety by firefighters and their equipment in the event of a blowup in the vicinity.

Scratch Line: An unfinished, preliminary fire line hastily established or built as an emergency measure to check the spread of fire.

Slash: Debris left after logging, pruning, thinning, or brush cutting; includes logs, chips, bark, branches, stumps, and broken understory trees or brush.

Sling Load: Cargo carried beneath a helicopter and attached by a lead line and swivel.

Slop-Over: A fire edge that crosses a control line or natural barrier intended to contain the fire.

Smokejumper: A firefighter who travels to fires by aircraft and parachutes into the site.

Smoke Management: Application of fire intensities and meteorological processes to minimize degradation of air quality during prescribed fires.

Smoldering Fire: A fire burning without flame and barely spreading.

Snag: A standing dead tree or part of a dead tree from which at least the smaller branches have fallen.

Spot Weather Forecast: A special forecast issued to fit the time, topography, and weather of a specific fire. It is issued upon request of the user agency and is more detailed, timely, and specific than zone forecasts.

Spotter: In smokejumping, the person responsible for selecting drop targets and supervising all aspects of dropping smokejumpers.

Spotting: Fire behavior in which sparks or embers are carried by the wind and start new fires beyond the zone of direct ignition by the main fire.

Staging Area: Location established at an incident where resources are placed while awaiting a tactical assignment on a 3-minute available basis. Staging areas are managed by the operations section.

Surface Fuels: Loose litter on the soil surface, normally consisting of fallen leaves or needles, twigs, bark, cones, and small branches that have not yet decayed enough to lose their identity; also grasses, forbs, low and medium shrubs, tree seedlings, heavier branch wood, downed logs, and stumps interspersed with or partially replacing the litter.

Temporary Flight Restriction (TFR): Requested by an agency and put into effect by the FAA in the vicinity of an incident; it restricts the operation of nonessential aircraft in the airspace around that incident.

Terra Torch: Trademark name for a device that throws a stream of flaming liquid; used to facilitate rapid ignition during burn-out operations on a wildland fire or during a prescribed fire operation.

Test Fire: A small fire ignited within a planned burn unit to determine the characteristics of the prescribed fire (fire behavior, detection performance, and control measures).

Torching: Ignition and flare-up of a tree or small group of trees, usually from bottom to top.

Uncontrolled Fire: Fire that threatens to destroy life, property, or natural resources.

Underburn: Fire that consumes surface fuels but not trees or shrubs (see **Surface Fuels**).

Water Tender: A ground vehicle capable of transporting specified quantities of water.

Weather Information and Management System (WIMS): An interactive computer system designed to accommodate the weather information needs of all federal and state natural resource management agencies. Provides timely access to weather forecasts, current and historical weather data, the National Fire Danger Rating System (NFDRS), and the National Interagency Fire Management Integrated Database (NIFMID).

Wet Line: A line of water (or water and chemical retardant) sprayed along the ground to provide a temporary control line from which to ignite or stop a low-intensity fire.

Wildland Fire: Any nonstructure fire, other than prescribed fire, that occurs in the wildland.

Wildland Fire Implementation Plan (WFIP): A progressively developed assessment and operational management plan that documents the analysis and selection of strategies and describes the appropriate management response for a wildland fire being managed for resource benefits.

Wildland Fire Situation Analysis (WFSA): A decision-making process that evaluates alternative suppression strategies against selected environmental, social, political, and economic criteria. Provides a record of decisions.

Wildland Fire Use: Management of naturally ignited wildland fires to accomplish specific, prestated resource management objectives in predefined geographic areas outlined in Fire Management Plans.

Wildland Urban Interface: The line, area, or zone where structures and other human development meet or intermingle with undeveloped wildland or vegetative fuels.

Wind Vectors: Wind directions used to calculate fire behavior.

Summing It Up

- Wildland fire is defined as any nonstructure fire that occurs in the wild. This type of firefighting may include setting fires to control fires, climbing hills and mountains, using helicopters to drop water onto fires, and living in temporary camps in the forest or near a fire site for extended periods. Wildland firefighters are trained specifically to handle forest fires.

- To familiarize yourself with wildland firefighting, learn and understand the terminology and basic concepts that are part of the trade.

- Most wildland firefighter jobs are temporary, seasonal, or part-time. Full-time positions are available, but you must have plenty of wildland firefighting experience before you can be hired for them.

- Federal agencies such as the US Forest Service, the Bureau of Land Management, the National Park Service, the US Fish and Wildlife Service, and the Bureau of Indian Affairs employ many wildland firefighters, as do state agencies, private companies, and local municipalities. Most jobs are concentrated in the western states.

- Federal wildland firefighting jobs are assigned job grade levels according to the General Schedule (GS). For example, a position for which you need no experience or education is a GS-01; a position for which you must have a bachelor's degree but not necessarily any experience is a GS-05 or GS-07, depending on your academic credentials and the hiring agency's policies.

- The Interagency Incident Qualification Card, or the Red Card, is part of the fire qualifications management system and is used by many state and all federal wildland fire management agencies. Without a Red Card, you are not permitted to fight forest fires. You must be part of a sponsoring agency to obtain one.

- All federal wildland firefighters must pass a work capacity test (WCT) to receive a Red Card. The WCT measures fitness, acclimatization, nutrition, skill, experience, motivation, and intelligence. Before taking the WCT, prospective candidates must complete a healthcare screening questionnaire (HSQ).

- You can raise your chances of being hired as a wildland firefighter by acquiring new skills, such as learning emergency medical procedures or obtaining a commercial driver's license. Being a knowledgeable, well-rounded candidate gives you an edge over the competition.

- Be sure to adhere to all deadlines in the application process. Follow all instructions and submit all required paperwork. Depending on the position you're seeking and your background, you may be required to submit a resume, college transcripts, or a copy of your Red Card or position task book (if you have one).

B